Jossey-Bass Teacher

Jossey-Bass Teacher provides educators with practical knowledge and tools to create a positive and lifelong impact on student learning. We offer classroom-tested and research-based teaching resources for a variety of grade levels and subject areas. Whether you are an aspiring, new, or veteran teacher, we want to help you make every teaching day your best.

From ready-to-use classroom activities to the latest teaching framework, our value-packed books provide insightful, practical, and comprehensive materials on the topics that matter most to K–12 teachers. We hope to become your trusted source for the best ideas from the most experienced and respected experts in the field.

Life Skills Activities for Secondary Students with Special Needs

Second Edition

Darlene Mannix

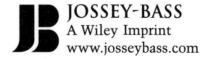

JOSSEY-BASS
A Wiley Imprint
www.josseybass.com

Published by Jossey-Bass
A Wiley Imprint
One Montgomery Street, Suite 1200, San Francisco, CA 94104-4594—www.josseybass.com

Jossey-Bass books and products are available through most bookstores. To contact Jossey-Bass directly call our Customer Care Department within the U.S. at 800-956-7739, outside the U.S. at 317-572-3986, or fax 317-572-4002.

Jossey-Bass also publishes its books in a variety of electronic formats. Some content that appears in print may not be available in electronic books.

PRINTED IN THE UNITED STATES OF AMERICA

SECOND EDITION

PB Printing   10 9

Contents

About This Book   xii

About the Author   xiv

Parent Activities and Suggestions   xv

Part One: Self-Awareness   1

Chapter 1: My Character   2
    Lesson 1.1: Qualities of a Good Character   3
    Lesson 1.2: Honesty   5
    Lesson 1.3: Kindness   7
    Lesson 1.4: Loyalty   9
    Lesson 1.5: Responsibility   12
    Lesson 1.6: Flexibility   14
    Lesson 1.7: What Are Values?   17

Chapter 2: Uniquely Me   19
    Lesson 2.1: Values Important to Me   20
    Lesson 2.2: My Ethnic Background   22
    Lesson 2.3: My Disabilities   24
    Lesson 2.4: What's a Reputation?   27
    Lesson 2.5: Changing Your Reputation   29
    Lesson 2.6: How You Appear to Others   31

Chapter 3: Personal Life Choices   33
    Lesson 3.1: Smoking: Is It for Me?   34
    Lesson 3.2: Marijuana and Other Drugs   37
    Lesson 3.3: Teens and Drinking   40
    Lesson 3.4: Changing Your Appearance   42
    Lesson 3.5: Tattoos and Piercings   45

Lesson 3.6: Rate the Date   48
Lesson 3.7: Ready to Move Out?   51
Lesson 3.8: Ready to Work Part-Time?   53

Part Two: People Skills   **55**

Chapter 4: Relating to Others   56
Lesson 4.1: Encouraging Others   57
Lesson 4.2: Working in a Group   59
Lesson 4.3: Working Toward a Common Goal   62
Lesson 4.4: Being Friendly   65
Lesson 4.5: Helping Others   68
Lesson 4.6: What Is a Mood?   71
Lesson 4.7: Noticing the Moods of Others   74
Lesson 4.8: How My Mood Affects Others   77

Chapter 5: Friendship Skills   79
Lesson 5.1: My Peer Groups   80
Lesson 5.2: Who Are My Friends?   82
Lesson 5.3: Making Friends   84
Lesson 5.4: People Who Are Like You   86
Lesson 5.5: People Who Are Different from You   89
Lesson 5.6: Where and How to Look for Friends   92
Lesson 5.7: Qualities of a Good Friend   95
Lesson 5.8: Social Situations   97
Lesson 5.9: A Positive Role Model   99
Lesson 5.10: What About Gangs?   101
Lesson 5.11: Social Networking Online   103

Chapter 6: Being Part of a Family   105
Lesson 6.1: My Family Tree   106
Lesson 6.2: Benefits of a Family   108
Lesson 6.3: Respecting Authority   110
Lesson 6.4: My Parent's Point of View   112
Lesson 6.5: My Sibling's Point of View   115
Lesson 6.6: Thoughts About Divorce   118
Lesson 6.7: Dealing with Stepparents   121
Lesson 6.8: Sharing the Chores   123
Lesson 6.9: Whom Can I Talk To?   125

Chapter 7: Communication Skills 128
    Lesson 7.1: Best Method to Communicate 129
    Lesson 7.2: Being a Careful Listener 131
    Lesson 7.3: Summarizing 133
    Lesson 7.4: Paraphrasing 135
    Lesson 7.5: Is This the Right Time and Place? 137
    Lesson 7.6: Communicating by Cell Phone 140
    Lesson 7.7: Giving Clear Directions 142
    Lesson 7.8: Verbal and Nonverbal Messages 145
    Lesson 7.9: Collecting Your Thoughts 147
    Lesson 7.10: Public Speaking 150
    Lesson 7.11: Expecting Respect 153
    Lesson 7.12: Being Convincing 155
    Lesson 7.13: Giving Your Speech 157

Part Three: Academic and School Skills **160**

Chapter 8: Reading Skills 161
    Lesson 8.1: Reading for School 162
    Lesson 8.2: Reading on the Job 164
    Lesson 8.3: Improving Reading Skills 166
    Lesson 8.4: Reading for Comprehension 169
    Lesson 8.5: Following Written Directions 172

Chapter 9: Writing Skills 175
    Lesson 9.1: Communicating Through Writing 176
    Lesson 9.2: Everyday Writing Tasks 178
    Lesson 9.3: Proofreading 180
    Lesson 9.4: E-mailing Dos and Don'ts 183
    Lesson 9.5: Using Computers to Improve Writing 186
    Lesson 9.6: Writing and More Writing 189
    Lesson 9.7: Writing on the Job 192

Chapter 10: Math Skills 194
    Lesson 10.1: Everyday Math Skills 195
    Lesson 10.2: Improving Math Skills 197
    Lesson 10.3: Common Math Situations 200
    Lesson 10.4: Understanding Graphs 202
    Lesson 10.5: Understanding Charts 205

Contents

Lesson 10.6: Sample Math Problems   208
Lesson 10.7: Using Computers for Math Information   211

Chapter 11: Study Skills   213
Lesson 11.1: School Tasks for Success   214
Lesson 11.2: Tools for the Task   216
Lesson 11.3: Taking Notes   218
Lesson 11.4: Studying Smarter   221
Lesson 11.5: Following Directions   223
Lesson 11.6: Doing Homework   226
Lesson 11.7: Managing Daily Assignments   228
Lesson 11.8: Managing Long-Term Assignments   230
Lesson 11.9: Completing Assignments   232
Lesson 11.10: Good Student Behaviors   234
Lesson 11.11: Requesting Help or Information   236

Part Four: Practical Living Skills   238

Chapter 12: Information Skills   240
Lesson 12.1: What Do You Need to Know?   241
Lesson 12.2: Where to Get Information   243
Lesson 12.3: Information from Newspapers   246
Lesson 12.4: Information from Magazines   248
Lesson 12.5: Information from the Internet   250
Lesson 12.6: Information from Books   253
Lesson 12.7: Information from Television   256
Lesson 12.8: Information from Other People   258
Lesson 12.9: Taking Classes   261

Chapter 13: Money Skills   263
Lesson 13.1: What Is a Budget?   264
Lesson 13.2: Making a Budget   267
Lesson 13.3: Paying Interest   269
Lesson 13.4: "On Sale"   272
Lesson 13.5: Unit Pricing   275
Lesson 13.6: How Much Do Things Cost?   278
Lesson 13.7: Writing a Check   280
Lesson 13.8: Maintaining a Checking Account   283
Lesson 13.9: What Is a Savings Account?   286

Lesson 13.10:   Credit Cards   288
Lesson 13.11:   Using Debit and Credit Cards and ATMs   290
Lesson 13.12:   How Much Money Will You Need?   293
Lesson 13.13:   Making Change   295

Chapter 14: Travel   298
Lesson 14.1:   Local Transportation   299
Lesson 14.2:   Overnight Travel   301
Lesson 14.3:   Traveling by Plane   303
Lesson 14.4:   Planning a Trip   305
Lesson 14.5:   Estimating Costs   307
Lesson 14.6:   Using a Timetable   309
Lesson 14.7:   Reading a Map   311

Chapter 15: Clothing   313
Lesson 15.1:   Caring for and Repairing Clothing   314
Lesson 15.2:   Buying Appropriate Clothes   316
Lesson 15.3:   Organizing Your Clothes   319
Lesson 15.4:   Washing and Drying Tips   321

Chapter 16: Living Arrangements   324
Lesson 16.1:   A Place to Live   325
Lesson 16.2:   Living with Parents   327
Lesson 16.3:   Home Upkeep   329
Lesson 16.4:   Home Repairs   332
Lesson 16.5:   Going Green   335
Lesson 16.6:   Decluttering   337

Chapter 17: Eating and Nutrition   340
Lesson 17.1:   Nutrition   341
Lesson 17.2:   Making Good Food Choices   344
Lesson 17.3:   Eating Out versus Eating In   346
Lesson 17.4:   Preparing a Meal   349

Chapter 18: Shopping   351
Lesson 18.1:   What Do I Need?   352
Lesson 18.2:   Smart Shopping   354
Lesson 18.3:   Comparison Shopping   356
Lesson 18.4:   Returning Items   358

Contents

Chapter 19: Exercise/Health and Hygiene   360
    Lesson 19.1: Exercise in Daily Life   361
    Lesson 19.2: Exercise Excuses   363
    Lesson 19.3: Personal Health Habits   365
    Lesson 19.4: Stress and Stressors   367
    Lesson 19.5: Stressful Events and Situations   370
    Lesson 19.6: Coping with Stress   372
    Lesson 19.7: Depression   377

Part Five: Vocational Skills   380

Chapter 20: Present Skills and Interests   381
    Lesson 20.1: My Strengths   382
    Lesson 20.2: My Interests   385
    Lesson 20.3: My Hobbies   387
    Lesson 20.4: Realistic Vocational Goals   389
    Lesson 20.5: Academic Strengths   392
    Lesson 20.6: Working with a Disability   394
    Lesson 20.7: Finishing High School   397
    Lesson 20.8: Extracurricular Activities   400

Chapter 21: Getting a Job   403
    Lesson 21.1: Searching for a Job   404
    Lesson 21.2: Vocational Vocabulary   407
    Lesson 21.3: Filling Out an Application   411
    Lesson 21.4: What Is a Résumé?   415
    Lesson 21.5: Interviewing for a Job   418
    Lesson 21.6: First Impressions   421
    Lesson 21.7: Getting Work Experience   423

Chapter 22: Working   425
    Lesson 22.1: Having a Good Attitude   426
    Lesson 22.2: Being a Great Employee   429
    Lesson 22.3: Making a Mistake on the Job   431
    Lesson 22.4: Handling Criticism on the Job   434
    Lesson 22.5: Being Prepared for the Task   436
    Lesson 22.6: Changing Jobs: Why?   439
    Lesson 22.7: Changing Jobs: How?   441

Contents

Part Six: Problem-Solving Skills   444

Chapter 23: Handling Problem Situations   445
    Lesson 23.1: Understanding the Problem   446
    Lesson 23.2: Coping with Surprises   450
    Lesson 23.3: Adjusting to Change   453
    Lesson 23.4: When the Problem Is You!   456

Chapter 24: Making Decisions   459
    Lesson 24.1: Decision-Making Factors   460
    Lesson 24.2: Needs versus Wants   463
    Lesson 24.3: Immediate Needs versus Waiting   466
    Lesson 24.4: Following Through   469
    Lesson 24.5: Changing Bad Decisions   473

Chapter 25: Resource Management   476
    Lesson 25.1: What Are My Resources?   477
    Lesson 25.2: Reliable Resources   480
    Lesson 25.3: Fact versus Opinion   483
    Lesson 25.4: Time Management   485
    Lesson 25.5: Staying on Task   488

Chapter 26: Goal-Setting   491
    Lesson 26.1: What Is a Goal?   492
    Lesson 26.2: Setting Priorities   494
    Lesson 26.3: Doing Things in Sequence   496
    Lesson 26.4: Realistic Goals   499
    Lesson 26.5: Adjusting Goals   502

Chapter 27: Risk-Taking   504
    Lesson 27.1: What Is a Risk?   505
    Lesson 27.2: Why Take Risks?   507
    Lesson 27.3: Acceptable Risks   510
    Lesson 27.4: Handling Fear   512

Contents

About This Book

Life Skills Activities for Secondary Students with Special Needs is a resource for special education and regular education teachers, counselors, parents, paraprofessionals, and others who are involved in the education, training, employment, or socialization of students.

What Are Life Skills?

Basically, life skills are a group of skills that an individual needs to acquire for an independent life, as far as that life is possible. One could argue that the most important skills one acquires in life are the skills of sound character, such as honesty, kindness, and being responsible. At school, students need to acquire the whole realm of academic skills, including reading, writing, and solving math problems. In addition, school is a microcosm of society that demands the acquisition of appropriate social skills. Life skills also includes the many tasks that make up daily living, such as shopping, saving money, traveling, or eating. Vocational skills are another component of what a special needs child will need to acquire—finding and maintaining an appropriate job. Problem-solving skills are a vital thinking technique that can be superimposed on all of the other areas.

Why Teach Life Skills?

The teaching of life skills is an ongoing process for children. It can take place in many campuses (at school, at home, in the community) and be taught by many teachers (including professional educators, the bus driver, your neighbor, other children, and community leaders). Sometimes, however, it is best to have a directed goal with a target in mind to help stay focused on what your child needs to learn. Having a specific goal helps not only the student, but the teacher or parent as well.

What Students Will Use This Book?

The lessons in this book are primarily directed toward middle school or younger high school students who have a special need for learning. This special need might be a social disability, learning disability, or moderate mental or physical handicap that requires slowing down the pace of the task, going step-by-step toward a goal, needing extra practice, learning through targeted discussion, and/or simply steering them toward the core skill.

The material can be adapted for a variety of uses. Answers can be oral or written, students can work individually or in groups, activities can be tailored to fit whatever needs are more pressing.

How Do I Use This Book?

As a teacher or parent, you have many options as far as using the material in this book. A typical lesson contains these elements:

- A specific objective for the lesson
- Brief comments about the nature or importance of the skill
- An introductory activity or two
- Discussion questions pertaining to the skill
- Answer key or suggested responses
- An extension activity or two
- Evaluation items

In addition, there are parent activities and suggestions for each of the six sections.
The book is organized into six main parts:

Part One, Self-Awareness, contains twenty-one lessons on character (being responsible, loyal, kind, and so on), individual uniqueness (ethnicity, disabilities, reputation, and so on), and personal life choices (such as smoking, drinking, tattoos, moving out).

Part Two, People Skills, contains forty-one lessons on relating to others (such as working with others, being in a good mood), developing friendship skills (recognizing people who are the same as or different from you, social networking, and so on), and being part of a family (such as understanding another's point of view, sharing space), and communicating (being a good listener, understanding verbal and nonverbal messages, and so on).

Part Three, Academic and School Skills, is primarily related to education and contains thirty lessons on reading, writing, math, and study skills. Teachers in a school setting may find this section helpful for their students.

Part Four, Practical Living Skills, is a longer section containing fifty-four lessons on acquiring information, handling money, travel, clothing, living arrangements, eating and nutrition, shopping, and including exercise and hygiene in your life. Parents of special needs teens may use this section in a home environment.

Part Five, Vocational Skills, contains twenty-two lessons on understanding present skills and interests (hobbies and strengths), getting a job (filling out an application, interviewing, and so on), and actual working (skills needed to be a good employee).

Part Six, Problem-Solving Skills, has twenty-three lessons on skills such as handling problem situations, making decisions, using good resource management, goal-setting, and risk-taking. The examples in these lessons come from home, school, work, and community settings.

Life Skills Activities for Secondary Students with Special Needs was first published in 1995. To reflect changes in education and current social needs, many lessons have been added or updated.

Part One, Self-Awareness, includes a chapter on My Character, which brings into focus character-building skills such as kindness, honesty, and responsibility. These skills are timeless in their value in any program for any student. Other lessons address tattoos and piercings, having a disability, and making life choices about moving out or getting a part-time job.

Part Two, People Skills, includes updated material about social relationships, including noticing the moods of others and how one's mood affects others, places to find friends, social networking online, understanding another's point of view, and using a cell phone.

Part Three, Academic and School Skills, has lessons on e-mailing, using computers to improve school tasks, and using computers to find information online.

Part Four, Practical Living Skills, now includes obtaining information from the Internet; taking classes for further learning; using debit, credit, and ATM cards; overnight travel; care of clothing; "going green" smart shopping; learning about nutrition; and the importance of daily exercise.

Part Five, Vocational Skills, includes revisions to the sections on interviewing for a job, searching for a job, creating a good first impression, and how to handle making mistakes and criticism on the job.

Part Six, Problem-Solving Skills, has lessons about seeing oneself as the problem, taking risks, and handling fearful situations.

There are a total of 191 lessons, 62 of which are new, for a total of 32 percent revised material. There are numerous minor updates and revisions on many of the retained lessons as well.

I hope that you find the lessons to be helpful and appropriate for your students or child!

Darlene Mannix

About the Author

Darlene Mannix has worked as an educator for more than twenty years and has taught a wide range of children, including learning disabled, emotionally disturbed, language-disordered, and multiply disabled students. She received her bachelor of science degree from Taylor University and her master's degree in learning disabilities from Indiana University. A past presenter at numerous educational conferences including the Council for Exceptional Children, she has authored many books, including *Writing Skills Activities for Special Children* (Jossey-Bass, 2004); *Social Skills Activities for Special Children,* second edition (Jossey-Bass, 2008); *Social Skills Activities for Secondary Students with Special Needs,* second edition (Jossey-Bass, 2009); and *Life Skills Activities for Special Children,* second edition (Jossey-Bass, 2009). She currently works as a Title 1 reading teacher at Indian Trail Elementary School in La Porte, Indiana.

Parent Activities and Suggestions

Part One: Self-Awareness

My Character

- Emphasize that a child's character is more important than anything else that he or she will ever develop. Being a good person is what really counts.

- Give your child opportunities to take on responsibility around the house. After giving an assignment or chore, act as though you *expect* him or her to do it; don't keep nagging.

- Talk about what values you think are important. Share experiences that have helped shape your values.

- Praise your child when you catch him or her doing something thoughtful or kind for others.

- When you introduce your child to others, use the opportunity to add a positive comment about your child.

- Practice acts of kindness all of the time. Invite your child to be a part of this.

Uniquely Me

- Share with your child any details that are appropriate about his or her birth. A birthday is a special day to every individual—it is the one day of the year that is earmarked for that person alone.

- If your child has a diagnosed disability, talk about what that means as far as expectations for his or her future. Even though he may have a disability, he still has the ability and the expectation to go as far as he can to succeed in life. If appropriate, talk about the causes of a disability.

- Make it a family project to participate in something that is of interest to your particular ethnic background—Irish dancing? French cooking?

Personal Life Choices

- You, of course, are a very important role model to your child. If you are trying to quit smoking, for example, share your decision with your child and explain why.

- Decisions about drinking, especially drinking and driving, can be some of the most crucial decisions your teen makes. Give your child a way out if confronted with a situation in which she needs a ride home. Let your child know that you'd much rather get a call for a ride home than have her get into a car with an impaired driver.

- Encourage your child to think and talk about future events such as moving out or working part-time. This can be scary—but it can also be exciting as you plan future independence together.

Part Two: People Skills

Relating to Others

- Point out good service (or poor service) as you interact with others around you. Compliment a server for refilling your drinks. Notice a cashier who is efficient. Let your child observe you modeling positive interaction with others.
- Get to know your neighbors. Even if it's just a friendly "Hello," encourage your child to get involved in the neighborhood. Perhaps he or she can help with a neighborly errand.
- Join in a community party, fund-raiser, or volunteer organization. Share a positive focus as a family and as a community.

Friendship Skills

- Encourage your child to host a party. It can be a simple get-together to play games or watch a movie, or an elaborate themed event.
- Talk to your child about gang activity. Stay in close contact with your school to keep communication and information lines open.
- Find out who your child's friends are. Invite them over and get to know them.

Being Part of a Family

- Attend or plan a family reunion.
- Get a family photograph taken. Frame it and display it.
- Give your child a sense of family history by going through old family photo albums. Show your child any memorabilia that was important to someone in your family.
- Spend an evening watching family videos. There will be lots of laughter, embarrassing moments, and good memories.
- Have family meetings on a regular basis. Make this a time for family members to share their concerns. This may be a good time to review lists of chores, talk about upcoming family projects or vacations, or make resolutions to improve problem situations.
- Don't hesitate to attend parenting workshops or family groups, or use other community resources if your family is going through a divorce or if there are problems with stepparents. This is more common than you may realize.
- Stay in touch with the school counselor or an administrator who may be the person most likely to work with your child if there are family problems that show up at school.
- Eat a meal together on a regular basis. Make it a point to do something together as a family. No one can miss, no excuses. This is a priority.

Communication Skills

- Resist the urge to speak for your child in social situations. Instead of telling about your child's accomplishments or activities, encourage him or her to talk (prompting is fine).

Life Skills Activities for Secondary Students with Special Needs

- Watch a movie or TV show together and discuss it afterward.
- Ask your child's opinions about things that are happening. Don't jump in too quickly to judge or overrule your child's opinion. Listen.
- Ask your child to give directions for how to do something or how to get somewhere. He or she will learn that directions need to be clear and sequential or it won't make any sense.
- If your child is moody or unusually quiet, ask if he or she can put the feelings into words. Model how sometimes you feel worried, tense, confused, and so on.
- Remind your child that moods change. Just because he or she is feeling sad or angry right now, that is not going to be the case forever. That is what a mood is—something that lasts for awhile and then will change.
- Encourage your child to write in a "mood journal" and express the feelings that are being experienced. This can be used to read later when the mood has passed and the situation may look different.

Part Three: Academic and School Skills

Reading Skills

- Take weekly trips to the library or bookstore to bring reading materials into your home. Second-hand bookstores are a great source for inexpensive books.
- If your child is having problems with reading, look for a peer tutor who may be interested in helping you out. Depending on the age of your child and the extent of the problems, you may want to contact your child's school or teacher to get some ideas.
- Order your child a subscription to a magazine that he or she enjoys.
- Be a good example of a reader by taking the time to read every day—demonstrate that this is a pleasurable activity (if it is for you!).

Writing Skills

- If your child takes phone messages and sometimes misses important things (such as the callback number), provide a ready-made phone pad with lines or spaces for the caller, time of call, message, and callback number.
- Keep lists around your house of things that are purchased on a regular basis, such as food items, cleaning supplies, and the like. Ask your child to add what is needed to each list by writing it down.
- If your family takes a trip or participates in a special event, have your child help record impressions and details about the event. You might want to remember who attended a family reunion, comments about a rock concert, anecdotes from a trip, humorous memories or predictions, and so on.
- Your child might be interested in starting a blog—an online journal. He or she may not want you to read everything that is on it, but show an interest, and if you're allowed to read it, add positive comments and don't insist on perfect spelling or grammar.

Math Skills

- Set aside ten to fifteen minutes each evening to focus on one particular math skill, such as reviewing math facts with flash cards, drawing pictures to go with a story problem, or helping set up an educational computer game that addresses a skill.

- When reviewing math homework, ask your child to tell you the specific directions and steps for an assignment. The procedures for math problems may be a little different now from when you were in school.

- Bring along a calculator to the grocery store and have your child keep a running tab or estimate of how much you are spending.

- Graphs and charts are everywhere—from the newspaper to the gas station to your electric bill. As you find them on everyday occasions, point out the purpose of the graph or chart and see if your child can identify the information.

- Help your child set up and maintain a personal graph or chart for a project, as an ongoing record or just to keep track of how much time is spent on a certain activity (how many minutes spent on chores, how many miles walked, how many inches grown, and so on).

Study Skills

- Find a calendar that introduces and uses one new vocabulary word a day. Have every member of the family learn the definition and use the word in conversation several times that day.

- Make sure your child has a designated place in which to study. Include a spot for all of the necessary tools—pencils, extra paper, a dictionary, calendar, stapler, a good desk lamp, bulletin board, and space for a computer/printer (if possible). Preferably, find a location that is relatively peaceful, free from distractions, and comfortable yet not so relaxing that nothing will be accomplished.

- If television, video games, or cell phones and their accessories are problems in competing for your child's time, find or negotiate a way to make their use contingent on how well your child's grades are kept up, chores are completed, attitude is acceptable, and so on. Do not feel that you "owe" these things to your child if he or she is not keeping up the other end of the bargain.

- Keep in close contact with your child's teachers and know when to expect report cards and midterm reports.

- Volunteer, if possible, to help out in your child's school with occasional projects or on a regular basis. Let your child know that school is important to you.

- If you have a problem or question about something that has happened at school, reserve judgment until you have contacted the school or principal and heard another viewpoint. Model showing respect for authority and understanding another's point of view in front of your child. Many issues are quickly resolved once communication lines between school and home are opened.

Part Four: Practical Living Skills

Information Skills

- If you can find a good set of encyclopedias or have access to the Internet, spend some time looking up information with your child. Show your child how the encyclopedia is organized (alphabetically) and, similarly, how to find information on the Internet.

Life Skills Activities for Secondary Students with Special Needs

- Encourage your child to watch local or regional news with you on TV. Talk about what is going on in your community.

Money Skills

- Encourage your child to make a savings plan to save up for a desired item. Map out how much needs to be saved weekly in order to buy the item within a reasonable amount of time.
- Help your child come up with a budget for spending and saving. If you pay your child for chores or grades, include that in the overall plan. Talk about what factors can be adjusted.
- Open up a savings or checking account for your child. Go over the monthly statements so that he or she can see growth, spending habits or trends, and fees that are assessed.

Travel

- Before taking a family trip, map out the plan using maps or an atlas. Calculate the mileage, expected travel time, and best route. Locate interesting side trips that your family might want to take.
- Make a list of what items are necessary for weekend travel, overnight travel, or plane travel. Keep the list handy for at least a week before you go on a major trip, and add items as they come to mind.
- Select several community destinations and have your child figure out how public transportation could be used to get there. Obtain a copy of timetables.

Clothing

- Periodically go through closets (spring cleaning?) and have your child choose what clothing is needed and what items can be given away or stored.
- Give your child opportunities to wash and dry clothing. Realize there might be a few mistakes along the way!

Living Arrangements

- Have a daily or weekly schedule of who is responsible for which chores in the house.
- Monitor your family's heat, electric, and phone bills for a period of several months. Analyze what factors account for the bill and talk about how to keep costs down.

Eating and Nutrition

- Set aside one evening a week for your child to host and prepare a meal. Help in whatever way is appropriate—shopping, planning, organizing, preparing, hosting—but increasingly give your child more independence.
- Set aside a particular place for coupons or weekly shopping ads so they are easily accessible before shopping.
- Collect family recipes or favorite meals that have been successfully prepared. Laminate them or use index cards or plastic sleeves to keep them protected.

Shopping

- Look for sales of needed items before buying them. Give your child a reasonable estimate of how much he or she should expect to spend on something. If the item comes in under budget, let your child keep the savings.
- Have a place to keep receipts so that you can return purchases easily if they don't work out.

Exercise/Health and Hygiene

- Set a good example of staying healthy by exercising. Include your child if possible, in your own activities.
- Look for opportunities for your child to participate in sports, on teams or through lessons or neighborhood game-playing in the park.
- Be aware of the changes your child will be going through as far as puberty. Prepare your child for the changes in hygiene and self-esteem that may be experienced.
- You are responsible for getting your child to the dentist and to the doctor when necessary.
- If you are concerned about your child's level of stress or possible depression, check in with your school counselor or a teacher whom you trust. Don't ignore warning signs if your child seems unusually unhappy or has developed odd or unexpected new behaviors.

Part Five: Vocational Skills

Present Skills and Interests

- You are in a unique position to note your child's strengths and weaknesses. Think about what you have noticed about his or her vocational interests over the years. When he was little, what did he want to be when he grew up?
- Expose your child to job possibilities. Take advantage of friends of yours who might be willing to take your child to work for a day—or a few hours.
- Does your child know what his parents do for a living? How do you feel about your job? What you say and your attitude about work can affect how your child will view the world of work.
- If possible, allow your child to participate in activities that reflect her or his interests. Lessons (music, riding) can be expensive, but look for ways to involve your child in things he likes in natural ways. (Can you trade riding lessons for stall cleaning? Are there teen programs at the YMCA or through scouting?)

Getting a Job

- Your child may need your help to pull some strings to land that first job. Help him or her by keeping an eye out for entry-level positions with your friends, neighbors, or even your own employer.
- Encourage your child to have character references ready to go. Think about who would give a glowing reference for a job application. Make sure your child asks permission to use this person as a reference.

Life Skills Activities for Secondary Students with Special Needs

- Sometimes employers will let the applicant take the paperwork home to complete. If your child needs practice in filling them out, grab a few samples and help her prepare to find the information that will be needed (school information, references, personal information, and so on).
- Your child may need to think creatively to land a job—work for free for a trial period? Show enthusiasm? Keep calling back (without being a pest)?

Working

- The first job may not be your child's ideal experience—but emphasize that he or she must perform as though it is the greatest job in the world. That kind of attitude will get your child noticed.
- If your child complains about things about the job, remind him that everything he learns and does can affect what happens later. He can take advantage of the "bad" things to learn how to accept criticism, learn from mistakes, gain new skills, and take pride in sticking it out!
- Emphasize again and again how important it is to get to work on time, have good attendance, and start the day with a smile.
- Remind your child that he or she is not the boss (yet).

Part Six: Problem-Solving Skills

Handling Problem Situations

- Most special needs students do not handle change very well. When you know that a major change is coming (such as a move, divorce, or new baby), let your child know well in advance, or with appropriate notice (some students will then perseverate about the change relentlessly). Stress positive aspects of the change and allow your child to be a part of it as much as possible.
- If your child is often the one causing a problem in a social situation, help her take ownership of that behavior. There is some degree of perceived power in being able to change what happens or control others' behavior. Encourage her to use this perceived power to control the most important person: herself.
- Give your child problem-solving activities to work on, such as Sudoku puzzles, word searches, jigsaw puzzles, and minute mysteries. Talk about techniques for problem solving—trying another approach, looking at something from another perspective, trial and error, thinking critically. These are skills that can be applied to life situations as well.

Making Decisions

- Make a pro/con chart when your child has a nonroutine decision to make. Help him consider both sides of the decision—the investment, the process, the consequences—before making a decision.
- Although it may be hard, sometimes it is better to stand aside and let your child make a poor decision (as long as it doesn't affect safety or too much self-esteem). Ideally, you can both laugh about it later.
- Sometimes it is helpful to involve a third party for making decisions. This might be someone who is familiar with the situation, someone respected by both sides, or someone who is objective enough to help with making a decision.

Resource Management

- As situations come up, have your child identify whether something is a *need* or a *want*.
- If your child works for you or gets an allowance, help her learn that this is not an endless resource. When the job is finished, she gets paid. When the job is not done, no pay.
- Have your child make her own personal resource list. What people in her life are there for her? What are her talents and skills?
- Use opportunities to differentiate between *fact* and *opinion*. While watching the news at night or reading an article about something going on, you might find opportunities to explain when someone is giving an opinion versus presenting carefully documented facts. When your child wants to argue, ask for facts.

Goal-Setting

- Set a monthly family goal. Write it, display it, review it, revise it, complete it!
- When there seem to be many things to do, practice prioritizing the goals. Talk about what needs to be done first. Sometimes just getting the first step done will get the ball rolling. Clean out one drawer, vacuum one room, write one letter, start one load of laundry.

Risk-Taking

- Break up your routine. List five things that your family has never done before and take a family risk. Learn to bowl. Run a 5K. Visit a nursing home. Plant flowers in the community park. Wear something currently in fashion. Have some fun.
- Some risks are not worth even considering. Being in a dangerous situation (taking drugs, being out late at night alone, getting into a car with a drunk driver) is not worth the risk. It is better to learn that lesson by example, not by experience.
- Be supportive of your child if he or she is in a frightening situation. You can't protect your kids from everything, but if you know your child is going to be in a frightening situation, have a plan ready to execute. And have a backup plan in case Plan A fails!

Part One

Self-Awareness

Chapter 1: My Character

1.1   Qualities of a Good Character

1.2   Honesty

1.3   Kindness

1.4   Loyalty

1.5   Responsibility

1.6   Flexibility

1.7   What Are Values?

Chapter 2: Uniquely Me

2.1   Values Important to Me

2.2   My Ethnic Background

2.3   My Disabilities

2.4   What's a Reputation?

2.5   Changing Your Reputation

2.6   How You Appear to Others

Chapter 3: Personal Life Choices

3.1   Smoking: Is It for Me?

3.2   Marijuana and Other Drugs

3.3   Teens and Drinking

3.4   Changing Your Appearance

3.5   Tattoos and Piercings

3.6   Rate the Date

3.7   Ready to Move Out?

3.8   Ready to Work Part-Time?

Chapter 1

My Character

1.1 Qualities of a Good Character

Objective:

The student will identify examples of a person showing good character traits.

Comments:

The notion of having good *character* is somewhat intuitive—you know good character when you see it. In this lesson, students are introduced to the idea of character as something positive, whether it is an action or a thought that leads to an action. It has nothing to do with physical attributes such as how someone looks or their physical limitations.

Introductory Activities:

1. Write the word *character* on the board and ask students what they think "good character" means.
2. As you go through their ideas, ask if they think character is something *inside* a person; that is, how they think or act—or *outside* a person; that is, the way a person looks.
3. Come up with a working definition of *character*: traits or inner qualities of a person that would make them outstanding or worthy of positive attention.

Activity:

"Qualities of a Good Character" is an introductory worksheet for students. The concept of character is presented by examples showing good citizenship, treating others well, or making good choices. Students are to match these three traits to the examples. Several answers can be correct as long as students can justify them.   *Answers:* 1. B (or C) 2. A 3. C (or B) 4. A 5. B 6. C 7. B 8. A (or C)

Discussion:

Go through the worksheet items and discuss why students selected their answers.

1. Did any of the examples mention the way a person looked? (No.)
2. In examples 3 and 6, what choices did the people have? (Be angry or wait; skip school or not.) How did the good choices help the people? (Avoided a possible argument; allowed Denny to take the test he needed to take.)
3. How do examples 2, 4, and 8 consider others while being a good citizen? (Make the park a nicer place for others; safety issue for the person and the drivers; provide relief for the man who lost the wallet.)

Extension Activities:

1. Have students search through photographs, magazines, or the Internet to find pictures that portray someone in the act of showing good character.
2. List characters familiar to students in movies, books, or other common venues who are good examples of someone with good character. Discuss why this person seems to have good character. What about this person is outstanding?

Evaluation:

1. Give an example of someone being a good citizen.   2. Give an example of someone treating others well.   3. Give an example of someone making a good choice.

1.1   Qualities of a Good Character

Directions:

These students are showing good character traits. Write the letter of the trait next to each example.

A = Good citizen   B = Treats others well   C = Makes good choices

_____ 1. Eloise's father asked her to be at home right after school so she could babysit for her little sister and brother. She told her friends that she wouldn't be able to go out with them after school and came home.

_____ 2. Danny and Henry were walking through the park near their home and noticed a lot of litter. They picked up some cans and threw them into a bag to be recycled.

_____ 3. Alison was angry at her best friend for forgetting to return a necklace that she borrowed. Alison wanted to yell at her friend, but decided to calm down and wait before talking to her friend. The next day she didn't feel angry, and her friend apologized.

_____ 4. Tony needed to cross a busy street to get to the store, but instead of rushing into the street to make the cars stop for him, he went to the street corner and waited for the crosswalk light to change. Then he walked across.

_____ 5. Sara knew that her mother was worried about losing her job. Sara decided to make her mother a nice salad when she came home, and she cleaned the house without being asked.

_____ 6. Denny's friend wanted him to join them in skipping school. Denny had a big test that day and told his friends that he needed to go to school.

_____ 7. Kara was walking down the hall when a girl accidentally knocked into her and made her drop her books. The girl felt very bad and almost started to cry. Kara laughed and told her not to worry about it.

_____ 8. Pete and Devon noticed a wallet on the street with some money, credit cards, and photographs inside. They picked it up and found enough identification to locate the owner, so they called him and returned the wallet.

1.2 Honesty

Objective:

The student will identify ways that someone could show honesty in given situations.

Comments:

To be thought of as an honest person, someone needs to continually demonstrate that quality, including (especially?) in situations that are not readily observed by others. Think honesty at all times! This worksheet offers examples of situations in which a person has an opportunity to act honestly.

Introductory Activities:

1. Talk about what *honesty* means—telling the truth or behaving in a way that is consistent with what is true.   2. Ask students to share examples of observed honesty in others.   3. Ask students to share examples of their own honesty.

Activity:

Explain that students will read about honesty in the examples on the worksheet "Honesty."   *Answers (Examples):*   1. Return the money.   2. Tell your mother why you didn't get the chores done. 3. Tell your friend that you already committed to an event but will spend time with him or her later. 4. Take the boxes to the post office.   5. Discreetly let the usher know which kids were involved. 6. Better to admit that you didn't get your math done.

Discussion:

Discuss how each example showed honest behavior and the positive results that came from that act.

1. How are other people affected by the honest behavior in these examples?
2. In item #1, why would returning the money matter if the clerk didn't know she had made a mistake? (Might catch up with her later and she would have to pay for the mistake.)
3. How was being honest taking a risk in #5? (Could be anger on the part of the kids if they found out.) Why would it be worth the risk? (So the theater would be a friendly place for others in the future.)

Extension Activities:

1. Discuss the difference between being "brutally honest" and being tactful.
2. Have students think of someone whom they consider to be a very honest person. Write a short paragraph describing the person and the person's honesty.

Evaluation:

How could you show honesty if you bought a sweatshirt at the store and when you looked in the bag, you had accidentally taken some socks that you didn't pay for?

1.2

Honesty

Directions:

How could these people demonstrate good character by using *honesty*? Write your answer next to each item.

1. I gave the clerk a $10 bill and she gave me way too much money back.

   _____

2. My mother asked if I finished all of the chores I was supposed to do. I didn't get them done, but it was because I had to help my next-door neighbor. I am not sure my mother will listen to my excuses, though.

   _____

3. My friend invited me to go bowling, but I already promised someone else that I would go out with him. I don't want to hurt my friend's feelings.

   _____

4. My aunt asked me to take these boxes to the post office before noon so they could get out in today's mail. She is gone, so she won't know whether I did it or not.

   _____

5. Some kids were throwing popcorn around in the movie theater. The usher asked me which kids were causing the problem.

   _____

6. I was rushing to get my math assignment done. Carol said I could copy her paper if I wanted to.

   _____

Chapter 1: My Character

1.3 Kindness

Objective:

The student will identify an act of kindness that could be shown to someone else in a given situation.

Comments:

A popular idea going around is that of doing a "random act of kindness" toward others—usually a surprising and pleasant act, going way beyond what is necessary to show kindness to someone. The act of kindness is not expected, is not necessary, and in many instances is not even acknowledged. Encourage students to be creative in their ways of showing kindness toward others.

Introductory Activities:

Give students plenty of examples of random acts of kindness and the spirit behind the movement by using the books *Random Acts of Kindness* (Daphne Rose Kingma and Dawna Markova, Conari Press, 2002) and *Kids' Random Acts of Kindness* (Conari Press, 1994).

1. Ask students to tell about acts of kindness that have been done to them.   2. Ask students to give examples of any acts of kindness that they have done to others.

Activity:

Students are to read each example of a situation in which an act of kindness could be done. Students should use their own unique personalities to come up with their responses. Encourage students to be creative, yet realistic. What would they really do?   *Answers (Examples):*   1. Pay the cashier and don't tell the girl that it was you.   2. Write Ben an anonymous note telling how much someone liked his work. 3. Send the girl flowers.   4. Make sure that Mrs. Miller receives a card from every student in her class.

Discussion:

There is no single correct answer to these situations. Some students may be able to describe an act of kindness, but would never follow through on it. Ask students to be honest about their responses.

1. Would you want someone to know if you did something kind for somebody? Why would you want to be recognized?   2. How much did each of your deeds cost in terms of time, money, energy? 3. Does doing an act of kindness make the kind doer feel good? Is that why people do these things? 4. After hearing what other people came up with as far as ideas, would you change what you would do? Do you like other ideas better now than your own?   5. Which of these acts of kindness would you ever really do?

Extension Activities:

1. Plan to do a wild, exuberant act of kindness. Plot whom you will target and what you will do, then carry it out. What was the reaction of the person you targeted? How did it make you feel? Did you do it secretly or did you want to be discovered?   2. Read the book *Random Acts of Kindness*. Which were your favorite anecdotes? Why?   3. Compile a class book of acts of kindness. What starts happening when people start being outrageously kind to each other?   4. Refer to www.actsofkindness .org to investigate lots of ways people have shown kindness to others.

Evaluation:

1. Give a general example of a random act of kindness.   2. Give a very specific example of an act of kindness that you have personally been involved in.

1.3   # Kindness

Directions:

How could the person in each picture below demonstrate an act of kindness? On the back of this sheet, draw or write about a good example.

                     Chapter 1: My Character

1.4 Loyalty

Objective:

The student will give an example of loyalty to someone or something.

Comments:

Being loyal to someone or something involves providing your support even during times of turmoil or misunderstanding. It is important to develop loyalty within friendships, family, and other groups that share a common bond or passion. Knowing that someone will stick with you or stick up for you whether you are there or not, whether you are having a good day or a bad day, is a true test of loyalty.

Introductory Activities:

1. Ask students to share the name of their favorite sports team. Why do they support this team?
2. Talk about what *loyalty* means—being supportive of someone or something in good times or bad. What does this actually look like?

Activity:

The worksheet "Loyalty" gives examples of students who are/are not showing loyalty to someone or something. The student is to circle the names of the loyal students.   *Answers:* 1. Allan   2. Jill   3. Katie   4. David

Discussion:

Go through each example and discuss why each person is or is not showing loyalty.

1. In each example, are the people showing loyalty to a person or to a team or organization? (To people: 2, 3, 4; to a team: 1.)
2. Why does it matter if Frank changed his mind about cheering for the team? (It shows he only cares about who is winning.)
3. In example 2, how would the sister feel in each case? (Loved; alienated.)
4. How does example 3 show a good solution? (Katie wants to invite the friend.)
5. Why would it be hard to be loyal to someone like the boy in example 4? (He is not a fun friend.) Do you think it is a good time to be loyal? (Probably; it might help him.)

Extension Activities:

1. Dogs are often given the label "man's best friend" because of their loyalty. Talk about what this means. Example?   2. Have students find examples in stories or movies of extreme loyalty. 3. In what ways do we show loyalty to our school, family, house of worship, country, and so on? 4. Collect items that depict loyalty, such as: sweatshirts, baseball caps, pins, pennants, school colors, bumper stickers, and so on.

Evaluation:

1. How could you show loyalty to a member of your family?   2. How could you show loyalty to an organization such as a house of worship, school, or team?

1.4   **Loyalty**

Directions:

Which of these students is showing loyalty to someone or something? Circle the name of the loyal student in each case.

1.

ALLEN: Go team! I will support our team, win or lose!

FRANK: Oh man, they are losing terribly! I think I'll start cheering for the other team.

Frank   Allan

2.

JILL: You are my sister, and no matter what, I care about you.

MEGAN: You look really weird. Don't tell anyone we are related.

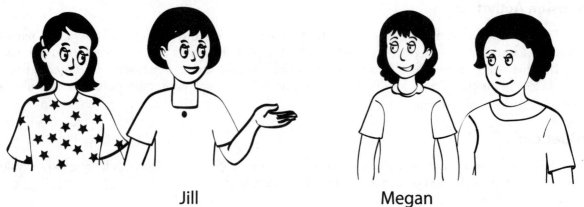

Jill   Megan

3.

ELLEN: Hey, we are going to Pat's house after the game. Want to come?

KATIE: Do I! Yes! Hang on . . . Hello, Sue? Something came up, and now I can't go out with you.

ABBY: Sorry, I already have plans.

Ellen   Katie   Abby

4.

MICHAEL: Rick is acting strangely these days. I don't think I'll hang out with Rick anymore. He is boring and doesn't want to do anything.

DAVID: I think he needs a friend, so I'll spend some time with him.

David   Michael   Rick

1.5 Responsibility

Objective:

The student will give an example of showing responsibility in a given situation.

Comments:

Being responsible means that you will do or be whatever is needed, whether or not someone is there to supervise you. It is important to be trusted to do what needs to be done, with or without someone directing you.

Introductory Activities:

1. What is the most important job you have ever been given? Who gave you the job? What did you have to do? How did it go?   2. Have you ever disappointed someone by not doing what they expected you to do?   3. What does being *responsible* mean to you?

Activity:

The worksheet "Responsibility" shows examples of a person being given a task to do in settings of home, school, and work. The students should write how they could show responsibility in each situation. *Answers (Examples):*   1. Make sure everything is cleaned up and the door is locked.   2. Stay at home until your sister is there, then leave with friends (or don't leave at all).   3. Make a daily schedule to walk the dog; walk the dog with friends.   4. Take out your assignment book and write the dates on a calendar.   5. Be careful driving; fill the car up with gas when done.

Discussion:

For each example, identify the task involved, who assigned the task, and how to make sure it is carried out responsibly.

1. In these examples, the task is specified by a boss, adult, or another person. Can you think of some tasks that you just have to be responsible for on your own, without a reminder from a person? (Habitual chores, paying bills, exercising.)
2. What are some consequences that could happen in each example if the person did not take responsibility?

Extension Activities:

1. Research the responsibilities and job descriptions of several different occupations (perhaps the president, a surgeon, a cashier). Why is it important to take any responsibility seriously, whether it involves "big" issues or somewhat smaller issues?
2. Invite guest speakers from different types of careers to talk to your class about their responsibilities. When they are looking to hire someone, how important is the characteristic of responsibility?

Evaluation:

1. How could you show responsibility at home?   2. How could you show responsibility at school?
3. How could you show responsibility at work?

1.5

Responsibility

Directions:

How could you show responsibility in each of these situations?

1. BOSS AT WORK: I won't be here when you leave, so would you please put everything away and lock up when you go?

   _____

   _____

2. FATHER: Make sure your little sister gets home safely before you go out with your friends.

   _____

   _____

3. MOTHER: You said you wanted a dog. Well, this one needs to be walked every day or he'll tear up the room.

   _____

   _____

4. TEACHER: Here are the dates of the next two tests. I am not going to remind you every day, so do what you need to do to remember.

   _____

   _____

5. FRIEND: Here are the keys to my car. You can borrow it tonight, since you don't have one.

   _____

   _____

Chapter 1: My Character

13

1.6 Flexibility

Objective:

The student will give an example of how someone could show flexibility in a given situation.

Comments:

Being flexible involves being able to make changes to existing plans (such as going to a later showing of a movie), accommodating things that you weren't expecting (such as sitting with your unexpected cousin instead of your friends), or making something work that wasn't originally in the plans (such as finding out the movie was cancelled). In all respects, it involves being able to change with as much ease and grace as possible. Special learners often find comfort in regular, predictable patterns. It requires flexibility to deal with a change in routine.

Introductory Activities:

Write the word *flexibility* or *flexible* on the board and have students give examples of what they think this means. What does *flexible* mean to a gymnast? What does it mean when applied to a rubber band? What do those examples have to do with a personality trait?

Ask students to give examples of times when they have had to be flexible in a situation.

Activity:

On the worksheet "Flexibility," students will read examples of people who have had to show flexibility in order to make an unexpected situation be acceptable. In some cases, it might mean giving up something in order to reach the best outcome for all parties.

Answers (Examples):

1. Jacob could see a different movie, go by himself, or go later in the week.
2. The girls could make separate books, or Emily could negotiate and have Emma change only three photos.
3. Joshua could play his position as well as possible, but ask to be a backup quarterback.
4. Madison could explain what happened and ask for time to redo the messy pages.
5. Andrew could be considerate and make his cousin happy.
6. Hannah could wear something else, or Hannah could change her outfit to be mainly pink.

Discussion:

As you discuss the questions, talk about how change might be a factor caused by other people, as in some of the examples, but that flexibility might be required when unexpected things happen that are not specifically caused by people (for example, a train running late, bad weather spoiling a picnic, a tree falling)

1. In examples 2 and 5, other people could possibly be flexible to change the situation. How?
2. Flexibility can show up in many different ways. How could example 1 be resolved in several different ways? (Change movie, change time, change date.)
3. What good things could come from showing flexibility in these situations? Are there any that are no-win situations even if the person is trying to be flexible?

Extension Activities:

1. Have students keep track of how many changes of plans happen to them in a single day. Try to categorize the events—people, schedules, weather?

2. Find out contingency plans for an organization that is driven by schedules, such as a train or bus station. What happens when a train runs late? What is the backup plan for equipment failure? How does flexibility help in keeping the overall system working well?

Evaluation:

1. How could you show flexibility if you had made plans to go swimming and it turned out to be a rainy day?

2. How could you show flexibility if you were planning on meeting two friends for pizza, but five friends showed up?

1.6   # Flexibility

Directions:

How could each of these people show the quality of flexibility? Write your answer on each line.

1. Jacob was expecting his friend Michael to show up at 6 o'clock so they could walk to the movie theater. Michael called and said that his family had unexpected company, so he wouldn't get to Jacob's house in time to walk with him to the movie. Jacob was counting on seeing the movie that night.

   _____

2. Emily and her sister Emma were working on a family photo project. Emily decided to change all of the photos of herself because she didn't like the way she looked in them. Emma had a plan made up for how the photos should go in the book, and now that Emily wanted to change them, it wouldn't be the way she wanted.

   _____

3. Joshua had his heart set on being the quarterback for the team he played with, but the coach told him he thought Joshua would be a better running back, at least for this season.

   _____

4. Madison finished her homework and had it all set next to the door so she wouldn't forget it. When she got to school, she noticed that her dog had walked across her paper—the one that was supposed to be turned in today. There were brown footprints across the first three pages.

   _____

5. Andrew hated to get his hair cut because he liked the way it looked. His mother said that he had to at least get a trim before the family went to his cousin's wedding. In fact, his cousin had specifically asked whether Andrew would take the pink dye out of his hair before they did the wedding pictures.

   _____

6. Hannah ordered a blue-and-white-striped sweater online. She ordered it in plenty of time to wear it to a big party that weekend. When the box arrived the day before the party, she opened it to find a lovely pink-and-white-striped sweater.

   _____

1.7 What Are Values?

Objective:

The student will list at least five common values and give an example of each.

Comments:

Each of us has a value system. There are certain things we place great importance on, and we act accordingly. Our values may be gained from our parents, our experiences, our education, and other sources, but it is important to know what we value. In this lesson, students are introduced to the concept of values and are given examples.

Introductory Activities:

1. Tell students you are going to say some words. Have them write one word that comes to mind that seems to include your examples.

$1,000,000 . . . gold coins . . . winning the lottery $\rightarrow$ Money, wealth

mom . . . dad . . . uncle . . . brother . . . Aunt Ginny $\rightarrow$ Family

blue ribbon . . . trophy . . . diploma $\longrightarrow$ Achievement

2. Define *value*. (Something of great importance to someone.)

Activity:

On the worksheet "What Are Values?" students are to match examples of values in action with the value listed.   *Answers:* 1. e 2. h 3. c 4. i 5. b 6. g 7. j 8. a 9. k 10. d 11. l 12. f

Discussion:

Have students discuss any of the items that are unclear to them. Explain that these are just examples—there are lots of other ways to demonstrate the value.

1. Which of the values on the worksheet are important to you?
2. What are some other examples of demonstrating the values on the worksheet?
3. Which values do you think would be important to these people?

   Elderly Person   Mother   Athlete   Teacher   Lawyer   Model

Extension Activities:

1. Have students collect or record bumper stickers they have seen or heard of. What values are indicated by the stickers? What clues were given?   2. Listen to speeches by politicians or school board members (election times are good times to work on this activity). What values are brought up?

Evaluation:

1. List five to seven common values.   2. For each value listed in (1), give an example of how someone could demonstrate that value.

1.7   ## What Are Values?

Directions:

Match the value on the left with an example on the right of your demonstrating that value.

1. Health _____

2. Wealth _____

3. Family _____

4. Friendship _____

5. Humor _____

6. Education _____

7. Beauty _____

8. Space _____

9. Food _____

10. Exercise _____

11. Music _____

12. Happiness _____

a. Wanting your own bedroom

b. Watching a comedy show on television

c. Spending time at the movies with your brothers and sisters

d. Working out at a health club three times a week

e. Making sure you have had your flu shot

f. Doing what you enjoy, allowing yourself to have fun

g. Going to graduate school

h. Opening a savings account

i. Sticking up for your friends, even when nobody else will

j. Planting flowers in front of your house

k. Preparing a gourmet meal

l. Learning to play the piano

Chapter 2

Uniquely Me

2.1 Values Important to Me

Objective:

The student will state or list at least five values that are personally important to him or her.

Comments:

Everyone has values, whether they are specifically stated or not. Just by observing a person and listening to what he or she says, you can determine some things that are of great importance to that person. In this lesson, students are to think about specific values that are meaningful to them.

Introductory Activities:

1. Have students write the name of a person who is important to them.   2. Have students write the name of an important possession.   3. Have students write what they think is the most important characteristic a person can have.

Activity:

Students look at a list of values and indicate which are either somewhat or extremely important to them personally.

Discussion:

Because this is an individual activity, responses will be quite different. It might be interesting to find out (with a show of hands) which items were most often selected as being important to students within the class.

1. Why are the things that people value different for everyone? (People have had different upbringings, different experiences, and so on.)
2. What values do you think are probably the same for most people? (Health, happiness, and so on.)
3. What people or kinds of people would not value wealth? (Clergy, homeless.)
4. What problems could arise between people who have very different value systems? (Depends on the value, but there could be a lot of conflicts.)
5. Do you think a person's values change as the person gets older? Why? (Probably needs change as we get older; need to have a job, money.)
6. How could a traumatic experience such as being saved from a life-threatening situation affect a person's values? (The person might tend to value life/health more.)

Extension Activities:

1. Have students consider the items on the worksheet and try to reduce them to a single word; for example, doing well in school, being well-educated could both be covered by Education.
2. Have students add items to the list. Which are the result of specific experiences they have had?
3. Have students conduct a survey of a cross-section of the population: adults, students, elementary children. Make a list of ten items to give as the survey. Which values are more predominant in certain age groups? (For example, do children value health and wealth? Do adults value being good at sports?)

Evaluation:

1. List five personal values.   2. Give an example for each value in (1) of how you demonstrate that value in your life.

2.1   Values Important to Me

Directions:

Put a check mark next to the items on the list that are somewhat important to you. Put two marks next to those that are extremely important to you. Leave items blank if you are not particularly interested in that value.

1. Having a lot of money _____

2. Doing well in school _____

3. Having a lot of friends _____

4. Having one close friend _____

5. Getting along with my parents _____

6. Getting along with my family _____

7. Having time to myself _____

8. Not worrying about having enough to eat _____

9. Getting/having a good job _____

10. Liking my job _____

11. Respecting myself _____

12. Being respected by others _____

13. Having my own space/room _____

14. Being good at something _____

15. Having a clean room _____

16. Breathing clean air _____

17. Recycling _____

18. Being well-educated _____

19. Being in good health _____

20. Being handsome/pretty _____

21. Knowing that someone loves me _____

22. Being in love _____

23. Having nice clothes _____

24. Having a lot of possessions _____

25. Being in good physical shape _____

26. Having a boyfriend or girlfriend _____

27. Being good at sports _____

28. Helping others _____

29. Being recognized for helping others _____

30. Believing in God or some other Supreme Being _____

31. Being happy _____

32. Being right about something _____

33. Being able to handle responsibility _____

34. Setting goals for myself _____

35. Having control of what happens to me _____

Chapter 2: Uniquely Me   **21**

2.2 My Ethnic Background

Objective:

The student will state and briefly describe his or her ethnic background.

Comments:

Many people identify themselves as being part of a particular ethnic group or originally descending from people of a certain country. Part of knowing yourself is being familiar with your ethnic background, particularly if customs and habits are still part of your day-to-day life. This lesson focuses on awareness of our individual backgrounds and taking pride in those origins.

Introductory Activities:

1. Have students indicate by raising hands if there are members of their family who recently (in the last generation or two) have come from another country. Perhaps some students may have heard about how their parents arrived in this country and would like to share with the class. Discuss this event.

2. Have students volunteer to discuss and describe any traditions their family has celebrated. (Do not force students to participate; some may not wish to emphasize their differences!)

3. Ask students if any of them speak a second language or have family members who do. Have them describe how this is helpful or difficult.

Activity:

Students are to complete the survey "My Ethnic Background" by individually writing answers to the questions. They may wish to take the sheet home and have their family members help them fill out the information. Assure students that if they do not wish to reveal their personal lives in class, they will not have to, but encourage them to think about the questions and complete them—at least for their own benefit.   *Answers:* Will vary.

Discussion:

Have students volunteer to share the information they completed on the worksheet. Emphasize that just because traditions may differ, this does not mean one is right or wrong.

1. Was this information easy to obtain? Who were your sources?   2. Are you part of a large ethnic group in your community? Do you feel you are accepted in the community?   3. Do you feel your ethnic group is stereotyped in any way? How?

Extension Activities:

1. Have students compile family photographs or newspaper clippings on a poster or collage. Have students volunteer to explain to the class the significance of the people on the poster.   2. Have students collect newspaper articles featuring their particular ethnic group in the news.   3. Make a class map of the world highlighting the countries where students in the class originated from. They may be surprised to find out the diversity within even one classroom.

Evaluation:

1. What is your primary ethnic background?   2. How did your family originally come to live in the community where you now reside?   3. What are some characteristics about your family that reflect your ethnic background?

2.2   **My Ethnic Background**

Directions:

Complete this activity by focusing on your own family background. Perhaps you have two or more nationalities represented in your family's history. Talk to your parents, grandparents, or other relatives who can help fill you in on your past.

Find out the following:

1. What ethnic groups are in your family? How did your family come to live where you do now? Did anyone come originally from another country?
2. What holidays or traditions do you celebrate? Are these different from your neighbor's customs?
3. Does anyone in your family speak a second language? What? When?
4. Are your closest friends of the same ethnic group as you? If not, does this present any problems? What?
5. If someone from another country were to visit your home, what do you think he or she would find most interesting? What object would he or she pick out as being unusual? Would any of your customs seem strange to that person? Which ones?

2.3 My Disabilities

Objectives:

(1) The student will identify common physical, mental, or emotional disabilities and state a characteristic of each. (2) The student will identify and briefly describe a personal disability.

Comments:

There are many types of recognized disabilities—learning disabilities, emotional disabilities, physical disabilities, and so on. Although we don't want students to cling to their disability as a crutch or excuse in any way, it is important for them to know, as much as is possible and appropriate, about their disability and how it affects them, their family, and their success in life. This lesson is a general introduction to the idea of having a personal disability, what that means, and how to take steps to deal with it positively.

Introductory Activities:

(*Note:* Select activities that are appropriate for your students, as some students may not be willing to discuss personal issues.)

1. Discuss: What is a disability? (Not being able to do something as well as others, primarily based on physical restrictions or cognitive/behavioral issues.)
2. What are some common types of disabilities that you know about? (Learning disabilities, attention deficit disorder, physical disabilities, and so on.)
3. Do you have a disability that you can share information about with us? Or is there someone in your family who has a disability? How has it affected you?

Activity:

On the worksheet "My Disabilities," students are to write one way that the disabled person is doing something positive to help himself or herself. Remind them to think about their own disabilities and ways that they have learned to be positive.

Answers:

1. Getting involved in wheelchair sports
2. Getting the information in a different way
3. Controlling the environment for success
4. Continuing to work with the speech teacher
5. Spending time socializing in fun ways
6. Doing things in his strong area

Discussion:

As you discuss the examples, encourage students to relate to the disabilities that are similar to their situations and experience.

1. In item 1, the boy is physically disabled. How has he continued to have a good life? (Enjoys sports, seems to have a good attitude.)
2. If someone has a speech disability, such as the girl in item 4, how could that affect them socially? (Embarrassing.) How did the girl handle the problem? What are some other ways that she could continue to be positive around others?

3. People with emotional or social disabilities, such as in items 3 and 5, have issues with others. What are some suggestions that you might make to these individuals? Perhaps you know of someone who has difficulty in this area and has developed some coping strategies.

4. Language or reading disabilities, such as in items 2 and 6, can be hard to deal with, especially in school, but what are some ways that these people have overcome their disabilities? (Learning in other ways, using their strengths.)

5. If you have any of these disabilities, what could you share as far as difficulties and successes?

6. Do you feel that others have to help you with your disability or that you can be in control of what happens to you and how to help yourself?

Extension Activities:

These websites contain ideas and actual experiences for simulating disabilities:

- www.pbs.org/wgbh/misunderstoodminds/

  Attention deficit; reading, visual, auditory disabilities

- www.addchoices.com/it_feels_like_.htm

  Visual and fine motor disabilities

- http://library.thinkquest.org/5852/activitiesandsimulatons.htm

  Activities and simulations for visual impairment and mobility disabilities

Evaluation:

1. Give an example of a physical disability. Describe something that a person could do with an adaptation.

2. If you have a disability, describe something positive and something negative about your disability.

2.3   My Disabilities

Directions:

How are these students doing positive things even though they have a disability?

1. I can't walk, but I can sure play basketball!

2. Listening to a recorded book is a lot easier for me. I can understand things a lot better when I hear them.

3. I know that I will get angry when Jeff gives me a nasty look. I want to punch him, but I will control myself by sitting on the other side of the room. I can talk to the counselor later today about how I can stay in control.

4. It's embarrassing for me to have to keep repeating words when people can't understand what I'm saying. But I will work hard with my speech teacher. I know I am getting better.

5. I find it hard to talk to people, but when I'm in a group and we go roller skating or bowling, it's a lot easier for me to fit in.

6. I don't like to read, but I sure am good at math. I'm on our school's Math Bowl team. I even help some of the younger kids at our school who need a tutor.

2.4 What's a Reputation?

Objective:

The student will make assumptions about a character's reputation based on given clues.

Comments:

A reputation is a judgment about a person made by others. Whether deserved or not, people make decisions about a person's character. In this lesson, students are given comments about others to consider. They are to decide what it tells about the person's reputation.

Introductory Activities:

1. Define *reputation* (a person's character as judged by other people).   2. Write one comment you think people say about you to others.

Activity:

Students are to read the comments on the worksheet "What's a Reputation?" and make a judgment about some aspect of the person's reputation.   *Answers (Examples):*   1. She is a good student; gets good grades.   2. He is a poor driver.   3. He knows about cars.   4. He cheats.   5. She's a bad player.   6. He's a good salesman.   7. She is honest.   8. He lies.   9. He's a poor carpenter. 10. She's fun.   11. She has a bad temper.   12. He eats a lot.

Discussion:

After students have completed the worksheet, compare their responses. Did they come up with the same conclusions?

1. How do other people come up with ideas about a person's reputation? (Things they observe, things they hear from others.)   2. What is an example of a good reputation?   3. What is an example of a bad reputation?

Extension Activities:

1. Have students consider some political figures or celebrities. What reputations are they known for? How did they get these reputations?
2. Have students think of famous people (or, if appropriate, students within the school's student body). Who has a reputation for being a good sport? For being friendly? For being rich? For being athletic? Have students think of other categories. Try to emphasize the positive.

Evaluation:

1. Define *reputation*.   2. If someone had a reputation for being a good cook, what are some possible clues that would lead you to think that?

2.4   What's a Reputation?

1. "She's such a brain!"

   _____

2. "Don't ever get in the car with Tom if you value your life."

   _____

3. "Fred is the one to ask if you have a question about cars."

   _____

4. "Oh, no—do I have to sit next to him in this class? I'll have to hide my paper so he doesn't copy everything."

   _____

5. "I hope we don't have to have Sheila on our team. She's awful."

   _____

6. "If you want a good deal, buy your cars from Mr. Alvarez."

   _____

7. "If Angie says it's true, it's true."

   _____

8. "Don't believe anything Mark says."

   _____

9. "John built your back porch? I hope it doesn't fall down."

   _____

10. "Be sure to invite Kim to the party. She's a lot of fun."

    _____

11. "I'm afraid to admit that I messed up on this paper. Mrs. Gabler will have a fit."

    _____

12. "Let's make sure we eat dessert before Randy gets here. There won't be any left."

    _____

2.5 Changing Your Reputation

Objective:

The student will identify reasons or ways for individuals to change a reputation in specific examples.

Comments:

Reputations are gained and lost all the time. If someone makes a concerted effort to change a reputation, that can happen. There are also other ways to make changes. Sometimes other people make that determination for us by providing training, guidance, or a model. In this lesson, students are given examples of reputations that have changed and are to determine what factors were involved.

Introductory Activities:

1. Have students give an example of something that could change a good reputation to a bad one.

2. Have students give an example of something that could change a bad reputation to a good one.

Activity:

Students are to read the four examples of reputation changes on the worksheet "Changing Your Reputation" and decide which was the "old" reputation and which is now the "new" reputation. *Answers:* 1. good student / apathetic student   2. unathletic / good athlete   3. school skipper / regular attendee   4. unskilled / good worker

Discussion:

Have students give their ideas about what caused the changes in the characters, reputations:

1. How did Cindy's reputation change among her friends? Among her teachers? Which reputation did she care more about? (Friends.)   2. What changes besides reputation did you think happened for Alfredo? (Became goal-oriented; self-esteem probably improved.)   3. How did the court system help Geno improve his attendance at school? Do you think that will help his reputation even though he didn't do it on his own at first?   4. Maria's bosses did not give up on her. How did that help Maria's reputation? (She was trying to live up to what they wanted for her; probably felt more important knowing that they valued her.)

Extension Activities:

1. Have students examine the changes in reputation of some popular celebrities who have gone up and down in the public eye. What events have caused people to change their minds about them?
2. Show students the classic movie *My Fair Lady* in which a dramatic transformation is achieved in an uncultured flower seller. Discuss how her reputation changed.

Evaluation:

1. List two ways that a person can change his or her reputation.   2. Describe a famous person who has undergone a change in reputation. Explain.

2.5   Changing Your Reputation

Directions:

Read the following examples of people who have had a change in reputation. How would these events change what someone thinks of a person?

BEFORE   AFTER

1. Cindy always had good grades and was a pretty good student. Her teachers liked her because she was bright and polite. As she got older, she started to hang around with a group of girls who liked to party more than they liked to study. When teachers tried to talk with Cindy about what was happening, she ignored them.

   Old reputation:

   New reputation:

2. Alfredo was picked last on any athletic team. He hated going to gym class because it always made him feel like a loser. Then he joined a karate class after school and began working out. He developed muscles, energy, and a spirit to compete. After a few months, Alfredo began trying out for some after-school teams. He found that he enjoyed them and was getting pretty good at them. Other kids began asking him to join them when they played.

   Old reputation:

   New reputation:

3. Geno had a terrible attendance record at school. He just didn't care about attending. Then he found out that the courts decided he had to see a probation officer once a week to discuss some of his other problems. Now that he didn't have a choice, he began attending every day. Now everyone expects Geno to show up—which he does.

   Old reputation:

   New reputation:

4. Maria was "all thumbs" when it came to typing. She worked at a job in which she had to do some work with word-processing software. Her bosses were frustrated, too, at all of her mistakes, although they really liked Maria and wanted to see her succeed. They decided to pay for her to attend night-school classes to learn how to operate a computer. Once she received the training, she understood how to do her job better. Now Maria looks forward to doing the paperwork!

   Old reputation:

   New reputation:

2.6 How You Appear to Others

Objective:

The student will describe how he or she appears to several other specified individuals.

Comments:

We have many sides, many faces. Although we may seem sweet and kind to our best friend's mother, we may be nasty and mean to that little brother whom we see every day. We give different people different views of how we behave and what we think. Sometimes when two people are discussing the same person, the views are entirely different, and you wonder if they are talking about the same individual! Part of what makes us complex, interesting individuals is the different attributes we reveal to others. In this lesson, students examine the different reputations other people might have in mind for the same person.

Introductory Activities:

1. Ask students how they feel about [select a winning football or basketball team]. Many students will probably indicate it is their favorite team. Ask why? (We like to be associated with winners.)
2. Ask students how they feel about [select a team with a somewhat bad reputation]. Comments will probably be negative!

Activity:

Using the worksheet "How You Appear to Others," students are to examine their reputations in light of how they appear to several different individuals. The individuals are chosen randomly, and you may wish to add or change the people. Encourage students to be objective!

Discussion:

Students may consider this a rather personal activity, so ask for volunteers to divulge information if they wish.

1. How much control do you have over your reputation among other people?   2. Do you think your reputation is more accurate as reported by people who are close to you, such as a family member or your best friend?   3. Do you think people who know you only through school or work would have valid observations about you? Why? (They may be more objective, different circumstances.)   4. Do others see you as they want to see you? Are they accurate?   5. Do you think others see you as you would like them to see you? Are you effectively giving them the right information to have whatever reputation you want?   6. Have you ever tried to make a good impression in front of someone and ended up feeling like you were being a phony?   7. When you described your reputation as if you were another person, did you tend to list your accomplishments? Your personality? Your physical appearance?   8. Are you happy with the reputation you feel most people have given you?

Extension Activities:

1. Have students spend some time talking to a close friend about how they appear to others. Find out what their reputation is. Are they surprised?   2. Collect and read some yearbooks (with permission). A lot of the comments may reveal some insights into the people's reputations. It would be interesting to look through those of parents! Again, get permission.

Evaluation:

1. In general, what kind of reputation do you think you have among your closest friends?   2. What kind of reputation do you have within your family?   3. What kind of reputation do you have at school or work?   4. Which reputation most reflects you? Why?

2.6 How You Appear to Others

Directions:

Different people have different perceptions of what you are like. Fill in the following information about the picture shown. How would the following individuals describe you or your reputation?

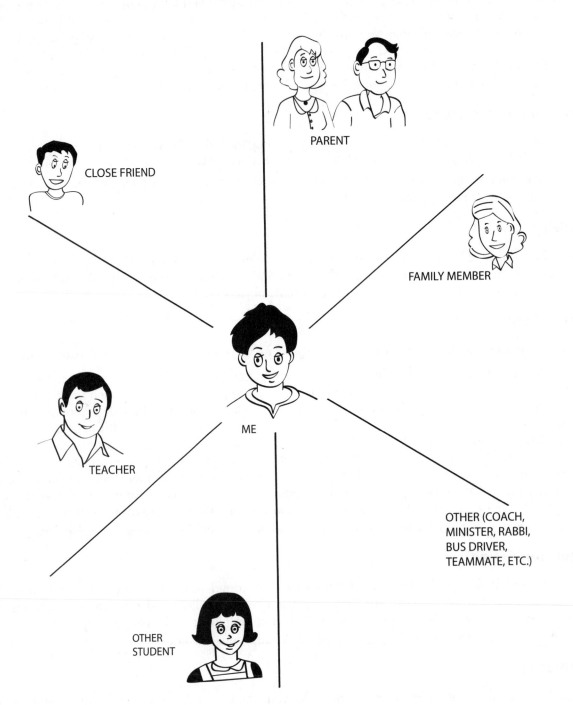

Chapter 3

Personal Life Choices

3.1 Smoking: Is It for Me?

Objective:

The student will identify several reasons why people choose to smoke or not smoke.

Comments:

By this age, many students are probably already smoking and are tired of listening to adults lecture them about the dangers of this habit. There are lots of reasons why smoking is unhealthy. On the other hand, the decision to smoke or refrain from smoking is tied into factors such as peer pressure, parents' attitudes about smoking, desire to appear "cool" or mature, and so on. At this point, students have probably already made up their minds. If we can educate them with the facts about smoking, perhaps some of them will make informed decisions about smoking.

Introductory Activities:

Have students complete a secret survey by indicating whether (1) they consider themselves to be smokers, (2) one or both of their parents smoke, and (3) they know of someone who wishes he or she could quit smoking but is having difficulty.

Activity:

On the worksheet "Smoking: Is It for Me?" students are to read the situations that involve smokers and nonsmokers and indicate the essence of the situation.

Answers (Examples):

1. Enjoys smoking.
2. Had experience with father's death from cancer.
3. Finds the smell offensive.
4. Wants to appear "cool."
5. Wants to appear older.
6. Probably addicted.
7. Has health problems.
8. Smokes to relieve nervous tension.

Discussion:

Students probably have some personal anecdotes either pro or con regarding smoking. Allow them equal time to express their opinions, but feel free to question the basis of their decisions.

1. If you smoke now, do you think you will still be smoking in ten years? Why or why not?
2. Do you believe there are serious dangers associated with smoking?
3. Does knowing the facts about the dangers of smoking affect your decision to smoke or not to smoke?
4. If parents smoke, do you think that would increase the chances of the children in the family smoking? Why?
5. What experiences do you know of people who have tried to quit smoking? What success stories are you aware of?
6. About what percentage of the people you hang around with would you classify as smokers?
7. About what percentage of people who are smokers do you think would like to quit?

Extension Activities:

1. Assign students the task of finding out recent facts and statistics about smoking. What diseases are associated with smoking? How is nicotine addictive?

2. Have students take a pro/con stance as to whether the government should regulate smoking and the rights of smokers.

3. Have students calculate how much money would be spent on cigarettes if a person smoked two packs a day for one year.

4. Cigarette smoking is associated with at least 85 percent of all cases of lung cancer. It is also a leading cause of heart disease. Obtain information from your local heart association or cancer centers about smoking. Get the facts.

5. Have students research the different methods and effects of quitting smoking (hypnosis, behavior modification, group support, and so on). What results and conclusions can they reach?

6. Collect different forms of advertising for cigarette ads. What is the point of each? To whom does each appeal? How effective is it?

7. What brands of cigarettes are popular among students? Research the amount of tar and nicotine in some popular brands. What exactly is being taken into the body?

Evaluation:

1. List at least three reasons why people choose to smoke.

2. List at least three reasons why people choose not to smoke.

3.1   **Smoking: Is It for Me?**

Directions:

What reasons do these people give for smoking or not smoking? Write your answer on the lines.

1. _____

2. _____

3. _____   4. _____

5. _____   6. _____

7. _____   8. _____

3.2 Marijuana and Other Drugs

Objective:

The student will be able to give factual information about specific drugs.

Comments:

As with smoking, the choice to smoke marijuana and take other drugs is one that students may already have made. Peer pressure, availability, lack of thought, and other factors play a part in this behavior. There are many programs available to fight drug abuse. Ideally, your school and community are aware of this widespread problem and are taking steps to combat it. In this lesson, students are given factual information about some commonly abused drugs.

Introductory Activities:

1. On a scale of 1 to 10 (with 10 the most severe), have students rate the drug problem as they see it in their school.
2. On a scale of 1 to 10, have students rate the drug problem as they think the adults (parents, teachers, school administrators, police) in the community would perceive it.
3. Have students volunteer to explain any discrepancy between (1) and (2).

Activity:

On the worksheet "Marijuana and Other Drugs," students are given short paragraphs to read about several commonly abused drugs. Questions about them are contained in the following discussion.

Discussion:

Some students may not want to reveal their thoughts about drug usage, particularly if they are known to be users in their crowd. Encourage them to at least answer the factual questions.

1. How would you answer people who say that smoking marijuana is no more harmful than smoking cigarettes? (It contains more cancer-causing agents than cigarettes.)
2. The marijuana produced today is from five to twenty times stronger than that from a decade ago. How would you answer people who argue that they used marijuana years ago and it never hurt them any? (They probably had a less-potent product.)
3. Cocaine is sometimes promoted as a recreational drug, often used by celebrities and wanna-be celebrities for fun. What are some of the dangers of using cocaine? (Damage to the membrane of the nose, disruption of the heart and respiratory functions.)
4. What is the problem with unsterile equipment associated with drug use? (Sharing needles puts users at risk of acquiring AIDS or other diseases that are transmitted through the blood.)
5. How can unborn children be victims of drug abuse? (Pregnant women can have premature or addicted children.)
6. What is an example of an inhalant? (Aerosol spray cans, paint cans, containers of cleaning fluid, and so on.)
7. What are some immediate effects of inhaling vapors? (Nausea, sneezing, nosebleeds, and so on.)
8. What are hallucinations? (Perceptions of an object or event that does not really exist, usually due to drug use.)

9. Have you heard of anyone having "flashbacks" due to previous drug use?

10. Many of these drugs have legitimate medical uses. Can you think of any? (Pain control, antidepressant uses, appetite control, and so on.)

11. How can being involved with drugs negatively affect your performance in school or at work? (Memory loss, attitude, depression, and so on.)

Extension Activities:

1. Interview a social worker in a drug treatment center. Listen to anecdotes of people whose lives have been affected by drug abuse.

2. Research the drug problem in your community. What steps are being taken to recognize this situation and prevent its worsening?

3. What educational programs are in the schools at the elementary, middle school, and high school levels? How effective are they?

4. Have students research specific drugs. Find out the attractions, effects, and problems associated with each.

5. Have students design a puppet show to present to younger children about alternatives to drug use.

6. Have students research the price of drug abuse in personal pain, business loss, affects on the family, courts, hospitals, and social agencies.

7. Find out the community penalties for possession of controlled substances. If possible, talk to a police officer involved with this aspect of drugs in your community. Do you think the penalties are severe enough?

8. What drug rehabilitation programs are available in your community? Contact your local mental health agency or hospital to get more information.

9. Do some research on the facts about drugs. These websites may be helpful:

   http://www.freevibe.com (Facts and teen stories)

   http://teenshealth.org/teen/ (Take the link for Drugs and Alcohol)

Evaluation:

1. List at least three drugs that are commonly abused.

2. For each drug listed in (1), describe the possible effects.

3.2   Marijuana and Other Drugs

Directions:

Carefully read the following information about specific drugs and the effects they have, and be prepared to answer questions about them.

Cannabis (Generic Name: Marijuana)

The use of cannabis may affect your short-term memory and ability to understand things. It can reduce your ability to perform tasks requiring concentration, such as driving a car. It is damaging to the lungs and contains more cancer-causing agents than cigarettes.

Cocaine

Cocaine is usually sold as a white powder that is inhaled through the nasal passages, although it can be injected or smoked. It stimulates the central nervous system, which is evidenced by dilated pupils, and it raises the blood pressure, heart rate, respiratory rate, and body temperature. Chronic use by inhalation can cause damage to the mucous membrane of the nose. If injected with unsterile equipment, the user can get AIDS and other diseases. The use of cocaine can cause death by disrupting the brain's control of the heart and respiration.

Narcotics (Heroin, Codeine, Morphine, Opium, and so on)

These drugs produce a feeling of euphoria followed by drowsiness, nausea, and vomiting. An overdose can affect breathing and lead to convulsions, coma, and possibly death. Tolerance develops rapidly. Addiction in pregnant women can lead to premature, stillborn, or addicted children.

Inhalants (Nitrous Oxide, Hydrocarbons, and so on)

When vapors are inhaled, the immediate effects can include nausea, sneezing, nosebleeds, and lack of coordination. These drugs can also decrease heart and respiratory rates. Long-term use may result in disorientation, violent behavior, brain hemorrhage, or death. Repeated sniffing can permanently damage the nervous system.

Hallucinogens (LSD, PCP, and so on)

LSD can produce illusions and hallucinations. These sensations and feelings can change rapidly and the user may experience panic, confusion, and loss of control. Chronic users of PCP report memory problems, speech difficulties, and mood disorders including depression, anxiety, and violent behavior.

3.3 Teens and Drinking

Objective: The student will state five to eight facts about teens, alcohol, and drinking.

Comments: Underage drinking is on the rise and is certainly not a positive choice for special students. One survey (Monitoring the Future survey, 2005) estimated that three-quarters of twelfth graders, more than two-thirds of tenth graders, and two-fifths of eighth graders had consumed alcohol. Other studies have found that the average age of a teen's first drink of alcohol is fourteen. The purpose of this lesson is to alert students to the facts about alcohol and making good choices.

Introductory Activities:

1. Ask students to list facts about alcohol and drinking. Many will probably have a vague idea about the dangers of alcohol, but probably not a clear idea of the extent and range of those dangers.
2. Ask students to give their opinions about alcohol and teen drinking. List reasons why students feel that it is acceptable or not acceptable.

Activity: Students should be given the worksheet "Teens and Drinking" and asked to fill out their responses before further teaching or discussion is given.

Answers: 1. twenty-one 2. car crashes 3. 1.5 oz., 5 oz., 12 oz. 4. bloodstream 5. brain 6. false 7. in full control 8. eaten; food 9. accepted, older, popular 10. poor

Discussion: Have students score their own papers as you lead a discussion about the facts of alcohol and drinking.

1. What are some ways that teenagers can get alcohol? (Parents, older friends.)
2. Why do you think underage kids want to drink? (To have fun, fit in, fight depression.)
3. Do you know of anyone who has been involved in a car-related accident that involved alcohol?

Extension Activities:

1. Invite someone from a community agency to speak to your class about alcohol and the effects of underage drinking.
2. Track coverage in your local newspaper about incidents involving teenage drinking.
3. These websites have kid-friendly activities, stories, quizzes, and information about alcohol and teens:

    www.checkyourself.com/Alcoholmyths.aspx

    www.thecoolspot.gov

Evaluation: List five facts about alcohol and/or teenage drinking.

Name _____ Date _____

3.3   Teens and Drinking

Directions:

See how much you know about teens, alcohol, and drinking. Fill in the blanks with your answers.

1. The legal age to buy or possess alcohol is _____ years old.

2. The three leading causes of death for fifteen- to twenty-four-year-olds are _____, homicide, and suicide. Alcohol is the leading factor in all three causes.

3. One "drink" consists of: _____ oz. of liquor, _____ oz. of wine, or _____ oz. of beer.

4. After you take a drink, the alcohol is absorbed into your _____.

5. From there (#4) it goes to your central nervous system, which consists of your spinal cord and your _____.

6. True or False: A teenager's brain is fully developed. _____

7. Alcohol is a depressant, which means it slows down functions such as perception, movement, vision, and hearing. Someone who is driving a car too fast might think that he or she is _____.

8. How fast alcohol is absorbed into the blood depends on what you've _____

   recently. The less _____ in your body, the faster you will get drunk.

9. Reasons why teens drink include curiosity, peer pressure, and wanting to feel _____.

10. Alcohol can lead you to make _____ decisions.

3.4 Changing Your Appearance

Objective:

The students will state at least three to five ways that a person could make changes in his or her appearance.

Comments:

Perhaps we all dream of waking up one morning and being that beautiful or handsome creature to whom everyone is attracted. We are often our own worst critics when it comes to judging our appearance. We may feel we are too tall, too fat, not pretty enough, and so on. Although physical appearance is only one dimension (and perhaps not even that important a dimension!) of an individual, there are some things that can be changed to improve one's physical appearance. In this lesson, some of those changes are investigated.

Introductory Activities:

Have students raise their hands if they:

1. Have ever used a tanning booth.
2. Have ever experimented with hair color.
3. Are wearing contact lenses.
4. Are wearing braces on their teeth.

Activity:

Several ways to change one's physical appearance are listed on the worksheet "Changing Your Appearance." Students are to match the change desired with a method (in the box) that could promote or make that change. Be sure students understand that these changes are not necessarily desirable for everyone; they are merely suggestions that one might investigate if one wanted to make physical changes.

Answers: 1.c   2.h   3.g   4.l   5.e   6.a   7.k   8.d   9.i   10.b   11.j   12.f

Discussion:

Avoid focusing on students who may have particular problems with their physical appearance, such as excessive acne, obesity, and so on. Try to keep things on general terms.

1. Do you think men or women are more conscious of how they look and how to improve their looks?
2. What are some methods that are different for men compared with women?
3. If someone really wanted to change his or her appearance, what might stand in the way? (Money to visit a doctor or get a fashionable hair style, not knowing how to go about starting an exercise program, and so on.)
4. What are some physical problems that are common to most students? (Probably pimples, improper eating habits, need for straightening teeth, and so on.)
5. If someone didn't have a lot of money, how could he or she still be fashionable? (Do some of the hair styling at home or with friends, buy fewer but better clothes, and so on.)
6. Is it important for girls to wear a lot of makeup? (Depends on the individual case; some look better without a lot on.)

Extension Activities:

1. Invite a beauty specialist to come to the school to do a face or hair makeover on some volunteers. Have the specialist point out techniques for enhancing one's best features to look good.
2. Have students find out the cost (and duration) of basic orthodontic work.
3. Contact lenses are now quite affordable. Have students contact a local eye care specialist to find out the cost of getting contacts.
4. Have students take a pro/con view of plastic surgery procedures. What are the costs, benefits, risks, results?
5. Have students research the effects of visiting a tanning booth, both short-term and long-term.
6. Have some ambitious students put together a fashion show for both boys and girls. What "look" is popular right now? Recruit a few "models" to demonstrate some fashion looks that suit different body types. Have fun!

Evaluation:

1. List three to five physical changes that a person could make in his or her appearance.
2. Write a paragraph explaining what you like best about your appearance and what you would change if you could (or what you are working on changing).

3.4   Changing Your Appearance

_____ 1. You want your hair to be shorter.

_____ 2. You want your hair to look blonder and curlier.

_____ 3. You hate wearing glasses.

_____ 4. Your striped shirts make you look heavy.

_____ 5. You are heavy!

_____ 6. Your teeth are crooked.

_____ 7. Your skin is very pale.

_____ 8. You have pimples all over your face.

_____ 9. Your eyebrows are very bushy.

_____ 10. Your skin is blotchy.

_____ 11. You are very thin and have no muscle tone.

_____ 12. People tell you that you dress very sloppily.

BEFORE

AFTER

---

a.   Get braces or another orthodontic appliance.

b.   Use facial makeup to even out the color of your face.

c.   Get a haircut.

d.   Use acne medication and/or visit a dermatologist.

e.   Watch what you eat; try to lose weight slowly so you can keep it off.

f.   Update your wardrobe by buying some new clothes; get advice from a salesperson.

g.   Try some contact lenses.

h.   Try some hair coloring; get a perm.

i.   Thin your eyebrows with tweezers.

j.   Start an exercise program to build up some muscle.

k.   Get some fresh air and sunshine, but remember your sunscreen!

l.   Wear clothes that are more flattering to your body type.

3.5 Tattoos and Piercings

Objective:

The student will describe an appropriate type of body art for a given situation.

Comments:

Love 'em or hate 'em, body art is everywhere! Some sources estimate 50 percent of people in their twenties have a tattoo or a body piercing. Piercings are basically nonmedical holes for the purpose of inserting jewelry or other decorations. State laws vary, but although tattooing and piercing is legal in all fifty states, most states require the customer to be at least eighteen or, if younger, to have a parent or guardian's written consent. (See http://www.ncsl.org/programs/health/minorbodyart.htm for state-by-state information.) Some things to consider before getting body art are safety, permanence of the procedure, and its effect on future issues (where you will work, public opinion regarding tattoos, changing fads, and so on).

Introductory Activities:

1. Ask students to describe interesting tattoos that they have seen.
2. Ask students to share any experiences about acquiring a tattoo or piercing.

Activity:

The worksheet "Tattoos and Piercings" includes situations in which a person has or is considering a tattoo or piercing. The student is to write an opinion about how this situation could be handled in the best interest of both parties.

Answers Examples:

1. Wait under she is sure about the relationship, or get a smaller tattoo.
2. Wait until they reach age eighteen.
3. Talk to the employer to see if the piercings would be offensive for that job—they may not be.
4. No! No! No!
5. Remove the stud when at work.
6. If they have a policy regarding body art, apply for one of the jobs that doesn't involve a lot of contact with customers.
7. Get something small or one that can be easily concealed.
8. A tattoo would be fine there. However, Rick should make sure he likes that line of work—he may change jobs someday.

Discussion:

If there is a policy in place about body art, that must be considered and adhered to. On the other hand, if there is no policy, then an inoffensive tattoo should not be a problem.

1. In example 1, why would it not be a good idea for Angel to have her boyfriend's name tattooed on her shoulder or anywhere? (Doesn't seem like a stable situation; he has a long name.)
2. What are some cute, interesting, or attractive tattoos that you have seen?
3. How much is "too much"? What do you think makes body piercing unattractive?
4. For what jobs might a lot of body art be welcome? (Sales of items that appeal to young people, performers.)
5. What concerns might you have about tattoos and piercings? What concerns might your parents have?

Extension Activities:

1. Find out the state or city laws for tattooing in your community.
2. Arrange for a visit of a tattoo artist. If this is not possible, you can view a video on getting a tattoo and a lip piercing on this website: http://tattoo.about.com
3. Do a report on how tattooing works. Include some colorful designs.
4. Do a random, informal survey of the prevalence of tattoos or piercings in your community. Sit at a busy mall for an hour and just count and tally your observations.

Evaluation:

1. Describe three types of body art.
2. Give an example of a tattoo that is inappropriate for a situation.
3. Give an example of a tattoo that is appropriate for a situation.

3.5   **Tattoos and Piercings**

Directions:

How could these body art situations be handled in a positive manner?

1. Angel wants to have her boyfriend's name (Christopher) tattooed on her shoulder. Her mother pointed out that she has had several boyfriends and she just started dating Christopher.

2. Sarah and Hailey want to get matching butterfly tattoos on their ankles. They are both seventeen years old. Sarah's mother asked her to wait until she is eighteen, but Hailey's mother said it is fine with her.

3. Austin wants to get his eyebrow, lip, nose, and ear pierced. He also wants to get a part-time job working at a nursing home. He is a friendly guy who really likes older people.

4. Sydney wants to get her belly button pierced. She has a friend who said she knows how to do piercings and she will do it at her home for free.

5. Kayla has a nose stud that she really likes. She applied for a job as a waitress at a restaurant that has a policy for no piercings.

6. Jordan wants to work at a five-star hotel. He has skull-and-crossbones tattoos on the backs of his hand and a star tattooed under his eye. There are several openings at the hotel, including a dishwasher at the restaurant, busboy, valet parking attendant, and hotel receptionist.

7. Danielle wants to get a tattoo, but she doesn't want to get in trouble at work for having a feature that everyone will stare at.

8. Rick works at a bookstore that sells graphic novels/comic books and art posters. There is no dress code. Rick would like to get a tattoo that is fun and gets attention.

3.6 Rate the Date

Objective:

Given various dating examples, the student will rate each on a scale of 1 to 10 and give reasons for his or her rating.

Comments:

As adults, looking back, probably all of us have had dating disasters that now appear humorous (after the passage of time). On the other hand, don't you remember some good times, moments you wish you could relive again and again? Some students may not actually be dating, but they can still identify good and bad aspects of going on a date. In this lesson, they are to read some episodes of students on dates and then rate them on a scale of 1 to 10.

Introductory Activities:

1. Ask students to volunteer to describe the most awful dating experience they've ever had. (Encourage humor!)

2. Ask students to tell about a particularly fun or interesting date they've had.

Activity:

Students are to read the anecdotes of seven different dates and then score them (1 to 10, 1 = disaster, 10 = wonderful) on the worksheet "Rate the Date." They will discuss their rating scales.

1. In example 1, what factors were not important to the girl on this date? (Wind, cold.)

2. What factors were important to the girl in example 1? (A considerate date.)

3. In example 2, what did Jennifer do that the boy found annoying? (Ignored him.)

4. In example 3, what was important to the girl? (Seeing the movie.) What did she find irritating? (The boy's behavior.)

5. In example 4, why did Amy surprise the boy? (She turned out to be a lot of fun and a good listener.)

6. Did you rate the date pretty high in example 5? Why? (Probably because both people had a good time.)

7. Do you think Janine was inconsiderate in example 6? (Ordered expensive items, didn't thank him.) Do you think the boy will ever ask her out again? (Probably not.)

8. In example 7, what could have prevented that date from ending up so bad? (Jeff could have tried to avoid the fight.)

9. What factors did you include in your ratings? What did you consider to be important about a good date?

10. Do you need to spend a lot of money to have a good date?

11. What do you appreciate from the other person when you go on a date? (Courtesy.)

12. Would you go out on a blind date? What information would you want to know ahead of time?

13. Do you think girls and boys should split the cost of dating?

Extension Activities:

1. Set up a "Dating Game" in which students ask questions of each other, but do not know to whom they are talking. (You could use a room divider, having students answer in writing, and so on.) Students might find it interesting to determine what girls or boys find appealing about them.

2. Have students conduct an informal survey or poll asking ten friends or classmates to tell the best or worst thing they've had happen to them while on a date. Information should remain confidential, of course, and be used simply for fun.

Evaluation:

Rate the following date. Include what factors you used to determine your rating.

I was really excited about going on my first date with Bill—on a ride in his brother's four-seater airplane. I had never been in an airplane, so I was really excited. What I didn't know was that I would get so airsick I spent the whole time vomiting into a little bag. I was so embarrassed, but I remembered to thank Bill and his brother and told them that I would always remember this very memorable experience. Bill couldn't stop laughing. He said I was a great sport and that our next date would be on the ground.

3.6   Rate the Date

Directions:

Rate each date described below on a scale of 1 to 10, with 1 being a disaster and 10 being wonderful. Think about what you are considering to be important!

1. "Andy and I had our first date at Homecoming. It was 30 degrees outside and windy. We were so cold! Andy was really thoughtful, though. He kept asking if I was warm enough and made sure I kept drinking hot chocolate. I remember thinking, 'This guy is so considerate! Is he always this way?'" _____

2. "Jennifer and I had been going out casually for awhile, so I felt like I knew her pretty well. But one night we double-dated with her best friend and her boyfriend. Jennifer and her girlfriend talked and laughed with each other the whole night. The other guy and I felt like we weren't even there! They kept talking about people and things we didn't know anything about." _____

3. "I had been looking forward to going to the movies with Ricardo. I really wanted to see the movie! But all he wanted to do was hang all over me and make out. I couldn't wait until it was over. I went back the next day to see the movie I had missed while I was being pawed." _____

4. "People told me Amy would really be a dud because she's so quiet. I just found myself talking and telling her things about myself that I had never told anyone else. She's such a good listener—I was fascinated just sitting around in the library, talking for hours." _____

5. "Pete and I took off on his motorcycle and went all around the county. It was a blast. We both love to be outdoors and feeling free! We made plans to work on fixing up his car next weekend." _____

6. "I don't think Janine dates very much. When we went out to dinner, she ordered the most expensive items on the menu. I hardly had enough cash to pay for it. Then when it was over, she didn't even thank me." _____

7. "Jeff and I went roller skating at the community rink. Another guy he knew from high school knocked into him, so Jeff shoved him back. One thing led to another until there was a full-fledged fight and the cops came. That date really made an impression on me!" _____

3.7 Ready to Move Out?

Objective:

The student will identify some positive indications that a person might be ready to move out or to a more independent setting.

Comments:

Our desire for older teens is to prepare them for as much independence as possible. At what point are they ready to move out from close parental supervision? Next steps for special teens might include a sheltered apartment, living with a different family member with fewer restrictions, or actually maintaining a safe environment on their own. Teens need to think about what factors are important before they can consider moving out. This might include mastery of independent living skills, financial support, and commitment to a safe lifestyle.

Introductory Activities:

1. Ask students to think about where they will be living, or hope to live, in the next five to ten years. Have them describe their future living environment.   2. Ask students to list what factors they think are necessary in order to move out on their own.

Activity:

The worksheet "Ready to Move Out?" has examples of teens who desire to move out of their present situation, which we will assume is that of living with a parent. Students should read each scenario and pick out the clues that indicate whether or not that person seems ready to move out.   *Answers:*

1. No (there will probably still be parental issues).   2. Yes (she has a job, the financial situation seems good).   3. Yes (factors of finance and the school).   4. Maybe (might continue to have problems if he has a bad attitude, but there's a possibility the move could be good for him).
5. No (forgets her medication, is not responsible).   6. No (doesn't have a job lined up).

Discussion:

Talk about the pros and cons of each example on the worksheet. What factors are favorable in each case? What factors indicate the student is not yet ready to become independent of a parent?

1. Which examples show someone who is probably in a good financial situation to move out? (#2, #3.)
2. Which examples show someone who can rely on a supportive adult? (#3, #4 maybe, #5.)
3. Which examples show someone who thinks that a change of environment will change his or her life substantially? (#1, #3, #4.)   4. What advice would you give to the boy in #6? (Don't move until you have a secure job.)

Extension Activities:

1. Have students interview a parent or custodial adult to ask for help in making a list of skills that the adult thinks are needed for independent living.   2. If possible and appropriate, take a tour of an assisted-living home, sheltered apartment, or other place that might be a possible next step for independence for your students.

Evaluation:

1. What is one indication that someone is ready to move out on his own?   2. What is an indication that someone is not ready to move out?

3.7   **Ready to Move Out?**

Directions:

Do you think these students are ready to move out?

Write Yes or No next to each description.

1. Madden is tired of his parents' always wanting to know where he is and what he is doing. He thinks things would be a lot better for him and for his parents if he moved in with his friend Hunter. Hunter's parents are not home very much, so Madden thinks that there won't be any problems.

    _____

2. Juliet is taking night classes at her local high school so she can get a high school equivalency degree. During the day she works at a shopping center. She has a chance to move into an apartment with two other girls who also have jobs and are going to school part-time. The rent is not very

    high, and the girls all want to finish high school. _____

3. Victoria is fourteen and her sister Natalie is sixteen. They want to live with their father in California instead of with their mother in New York. Both parents agree that the girls would be welcome to make the move. Natalie is excited about going to a special school that has classes for art students, which is something she is very interested in. She can also apprentice at her dad's

    office and earn some extra money. _____

4. Ethan has had problems at his school in the city. His grades are not good, he does not get along with most of the other kids, and he is getting in trouble in the community. He wants to move in with his older brother who has an apartment with several other guys. The move would put Ethan in a different school district. His brother said he would make sure that Ethan gets off to a good start.

    _____

5. Maria needs to take medication to control her seizures. Sometimes she forgets to take her pills, so

    her mother has to make sure that she takes them every day. _____

6. Cameron wants to move out of his parents' home, so he applied for a job at the local plant nursery. They told him that they would be hiring workers in the summer, but couldn't promise anything yet. He has a little money in a savings account, but not enough to pay rent. The fast-food restaurants

    are hiring, but he doesn't want to work on weekends. _____

3.8 Ready to Work Part-Time?

Objective:

The student will identify at least two conditions that would be important in determining readiness for a part-time job.

Comments:

Working is a great way for a student to test the waters of the working world. Some conditions that you need to think about are (1) the appropriateness of the job (are you qualified?), (2) the amount of time it will involve, (3) the logistics of the actual workplace (can you walk to work, or do you need to be able to drive?), (4) other commitments (sports, family obligations), and (5) motivation for working (to be with friends?).

Introductory Activities:

1. Ask students to list some part-time jobs that they know about.   2. Ask students to give some advantages of working part-time rather than full-time.

Activity:

Students should read the examples on the worksheet "Ready to Work Part-Time?" and decide whether or not each person is a good candidate for working part-time.   *Answers:*   1. Yes (good opportunity to work for a relative, only weekends)   2. No (the job will not fit Lauren's desires)   3. No (needs to study)   4. No (not qualified)   5. Yes (wait until summer)   6. Yes (flexible job)

Discussion:

Some of the situations may not be clearly yes or no. Have students speculate about how the part-time jobs might work for the students, with some adaptations.

1. What are some part-time jobs that have flexible hours or working conditions?   2. Why is it important to balance work, school, and social time?   3. Why were some of the jobs not a good fit with the students on the worksheet?

Extension Activities:

1. Have students look through local newspaper ads for part-time jobs to get a sense of what employment opportunities there are in the community.   2. Have students complete a time management schedule to see what type of part-time employment would best fit their individual situation. Nights? Weekends? Summer only?

Evaluation:

List two conditions that would indicate that someone is ready to find a part-time job.

3.8   Ready to Work Part-Time?

Directions:

Read each of the following situations. For each, would you recommend
that the student try to get a part-time job at this time? Why/why not?

1. Christopher has a chance to work at his uncle's garage on the weekends. Chris knows that he will
    have to get all of his school work done during the week, but he has been keeping his grades up
    and thinks he can handle it.

    _____

2. Lauren's friend Samantha got a job working at a tanning salon and said it would be fun if Lauren
    worked there, too. Lauren doesn't like to work evenings or weekends, but thinks it will be fun to
    work when Samantha works so they can talk.

    _____

3. Ryan really wants to go to a community college after high school, so he needs to keep his grades
    up. He studies about three hours every night after school and also spends a lot of time on week-
    ends studying. He found a job at a pizza parlor that requires working a lot of weekends.

    _____

4. Tyler found an ad for a part-time lifeguard at the local pool. The pay is good and the hours would
    work out well for him, too. He thinks he can learn to swim and pass the certification quickly so he
    can apply for the job.

    _____

5. Jasmine is co-captain of her cross country team. She has to run every day to stay in shape. She is
    thinking about trying to get a part-time job working with kids at a camp in the summer.

    _____

6. Jose's family owns and runs a restaurant in town. Jose's parents said that he can come out to the
    restaurant and help clean off tables on the evenings that he doesn't have any homework.

    _____

Part Two

People Skills

Chapter 4: Relating to Others

4.1   Encouraging Others
4.2   Working in a Group
4.3   Working Toward a Common Goal
4.4   Being Friendly
4.5   Helping Others
4.6   What Is a Mood?
4.7   Noticing the Moods of Others
4.8   How My Mood Affects Others

Chapter 5: Friendship Skills

5.1   My Peer Groups
5.2   Who Are My Friends?
5.3   Making Friends
5.4   People Who Are Like You
5.5   People Who Are Different from You
5.6   Where and How to Look for Friends
5.7   Qualities of a Good Friend
5.8   Social Situations
5.9   A Positive Role Model
5.10 What About Gangs?
5.11 Social Networking Online

Chapter 6: Being Part of a Family

6.1   My Family Tree
6.2   Benefits of a Family
6.3   Respecting Authority
6.4   My Parent's Point of View
6.5   My Sibling's Point of View
6.6   Thoughts About Divorce
6.7   Dealing with Stepparents
6.8   Sharing the Chores
6.9   Whom Can I Talk To?

Chapter 7: Communication Skills

7.1   Best Method to Communicate
7.2   Being a Careful Listener
7.3   Summarizing
7.4   Paraphrasing
7.5   Is This the Right Time and Place?
7.6   Communicating by Cell Phone
7.7   Giving Clear Directions
7.8   Verbal and Nonverbal Messages
7.9   Collecting Your Thoughts
7.10 Public Speaking
7.11 Expecting Respect
7.12 Being Convincing
7.13 Giving Your Speech

Chapter 4

Relating to Others

4.1 Encouraging Others

Objective:

The student will give examples of ways to encourage or praise others in given situations.

Comments:

People handle the skill of encouraging and praising others in different ways; some are comfortable with being verbally affectionate, others are not so vocal. But each individual can find a way to demonstrate encouragement to others in a manner that he or she feels comfortable with. In this lesson, students are to use their unique personal qualities to demonstrate how they could show encouragement to others.

Introductory Activities:

1. Define *compassion* for students. (Showing sympathy toward someone else's misfortune or distress.)
2. Have students give examples of situations in which someone has been distressed or needed encouragement.

Activity:

Students are to read examples of young people who are going through some distressing circumstances. The student will offer words of encouragment for each example.   *Answers (Examples):*   1. We'll still stay in touch; I'm here if you need to talk.   2. It was hard for me at first, too, but let's keep trying, OK?   3. Would you help me practice for my part? I could really use your help.   4. May I get you anything? Would you like me to mow the lawn for you?

Discussion:

Have students compare their responses. Remember that each student might view the given situations a little differently—perhaps he or she has been through a divorce in the family or been the friend who was disappointed.

1. Have any of these situations happened to you? Can you tell about how it made you feel? 2. What if the people in each example really didn't want to talk about the problem? How would you handle that?   3. Do you think people know if you are just saying something to try to be kind or if you really feel sympathetic toward them?   4. Are there times when it is better to say nothing than to say something that sounds made up or insincere?

Extension Activities:

1. Have students pair up and create a list of 50 to 100 phrases of encouragement such as: "Good job!" "Keep trying!" "You'll get it!" Write the phrases or words on colored poster board or strips of construction paper and hang them around the room. You'll never be at a loss for something positive to say!   2. As a writing activity, have students pretend to be a "Dear Abby" columnist and write their advice in response to problems that are submitted.

Evaluation:

1. Give a simple definition for the word *compassion*.   2. Give three examples of words or phrases of encouragement.

4.1   Encouraging Others

Directions:

Read and think about the following situations. What is something that you could say to encourage, support, or praise the person in the example? Write your answers on the lines provided.

1. Your best friend just found out that his parents are getting a divorce. There is also talk of him moving to another state to live with one of his parents (who are not speaking to each other). What would you tell him?

    _____

    _____

2. You are supposed to be helping your little sister with her math homework. You try and try to explain division to her, but she just doesn't seem to catch on. She'll listen for a little while, then just throw her paper down and give up, saying it's just too hard. What might you say to her?

    _____

    _____

3. You and a friend both try out for speaking parts in the school play. The results are posted, and you made it! Your friend, however, did not get any part at all. The friend says that it doesn't matter, but you know better. What will you do or say?

    _____

    _____

4. Your father just lost his job—at a company where he has worked for almost twenty years. He always seems to be in a bad mood and doesn't want to talk about it, especially to you. What will you say to your dad?

    _____

    _____

4.2 Working in a Group

Objective:

The student will successfully complete a given task as a member of an assigned group.

Comments:

An important life skill that carries through to adulthood is the ability to complete tasks as a member of a group. In this lesson, students are assigned to work as part of a group to complete a given task. Afterward, students will evaluate their own performance and the ability of the group to complete the work.

Introductory Activities:

1. Have students list tasks that are easier to complete when they are performed by a group, rather than an individual. (Lawn work, cooking a meal, practicing for basketball, and so on.)
2. Have students think of why some tasks are easier when performed in a group.
3. Have students think of some drawbacks to working in a group.

Activity:

Students are to work on an assigned task as a group. Groups should be small, perhaps three to five students. All groups should work on the same task. Many tasks lend themselves to group work, but some ideas are:

- Assemble a hundred-piece puzzle.
- Color in a map of the United States with all states labeled.
- Solve a crossword puzzle.
- Complete a page of math problems (can be coded to reveal a secret message).
- Write a poem (must be twenty lines long).

Do not give students any more directions other than to assign the task, help them complete the information on the worksheet "Working in a Group," and tell them the length of the time for this activity. Allow the students to proceed with the task with a minimum of teacher intervention. Just observe!

Materials: Will vary depending on the task.

Discussion:

After all groups are finished (or time has run out), have students come together to discuss the following questions about working in their group.

1. Did your group select a leader? Who was it and how was he or she selected?
2. How did your group determine who would work on each part of the task?
3. Did anyone not participate? Did one person do everything? Was the work divided fairly?
4. What was fun or interesting about working in a group? Was your task completed efficiently because there were many workers?

5. What problems did your group encounter?

6. Which group put the most effort into the assignment? What good ideas did that group come up with?

7. If you had the same task to do over again with the same group, what would be done differently?

Extension Activities:

1. Repeat the assignment with another task and with different group members. Have students record or reflect on what was managed better on the second try.

2. Keep the same groups for several tasks, but alternate the students as being a leader of the group. Select one person from each group, take them aside, and inform them that they have a special, secret task: to act as a "recorder," to note how many comments of praise or encouragement are given by each leader. When all students (except for the recorders) have been the leaders, have the recorders share their findings.

Evaluation:

1. Give an example of a task that is better performed by a group than an individual.

2. Give two reasons why group work can be more efficient than individual work.

3. Give examples of at least two problems that need to be worked out when a task is performed by a group.

4.2   Working in a Group

Directions:

Each student will be assigned to work on a given task as part of a group. After the activity is completed, you will discuss and answer some questions about the activity. Fill out the following required information below before you begin.

Task: _____

Members of the group: _____

_____

Materials needed: _____

_____

_____

Time allowed for the task: _____

Additional information or comments: _____

_____

_____

_____

_____

4.3 Working Toward a Common Goal

Objective:

The student will identify the importance of using strengths of self and others in working on completion of a common goal.

Comments:

In this lesson, the entire class is to work on a project. This could be a major project, incorporating a lot of time and energy, or a smaller project, completed in one lesson. Students should be aware of using the strengths of each member of the group to efficiently carry out the project.

Introductory Activities:

1. Have each student list on a piece of paper two or three general strengths or skills they possess. These could be athletic, social, or artistic skills, as well as character strengths—organized, smart, patient, and so on.
2. On the same paper, have students classify themselves as someone who enjoys being in charge (leading others), or likes carrying out assigned jobs (following instructions from others), or who prefers to work independently. Students may have characteristics of more than one group, but try to have them narrow it down to their predominant trait.

Activity:

Inform students that the entire class is going to be working on one project for which they will all be accountable. The project assigned should be something that is large enough for many students to find an opportunity to participate. Be sure you have administrative and parental support for your activity! Examples:

- Design a huge poster for the hallway to promote a school event (school fair, football game, library week, and so on).

- Organize a school-wide food drive to collect canned goods for a charitable organization.

- Design and sell T-shirts, bumper stickers, or pinned buttons with a school motto or logo on it.

- Challenge another class to a *Jeopardy*-type game dealing with information on a certain subject (history, geography, spelling words, and so on).

- Organize an auction in which people donate items to be bid on to raise money for the local animal shelter.

Have students complete the worksheet "Working Toward a Common Goal" with information supplied about the project that they will be doing. Encourage them to use the strengths and resources of the members of the class when organizing the project. Also, have them use ideas and lessons learned from the project in Lesson 4.2 (Working in a Group) to include everyone in the project.

Materials: Will vary depending on the project.

Discussion:

After the project is completed, have students discuss the questions on the worksheet and the following questions:

1. When you first began the project, how did you feel about doing it?
2. Now that you are finished, are you disappointed in the results or happy?
3. How did the class organize this task?
4. Were the individual strengths of the members of the class used to full advantage? How?
5. Was the project successful?
6. Did you choose a leader?
7. What would you change if you did this project again?
8. Did you like having one grade for everyone or did it seem unfair?
9. How did members of the class help each other?
10. What did you learn from this activity?

Extension Activities:

1. For one week, have students work cooperatively on all assignments, knowing that they will be given one grade. After a week, evaluate the pros and cons of this type of structure.
2. Have students come up with a pool of project ideas and select a second class project to work on. Allow students to design, plan, carry out, and evaluate the project. Look for use of individual strengths and more efficient work.

Evaluation:

1. Name two projects that can efficiently be completed as a large group.
2. List two personal strengths you can contribute to a large group project.

4.3   **Working Toward a Common Goal**

Directions:

You will be working on a class project. All students will be expected to participate and all will be given one grade—the SAME grade for everyone. Complete the following information about your class project. After you are done with the project, you will be asked to discuss the activity.

Project: _____

Materials needed: _____

_____

_____

Plan for carrying out the project: _____

_____

_____

Who will do what: _____

_____

_____

Time allowed for project: _____

How will we evaluate the success of our project? _____

_____

_____

4.4 Being Friendly

Objective:

The student will identify ways to show friendliness to others, given specific situations.

Comments:

Not everyone is naturally friendly and outgoing. But even those of us who tend to be withdrawn and shy can learn to appear friendly to others simply by making the first nonthreatening move or just saying "hello." In this lesson, students are given examples of people who are somewhat approachable and would be good targets on which to practice developing this social skill.

Introductory Activities:

1. Have students list three to five people whom they think of as being especially outgoing and friendly.   2. Have students indicate by show of hands whether or not they would be the first one to speak if on the street they passed: (a) a complete stranger; (b) someone they recognized by sight but didn't know his or her name; and (c) someone unknown who looked grumpy or distressed.

Activity:

Students are to draw or write their responses to examples on the worksheet "Being Friendly" in which a person could easily demonstrate initiating friendliness.   *Answers (Examples):*   1. You could ask if the puppy is friendly and remark about how cute it is.   2. You could smile at the girls and say "Hi." 3. You could ask the man if he's in a hurry and would like to go in front of you.   4. You could go up to your teacher and ask if he or she remembers you.   5. You could offer to take your cousin outside to play catch.   6. You could just say "hello" if he is busy, or ask for an autograph if it seems he is happy to have the attention!

Discussion:

Have students compare their ideas to these situations.

1. Do you like it when people who are friendly approach you and begin talking to you, or are you distrustful?   2. Do you think some people would rather be left alone than talked to? (For example, the man in the grocery line.) How would you be able to tell whether or not someone would be approachable?   3. If the famous person in situation 6 looked as though he just wanted to go shopping, how could you show friendliness without being annoying?   4. Do you think young children in particular are taught to avoid strangers, especially ones who try to appear overly friendly? 5. Do you think the expression "Have a nice day" is overused and empty of feeling? What friendly expression might you use instead?

Extension Activities:

1. Have students make an assignment for themselves: to demonstrate or initiate a friendly behavior toward someone every day for a week. Have them record what they did, how they felt about it, and how the person reacted. Does it get easier with practice?   2. Designate one person in your classroom

each day to stand outside the classroom and greet every person who enters the class. This greeting could consist of a simple hello, shaking of hands, pat on the back, or whatever seems appropriate. How do students feel when they know they are going to be met with a greeting (ideally, a sincere one) before class each day? How does it feel to be the greeter?

Evaluation:

1. Give two examples of friendly, nonthreatening comments that you could make to anyone in any type of social situation.   2. Give the name of someone whom you consider to be a friendly individual and explain why you think this.

4.4   **Being Friendly**

Directions:

How might you show friendliness in each of these situations?

1. You are walking along the sidewalk and pass a woman who is walking an unusual little white puppy.

   _____

   _____

2. You are sitting in the park, reading a book, when two little girls go by, laughing, skipping and hopping.

   _____

   _____

3. You are standing in a very long line at the food store ahead of an eldery man who has two items in his cart.

   _____

   _____

4. You are at a party with people from your neighborhood and see your first-grade teacher.

   _____

   _____

5. You are at a family reunion (borrrrrring) and notice that your younger cousin looks just as miserable as you are.

   _____

   _____

6. You are at the shopping mall when you notice the quarterback from your favorite professional football team walking around with his wife and children.

   _____

   _____

4.5 Helping Others

Objective:

The student will identify appropriate ways to assist others in given situations.

Comments:

It is a nice idea to think we can always be helpful to others; however, it is important to be cautious as well. There are some situations in which we are unable to help and indeed, should not even attempt to dabble in something beyond our skills (car accidents, dangerous situations, and so on). In this lesson, students are to evaluate the given situations and decide what type of assistance is needed and who should provide that assistance.

Introductory Activities:

1. Have students raise their hands if they would give a stranger verbal directions for how to get to the post office.
2. Have students raise their hands if they would draw a map for someone who wanted to get to the post office.
3. Have students raise their hands if they would allow a stranger to follow them while they were riding a bike to show that person how to get to the post office.
4. Have students raise their hands if they would get in the car with a stranger who wanted to know how to get to the post office.

Activity:

There are different levels of involvement regarding how far someone will—or should—go to provide help for another person. On the worksheet "Helping Others," the student is to indicate what level of help he or she thinks is appropriate for the situations given. #1 indicates that the student would directly help the person; #2 indicates that he or she would find someone else to help; and #3 indicates that he or she would not become involved in the activity at all. Inform students that they are to select only one of the options. Their choices will be discussed.

Answers (Examples):

1. #2—call 911.
2. #2—call a gas station if it looks like he needs help; he may be fine by himself.
3. #1—chase the dog away.
4. #2—offer to call someone for him.
5. #1— if you know how to do algebra!
6. #2—recommend a good French tutor.
7. #2—encourage him to talk to the school counselor.
8. #2—call a lifeguard if one is close by unless you know water safety.
9. #3—your help will probably not be necessary if the door swings open automatically.
10. #1—help her out.
11. #2—get a salesperson to help.
12. #2—encourage him to talk to someone; it sounds like there's trouble involved.

Discussion:

Although there is room for individual variations, probably most of the students will agree on the majority of the situations. Ask for their thinking on each.

1. How is situation 1 different from situation 2?
2. How would you handle situation 4 if your parents were home?
3. How would you handle situation 4 if you were home alone and it was night?
4. How are situations 10 and 11 alike and different?
5. Were there many people who used response #3 (avoid the situation entirely) for any of the situations? Do you think most people want to help others, even if it is just by referral?
6. Can you think of examples of #3-type situations that probably should be avoided?

Extension Activities:

1. Make a directory of agencies, people, and local social services that can be used as a referral resource for several types of problems. What community services are there for helping students who are having financial, social, parental, drug, or school problems?
2. Interview your school counselor. Find out what types of referrals he or she deals with and what kinds of advice he or she would give for situations such as dealing with kids who are experiencing school and home problems.

Evaluation:

1. Give two examples of situations in which you could provide direct assistance to help someone else.
2. Give two examples of situations in which you could refer a person with a problem to someone else.
3. Give two examples of situations in which you should not become involved.

4.5

Helping Others

Directions:

Read the following situations. In the space provided, write: #1 if you would provide direct assistance, #2 if you would refer the person to someone or something else for help, #3 if you would avoid the situation entirely.

_____ 1. At night, you pass a car accident in which a woman is injured and bleeding.

_____ 2. You pass a car that is by the side of the road with a flat tire. A man is outside on the highway pulling out the jack from the trunk.

_____ 3. You and your little sister are walking through the park when a large dog runs up and begins to chase her.

_____ 4. An unfamiliar man comes to your door and knocks. You open the door and he says he has car trouble and wants to use your phone.

_____ 5. A friend calls and doesn't know how to do his algebra homework.

_____ 6. A friend of a friend calls and needs help translating a paper from English to French.

_____ 7. A friend is thinking of running away from home because he can't get along with his parents.

_____ 8. You are swimming in the pool at the neighborhood park and see a little kid who looks like he is drowning.

_____ 9. A man in a wheelchair is approaching the door to the grocery store. You are several feet behind him.

_____ 10. In the grocery store, an elderly woman is trying to reach a box of cereal on a high shelf.

_____ 11. In a sporting goods store, a young boy is trying to reach a bowling ball on a high shelf.

_____ 12. Your best friend calls and says that he or she needs a lot of money in a hurry and begs you not to ask any questions.

4.6 What Is a Mood?

Objective:

The student will identify five to ten different moods/emotional states.

Comments:

We sometimes group people into "good" moods or "bad" moods, when there are actually many different emotional states in between. Technically, a mood is an emotional state that lasts for a length of time such as hours or days, whereas emotions (especially in teens) can fluctuate frequently. For the purposes of these worksheets and discussion, we will treat "mood" as an emotional state that typifies a person for at least a specific length of time that is long enough to cause attention or warrant the label.

Introductory Activities:

1. Have students list as many types of moods as they can think of—try starting with "a" (amused, annoyed) and go as far as you can!
2. Good mood/bad mood: Have students write examples on the board of things or situations that would "put them" in a good or bad mood.

Activity:

Using the worksheet "What Is a Mood?" have students give an example by writing, drawing, or orally stating someone who is showing the moods on the activity sheet.

Answers: Will vary.

Discussion:

There are many types of emotions and many reasons why someone would feel that emotion for a prolonged length of time. As you discuss the moods, look for specific examples that will help convey each mood.

1. If you were going to label these moods simply Good/Bad, which side would you put them on? (Perhaps 1, 2, 4, 6, 7, 8, and 10 would be "bad," and 3, 5, and 9 would be "good.")
2. Are some moods something other than good/bad? Are there neutral moods?
3. Do you have some really good examples for some of the moods? Share.
4. Could being in a "bad" mood lead to something good? Explain. (Maybe being confused could lead to understanding; being broken-hearted could lead to going out and trying to find new friends; and so on.)
5. What do you think it means to be a "moody" person? Is that good or bad or neutral? (Someone who changes moods a lot; could be either.)
6. What kind of mood do you think describes you most of the time?

Extension Activities:

1. If students are computer-savvy they probably already know about emoticons—little faces or pictures that can be downloaded to express an emotion. One website is www.aeddemotions.com/emotions.html. Or this site uses only variations of smiley faces: www.instantsmileys.com. This site uses the keyboard to express emotions, including blowing a kiss, winking, pouting, yawning, and others: www.livejournal.com/moodlists.bml.

2. A word of caution: some sites also provide easy access to adult-themed emoticons and some that are just not polite!

3. Mood rings used to be popular in the late 1970s. Assign a group of students the topic of researching this fad and discover the fun and science of how a mood ring works. Check out www.howstuffworks.com/question443.htm.

Evaluation:

1. List five to ten (teacher specifies) different moods and give an example of each.
2. Write a paragraph telling about a time when you experienced one of the moods you listed in (1).

4.6 What Is a Mood?

Directions:

Give an example of someone showing the following moods:

1. Stressed

_____

_____

2. Broken-hearted

_____

_____

3. Amused

_____

_____

4. Distressed

_____

_____

5. Creative

_____

_____

6. Confused

_____

_____

7. Bored

_____

_____

8. Sarcastic

_____

_____

9. Cheerful

_____

_____

10. Annoyed

_____

_____

4.7 Noticing the Moods of Others

Objective:

The student will identify a specific mood of a character when given written and facial clues.

Comments:

Sometimes teens (or all of us, at one time) are so wrapped up in their own emotional state that they do not notice the moods of others. Noticing and then correctly identifying someone else's mood is a good social clue as to whether or not this is a good time to ask for something, offer to help out, stay away, or join in the fun. In this lesson, students are given some examples of a person who is in a specific mood.

Introductory Activities:

1. Have students think of a movie or TV character who is a good example of someone who is usually in a good mood, bad mood, sad mood, or other type of mood.   2. Have students take turns (on a volunteer basis) demonstrating a mood with only facial cues or by using body language (such as crossing arms, pouting, tapping foot).

Activity:

Students are to use the worksheet "Noticing the Moods of Others" to match people with an appropriate mood.   *Answers:* 1. b   2. e   3. a   4. d   5. c

Discussion:

After students have completed the worksheet, they can discuss the following questions:

1. In example 1, the boy is frustrated. Does this mean he is also angry? (Not necessarily.) 2. What would be a solution to help the boy change to a better mood? (Ask for help on his math problem.)   3. In example 2, the girl is bored. What is an alternative for her to get out of her bored mood? (Find something else to do, invite a friend over, read a book.)   4. In example 3, the girl is excited. What clues did you pick up on? (Facial excitement, tone of voice, hands waving.) 5. In example 4, the boy is angry. Do you think he is always in an angry mood or is this because of the situation? (This situation triggered angry behavior—we would need to know him a little better to know whether he is an angry person in general or just set off because of this situation.) 6. In example 5, the girl is happy. What is the specific reason? (She got a present from her parents.) 7. Can you think of people who always seem to be in a good mood? What does it feel like to be around them? How do you think they would explain their good mood?   8. When something specifically good or bad happens to you, how does that affect your mood? (Can throw you into a good or bad mood temporarily, but you can bounce back to your normal mood.)

Extension Activities:

1. Have students make a small chart with several moods listed (such as happy, bored, silly, amused, stressed) and observe others who seem to be expressing that mood. Jot down the circumstances that

might be contributing to that mood.   2. Have students look for examples in books, short stories, or other written examples that have a character clearly expressing a mood. Share how the author uses words to depict a mood clearly.

Evaluation:

What mood do you think each of these people might be experiencing?

1. A person with tears on her face, mouth trembling. _____ (sadness)   2. A person yawning, drumming fingers on a table. _____ (boredom)   3. A person rolling on the floor, laughing and playing with a dog. _____ (happy)

4.7   Noticing the Moods of Others

Directions:

Match the person on the left with the mood he or she is in from the choices on the right. Write the letter next to each person.

_____ 1. Dang it! I can never get these numbers to add up right!

a. Excited

_____ 2. Ho, hum. I've seen this show at least twenty times already.

b. Frustrated

_____ 3. I can't WAIT 'til you come over!! Can you hurry??? Please hurry!

c. Happy

_____ 4. When I find out who spilled coffee on my research report, there will be some screaming going on around here and it won't be me!

d. Angry

_____ 5. I just had the best day! My parents gave me a gift card for some new jeans.

e. Bored

4.8 How My Mood Affects Others

Objective:

The student will state how one person's mood might affect another person.

Comments:

For better or worse, our moods affect other people around us. If I am in a really bad mood, my students know to be quiet and give me some room. If I am cheerful and silly, my students are more likely to open up, talk more, and feel relaxed. It is important for students to have the awareness of how their mood affects others—positively and negatively.

Introductory Activities:

1. Ask students to give feedback as to how they know their parent's, teacher's, or sibling's mood first thing in the morning. What are some clues?   2. Role-play a situation in which you (the teacher) enter the classroom in each of several moods. Discuss how that affects the students' first impression of how the day is going to go.

Activity:

Students are to complete the worksheet "How My Mood Affects Others" by identifying the mood of a person and a typical response to that mood.   *Answers (Examples):*   1. happy / happy also 2. frustrated / angry   3. grieving, sad / annoyed

Discussion:

How we feel and show our emotions can and does affect how others feel. We can't control things around us, but we can try to control our moods, especially as they affect other people.

1. In example 1, Theo shared his happiness with a friend. How would Theo have felt if Mike didn't want to come over or said that his aunt sent him a lot more than $50 on *his* birthday? (Happiness buster!) 2. In example 2, Angel's bad mood was brought on by oversleeping. How else could she have handled this situation with her brother? Could her brother have done anything different to help Angel's mood? 3. In example 3, Stefano was grieving over his dog. Have you ever felt the loss of a pet or a friend? Has this sadness been misinterpreted by others? Did anything help to make you feel better?

Extension Activities:

1. Ask for volunteers to role-play two-person situations in which Person A is in a specific mood (list the choices and have students pick them at random). Have Person B participate in the role-play and (a) just listen without giving feedback, then (b) try to interact with Person A to join in a good mood or lessen the bad mood.   2. Finish the story: Give students a scenario for the beginning of a story (for example, invited to a party, hiking in the woods, participating in a play) and have them finish it with alternate endings. In one, for example, the narrator is in a crazy/sad/happy/sarcastic mood. Complete the story, staying true to the mood. Compare endings.

Evaluation:

1. How could a person in this mood affect someone else in a positive way? (Being patient while waiting in a long line to buy something.)   2. How could a person in this mood affect someone else in a negative way? (Being sarcastic while at the tryouts for a cheerleading squad.)

4.8   **How My Mood Affects Others**

Directions:

Read each of the following stories. Identify the mood, then write a short answer that describes how the first person's mood affected the other person or people.

1. Theo got a birthday card from his aunt with a $50 bill inside it. He began to dance around the room! He called his friend Mike and invited him to go out for pizza, Theo's treat. Mike said he would be over in two minutes.

   Theo's mood: _____

   Mike's response: _____

2. Angel overslept on the day of a big math test at school. She ran downstairs, pushing her brother, Tom, out of the way as she grabbed some lunch meat out of the refrigerator. "Hey!" yelled her brother. "That was for my lunch!" "Too bad," yelled Angela. "You are out of luck today! Now, *move!*" Tom threw a banana at her as she dashed out of the house.

   Angel's mood: _____

   Brother's response: _____

3. Stefano had to take the old family dog to the vet to be euthanized. He didn't want people to notice that he had been crying. When Sandra asked him if he wanted to help out on a school project, he said no and walked away. Sandra told the other friends in their group that Stefano was acting really weird and that they should stay away from him because he was in a bad mood.

   Stefano's mood: _____

   Sandra's response: _____

Chapter 5

Friendship Skills

5.1 My Peer Groups

Objective:

The student will define and give examples of members of a peer group.

Comments:

Peers have a tremendous influence over children, particularly as they enter adolescence. It is important for students to recognize that they are part of larger social groups and that these groups can and will affect them. In this lesson, students are to think about what people compose their peer groups.

Introductory Activities:

1. Have students list five or six of their closest friends.   2. Have students add to that list by including people with whom they spend a lot of time (because of the activity), though they may not necessarily be "friends" with them.   3. Define *peer* for students. (Someone who is equal to another person, either in social standing or because he or she is in the same age group or has the same status.)

Activity:

Each student will think of peers who have something in common with him or her, such as family background, interests, or school activities.   *Answers:* Will vary.

Discussion:

Be aware that some students may be perceived as low status or outcasts within the group. You may not want to have students reveal the names they put on their worksheets. What is important is that each student is aware of his or her peer group(s).

1. Did you tend to write names of people who are the same age as you?   2. Except for item 3, did you tend to write names of people who are the same sex as you?   3. Do you consider yourself to be friends with everyone whose name you wrote down, or were there people who are part of your groups but not necessarily someone you were close to?   4. What does this phrase mean: "a jury of your peers"?   5. Do you think you would have the same names written if you filled this out ten years from now?

Extension Activities:

1. Make a banner or several separate posters of peer groups within the school. Use copies of yearbooks or newspaper photos to get you started (softball team pictures, pep club, and so on). 2. Have students bring in photographs that portray themselves with at least one or two other people. What is the common thread between the people in the photo?

Evaluation:

1. Define *peer* or *peer group*.   2. Give two examples of someone in your peer group and state why that person is considered to be a peer.

5.1   My Peer Groups

Directions:

Write the name of someone who fits the description of each of the following comments. Try to pick different people for as many as you can.

1. Someone who is the same age as I am:

   _____

2. Someone who is interested in the same hobbies as I am:

   _____

3. Someone who is the same sex as I am:

   _____

4. Someone who gets about the same grades as I do:

   _____

5. Someone who works with me or does about the same job as I do:

   _____

6. Someone who comes from a family that is a lot like mine:

   _____

7. Someone who is on the same team as I am:

   _____

8. Someone who feels the same way I do about something very important to me:

   _____

Chapter 5: Friendship Skills   **81**

5.2 Who Are My Friends?

Objective:

The student will list at least five individuals whom he or she considers to be a friend.

Comments:

Having a good friend can go a long way in terms of having a happy life. Many people are very lucky to have just one good friend. Not everyone needs to be popular, with their cell phone ringing constantly with invitations, to be a part of things. Yet sometimes we overlook the people in our lives who are there for us, who really are the steady friends whom we can count on. In this lesson, students are focusing on identifying people in their lives who are already their friends.

Introductory Activities:

1. Discuss with students the notion of being "popular"—what does that mean? How many friends are needed in order to be popular?   2. Discuss the notion of a "best friend." Is there one certain individual who stands out from the rest, who is a critical person in someone's life? For what reason(s)?

Activity:

Students are to identify possible friends who are already in a person's life on the worksheet "Who Are My Friends?"   *Answers:* Will vary.

Discussion:

Using the worksheets, guide students through a discussion on what people are already established as being friends in their lives.

1. Which of the items on the worksheet were easy for you to complete?   2. Which items were more difficult for you? Why?   3. Do you see any kind of pattern on the list? Are the same names popping up several times on your sheet?   4. When you think about the names on your list, did any of them surprise you?   5. Do you think your name would appear on the list of questions if your friends were to fill out the list? For what categories?

Extension Activities:

1. Have students make a list of their friends. Then, using a target image, have students arrange their friends with the closest friends in the middle of the target. Place the others accordingly. Discuss the idea of best or close friends compared with casual friends A student may have many casual friends, but out of this group there will most likely be one or two who are especially close to the student.   2. Discuss the idea of *age*. How many students have older people on their list as a friend? How many friends are younger than they are? How does this contribute to an interesting array of friends?

Evaluation:

1. List three to five people whom you consider to be your friends.   2. For three of the friends, write a reason why that person is a special friend to you.

5.2   **Who Are My Friends?**

Directions:

Read each description and write a name or names of someone who comes to mind.

1. Someone who makes me laugh

2. Someone I can talk to about school problems

3. Someone I can talk to about family problems

4. Someone who likes to do the same activities as I do (sports, hobbies)

5. Someone who goes to my house of worship

6. Someone who is in a club or organization with me (4-H, scouting, cheerleading).

7. Someone who is friendly to me

8. Someone who calls me or contacts me first

9. Someone who invited me over to their house

10. Someone who invited me to a party or an event

11. Someone who is a good listener when I talk

12. Someone who can keep a secret

13. Someone who makes me feel included in things

14. Someone who buys me things

15. Someone who likes my gifts

5.3 Making Friends

Objective:

The student will identify three or four ways to initiate a friendship.

Comments:

Some students have difficulty making friends. Perhaps they are shy, too loud, or simply try too hard. In this lesson, several ways to initiate a friendship are discussed.

Introductory Activities:

1. Have students list two people who have recently become their friends.   2. Have students write the names of two people whom they consider to be friendly.

Activity:

Students are to examine the ten cartoon situations on the worksheet "Making Friends" and evaluate how good a way each is to initiate making friends with someone else. In some cases, "maybe" is an appropriate answer.   *Answers (Examples):*   1. No—may be too aggressive.   2. Yes—acting first. 3. Yes—go where people are.   4. No—isolating self.   5. Yes—acting friendly.   6. Yes—being helpful.   7. Yes—acting first.   8. No—critical comment; or Maybe—teasing in a friendly way. 9. Yes—acting first.   10. Yes—being resourceful.

Discussion:

Students should be prepared to explain their answers and try to come up with some general ideas for making friends, such as: look and act friendly toward others, include others, be available, go where other people are, and make the first move.

1. Which of the ways on the worksheet would you try?   2. Which of the students on the worksheet would you find irritating or offensive?   3. When is the last time you picked out someone whom you would like for a friend? How did you become friends?   4. Is it harder to initiate friendships with someone of the opposite sex?   5. If you are basically a shy person, what are some quiet ways you could initiate talking or contact with someone else?

Extension Activities:

1. Have students target someone whom they would like to befriend. Have them practice friendship-making skills to initiate contact with the person. Keep a journal of progress!   2. By secret ballot, have students write the names of three people in the class, school, or group who they consider to be good at making friends. Analyze why these people are friendly.

Evaluation:

1. List three good ways someone could initiate a friendship with another person.   2. List one way that would probably not be a good way to make friends with someone else and explain why.

5.3   **Making Friends**

Directions: Read each situation and decide whether it is or is not a good way to approach someone to initiate a friendship. Write YES, NO, or MAYBE next to each item. Be prepared to explain your answers!

1. Hi! Let's be friends.

2. I need a study buddy for the test. Want to work together?

3. I think I'll join the volleyball team. It looks like it might be fun.

4. I'll just eat lunch by myself and work on my homework.

5. May I join you?

6. You look like you could use a hand. Would you like some help?

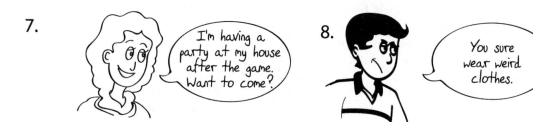

7. I'm having a party at my house after the game. Want to come?

8. You sure wear weird clothes.

9. Let's include the new kid.

10. Would You introduce me to your cousin? WOW!

Chapter 5: Friendship Skills   **85**

5.4 People Who Are Like You

Objective:

The student will find something in common with the descriptions of two individuals who are friends.

Comments:

One way to make friends is to hang around with people who are similar to you. At least you know there will be some kind of common interest. Encourage students to think about ways that they are like other people. These similarities can lead to friendship.

Introductory Activities:

1. Make a Venn diagram with two names for the circles. Choose two students at random in the class. Ask for descriptions of the students in terms of what they like to do, where they live, what they look like, and so on. Emphasize the overlapping area of the diagram as something that they have "in common."   2. Have students pair up and complete a Venn diagram with another person in the classroom. Discuss the common areas.

Activity:

Students will read descriptions of two people on the worksheet "People Who Are Like You" and then find what the individuals have in common. They can write or discuss the common areas.   *Answers:* 1. Both enjoy football.   2. Both have an interest in dogs.   3. Both enjoy boats and lakes. 4. Both enjoy winter sports.   5. Both enjoy reading.   6. Both enjoy the outdoors.   7. Both know what it feels like to struggle in school.   8. Both like food.

Discussion:

For each of the pairs on the worksheet, there is something in common but also a variation of how they share the enjoyment or struggle that they each feel.

1. In example 1, what could the boys do together that involves football? (Talk about their favorite teams.)   2. In example 2, the girls both enjoy something with dogs, but their interests are different—one wants to be directly involved and the other enjoys drawing. Yet how can their common interest bring them together as friends? (They can talk about the different breeds, what makes them laugh when watching them.)   3. For the other examples, how does a common interest show up in a different way?   4. In example 7, the boys have something in common— they are both having trouble in school. How can that common struggle draw them together? (They both know what it's like, might need tutoring, perhaps can help each other with their strengths.) 5. Do you think any two people can find something in common with each other?

Extension Activities:

1. Have students make a Venn diagram for themselves and several of their friends. What areas overlap? 2. Have students ask others who know them to give a brief description of what they (the students) are like; perhaps a "Top Three list" of what traits or interests best describe them. Have the students compare the list provided by several different people and discover which trait(s) are most obvious to others. Any surprises?

Evaluation:

What do these individuals have in common?   1. Mike likes to roller skate; Jenna likes to skateboard. 2. Anna used to live in Paris, France, while her parents worked over there. Janelle has always wanted to learn to speak a foreign language.

5.4 **People Who Are Like You**

Directions:

Read the following descriptions and find something that the people have in common.

1. Eric loves to watch professional football. Jerris likes to play football, but he doesn't really like to watch teams play.

2. Amy loves dogs; in fact, she volunteers at the local animal shelter. Her friend Cami is allergic to most dogs, but she is a good artist and draws pictures of dogs and other animals.

3. Mark has always wanted to go sailing, but there are no lakes near him. Derrick lives on a lake and has a rowboat and a canoe.

4. Denise ice skates in the winter. Alyson can't skate at all, but she loves to go tobogganing down the biggest hills in the park.

5. A perfect day for Alex is to sit in a comfortable chair and read a good book about cowboys and the Old West. Tina can spend hours reading mystery books.

6. Jenni just got a twelve-speed bike and can't wait to go biking. Karlie loves to run outside and likes to keep in shape for the cross-country team.

7. Benny is struggling to keep up in his math class. It just seems so hard! Juan doesn't have any trouble in math, but he is failing his English class.

8. Robert's family is Italian and they make the best lasagna! Serena is from Mexico, and she loves any kind of food with cheese on it.

5.5 People Who Are Different from You

Objective:

The student will list three to five ways in which people can significantly differ from each other.

Comments:

In these days of celebrating cultural diversity, it is apparent that even small details of one's life are scrutinized for political correctness. Although this can be carried to annoying extremes, the underlying theme of getting to know someone, including their differences, is still a valid task. It really is important to understand where someone is coming from in terms of their cultural background, opinions, upbringing, and choices.

In this lesson, a few differences are highlighted.

Introductory Activities:

1. Talk about how different cultures celebrate holidays. There are so many to choose from—perhaps Hanukkah, Martin Luther King Jr.'s birthday, Kwanzaa, and May Day are a few that would spark some discussion. If appropriate, open it up to a discussion about religious celebrations.
2. Have students offer to share how to say a common greeting or count to ten in a foreign language. How many different languages are students familiar with?

Activity:

Students are directed to think about ways in which people can differ in terms of activities, language, ethnicity, family, and how they spend time on weekends on the worksheet "People Who Are Different from You."

Answers: Will vary.

Discussion:

People differ in many ways other than ethnicity, although that is probably one of the most prominent themes. Encourage students to realize that differences are a good thing—diversity is what keeps things interesting at the very least!

1. What are some examples of different things that your friends like to do? Why is it important to try some new things? (Expand your horizons, you might find a new activity for yourself.)
2. What are your experiences with someone who speaks a different language from you?
3. How might it be difficult to speak one language at school and another at home?
4. How might it be helpful to know two languages?
5. What do you know about your own ethnic background?
6. What are some things you find interesting about a different ethnic background?
7. Can you name any famous people who are from a certain country?
8. Have you ever wished that your family was different in some way? How?
9. What are some good things about knowing people who are very different from you?
10. Do you think that you have learned something new about a different culture, religion, or philosophy in the last few years? Explain.

Extension Activities:

1. Invite a guest speaker from another country to visit the class and talk about customs, cultural differences, language, traditions, and any other topics that are appropriate. Allow a question-and-answer time for students to find out more about another country.

2. Encourage interested students to find a pen-pal (or "e-pal") from another country. Two sites that may be helpful are www.epals.com and www.studentsoftheworld.info (a French-based site, but in English).

Evaluation:

1. List three ways that people can be different from each other in terms of this activity.

2. Write a paragraph describing one of the ways that you and a friend are different and how that difference helps your friendship.

5.5   People Who Are Different from You

Directions: Here are some ways in which a person can differ from you. Write down the name of someone you know who fits the description.

Favorite things to do:

My favorite thing to do in my free time is _____.

Someone who likes to do something different is _____.

What does he or she like to do? _____

Language:

The language I speak at home is _____.

Someone who speaks a different language is _____.

What language? _____

Ethnic background:

My ethnic background is _____.

Someone who is from a different background is _____.

What background? _____

Family:

Here is a description of my family: (size, parents, siblings) _____

Someone who has a different family is _____.

What is his or her family like? _____

Weekends:

On a weekend, I am most likely to be/do _____.

Someone with different weekend plans is _____.

What are his/her plans? _____

Chapter 5: Friendship Skills   **91**

5.6 Where and How to Look for Friends

Objective:

The student will identify several examples of where or how he or she could find an opportunity to make a friend.

Comments:

Special needs teens may find it difficult to start up friendships. Although we try to group them and encourage them to participate in all kinds of activities, it does take a certain chemistry to find people who really get along with and actually like each other! By intentionally identifying some ways to search for friends (using common interests, sharing experiences), the student may increase the chances of being in the right place for a friendship to start.

Introductory Activities:

1. Ask students to list some places that they like to go to hang out with friends. (Shopping center, arcade, movies, and so on.) Why are these good places to get to know someone?
2. Go through the list and have students give ideas for how they could make a new friend or meet someone at each of the places. Sometimes having a friend introduce or include new people in a group is a good way to enlarge the social circle.

Activity:

Students are to read conversations between people on the worksheet "Where and How to Look for Friends" and try to figure out how they became friends.

Answers:

1. The girls share an interest in horses at the stable.
2. The boys play football on a team.
3. The kids worked together on a science fair project.
4. The girls didn't want to swim but will try another activity.
5. The kids both take their dogs for training.

Discussion:

Being in the right place at the right time can help someone find friendship with people who share an interest, problem, or situation. Encourage students to "think big" to come up with places and opportunities to meet others.

1. In example 1, the girls share an interest in horses. How could this start a friendship? (They could ride together, share chores.)
2. In example 2, the boys are on a team together. What are some other teams that are available in our area or at our school?
3. In example 3, the kids were working together and became friends that way. Who has any other examples of working with someone on a project?

4. In example 4, the girls did *not* like the activity they were doing together, but one suggested an alternative. So even an unpleasant activity led to something better. Has this ever happened to you or someone you know?

5. In example 5, how did the dogs serve as a starting point for starting a conversation? How would that make it easy to talk to someone? (Dogs are appealing to many people—good conversation starters!)

Extension Activities:

1. Encourage your class to take part in activities with older or younger groups of people in your community. Assisted-living facilities often welcome this age group to come and befriend older adults who may be looking for friendship as well. If appropriate, cross-age tutoring or being a buddy to a younger child within a school can also serve to let the student be a role model and friend to someone in need.

2. Get a copy of your community's local paper and have students identify possible activities that are open to the public throughout the week. This might include activities at the library, special events, community parties, and so on.

Evaluation:

1. List three places or activities that would be good places to find a friend.

2. Think about one of your friends and how you first met. Write a few sentences that explain how your friendship started.

5.6   Where and How to Look for Friends

Directions: Read the following conversations between characters and try to determine how they became friends. Write your answers on the lines.

1. "I started taking riding lessons at Paradise Riding Center."   "I love horses! I couldn't wait to get a job working at the stable!"

_____

2. "Here—try to catch the football!"   "Got it! See you at practice later."

_____

3. "We had so much fun working on the science fair!"   "Let's try to be partners for the Math-a-Thon planning committee."

_____

4. "I am only taking swimming lessons because Mother thinks I'm going to drown in the bathtub. I hate swimming."   "Me too. I would rather go bowling. Why don't we go to the alley after the lesson next week?"

_____

5. "Down, Ginger! She hasn't passed her obedience class yet!"   "What a beautiful dog! This dog training class is fun, isn't it?"

_____

5.7 Qualities of a Good Friend

Objective:

The student will identify several qualities he or she feels are important in a friendship.

Comments:

Many different qualities may draw friends together. Some are based on being thrown together in a time of crisis, having mutual interests, geographical convenience, or simply just enjoying the company of another person. In this lesson, students are to analyze qualities they feel are important in a friendship.

Introductory Activities:

1. Have students volunteer to tell about a particularly good experience they had with a friend.
2. Have students volunteer to tell about how a friend helped them through a difficult time.

Activity:

Students are to read over the list of suggested qualities on the worksheet "Qualities of a Good Friend" and rank from 1 to 5 (1 is the highest) those they feel are most important. They can add qualities to the list.

Discussion:

You may want to take a quick class survey to find out which were the top three qualities selected. Be sure to ask which additional qualities were added to the list.

1. Why did you select the qualities that you did? Did you have a particular experience or reason?
2. Which did you think was the single most important quality?
3. Do you think you also possess that single most important quality in being a friend toward others?
4. Are you as good a friend to others as you expect others to be to you?
5. How long do you think someone possesses these qualities (for example, is really loyal, trustworthy)?

Extension Activities:

1. Look for anecdotes of true friendship in books, newspapers, magazine stories, and so on (for example, a young man had cancer and lost his hair, so all of his close friends shaved their heads). What quality does it show as being important?
2. Target a friend and do something special to thank that friend for his or her special quality.

Evaluation:

1. List three qualities you think are important in a friendship.
2. Explain which of those qualities is the most important to you. Why?

5.7   Qualities of a Good Friend

Directions:

Which of these qualities do you think is important in a friendship? Rank each item from 1 to 5 (1 = most important). Feel free to add your own ideas.

- Is popular ____
- Has money ____
- Is a good listener ____
- Can be trusted with secrets ____
- Doesn't talk behind your back ____
- Is usually happy ____
- Is a good student ____
- Gets lots of attention ____
- Is funny ____
- Has good ideas for things to do ____
- Is interesting ____
- Understands how you feel ____
- Is respected by other people ____
- Is good at sports ____
- Comes through in a crisis ____
- Is loyal—keeps on being your friend even when you're not around ____

5.8 Social Situations

Objective:

The student will identify several social situations that are personally comfortable or uncomfortable for him or her and explain why.

Comments:

One way to make (and perfect) friendships is by spending time in social situations. Our comfort level differs, depending on what those situations are. Some students may enjoy dancing, while others fear it as a horrible situation. In this lesson, students are to think about social situations they enjoy and those they may find uncomfortable.

Introductory Activities:

1. Have students volunteer to tell about a situation involving other people in which they felt embarrassed or awkward.   2. Have students volunteer to tell about a situation involving other people in which they felt comfortable and possibly proud of themselves.

Activity:

Students are given examples of ten social situations on the worksheet "Social Situations." They are to indicate which make them comfortable, uncomfortable, or neither. The situations are smoking, dancing, playing cards, talking about sports, eating, talking about a controversial topic, talking positively about someone else, talking negatively about someone else, drinking, playing sports.

Discussion:

Be sure each student understands the context of each picture. There are no "right" or "wrong" answers; each student will respond according to his or her own comfort level.

1. Which situations would make you feel uncomfortable? Why?   2. In which situations would you feel quite comfortable or even look forward to participating?   3. Did you feel "neutral" about any of the situations?   4. What do your answers reveal about you? (Think of yourself as a risk-taker, enjoy sports, and so on.)

Extension Activities:

1. Write about your most embarrassing moment. Who was around? How did you handle it? What do you think people thought about you? Does it seem funny now?   2. The next time you are at a party or social gathering, observe the people around you. Pick out someone who seems to be very social and try to decide what qualities it is about him or her that make the situation fun for him or her. Is the person outgoing? A good listener? Does he or she move around a lot to talk to many different people? Observe!

Evaluation:

1. List two social situations in which you feel very comfortable.   2. List two social situations that make you feel uneasy, nervous, or bored.

5.8   Social Situations

Directions: Here are ten social situations in which people are involved in a lot of different activities. Circle those that show situations in which you would feel comfortable. Put an X on those in which you would feel uncomfortable. Leave alone those in which you would not particularly feel one way or the other.

5.9 A Positive Role Model

Objective:

The student will identify a personal positive role model and give at least one reason why this person was selected.

Comments:

It is important to have someone to look up to—to admire and to emulate. Part of growing up is modeling oneself after other people. If students can relate to someone who is a positive influence (for whatever reason), this can help them aspire to try to develop the same positive traits in themselves.

Introductory Activities:

1. Have students write the name of a peer whom they admire or wish they could be like. 2. Have students write the name of someone else whom they admire, but there are no restrictions—this could be anyone.   3. Have students write the name of an adult whom they admire.

Activity:

On the worksheet "A Positive Role Model," students are to pretend they are one of the people they selected as a role model and describe what a typical day would be like for them as this person. Some students may insist on selecting someone whom you may not think of as a "positive" person; however, encourage students to pick someone who in some way has a redeeming quality! Allow students to really exaggerate the details in their writing. This may help them use their imaginations and have some fun with the project. (You may want to provide parameters on the role model—living or dead, fictional or real-life person, and so on.)

Discussion:

Have students share who they selected as their role model. Ask for volunteers to read their entries if they desire. The bottom line in this activity is for students to identify what it is about their role model that makes that person a positive influence on them.

1. Who did you select for your role model?   2. What positive characteristic about this role model did you focus on?   3. Do you think you could really be like this person in some way? Is the characteristic you like really attainable for you?   4. Do you admire this person because he or she is somewhat like you or because he or she is different in some way from you?   5. Did you pick someone who is the same sex as you?   6. Did you pick someone with the same abilities (artistic, athletic, and so on) as you, only more pronounced or professional? What does this indicate about you?

Extension Activities:

1. Write a letter to a famous role model. What would you like to find out about him or her? 2. Read a book or magazine that contains information about your role model. What has he or she done that you admire? What background information did you find out that interested or surprised you?   3. Conduct an informal survey of your class or other group. Who are popular role models among these groups? Try to predict—Movie star? Musician? Athlete? Why?

Evaluation:

1. Identify a person who is a positive role model for you.   2. Give at least one reason why this person is a positive influence.

5.9   # A Positive Role Model

Directions:

You have just turned into your positive role model. Describe a typical day in your life. Ideas: What will you wear? What will you do today? Who will you talk to? How will people respond to you? Will you do anything surprising? (Use the back of this sheet if you need more space to write.)

_____
_____
_____
_____
_____
_____
_____
_____
_____
_____
_____
_____
_____
_____
_____
_____

5.10 What About Gangs?

Objective:

The student will define and give examples of membership in an organized gang.

Comments:

Students are exposed all too soon to the influence of gangs. Some are part of the "wannabes" and do not realize the danger they are putting themselves in. Though students may view gang membership as powerful or prestigious, there are serious social and criminal consequences linked to gang activity. This lesson is primarily for discussion of students' perceptions, experiences with, and decisions about gangs.

Introductory Activities:

1. Define *gang* for students. (A group of people associated together whose activities are primarily antisocial and delinquent.)   2. Have students list characteristics of gangs in general. (Wearing a certain color, special hand signals, signs, and so on.)

Activity:

The student will read some comments about gangs and decide whether he or she agrees or disagrees with the statement. Some of the statements are facts; others are opinions.

Discussion:

Students may have had some exposure to or experience with gangs in your community. Some may act like it is "cool" to be part of a gang and will disagree with the comments on the worksheet. At your discretion, you may want to have students share their anecdotes about gangs. Be prepared to back up your opinion!

1. What do you think are the good things a gang can offer a member? (Belonging, safety against others, and so on.)   2. Can these good things be gotten in other ways? How? (Join a different group.) 3. Do you think most kids who act like they are in a gang are truly gang members or are they "wannabes"? What's the difference?   4. What consequences are there to committing a crime? 5. What crimes are organized gang members often guilty of? (Drive-by shootings, knife fights, theft, and so on.)   6. What would be a way to convince someone to stay out of a gang?

Extension Activities:

1. Collect newspaper articles about gang activity. What type of activity is in your area or close to your community?   2. If possible, arrange for an interview with someone who was or is somehow involved in a street gang. (Clear this with your administration first!) Has this been a positive experience for the person?

Evaluation:

1. Define *gang*.   2. Give two examples of positive things that gang membership seems to promise. 3. Give two examples of negative consequences that can occur because of gang membership.

5.10   **What About Gangs?**

Directions:

Read the following comments about gangs. Circle "agree" or "disagree" to show how you feel about the comment.

1. There are gangs in my community.   **Agree   Disagree**

2. Organized gangs in the United States are in the business of crime.   **Agree   Disagree**

3. Gangs have special ways of showing membership, such as wearing a   **Agree   Disagree**
   certain color or having a hand signal.

4. People who join gangs want to belong to a group.   **Agree   Disagree**

5. Older gang members can recruit others by intimidation or by providing   **Agree   Disagree**
   a sense of belonging.

6. New members have to go through initiation to join some gangs.   **Agree   Disagree**

7. Once you join a gang, it is difficult to get out.   **Agree   Disagree**

8. People who join gangs have experienced some sort of hardship or abuse   **Agree   Disagree**
   as a child.

9. Some people act like they are members of a gang, but they are really not.   **Agree   Disagree**

10. Kids join gangs because they want to feel powerful.   **Agree   Disagree**

11. Joining a gang can be dangerous.   **Agree   Disagree**

12. Once you join a gang, you have lost your power to make choices.   **Agree   Disagree**

Copyright © 2009 by John Wiley & Sons, Inc.

5.11 Social Networking Online

Objective:

The student will describe the purpose and features of several online sites.

Comments:

Students are becoming increasingly familiar with online sites to make new friends, share information with peers, blog, carry on conversations, and share many aspects of their life. Although many sites are safe and fun, adults should always be careful to know what their children are doing on the computer and to teach them to be careful with what information they share. This site is helpful for safety guidelines for adults: www.onguardonline.gov/topics/safety-tips-tweens-teens.aspx.

Introductory Activities:

1. Ask students to tell you what they know about Facebook or MySpace. Some may have accounts on these or other sites for social networking.   2. Discuss what a blog is and visit several online. 3. Write and visit these websites as a group or in small groups: Facebook, LiveJournal, ePals, Horseland, Flixter. Have students talk about the purpose and features of these sites.

Activity:

After checking out the sites just listed, have students complete the worksheet "Social Networking Online" by selecting an appropriate site for the people on the list.   *Answers:* 1. Facebook   2. Flixter 3. LiveJournal   4. ePals   5. Horseland

Discussion:

After students have completed the worksheet and have some familiarity with the websites, discuss the features and attractions of the sites.

1. What are some of the things that you like about Facebook? (Can post pictures, can link to many other fun features, easy to add friends.)   2. How is LiveJournal different from Facebook? (It is a blog/journal, purpose is more to put thoughts into writing than to list social activities.) 3. What are some of the features that you noticed about ePals? (Helps you find people who may have similar interests but live somewhere else, safe e-mail, can join as a class or individually, has projects you can join.)   4. What are some of the features that you noticed about Horseland? (Has levels for younger and older kids, can connect with other horse lovers, games.)   5. What are some of the features that you noticed about Flixter? (Polls, movie reviews, movies online, quizzes.)   6. Why do you think some people enjoy making online friends, even though they might never meet? (Still fun to talk to someone, share interests.)   7. What are some safe sites that you have visited to make friends or share information with people you already know?

Extension Activities:

1. Compile a classroom list of favorite sites to visit that are safe, approved, and interesting. Have students fill out an information sheet with features, comments, and opinions about the site.   2. Join ePals.com as a classroom project and connect with another class in another geographical area. Explore!

Evaluation:

1. List two online sites that are safe and helpful for making friends.   2. Choose one of the sites and describe the features of that site.

5.11   **Social Networking Online**

Directions:

Read the description of the interests of each of the following people. Then select a site that could be a good computer match for him or her. Write your answer on the lines.

Facebook   **Horseland**

LiveJournal   **Flixter**

ePals

1. Tony likes to keep up with friends on the Internet, but he doesn't like to write very much—mostly he just likes to read about what's going on with them and look at their pictures.

   _____

2. Barb loves to go to movies and enjoys chatting with others online about which ones she likes.

   _____

3. Amy likes to write about her life. Pretty much every day she wants to tell the world about her thoughts and what she's doing.

   _____

4. Frank is interested in learning about what life is like for students in other countries. He has a computer and wants to start corresponding with someone his own age in Portugal.

   _____

5. Dolores and her younger sister both enjoy horses. They found a site where there are people to talk to about horses and also games that they can both enjoy.

   _____

Chapter 6

Being Part of a Family

6.1 My Family Tree

Objective:

The student will complete a brief family tree, including siblings, parents, and grandparents.

Comments:

It is interesting to research one's family tree. Through records, interviews with relatives, and perhaps old diaries, one can reconstruct a brief history of the people who helped create us! In this lesson, students are to attempt to research their own family tree, at least for a generation or two back.

Introductory Activities:

1. Define *genealogy* for students. (The study of family origins)   2. Define *family tree* for students. (A chart that lists the names of people in a family, showing the different generations)   3. Have students list names of their siblings, parents, and as many grandparents as they can.

Activity:

Students are to work on drawing and filling in names for an informal family tree on the worksheet "My Family Tree." Students can get information from parents or other relatives to complete the activity. You may wish to have students complete the chart using their natural parents (if they live with a stepparent). Students may wish to include stepsiblings as brothers and sisters. Decide how you want to have them complete the chart. Be sensitive to students who live in foster homes or who may be adopted.

Discussion:

Ideally, students will have learned a little about the people on their charts beyond simply noting their names. Allow time for discussion of what anecdotes they learned about the people in their past.

1. Who or what were some good sources for you to complete the chart?   2. What interesting or surprising things did you find out about the people on your chart?   3. How far back were you able to go; that is, how many generations?   4. Were there any common first names among the people in your family tree? Any common characteristics?

Extension Activities:

1. Add to your family tree by locating and including pictures of the people on your chart. 2. Write a biography about one of your ancestors.   3. Write a journal for your future grandchildren. Describe to them what your life is like. What is the present technology, food, prices, popular fads, television, and so on?   4. There are several online sites that can help you locate your ancestors through census, military, and vital records. A free site is www.familysearch.org that will get you started; www.ancestry.com requires membership.

Evaluation:

1. Define the word *genealogy*.   2. Define the term *family tree*.   3. Draw a sample family tree showing an individual, one sister, one brother, parents, and two sets of grandparents.

6.1   My Family Tree

Directions:

A family tree, or pedigree chart, lists a person's name and the names of his or her parents, grandparents, great-grandparents, and so on. On the back of this sheet, try to complete your own family tree, including brothers and sisters. Get information from your parents or other relatives. You can use the following sample chart to get started.

O   indicates a female

△   indicates a male

—   indicates people of the same generation (siblings, cousins)

| indicates different generations (parents, grandparents)

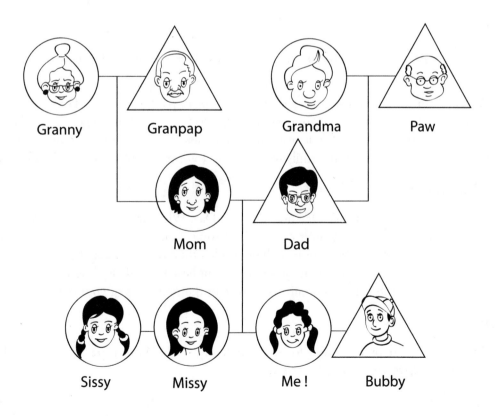

Chapter 6: Being Part of a Family

6.2 Benefits of a Family

Objective:

The student will list at least three ways that members of a family can help or benefit each other.

Comments:

Ideally, families provide more than shelter and financial security for each other. The members of a family share living space and problems, but they can also share support, encouragement, happiness, and time. Whatever the student's family situation is like, he or she is a member of a very special group that can be a lifelong benefit. (*Note:* Be sensitive to those students who might be in foster care, be adopted, and so on.)

Introductory Activities:

1. Ask students to think about what family they wish they could be a part of if they could choose one other than their own.   2. Have students list reasons why they chose that family.

Activity:

On the worksheet "Benefits of a Family," students are to read examples of how particular members of families have helped each other. They are to write the specific reason on the lines.   *Answers (Examples):*   1. Older brother walked her to school.   2. The whole family is saving for a vacation. 3. Older brother helped Bobby improve his football skills.   4. Sister helped Ann get ready for the prom.   5. The whole family worked together to make decisions.   6. The whole family spends a regular time together.

Discussion:

No family is ideal; every family has difficulties. But families share many bonds—genetic, lifestyle, experiences, and current events.

1. As kids gets older, why do they sometimes pull away from parents?   2. Do you think siblings of the same sex get along better than opposite-sex siblings?   3. What types of crises might bring a family closer together?   4. What are some activities that families can enjoy doing together? 5. Would you want your own future family to be similar to or different from your family now?

Extension Activities:

1. Find out the origins of Mother's Day and Father's Day. What are some creative ways to celebrate and honor these people?   2. Watch and analyze some family situation-comedy shows on television. How have members of the family helped each other or stuck together through problems? 3. A caricature is a cartoon-like drawing of a person emphasizing outstanding features (like wild hair or pointed ears) or interests. Make a family caricature of the members of your own family.

Evaluation:

1. List three needs a family can meet for its members.   2. Write a paragraph describing a time when your family helped you through a crisis.

6.2   Benefits of a Family

Directions:

Think about ways family members can help each other. Read each example and write one way the family involved demonstrates how being part of a family can be beneficial.

1. Sally is afraid to go to school because some of the older kids have been teasing her. Her older brother, Frank, has decided to walk to school with her to make sure she gets there safely.

   _____

   _____

2. The Morgan family wants to travel to Yellowstone National Park for a family vacation. Mr. Morgan is working overtime and the older children are earning money by doing odd jobs. Everyone is putting money into a special account at the bank so they can afford to go.

   _____

   _____

3. Bobby wants to join the middle school football team. His older brother, Tom, played for several years on the local high school team. Tom is spending weekends helping Bobby learn how to throw and catch the ball.

   _____

   _____

4. Ann wants to wear something special for the prom. She went through her sister's closet and found just the right dress. Her sister helped her get ready for the big day.

   _____

   _____

5. When Juan's father died, the entire family grieved for a long time. The family had to make important decisions together and realized that being close was comforting as well as necessary for them.

   _____

   _____

6. One of the favorite activities for the Johnson family is to rent movies on the weekend, make buttered popcorn, and spend an evening together. No one is allowed to have a friend over, and everyone is expected to be there. The Johnsons find that they really enjoy spending family time together.

   _____

   _____

6.3 Respecting Authority

Objective: The student will state at least two reasons why it is necessary to respect and obey parental authority.

Comments: Older students may find it difficult to follow rules that seem too restrictive or protective. Nevertheless, parents are responsible for the children's actions while they are minors. Rules are necessary for safety, efficiency, and discipline. Rules may change with the age of the child and the amount of responsibility that he or she can handle.

Introductory Activities:

1. Have students raise their hands to indicate who they view as the primary source of parental authority in their house: father, mother, other adult, and so on.
2. Have students list specific rules that apply in their families or households.

Activity: The student will read several anecdotal paragraphs about a teen and his or her parents and decide whether the teen is showing respect to the parent or not.

Answers: 1. No   2. Yes   3. No   4. No   5. Yes   6. No

Discussion: Have students discuss the examples and decide exactly what rule or request was given and then whether or not it was followed.

1. At what age should parents begin to give a child more authority? When should it be fifty-fifty?
2. Are parents responsible to higher authority systems themselves for care of their children?
3. In which of the examples were parents motivated by concerns for the children's safety?
4. What things could the people in the examples have done to try to change what they considered to be unfair rules?

Extension Activities:

1. Have students conduct a survey of their class or grade. What is the curfew time for most ninth graders? Twelfth graders? Girls? Boys?
2. Invite a probation officer or welfare worker to speak to the class about the legal responsibilities of parents for their children.

Evaluation:

1. List two rules that parents or adults in your household expect you to follow
2. List two reasons why it is necessary to obey parental authority.

6.3   Respecting Authority

Directions:

Read each of the situations. Decide whether or not the main person in the story is showing respect for parental authority or not. Circle YES or NO.

1. Tommy is five years old. His dad tells him not to play with matches. Tommy puts the matches away and gets his dad's cigarette lighter instead and begins to play with that.   **YES**   **NO**

2. Amy is in high school. She borrows her mother's car to go to work at the local dry cleaning store on weekends. Her mother needs the car at midnight on weekends to go to her job. Amy is supposed to fill up the car with gas each weekend and have it in by 10 p.m. Amy goes out to a party on Friday night with friends and has the car back at the house by 9:30. She then returns to the party by getting a ride with another friend.   **YES**   **NO**

3. Steve is fifteen. He has a curfew of 11 p.m. on weekends and 10 p.m. on school nights. He has been getting C's and D's on his report card, so his parents change the curfew to 9 p.m. every night until his grades improve. Steve thinks the curfew is too early and unfair, so he has been coming in at 10 p.m. on weekends.   **YES**   **NO**

4. There have been several robberies and other crimes in Marla's neighborhood over the past few months. Marla's dad decides he is going to pick her up at school and wants her to stay there to wait for him until he can get her. Marla finds this extremely embarrassing, so she tells him that she has a ride with friends and walks home instead.   **YES**   **NO**

5. Sally's older sister just found out she is pregnant. Their parents are extremely upset about this. Now Sally's parents refuse to let Sally even go out on a date at all. Sally is angry at her parents and thinks this is unfair. After all, she doesn't even have a serious boyfriend! She sees her friends at school and talks to them on the phone.   **YES**   **NO**

6. Robert Smith has been skipping school. The probation department is going to prosecute his father if he doesn't make sure that Robert gets to school every day. Mr. Smith leaves for work at 5 a.m. each morning but wants Robert to call him at work right before he leaves for school at 7:30 a.m. Robert calls, then goes to his friend's house to play video games.   **YES**   **NO**

6.4 My Parent's Point of View

Objective:

The student will give a plausible response to a situation from a parental point of view.

Comments:

In general, people respond to a situation from their own viewpoint unless given a reason not to. Teens may not view a situation from a parental point of view simply because they have never been asked to consider that viewpoint. Of course, this assumes that the parent is loving, careful, protective, and truly wants the best for each child. Unfortunately, this is not always the case; however, for this lesson the position of the "parent" should be assumed to be one that protects the child.

Introductory Activities:

1. List areas in which teens and parents may have differing opinions—think in terms of music, dress, activities, and so on.
2. Have students share short anecdotes in which they differed with their parents, but the parents turned out to be right.
3. Repeat the activity, but ask for examples in which the *student* turned out to be right.

Activity:

Students get to pretend to be the parent on the worksheet "My Parent's Point of View" by responding to situations as a parent.

Answers (Examples):

1. You don't have your license yet—it isn't even legal for you to drive.
2. Sorry, but we have a new baby in the family and it's just not a good time.
3. We have had company for two weeks, and not much has been normal in our house.
4. We have a lot going on that week, and you already are committed to doing other things.
5. We want you to learn from our mistakes.

Discussion:

Use the worksheet to start the discussion of these questions:

1. Think about activities such as the driving in example 1. Why does the boy want to drive so badly? What would you think of the parent if she let him drive and then he had an accident?
2. In example 2, the girl wants a large dog. Besides having a new baby in the family, why would the father tell her no? (Large dogs have special requirements, cost more to feed, maybe someone in the family is allergic.)
3. The teacher in example 3 is concerned about the son. What are some possible reasons that the adult could give? Do you think the teacher was threatening to the mother?
4. The girl is angry in example 4. Why do you think she feels angry at her mother? How else could she have this discussion with her mother?

5. In example 5, the boy wants permission to get into trouble. Do you think the parents care if he does? Even if they were parents who got into trouble as kids, do you think they want their son to have the same issues?

6. For all of these examples, did you write responses that showed parents who cared about their children?

7. What do you think might be hard for a parent when dealing with kids your age?

Extension Activities:

1. Role-play the situations on the worksheet and add others as appropriate. Have pairs of students take turns playing the role of the student (or teacher) and the parent.

2. Have students write a letter to their parents or to an adult, explaining what it is like to be a teenager these days and what life is like for them. You do not have to actually deliver the letters—it might be interesting and revealing to have students write to a hypothetical adult.

Evaluation:

1. How might your parent/guardian respond to the following situations:

   a. You want to borrow $100 to buy some new shoes the day after your father was laid off from work.

   b. You are invited to an overnight camping trip with a new family that just moved into your neighborhood.

2. In example 5, the boy wants permission to get into trouble. Do you think the parents care if he does? Even if they were parents who got into trouble as kids, do you think they want their son to have the same issues?

3. For all of these examples, did you write responses that showed parents who cared about their children?

4. What do you think might be hard for a parent when dealing with kids your age?

6.4   **My Parent's Point of View**

Directions:

Pretend you are the parent in each of these situations. Write something that you might say in each situation.

1. Mom, I am almost old enough to drive. Couldn't I just take the car out for a little ride if I'm really careful?

2. I really want to get a dog. Someone in my class is giving away a St. Bernard for FREE! Why can't we get it?

3. Mrs. Smith, I am really concerned about Johnny. He doesn't seem to concentrate in class and he hasn't turned in homework in two weeks. Can you help me?

4. You are so mean! I wanted to go to Cassie's party and you don't trust me. I hate you!

5. I bet you and Dad did some pretty wild things when you were my age, didn't you? So why do you care if I get in trouble once in awhile?

6.5 My Sibling's Point of View

Objective:

The student will give a plausible response to a situation from the point of view of a sibling.

Comments:

Almost everyone with a brother or sister runs into a conflict or situation in which opinions are very different. Age can make a difference, too, in terms of responsibilities, permission to do things, and experience. Gender also plays a factor—think about being the only boy in a family of five children or the youngest girl in a string of boys. But having a sibling is having a family member who is somewhat close to the same age and therefore overlaps in life situations. Again, teens may not try to see issues from another point of view unless asked specifically to do so.

Introductory Activities:

1. Have students raise their hands to show if they have a sibling. (You may include stepsiblings.) Narrow down the qualifications to include: an older or younger sibling, a brother or sister, and twins.

2. Continue to involve students in the sibling mind-set by asking "who" questions, such as: Who in here is an only child? Who has more than four brothers and sisters? Who is the youngest child? Who is the only boy or girl in the family? Who is a twin? Who has to share a room? Who has to babysit? Who has to do the worst chores? Who would trade their brother or sister for a dog? Who has a sibling who is your best friend?

Activity:

On the worksheet "My Sibling's Point of View," students can read a situation and respond in two ways—as themselves and as a sibling.

Answers (Examples):

1a. I felt happy that my dad was proud of me.

1b. I felt left out and jealous.

2a. It all happened because I was in a hurry; I didn't do it on purpose.

2b. My sister is careless and didn't care about the damage that was done.

3a. We are lucky to be able to go on vacation at all and anywhere would be great—so let's work out a way to make it happen.

3b. Maybe we could visit a theme park near a beach and two of us would be happy.

Discussion:

Having a sibling means giving things up, but also having a larger family. You may be familiar with the family dynamics of the students in your class and want to avoid or touch on some of the following questions.

1. The situations on the worksheet all involved a conflict of some sort between siblings. Why do you think there are problems between brothers and sisters in a family? (Roughly the same age group, involve sharing parent's attention, being compared to others.)

2. Do you think the kids in your family are typical in terms of getting along with others but having conflicts sometimes?

3. What are the biggest areas of conflict between you and your siblings?

4. Who works out resolving the conflicts—do your parents, or do you have to work it out between yourselves?

5. How would your family work out the conflict in example 3?

6. What would your siblings say about you in a conflict situation?

7. How would your siblings describe you as a member of the family?

Extension Activities:

1. Have students make a family collage—bring in pictures of past trips, events, baby pictures, and other items that could be put on poster board. If desired, you can have students talk about their siblings.

2. Have creative writing students write a short story in which they switch positions with a sibling for a day and write about what it might be like to be a completely different person within the same family. Share writings.

3. Using photos, have students bring in pictures and demonstrate strong sibling and family resemblances. It might be a physical characteristic such as red hair, blue eyes, or long legs. Talk about other ways in which siblings demonstrate the same traits—generosity, short-temper, quick grasp of math, and so on.

Evaluation:

How would you and a sibling respond differently to the following situations?

1. Acquiring a new pet
2. One of you winning an award for something you both like to do

6.5   My Sibling's Point of View

Directions:

Read each of the following situations and answer each question (a) from your point of view and (b) from the sibling's point of view.

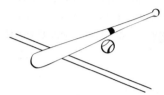

1. You and your brother Keith both play on a softball team with the park league. At one game you hit a home run but your brother struck out. On the way home, all your father could talk about was how great you played. Keith was very quiet on the way home. Your dad said it was the best you had ever played.

How would you describe this game and this ride home?

a. _____

b. _____

2. You and your sister have to share a bedroom. You were in a hurry to get to a meeting with your friends; you left the door open and left a bowl of potato chips on the floor. Sometime during the day the dog got in, ate the food, chewed up your sister's new shirt, and left muddy footprints all over the floor. You felt bad, but you were in a hurry, and sometimes your sister leaves the door open.

What might you talk to your parents about?

a. _____

b. _____

3. You and your two siblings get to vote on where to go for vacation. You want to go to the beach. Your sister wants to go skiing. Your brother wants to visit a theme park. Your parents say you all have to agree. You really, really want to go to the beach and you are the oldest so you should have more say in the decision.

What would your conversation be like?

a. _____

b. _____

6.6 Thoughts About Divorce

Objective:

The student will express—either in writing or orally—his or her opinion or experience regarding divorce.

Comments:

Statistics show that about half of all first marriages end in divorce. Second marriages have a 65 percent divorce rate. With such statistics, it is probable that almost all students have some experience with divorce. In this lesson, students are given the opportunity to collect their thoughts about divorce and to state their opinions.

Introductory Activities:

1. Have students raise their hands if they know someone who is divorced.   2. Have students raise their hands if someone in their immediate family (parent, sibling) is divorced.   3. Have students raise their hands if they think they will be divorced at some time in their lives.

Activity:

Students are given twenty statements on the worksheet "Thoughts About Divorce." There are really no right or wrong answers to these comments; they are provided to stimulate thought and discussion. Some students may be going through a divorce in their family and have negative or intense feelings. Be sensitive to this. Students can learn and benefit from the comments of others.

Discussion:

After students have responded to the statements, go through each and have students volunteer to give their experiences and feelings about them. Students will have a variety of comments, especially those who have come from divorced families. They may be able to see only one side of the situation, so encourage students to listen carefully to the comments of everyone else. Perhaps they will be made aware of other viewpoints and success stories that have come out of divorced situations.

1. What are some reasons why people get divorced?   2. How does having children in a marriage complicate a divorce?   3. What are ways that people can try to save their marriage and avoid a divorce?   4. Do you think it's better for people who don't get along to stay married for the sake of the children?   5. Would children from divorced families answer these questions differently from those from non-divorced families? Why?   6. What problems can arise after a divorce? (Financial problems, custody problems.)   7. Why do children sometimes feel responsible when their parents divorce?   8. What steps might people take to "divorce-proof" a marriage?

Extension Activities:

1. Research the topic of divorce using current periodicals (newspapers, magazines), Make a list of fifteen to twenty questions about divorce, predict what you will find, and then search for the answers. 2. Check with your local County Recorder's Office to find out the number of marriage licenses

applied for in the past year and the number of divorce cases filed during the same period of time. What ratio did you find?   3. If your parents have been divorced, write about your experience. How did you feel? How did you cope? How are things different in your life now? How has this experience affected you? What advice would you give to someone else who is in this position?

Evaluation:

1. List two or three reasons why people choose to divorce.   2. List two or three ways that people might try to prevent a divorce.   3. Write a paragraph describing your experience with a divorce and how it has affected you presently and how you think it will affect you in the future.

6.6   Thoughts About Divorce

Directions:

Read the following comments about divorce. Circle "Agree" or "Disagree" to show how you feel about the comment. If you are undecided, put a question mark next to the comment.

1. Divorce is always wrong.	**Agree**	**Disagree**
2. I will probably be divorced someday.	**Agree**	**Disagree**
3. Both people are at fault in a divorce.	**Agree**	**Disagree**
4. Parents should stay together for the sake of their children.	**Agree**	**Disagree**
5. Children should get to pick who they want to live with after a divorce.	**Agree**	**Disagree**
6. Counseling can keep people from getting a divorce.	**Agree**	**Disagree**
7. The mother should always keep the kids.	**Agree**	**Disagree**
8. Children can be part of the problem in causing people to get a divorce.	**Agree**	**Disagree**
9. Many divorces are about money.	**Agree**	**Disagree**
10. If someone has an affair, they will probably get divorced.	**Agree**	**Disagree**
11. People who are divorced once will probably get divorced again.	**Agree**	**Disagree**
12. Divorce is now considered to be socially acceptable.	**Agree**	**Disagree**
13. If only one person wants to stay married, the marriage will not work.	**Agree**	**Disagree**
14. Marital problems stem from couples who don't communicate with each other.	**Agree**	**Disagree**
15. Marital problems stem from couples who don't make commitments to each other.	**Agree**	**Disagree**
16. Second marriages are always better.	**Agree**	**Disagree**
17. People should get to know each other very well before they get married.	**Agree**	**Disagree**
18. It is very easy to get a divorce.	**Agree**	**Disagree**
19. It is expensive to get a divorce.	**Agree**	**Disagree**
20. Half of all marriages now end in divorce.	**Agree**	**Disagree**

6.7 Dealing with Stepparents

Objective: After interviewing a stepparent, the student will be able to identify two or three problem situations encountered in stepfamilies and offer solutions.

Comments: Students may have to deal not only with stepsiblings, but also with stepparents. Often this is a vaguely defined role that can be uncomfortable for parents and children alike. New roles are thrust upon everyone. Adaptations must be made. New living patterns are established. Discipline must be worked out. Making these adjustments can be difficult. In this lesson, students are to interview a stepparent to find out what difficulties he or she has encountered and what has been helpful.

Introductory Activities:

1. Have students compile a list of questions they could ask a stepparent about his or her new role.
2. Have students suggest a list of possible problems that would be common to stepparents.

Activity: Students are to interview an adult who has volunteered to participate in this activity. You may want students to find their own willing participant or you might have one adult speak to the class. Students are to ask questions during the interview and record the answers.

Discussion: Be sure to preview any additional questions that students want to add to the list on the worksheet "Dealing with Stepparents." Depending on how well you know the volunteer and how frank you want the discussion to be, you may want to tailor the questions to fit the situation. After the interview(s) are discussed, you may want to go over the following questions:

1. Do you think most stepparents and stepchildren get along?
2. What do you now think is the hardest thing for adults to deal with in a stepfamily?
3. What do you now think is the hardest thing for children to deal with in a stepfamily?
4. Was our list of possible problems accurate?

Extension Activities:

1. Write and perform several skits dramatizing a particular problem that might be encountered in a stepfamily. Show various outcomes.
2. Compile and review a list of fairy tales or common stories that have stepparents portrayed as wicked and uncaring. How do you think this got started? Rewrite the stories with a more contemporary character in the stepparent role.

Evaluation:

1. List two or three problems commonly encountered in stepfamilies.
2. Give an appropriate suggested course of action for each problem considered in (1).

6.7   Dealing with Stepparents

Directions:

Conduct an interview with someone who is a stepparent. You may want to add to this list of questions.

1. How long have you been a stepparent?

2. Do you have children of your own?

3. What is the hardest thing for you about being a stepparent?

4. Did you and your spouse make plans ahead of time for how you would handle having two families living together?

5. Do you feel free to discipline your stepchildren?

6. What do your stepchildren call you?

7. What problems have you encountered with your children and stepchildren living together?

8. How do you and your stepchildren get along in general?

9. What have you found that you really like about your stepchildren?

10. Do you have problems with shared visitation of your stepchildren?

11. Do your children and stepchildren get along with each other?

6.8 Sharing the Chores

Objective:

The student will identify at least ten chores that are necessary for running a household.

Comments:

There is a lot of work involved in running a household. Ideally, most of the chores are shared by family members! In this lesson, students are to identify common household chores and think about who is primarily responsible for that work in his or her home. Each student should then think about his or her own role in the running of the household.

Introductory Activities:

1. Have students volunteer to describe the most-hated chore at their home.   2. Have students tell about common chores they are responsible for in their home.

Activity:

Students are to complete the worksheet "Sharing the Chores," which lists various common household chores, by writing the name or identifying the person usually responsible. Students can make their own key to identify people and can add to the list.

Discussion:

After completing the chart, students may have a better idea of the amount of work it takes to effectively run a household. It may be revealing to actually figure out how much or how little certain individuals do.

1. Which chores are more efficiently done if they are usually performed by one person (rather than rotating the job)? Why?   2. Which chores do you personally find appealing? Distasteful? 3. What could or would happen if a particular chore on the list was neglected for two weeks? 4. Do you think children should be responsible for a lot of chores if they are busy with school or sports?   5. Do you think children should be paid for doing chores?   6. Are your family chores distributed equally? How are they selected for each individual?   7. Are chores basically the same for most families in your community?

Extension Activities:

1. Add to the chart by figuring out the following information: (a) the frequency with which each chore should be done (for example, weekly, daily), (b) how much time is involved in completing the chore, and (c) a rating of how much effort or enjoyment is associated with the chore. 2. Figure out how long it actually takes to complete each chore on the list. If someone were paid minimum wage to do each chore, which would be the most expensive? Least expensive?

Evaluation:

1. List ten common household chores.   2. Write a paragraph describing how to efficiently perform your favorite chore; then write a paragraph describing how to perform your least favorite chore. Give reasons for why you like or dislike the tasks you selected.

6.8   **Sharing the Chores**

Directions:

Who is responsible for doing these chores in your family? Indicate who does what. Add items to the list that apply to your family.

1. Sorting clothes _____

2. Vacuuming _____

3. Caring for pet(s) _____

4. Preparing meals _____

5. Shopping for food _____

6. Shopping for other household items _____

7. Dropping off dry cleaning _____

8. Car maintenance _____

9. Washing windows _____

10. Waxing and polishing the floor _____

11. Dusting _____

12. General errands _____

6.9 Whom Can I Talk To?

Objective:

The student will list three to five people in his or her life who would be possible sources of help in confidential situations.

Comments:

We have all had a situation or issue that is troubling, frightening, or confusing at some time in our lives. Knowing that there is a person who cares about you and about your problems is a great source of hope. In this lesson, students are asked to focus on identifying a person or persons who would be helpful and safe to talk with about their situations. It is great if there is someone within the family who knows the dynamics and the players and can help the student, but often it takes someone who is uninvolved to be objective.

Introductory Activities:

1. Think about a problem or something bothering you. You don't have to say it out loud, but raise your hand if you can think right away of a person whom you would feel safe talking to about your problem. Raise your hand if you are thinking of a friend. Raise your hand if you are thinking of an adult. Raise your hand if you are thinking of someone at school. Raise your hand if you are thinking of someone at home. It is great that there are so many people that you are thinking about who might be helpful to you.

2. We all like people who tell us we are great, we are right, we are the best! But think about a person who will tell you the truth about a situation or even about you, whether it is flattering and pleasing or not. Can you think of such a person?

Activity:

On the worksheet "Whom Can I Talk To?" the students are to identify the character in each pair who is a person who is being helpful to the person with the problem or question.

Answers: 1. grandmother   2. older brother   3. school counselor (or teacher)   4. pastor

Discussion:

There are many people who are available to students, but the student must take the initiative to identify and seek out help. It is important, too, to select someone who is trustworthy.

1. In example 1, the girl's grandmother was helpful to the girl. How? (She listened to her, she knows the mother, she identified an issue that the girl wasn't aware of—being stressed by the job.)

2. Why might an older person be helpful in talking about family issues? (An older person has a unique perspective, might know the members of the family quite well.)

3. In example 2, what is the boy's problem? (Feels unpopular.) How did the brother help him? (Told him the truth, gave advice.)

4. In example 3, the problem is probably one that needs some professional help. Why? (The girl can't control things happening at home, there might be abuse or some reason why she doesn't want to go home.)

5. Who are some professionals who might be available to help with family problems? (School counselor, Youth Service Bureau, other agencies.)

6. What is the boy's issue in example 4? (The worthiness of his life.) Do you think this is a common issue? (Probably.)

7. Do you think that most people really want to talk to someone about a problem or would they rather work it out by themselves?

8. When you talk to someone, you are really putting trust in them. What kind of personal traits would you want to see in someone you opened up to? (Honesty, kindness, able to keep a secret, knowing when to intervene in a situation.)

Extension Activities:

1. Make a list or bring in a page of resources that are readily available to students in the community for any kind of social/family problem, including phone numbers and names of contact people. Post it in your classroom or make sure that students know where to find this information.

2. Invite a social worker, counselor, pastor, or mental health worker to come to your class to talk about what they do in terms of counseling and listening to others.

3. As a teacher, try to confer individually with your students over projects, assignments, and other routine school-related items, but always make it a point to find out something that is going on in their lives. Teachers are often the first to pick up on erratic behavior, depression, and just "something wrong."

Evaluation:

1. List three people who would be helpful to talk to in a confidential situation.

2. List a family member who would be a good resource in a family problem situation.

6.9   **Whom Can I Talk To?**

Directions: Who did these characters find helpful in each of these situations?

1. "I am so mad at Mom. She doesn't understand why it is so important to me to dress like the other kids."

   "When she was a teenager, she and I had all kinds of discussions about clothes, believe me! But she wants you to fit in. She does know that it's important to you. Just don't make a big deal about it right now. She's stressed by her job."

2. "Why don't girls like me?"

   "Sometimes you act really stupid. Try being more quiet and listening for a change."

3. "My home life is really rotten these days, Ms. Astor. I just don't even want to go home."

   "Molly, you are a great girl. Let's meet during your study period tomorrow and we can talk about some ideas for you."

4. "Pastor Bob, I feel like I want to do something important with my life, but I just feel lost."

   "You are not the only one who feels that way. Things take time. Why don't you come to our discussion group?"

Chapter 7

Communication Skills

7.1 Best Method to Communicate

Objective:

The student will give an example of an appropriate way or method of communicating in a given situation.

Comments:

There are many ways to communicate with others; for example, via technology (e-mail, texting, cell phones), humans (letting someone deliver a verbal message), written messages (notes, letters), prewritten items (greeting cards, forms), public venues (bulletin boards, newspaper ads), and even unique ways such as skywriting, a message in a bottle, or using a secret code. The idea is to use the most appropriate method for the situation.

Introductory Activities:

1. Have students list as many ways to communicate as they can. Try to group the items by common features (writing, technology, and so on).   2. Have students suggest a message that would be a good example of how the method can be used; for example, an e-mail might be a good way to communicate plans to a friend or groups of friends quickly.

Activity:

The worksheet "Best Method to Communicate" gives examples of types of messages that need to go out. Students are to suggest a good method to communicate that message.   *Answers (May vary):* 1. Face to face / note   2. Phone / face to face   3. Greeting card   4. Message board   5. Another person (family member?) / note / phone   6. Face to face   7. Face to face   8. E-mail / cell phone 9. Newspaper / message board   10. Newspaper ad

Discussion:

There are usually alternative methods for delivering a message. Things to keep in mind are the circumstances surrounding the message, the means of sending a message, and the appropriateness of the message for the situation.

1. How would you want to receive the news that someone was breaking up with you? How about if someone liked you and wanted to go out with you?   2. What types of messages are best delivered in person?   3. What kinds of methods would be best if you wanted to communicate with just one individual? How about a small group of people? How about if you had a message for the community?

Extension Activities:

1. Have students investigate and report on other methods of communicating, such as speaking a different language or using a code, sign language, or other methods.   2. Have students keep track of how many different forms of communication they use in a day.

Evaluation:

1. List five common ways that people can communicate.   2. What would be a good way to communicate if you wanted an individual to know about something?   3. What would be a good way to communicate if you wanted the community to know about something?

7.1   # Best Method to Communicate

Directions:

What is a good way to communicate for each of the situations below?

• phone	• e-mail
• face to face	• greeting card
• letter	• message board
• through another person	
• note (on a piece of paper)	

John
East way Road
Washington D.C

1. Finding out your grade in math from your teacher

2. Asking someone out on a date

3. Wishing your aunt a happy birthday

4. Finding out your work schedule

5. Letting your mother know you will be home late

6. Being angry at your sister for taking your sweater

7. Wanting to know if you can borrow your dad's favorite belt

8. Letting a friend know that you are meeting at the mall at 7 o'clock

9. Letting the community know that you are having a yard sale

10. Trying to sell your bike

7.2 Being a Careful Listener

Objective: The student will demonstrate the ability to listen to a partner for at least two to three minutes without interrupting and to remember at least three main points.

Comments: Listening to what someone is saying is a logical prerequisite to understanding what is on that person's mind. In this lesson, the student is given an exercise in listening to another person.

Introductory Activities:

1. Have students raise their hands if they think of themselves as a good listener.
2. Have students list ways they can show they are actively listening to someone else who is talking. (Having eye contact, concentrating on what's being said, and so on.)

Activity: Students are to participate in an exercise with a partner in which they take turns listening to each other speak on a designated topic for two to three minutes. The worksheet "Being a Careful Listener" suggests several topics. You may want to tape record both speakers so that they can check for the accuracy of their memory of what was said. Remind students of the rules: (a) do not interrupt the speaker, and (b) concentrate on what the speaker is saying.

Materials: pen or pencil, tape recorder

Discussion: After students have had a turn being both the speaker and the listener, discuss the following questions:

1. How well did you listen? How much did you recall?
2. What helped you remember? Did you use any tricks to help you?
3. What distractions did you encounter that took your mind off of what the speaker was saying?
4. Did eye contact help?
5. Did you find yourself wanting to interrupt?

Extension Activities:

1. Target a person you do not know very well and try to engage that person in conversation. Practice being a good listener: use eye contact, ask good questions to keep the conversation going, and don't interrupt.
2. Practice tape recording short speeches or discussions from the radio or television, then write down the main points that you remember. Use these as exercises to work on being a better listener.

Evaluation:

1. List two ways you can improve your ability to be a good listener.
2. Listen to a tape-recorded message (prepared by the teacher) and write the main points.

7.2   Being a Careful Listener

Directions:

Perform the following activity with a partner. Listen to your partner talk about one of the following topics for two to three minutes. Tape-record the comments. Be sure to read the rules!

Suggested Topics:

My Most Embarrassing Moment

What I Think About Our School

My Favorite Recent Movie

The Best Place to Eat

If I Had a Million Dollars

Think of some other topics and write them here:

Rules:

1. Don't interrupt while the other person is talking.

2. Concentrate on what the other person is saying.

When your partner has finished, repeat as much as you can remember about what was said. You may want to tape record your comments. Then play back the original tape recording. How much did you remember? How well did you listen?

7.3 Summarizing

Objective:

The student will accurately summarize a short paragraph.

Comments:

Summarizing consists of preserving a message, but in shortened form. In this lesson, students are given short paragraphs to read (or listen to), and then they are to indicate which of the choices is the best summary of the paragraph.

Introductory Activities:

1. Have students define the word *summary*. (A shortened version of a longer passage that covers the main points) 2. Have students list various types of texts or comments that are often summarized. (Newscasts of speeches, teachers' lectures, and so on)

Activity:

Students are to read the four short paragraphs on the worksheet "Summarizing" and then mark the choice that is the best example of a summary of that paragraph. Remind students that a good summary should include the main point(s) of the paragraph; it does not have to be as long as the original paragraph!
Answers: 1. b 2. c 3. a 4. c

Discussion:

After students have completed the worksheet, discuss why the answer they selected was the most appropriate and why the other answer options were not the best summaries.

1. Does it help to come up with your own summary statement before looking for the choices given?
2. In some of the examples, the choice was true, but was only one small detail—it was not the main idea of the paragraph. Which are examples of this? (4a, 4b.) 3. Some of the choices included information that was partly true, but we don't really know if the rest of the sentence is true. Which choices were examples of this? (2a, 3b.) 4. How can a summary of something be helpful? (Don't have to read the entire text, just gives the main points.)

Extension Activities:

1. Have students practice taking summary notes of brief lectures or information presented in short paragraphs. Compare summaries among the students—what is the main idea they should have picked up on? 2. Practice reading paragraphs to a partner and have the partner give a one-sentence summary of what was read. Make sure students include the main idea!

Evaluation:

1. Give a one-sentence summary of a paragraph (provided by the teacher). Make sure you include the main point or points and do not include irrelevant details or inferences that are not specifically given.
2. Write a paragraph about a given topic. Then summarize your paragraph in one sentence.

7.3   # Summarizing

Directions:

A summary is a shortened version of what was expressed. Read or listen to the following paragraphs. Circle the letter of the best summary of each.

1. A huge black dog watched a cat cautiously approach a little brown bird. The cat's tail wagged slowly side to side as it focused on its prey. Just before the cat was about to pounce, the dog barked. The little bird flew away, leaving the cat without a target.

    a. A black dog wanted to catch a bird.

    b. A dog scared away a bird before a cat could get it.

    c. A dog chased away a cat who was chasing a bird.

2. Jeremy got an F on his chemistry quiz today because he forgot to study. Now he has found out he has a math test in the next hour. He also forgot to study for that test.

    a. Jeremy has a bad memory.

    b. Jeremy is not very good at chemistry.

    c. Jeremy was not prepared for his tests today.

3. The tall blonde girl picked up the basketball, dribbled it a few times, and then smiled as she watched it sail through the air and fall through the hoop.

    a. A girl made a basket while playing basketball.

    b. A girl had blonde hair and was very pretty.

    c. A girl was a good athlete.

4. I wanted my best friend to come over this weekend so we could go out for pizza and go to the soccer game, but my mother informed me that my aunt and uncle from Seattle were going to arrive and I would be busy cleaning my room.

    a. My aunt and uncle live in Seattle.

    b. My friend and I wanted to go to a soccer game.

    c. My plans for the weekend changed because we were having guests.

7.4 Paraphrasing

Objective:

The student will accurately paraphrase a given sentence or short paragraph.

Comments:

Paraphrasing differs from summarizing in that one is looking for different words to convey the same meaning (rather than simply shortening the text). By using different words that mean about the same thing, the student is showing he or she understands the speaker's or writer's intent.

Introductory Activities:

1. Define the word *paraphrase*. (To restate something in different words, keeping the same meaning.)
2. Have students compare and contrast a summary and a paraphrase of a text. (Both may be shortened forms; a summary could contain the same words, a paraphrase uses different words.)

Activity:

Students are to read the sentences on the worksheet "Paraphrasing" and select the answer that best paraphrases the intent of the sentence. Remind students that they are looking for the same meaning, but a different form or choice of words that means about the same thing as the original.   *Answers:* 1. b 2. a 3. a 4. b 5. b 6. b

Discussion:

Have students discuss why the selected answer is the best paraphrase and why the answer they did not select was not a good paraphrase. Some reasons may be that it was more of a summary than a paraphrase, too much was implied in the answer, or the answer was too vague.

1. Was this activity harder or easier than summarizing a sentence or paragraph? Were they about the same?   2. In sentence 1, why wasn't (a) a good answer, as it was true? (It didn't address the meaning of the sentence; the important fact was that the opponents made excuses for losing.) 3. Why wasn't (b) a good paraphrase for sentence 3? (It was possibly true, but didn't focus on roller coasters.)   4. How do you know the girl in sentence 5 was angry? (Clues such as her red face, yelling, hitting.)   5. What words in the sentences and the correct paraphrases could you match up as being about the same thing? (1. excuses, poor sports; 2. 100 degrees, temperature; 3. thrill, fun; 4. blank, didn't know; 5. yelled and hit, angry; 6. anytime and anyplace, love.)

Extension Activities:

1. Practice paraphrasing with a partner. Have a partner give a sentence. Then repeat the sentence b ut use different forms of the words to keep the meaning.   2. Write several sentences on the board. Have all students write a paraphrase of the same sentences. Compare the different versions.3. Practice paraphrasing by taking a nasty or impolite comment and turning it into something appropriate. For example:

   a. I hate your hat. *Paraphrase:* I don't care for that hat.

   b. You are really fat. *Paraphrase:* You're somewhat overweight.

   c. That perm looks horrible. *Paraphrase:* Your hair is different today.

Evaluation:

1. Explain the difference between giving *a summary* and giving *a paraphrase of* a sentence or paragraph.
2. Provide a paraphrase of given sentences (provided by the teacher).

7.4   # Paraphrasing

Directions:

Paraphrasing is stating something in a way that keeps the meaning, but changes the words. Read each sentence below and circle the letter of the better paraphrase.

1. Our opponents in football made all kinds of excuses when they lost to our team.

    a. We beat the other football team.

    b. The members of the other football team were poor sports.

2. The thermometer nearly hit 100 degrees today.

    a. The temperature was almost 100 degrees.

    b. It was a warm day today.

3. My friend and I loved the thrill of going up and down on the roller coaster.

    a. We thought that riding the roller coaster was fun.

    b. My friend and I like rides.

4. I just gave the baby a blank look when it cried.

    a. I don't like crying babies.

    b. I didn't know what the baby wanted.

5. The red-faced girl yelled at the younger girl and tried to hit her.

    a. A girl had a red face from yelling.

    b. A girl was very angry at another girl.

6. I could eat an entire pizza with three or four toppings all by myself anytime, anyplace.
    a. I am really hungry.
    b. I really love pizza.

7.5 Is This the Right Time and Place?

Objective:

The student will give examples of several situations that may affect how a comment or expression is interpreted adversely or unclearly.

Comments:

There are times when people may be in a hurry, in pain, running late, or feeling extremely depressed or extremely happy. These are situations that may also affect comments and actions. What is said during that time may not truly be what is meant; these are comments that can be misinterpreted and overreacted to. In this lesson, students are presented with situations in which the characters are in somewhat abnormal positions and their comments do not truly reflect what they would say or do in calmer, more normal situations.

Introductory Activities:

1. Have students give examples of times or situations in which they felt stressed or pressured.
2. Have students describe situations in which they knew they would get an undesired answer or response from a parent or teacher because of the bad timing or specific situation.

Activity:

Students are to read the situations on the worksheet "Is This the Right Time and Place?" in which characters are placed in stressful or abnormal situations. The responses the characters give are not reflective of what that character would probably normally say or do. The student is to decide what unusual or stressful situation is affecting the person.

Answers (Examples): 1. Embarrassment in front of a friend 2. In a hurry 3. Headache 4. Guilt 5. Extreme happiness

Discussion:

Discuss each item on the worksheet and have students conclude what factor(s) might be causing the situation to be abnormal for the characters.

1. How did the character feel in situation 1? (Embarrassed by his sister.)
2. What was abnormal about the situation? (Her outfit.)
3. How could the first boy in situation 2 misinterpret what the second boy said and did? (Left in a hurry, left out, rudeness.)
4. What factor in situation 3 could be responsible for the seemingly rude behavior of the girl? (Headache.)
5. In situation 4, what possible other responses could the girl who forgot to wait for her friend have given?
6. Under normal circumstances, how would the girl in situation 5 have reacted? (Probably distressed or angry.)
7. What are some situations that particularly throw you off or make you more irritable than usual?
8. What are some extremely happy situations that might cause someone to act in an unusual way?

9. How can you be sensitive to someone's mood before you approach him or her? What cues are there?

10. What is a more polite way that the rude people could have explained that it was a bad time to be approached?

Extension Activities:

1. Have students find, look for, make, or draw pictures of people in obviously stressful situations and then add captions (humorous, if desired!) to accentuate the absurdity of asking for a favor right then. (For example, a kid in three layers of snowsuits asking his mother if he could go to the bathroom.)

2. Have students keep a running classroom list of "Situationally Silly Questions," such as taking a spelling test and having someone raise his or her hand to ask, "How do you spell that?" You'll find that there are many silly questions that are asked. Emphasize that it is the situation that makes it funny or silly, not that there are bad questions. Look for cartoons that show situationally silly examples also.

Evaluation:

1. Give three examples of situations that may be stressful or abnormal, causing someone to react in an unusual manner.

2. Write a paragraph about a time when you felt you were misunderstood or treated rudely because the other person involved was in a stressful or unusual situation.

7.5   # Is This the Right Time and Place?

Directions: Sometimes a situation might cause a person to act or react differently than usual. In each of the following examples, what situation is causing the person to act or react in an unusual manner?

7.6 Communicating by Cell Phone

Objective: The student will identify whether or not a situation is appropriate for using a cell phone.

Comments: The use of a cell phone in public can be annoying if the situation is one that usually calls for quiet or peace (house of worship, a wedding, in class), if others are within earshot of a private or embarrassing conversation (having an argument, telling a joke), or if having a conversation with another person who is not present is rude (when you are ignoring others who are with you). On the other hand, a cell phone is a great way to communicate when you need directions, clarification about an imminent meeting or activity, or to report an emergency. Students need to decide whether the cell phone is the best way to communicate in each situation on the worksheet.

Introductory Activities:

1. Have students give an example of helpful cell phone use.
2. Have students give an example of rude cell phone use.

Activity: On the worksheet "Communicating by Cell Phone," students are to decide whether or not a cell phone is the best means of communication.

Answers: 1. no   2. yes   3. no   4. yes   5. yes   6. no   7. yes   8. no   9. yes   10. no   11. no   12. yes

Discussion: Talk about why the cell phone was or was not the best choice for each example. For each "no" response, discuss a better way to communicate.

1. What is rude about using a cell phone in examples 1, 3, 6, 8, 10, and 11?
2. What would be a better way to communicate in each of those examples?
3. In which cases would texting be acceptable rather than talking out loud?

Extension Activities:

1. Have students evaluate different types of phones and compare features. What else can you do with a cell phone besides talk?
2. Have students conduct a random survey of how many people they see using a cell phone in one hour's time at a public place.
3. Have students research how many driving accidents involve cell phone use by the driver.

Evaluation:

1. Give an example of a situation in which cell phone use is appropriate.
2. Give an example of a situation in which cell phone use is not appropriate.

7.6 Communicating by Cell Phone

Directions:

In which of these situations would a cell phone be a good choice to use to communicate? Write YES or NO next to each.

1. Waiting in a busy doctor's office

2. Calling a friend while you are sitting in a park

3. Having lunch with a friend and thinking about something you wanted to tell another friend

4. Seeing two cars collide while you are walking home from school

5. Letting your boss know that you will be a little bit late while you are getting ready to get on the bus for work

6. Sitting in church while the pastor is speaking

7. Calling your brother to let him know it's time to pick you up from your piano lesson

8. Sitting in the back of a classroom and wondering what your mom is going to fix for dinner

9. Talking to your friend who is somewhere in the water park while you are saving a place in line

10. Telling someone a joke while you are waiting for a wedding to begin

11. Chatting with a friend while you are in a movie theater waiting for the previews to be over

12. Calling home from the supermarket to ask your mother what kind of meat you were supposed to pick up for her

7.7 Giving Clear Directions

Objective:

The student will provide clear, accurate directions to enable another person to correctly complete a given task.

Comments:

Expressing oneself so that others can understand the message is a very important skill. In this lesson, students are given the opportunity to follow verbal directions and then must give directions for another person to follow. The tasks involved are simple drawing of figures. Through trial and error, students will experience how important it is to be very specific and use words the listener will understand.

Introductory Activities:

1. Give students the following set of directions as if you really expected them to comply: "Take out a pencil, put it in your left hand—no, make that your right hand—draw two or four concentric circles, shade the middle one in, fold your paper in half or thirds if you want to, and then place it in the upper right-hand corner of the desk and write your address in Chinese on the top." When students look at you in disbelief, ask them what was difficult about that task. (Too many directions, given too fast, directions were changed, directions were unclear, they were asked to do things they probably didn't know how to do, and so on.)

2. Have students come up with suggestions for how better to give instructions for that type of task.

Activity:

Students will be given oral directions (read by the teacher) for the first part of this activity on the worksheet "Giving Clear Directions." They are to draw geometric figures in a specific pattern. On the second part, they are to generate directions for someone else to follow.

Instructions for Part I:

1. You will be drawing three squares. Make the first square small. Leave a little space. Then draw a second square to the right of the first one. This square should be medium-sized. The bottom line should be in line with the first square. The third square should be a little bigger than the other two. It, too, should have the bottom line on the same level as the other two.

2. You will be drawing three circles, in a line. The first circle should be small. Color in the entire circle. The second circle is the same size as the first. Draw it to the right of the first one. Then draw a line in the circle to cut it in half. The line should go from top to bottom. Shade in the left half of the circle. The last circle should be bigger. Draw this circle so that the bottom of it is in line with the other two. Then draw a line going up and down that cuts the big circle in half.

3. Draw a medium-sized square. In the middle of the square, draw a small circle. Make sure the outline of the circle does not touch any part of the square. Cut the circle into four equal parts by drawing two lines, one up and down, the other sideways. Shade in the bottom right-hand section of the circle.

4. There are three figures in this drawing. First draw a small triangle. Cut the triangle in half by drawing a line from the point at the top to the base. Shade in the right half of the triangle. Now draw a small circle on top of the triangle, so that the point of the triangle touches the bottom of the circle. Divide the circle into four equal parts by drawing two lines: one up and down, the other sideways. Shade in the upper right-hand section of the circle. Then draw a rectangle on top of the circle so that they touch in only one point. Make sure the long part of the rectangle is going sideways. Cut the rectangle into four equal parts by drawing two lines: one up and down, the other sideways. Shade in the upper left-hand section.

Instructions for Part II:

The student should write directions that would enable someone else to draw the figures on the sheet. Examples:

5. There will be three figures in a row. The first one is a small square. Leave a small space to the right and draw the second, a medium-sized triangle with the base on the same line as the bottom of the square. The third is a square, the same size as the first square. Shade in the third square completely.

6. Draw a rectangle with the long side going across. Then draw another rectangle of the same size, but with the long side going up. The two rectangles should be touching each other like this: the short side of the second rectangle should be on the same line as the bottom of the first rectangle so that the whole short side of the first rectangle touches the second rectangle. Then go to the first rectangle and find the middle of the top long side. Draw a big black dot on that line so that half of the dot is below the line and half is above.

Discussion:

Students will probably have a lot to say about how hard or fun this task was. Go over the following questions:

1. What helped make the directions clear when you were given things to draw?
2. What directions seemed confusing?
3. How was using shapes an easier task than if you were supposed to draw a dog or a house? (Consistent, all agree on what a shape looks like.)
4. What was hard about writing directions for someone else?
5. What parts were most confusing when you had to direct someone else to draw a picture?

Extension Activities:

1. Have students draw three or four pictures (using shapes or other agreed-upon items) and write directions for someone else to follow. Trade directions and compare drawings.
2. Have several students go to the board and work on the same set of directions (given orally) at the same time by one person. See how differently people can interpret the same set of directions if the directions are not specific and clear.
3. Try this type of activity with other items. For example, use colored 1-inch blocks and direct students to place them in a certain pattern. Or have two students sit back to back so they cannot see each other and have one proceed to build something. As he or she puts the blocks in place, he or she should tell the second student what to do. The rest of the class can serve as a silent audience to see if the second student is complying with the directions accurately. Try it (a) without allowing the second student to ask any questions, and (b) allowing the second student to inquire of the audience: "Is this correct?" That is the only question that can be asked of the audience. Have fun with this!

Evaluation:

1. Given a specific geometric drawing, write out clear directions for how someone else could reproduce the drawing without seeing the picture.
2. Given specific written or verbal instructions, draw the pattern or figures described.

7.7   **Giving Clear Directions**

Directions:

Part I: For Part I, draw the figures you hear described.

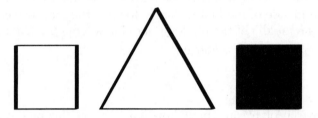

Part II: For Part II, you will write clear directions for someone else to follow in order to draw the figures you see. Use the back of this sheet for your directions.

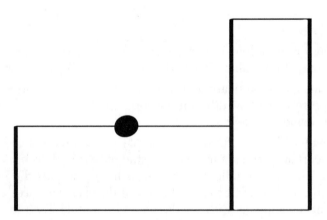

7.8 Verbal and Nonverbal Messages

Objective: The student will give an example of a verbal and a nonverbal message that convey the same meaning.

Comments: Tapping a foot, rolling eyes, wagging a finger, or shrugging shoulders all give nonverbal messages. Sometimes a nonverbal message is even more powerful than words. (Did your mother ever give you "the look"?) It is important to understand what the message is, whether the means is verbal or nonverbal.

Introductory Activities:

1. Pick two students to role-play situations in which they cannot speak but can use only nonverbal communication. Situations might be ordering food from a menu, picking out a DVD or CD in a store, playing a game or sport, and so on.
2. Have students take turns reading this sentence, emphasizing one italic word at a time. Talk about how the meaning changes, depending on which word is emphasized:

   "I would like to go to the game with you on Saturday."

Activity: On the worksheet "Verbal and Nonverbal Messages," students should show how a response to a question could be indicated by using a verbal answer and then by using a nonverbal message.

Answers (Will vary):

1. "Yes!"—Smile
2. "Lost it."—Scratch head
3. "To the left."—Point
4. "A salad."—Point to item on menu
5. "Oh, yeah!"—Thumbs up
6. "Ten."—Hold up both hands
7. "Not a clue."—Hands up, lost
8. "Go team!"—Fist in air
9. "Nope."—Shrug
10. "Thanks for coming!"—Applaud

Extension Activities:

1. Body language can reveal a lot about a person. These two websites have interesting information; however, you should preview what is appropriate for your students. The first, www.positive-way.com/body.htm, has a lot of information On www.howcast.com, search for How to Interpret Body Language for a short video with interesting commentary.
2. Have students come up with both ordinary and more exotic examples of using nonverbal communication. (Flagging down a taxi? Ballroom dancing? Teaching a dog to stay?)

Evaluation:

1. How could you give a verbal message to let someone know you like him or her?
2. How could you give a nonverbal message to let someone know you are angry?

7.8   Verbal and Nonverbal Messages

Directions: How could each question be answered (a) verbally and (b) nonverbally?

1. Do you like pizza?
   (a) _____
   (b) _____

2. What did you do with your homework?
   (a) _____
   (b) _____

3. Which way is the restroom?
   (a) _____
   (b) _____

4. What would you like to order for lunch?
   (a) _____
   (b) _____

5. Do you think that girl is cute?
   (a) _____
   (b) _____

6. What is 5 plus 5?
   (a) _____
   (b) _____

7. I think this math problem is really hard. Do you get it?
   (a) _____
   (b) _____

8. Aren't you happy that our team won?
   (a) _____
   (b) _____

9. Do you even care that you are getting an F on your test?
   (a) _____
   (b) _____

10. Here comes our special guest. Should we give her a big welcome?
    (a) _____
    (b) _____

7.9 Collecting Your Thoughts

Objective:

The student will state at least one reason why it is important to collect his or her thoughts before speaking or writing.

Comments:

Speaking spontaneously is fine in most occasions; however, at times it is beneficial for people to think before talking. Some situations might require a degree of delicacy or diplomacy, and taking a few seconds to think through what you really want to convey is well worth the effort. Students are given situations to think through before stating what they would say to handle the situation.

Introductory Activities:

1. Explain that you are going to give students a choice. They must write their choice immediately. State: "Vote A or B. A—we can skip homework for three weeks and you'll have one huge test at the end. B—you will have daily assignments for three weeks and no final exam. Write A or B."

2. Explain that you are going to give students another choice. This time they must think for thirty seconds before they indicate their choice. State: "You notice that a house is on fire. You have time to save one person. Would you save person A—a two-year-old boy who is screaming by a door on the second floor, or person B—a sixty-year-old grandmother who is in a wheelchair by a window on the first floor?"

3. Ask students which activity was more difficult. Did the extra thirty seconds to think about the situation make the choice harder or easier? Why?

Activity:

Students will be given several situations to consider on the worksheet "Collecting Your Thoughts." They must take thirty to sixty seconds to plan what they will say (and do). Then they should write their response on the worksheet.

Answers: Will vary.

Discussion:

The extra time, though short, should give students a chance to think through several alternative responses. After students have completed the activity, compare answers, emphasizing what they did with the "thinking time."

1. What would have been your first response if you didn't take the time to collect your thoughts?

2. Would your response have been the same or did the added time encourage you to change your first response?

3. Why do you think taking time to "think through" a situation would make someone change his or her mind? (Could think of more alternatives, new ways to look at a situation.)

4. Why would it be harder to decide which person to save—a baby on the second floor or an older person on the first floor—than deciding when to take a test? (Much more important consideration, more complicated.)

Extension Activities:

1. Make a list of ten questions other people must answer right away, without giving it any thought. Examples:
   a. Would you shave your head for $10 right now?
   b. Would you shave your head for $100?
   c. Are you a happy person?
   d. Should all students be given A's?
   e. Should school meet on Saturdays?
   f. Do you like pizza?
   g. Do you like snakes?
   h. Would you lie to your best friend to avoid hurting his or her feelings?
   i. Would you trade places with the President of the United States for a week?
   j. Are girls more sensitive than boys?

   Then pick three or four of the questions, reflect on them for a minute or two, and see if the answers change and why.

2. Begin using the phrase "Collect your thoughts" in class when assigning oral and written work. Encourage students to refrain from even picking up a pen or pencil until they have taken some "think time." Make this a practice so that students learn to expect to think first.

Evaluation:

1. State one reason why it is important to collect your thoughts before expressing an opinion.
2. Write a paragraph expressing your opinion about whether or not your school should have a dress code. Think first.

7.9   **Collecting Your Thoughts**

Directions:

How would you carry out the following tasks? Before you write what you would say, take thirty to sixty seconds to think it through. Collect your thoughts! Now write what you would say.

1. You have to tell your best friend that her very exotic tropical fish just died as a result of your having forgotten to feed it for a week while she was on vacation.

_____

_____

_____

_____

2. Explain to your teacher that your semester research project is not finished, and give your reasons.

_____

_____

_____

_____

3. Your little sister wants to know if the Tooth Fairy and Santa Claus are real. She trusts you and will believe whatever you tell her.

_____

_____

_____

_____

4. You must give a short talk to the Student Council on your opinion about whether or not you think fourteen-year-olds should be allowed to drive.

_____

_____

_____

_____

7.10 Public Speaking

Objective:

The student will complete items on a checklist in preparation for making an informal speech.

Comments:

Public speaking can be a terrifying experience for many (most?) people, yet it is an excellent way to express an opinion, especially if the comments made are well thought out and the speaker is prepared to deliver the speech. In this lesson, students will take steps to prepare a simple speech that will be given at a later time.

Introductory Activities:

1. Have students name or list some people who are good public speakers, or people whom they enjoy listening to. (Perhaps a stand-up comedian, a favorite teacher, and so on.)
2. Have students list reasons why it might be scary to speak in front of people.
3. Have students suggest techniques that make a good speaker seem interesting or easy to listen to. (Humor, interesting topic, pleasing voice, and so on.)

Activity:

The student is to select a topic he or she finds interesting or might know something about. If the topics on the worksheet "Public Speaking" do not seem appropriate for your class, have students suggest others. Students do not all have to pick the same topic! Students will then go through the checklist, item by item, to prepare themselves for giving a speech. You should specify the length of time involved in giving the actual speech (perhaps three to five minutes).

Materials: Have resources available such as books, encyclopedias, newspapers, or pamphlets. Also, instruct students to obtain note cards (3" × 5") and other materials (posters, markers, rulers, and so on) if they are going to include visual aids. *Time:* You may want to plan several days or a week to complete this activity. Depending on how much help the students need, this activity might take more time than the usual writing activities. You may want to assign specific due dates for items on the checklist. Have students be available to monitor each other's progress.

Discussion:

As students progress through the checklist, monitor them carefully to make sure they are not bogged down on certain steps. Some will need help with outlining, writing good introductions and conclusions, and preparing the visual aids. At this point, it is more important that they go through the steps and complete each item even if it is not completely "polished." An outline could be as simple as writing the topic sentence from each paragraph on individual note cards. Go through the following discussion questions to help students focus on the Activity:

1. Was it difficult to select a topic?
2. Were your resources readily available? Did you find resources other than printed material? (Such as individuals.)
3. Can you read your rough draft?
4. Do you feel you have outlined your speech adequately? What information should be put on the note cards?

5. How can you keep your note cards organized? (Number them, color-code.)
6. Why is it important to have a good introduction and conclusion?
7. What types of visual aids would be good for your presentation? Why?
8. How many times would you need to practice your speech before you feel comfortable with it?
9. Where are some places or who are some people who could help you feel comfortable with practicing your speech?
10. Why is it important to look at your audience rather than just reading the cards? (Gets audience involved.)
11. Why is it important to speak slowly and to remember to breathe? (Slows you down, makes sure people can understand you.)

Extension Activities:

1. If students are having particular difficulties with some aspect of this assignment (such as outlining, writing a conclusion, practicing), pair students with a buddy who is more competent and allow them to work together.
2. To make interesting visual aids, give students time to work in the computer lab (if available) or use other resources to create charts, graphs, or pictures.

Evaluation:

1. State the topic of your speech.
2. List at least two important features that will be included in your speech. (Visual aids, interesting statistics, and so on.)

7.10   Public Speaking

Directions: Select a topic about which you feel strongly or know a lot about. Go through the following checklist, marking off each item as you have completed or thought through what you plan to do.

Suggested Topics:

Professional Athletes Make Too Much Money

Students Should Have More Voice in the Way They Are Graded

Ways We Can Stop Pollution in Our Community

Exotic Animals Should Not Be Kept as Pets

Why We Need a Girls' Football Team

- [ ] 1.   I have selected a topic.

- [ ] 2.   I have several resources (people, newspapers, library books, and so on) to get information.

- [ ] 3.   I have jotted down some ideas about what I want to say.

- [ ] 4.   I have a rough draft outline of what I want to say.

- [ ] 5.   I have a more finished copy of the outline.

- [ ] 6.   I have put my outline on note cards.

- [ ] 7.   I have a good introduction.

- [ ] 8.   I have a good conclusion.

- [ ] 9.   I have some visual aids (charts, pictures, slides, and so on).

- [ ] 10.   I have practiced reading my speech.

- [ ] 11.   I practically know the speech without looking at my cards.

- [ ] 12.   I have practiced the speech, remembering to look up occasionally.

- [ ] 13.   I have practiced the speech, remembering to slow down and breathe occasionally.

- [ ] 14.   I have practiced the speech, giving it in front of a friend.

- [ ] 15.   I feel that I am ready to give my speech to a real audience!

7.11 Expecting Respect

Objective:

The student will state at least two techniques to help get the respect of an audience.

Comments:

Not everyone is a dynamic public speaker, but there are some techniques that can help shape the audience's expectation toward a speaker. Teachers know that sometimes giving the class the "silent treatment" can be an effective way to gain its attention. Several techniques mentioned in this lesson include waiting for the audience to be quiet, using eye contact, interacting with the audience, and having a sincere, serious demeanor—expect the audience to respect you!

Introductory Activities:

1. Have students give examples of different types of audiences and speakers they have observed during the past week.   2. Write the words **Respectful** and **Not Respectful** on the board. Underneath each, have students list examples of audience behavior from (1) that showed either respect or lack of respect toward the speaker.

Activity:

Students are to read the four techniques on the worksheet "Expecting Respect" that a speaker can use to obtain respect from the audience. The student is to first indicate (Yes/No) whether or not the speaker is behaving in such a way that he or she expects respect. Second, the student is to indicate which technique is illustrated.   *Answers:* A. No, 1   B. Yes, 3   C. No, 4   D. No, 2

Discussion:

Go through each illustration to determine what the speaker could have done to improve the attention and respect of the audience.

1. In situation A, what are several things the speaker could do to get the attention of the audience? (Say "Listen, please"; stop talking; make a joke; and so on.)   2. In situation B, how did the speaker include the audience in her comments? (Talked about what had happened to them.) 3. How else did the speaker in situation B get the audience's attention? (Showed a chart.)   4. Do you think the speaker in situation C had the attention of the audience? Do you think he had the respect of the audience?   5. In situation D, if the speaker had looked up, what would he have noticed? (The audience was bored.)   6. What else could have been improved to get the audience's respect in situation D? (Shorten the list.)   7. What techniques do your teachers use to get the class's attention and respect?

Extension Activities:

1. While students are practicing their speech, tell them to include several checkpoints on their note cards at the points when they should make sure they have eye contact with someone in the audience. 2. Assign students to observe a speech on television (perhaps a TV preacher, politician, or special lecture). Have students jot down audience reactions that show the audience is attentive and respectful to the speaker (or not). What specific techniques do the students observe the speaker doing to get respect?

Evaluation:

1. List two behaviors a speaker can use to try to get the respect of an audience.   2. Write a paragraph explaining why it is important to have the attention and respect of an audience.

7.11   **Expecting Respect**

Directions: You want your audience to respect you while you are giving your speech. Read the techniques for getting your audience to respect you. Then look at the following situations. (1) Write Yes or No to show whether the speaker is expecting respect. (2) Then write the number (1, 2, 3, 4) of the technique illustrated.

> 1.   Wait for the audience to give you its attention.
>
> 2.   Use eye contact with your audience.
>
> 3.   Interact with the audience by including questions or comments about them.
>
> 4.   Be sincere and serious.

7.12 Being Convincing

Objective:

The student will give at least two examples of convincing arguments to back up his or her opinion.

Comments:

In some cases, the audience that needs to be convinced of something may be a parent, friend, or stranger. Some techniques that can help strengthen a position include: being enthusiastic, using logic, being interesting, and showing how one's position will benefit the audience or other person.

Introductory Activities:

1. Have students list five things of which they wish they could convince their parents, teacher, or a rich relative. This may be an idea, an event, or purchase.   2. Have students list ways they could try to convince the people in (1) to agree with their position.

Activity:

On the worksheet "Being Convincing," students are to read the techniques for being convincing and then match the technique with the situation illustrated.   *Answers:* A. 4   B. 2   C. 1   D. 3

Discussion:

The audience in these examples consists of a single person, rather than a group. However, the principles can apply to any situation in which one person is trying to convince another.

1. How much of a role does sincerity play in trying to convince someone else of something? Is it more convincing if you act as though you truly believe in what you are saying?   2. Do you feel that someone who is very convincing usually believes in what he or she is saying?   3. If you know that someone is trying to sell you something (which is a form of convincing), what might you be cautious about? (Trying to figure out what the salesperson gains from this; being aware that he or she is looking out for his or her own interests too.)   4. What are some occupations that are based on being a good convincer? (Sales, law.)

Extension Activities:

1. Videotape and view ten television commercials. For each, discuss: (a) Who is the target audience? (b) What is the ad trying to sell?, and (c) What techniques for convincing are used? 2. Have students write and perform skits in which they demonstrate their ability to be convincing. Skits could include: (a) convince parents to let them stay out past midnight; (b) convince a sister/brother to let them borrow items such as clothes, CDs, magazines, cash; and (c) convince a teacher to put off a huge assignment until the next week.   3. Have students design a product and write a commercial to try to sell it to an audience. Videotape the commercials, if possible. Discuss what techniques were used. Evaluate how convincing is the commercial.

Evaluation:

1. List two techniques that can be used to convince someone else to agree with your position.
2. Describe your favorite commercial. Explain how it is convincing and what techniques it has used to convince and appeal to you.

7.12   **Being Convincing**

Directions: Read the technique for convincing your audience to agree with you. Write the number of the technique (1, 2, 3, 4) that is illustrated in each situation.

---

1.   Be enthusiastic!

2.   Use logic or common sense.

3.   Be interesting.

4.   Show how your ideas will benefit the audience.

A. Dad, I really need a car of my own. It would save you so much time and trouble from having to pick me up all the time!

B. If I had a room of my own, it would be much quieter for me to study. My two sisters and I wouldn't get our books mixed up.

C. I would absolutely LOVE to use your extra ticket for the rock concert. Wow!! Cool!!! Thanks for thinking of me!! Great!!

D. Nassau would be a great place to go for a winter trip. The temperature ranges between 69 and 82 in December. Nassau is the capital city of The Bahamas. There is a famous straw market.

7.13 Giving Your Speech

Objective:

The student will give a three- to five-minute speech on an appropriate topic.

Comments:

By the time this lesson is reached, the student should be well prepared to give his or her presentation to an audience. The important points are not only the delivery of the speech, but also how well the ideas are expressed to the audience. Because it is assumed that everyone will participate, an evaluation form is provided with space for each student to do a self-evaluation as well as view comments from a peer and teacher.

Introductory Activities:

1. Have students list factors they think are important when evaluating a speech or speaker. (Well prepared, good eye contact, other ideas from previous lessons.)
2. Have students give ideas for how a self-evaluation could be helpful in assessing a speech.
3. Have students give ideas for how having a peer do an evaluation could be helpful.
4. Have students give ideas for how a teacher's input could be helpful in evaluating a speech.

Activity:

Because this is quite an involved activity, the following order of events may be helpful:

1. Give each student a time at which he or she will be expected to present the speech to the class.
2. Review the items on worksheet 7.10 "Public Speaking" to make sure everyone is reasonably prepared.
3. Go over the items on the evaluation form "Giving Your Speech." You may want to pair students to do each other's student evaluations. Make sure students understand what is expected for an "Excellent," "Good," "Fair," and "Poor" rating. Students doing the evaluation are to indicate their rating in the appropriate box. Short comments would be appropriate.
4. If possible, plan to videotape the speeches, as this will be helpful when reviewing the ratings and the comments.
5. After the student has given his or her speech, the student should complete the self-evaluation portion of the worksheet immediately. The selected peer should also complete the evaluation at that time. This may be done on a separate sheet of paper and the results later transferred to the main sheet. Likewise, the teacher evaluation should be completed and transferred so that all information is in one place.

Materials: pen or pencil, videotaping equipment, sufficient copies of the evaluation sheet so that students and teacher have copies to complete

Discussion:

After students have participated in the activity by giving their speeches, distribute the evaluation forms (which now should have all respondents' comments attached and/or transferred to one main sheet). If students feel comfortable with this, play the videotape of their performance while discussing each presentation.

1. Which of your ratings (self-, peer, teacher) tended to be the highest? Which the lowest?
2. What would you change about your presentation?

3. What ideas did you get from listening to the speeches of other people about what to do or what not to do?

4. Do you feel you effectively communicated what you wanted to say?

Extension Activities:

1. Have students work in small groups to prepare a speech or presentation for specific groups—a kindergarten class about drug awareness, a commercial to another class, a short play or skit for parents, and so on.

2. Divide students into two groups to take a pro (for) side of an issue and a con (against) side. Have them come up with logical arguments and try to present each side clearly and effectively. Evaluate the effectiveness of the speech using the evaluation sheet from this lesson.

Evaluation:

1. List two or three things you felt went particularly well with your speech.

2. List two or three things you feel could be improved with your speech. How could you specifically change things to make these improvements?

3. Write a short paragraph explaining the value of having a self-, peer, and teacher evaluation done on the same speech.

7.13   Giving Your Speech

Directions: Read this evaluation form before you give your speech. You will evaluate yourself on the performance, have at least one peer evaluate your speech, and have your teacher complete an evaluation.

Ratings: Excellent   Good   Fair   Poor

	Self-Evaluation	**Peer Evaluation**	**Teacher Evaluation**
Was the speaker prepared?			
Did the presentation go smoothly?			
Did the speaker use his or her note cards smoothly and efficiently?			
Was the speech easy to listen to?			
Was the speech interesting?			
Did the speaker have the attention and respect of the audience?			
Did the speaker have a good, interesting introduction?			
Did the speaker have a logical conclusion?			
Did the speaker use effective visual aids?			
Was the overall performance good?			

Part Three

Academic and School Skills

Chapter 8: Reading Skills

8.1   Reading for School

8.2   Reading on the Job

8.3   Improving Reading Skills

8.4   Reading for Comprehension

8.5   Following Written Directions

Chapter 9: Writing Skills

9.1   Communicating Through Writing

9.2   Everyday Writing Tasks

9.3   Proofreading

9.4   E-mailing Dos and Don'ts

9.5   Using Computers to Improve Writing

9.6   Writing and More Writing

9.7   Writing on the Job

Chapter 10: Math Skills

10.1   Everyday Math Skills

10.2   Improving Math Skills

10.3   Common Math Situations

10.4   Understanding Graphs

10.5   Understanding Charts

10.6   Sample Math Problems

10.7   Using Computers for Math Information

Chapter 11: Study Skills

11.1   School Tasks for Success

11.2   Tools for the Task

11.3   Taking Notes

11.4   Studying Smarter

11.5   Following Directions

11.6   Doing Homework

11.7   Managing Daily Assignments

11.8   Managing Long-Term Assignments

11.9   Completing Assignments

11.10   Good Student Behaviors

11.11   Requesting Help or Information

Chapter 8

Reading Skills

8.1 Reading for School

Objective: The student will give examples of reading tasks in various school subjects.

Comments: Reading is a vital skill (in some respect) in every subject at school. Whether rules to a game, a summary of a class, or textbook information, reading is required in order to fully gain the information available.

Introductory Activities:

1. Have students list reading skills involved in their academic classes.
2. Have students list reading skills involved in nonacademic classes (for example, art, music, P.E.).

Activity: Students are to match the reading activity with its appropriate class.

Answers: 1. d   2. a   3. c   4. b   5. h   6. g   7. e   8. f

Discussion: Have students discuss the items on the worksheet. They may or may not be typical of reading assignments for their classes, but students should be able to identify the type of class with which they would be paired.

1. What alternatives to reading assignments are provided in some classes? (Taped books, oral discussions, making projects, and so on.)
2. How essential of a skill do you think reading is when you consider your classes? (Probably depends on the class and teacher.)
3. Do you think there are any classes in which the skill of reading is not a part or plays a minimal role? (Perhaps music, other arts classes.)
4. What provisions are made for students who have a lot of trouble with reading? (Partner-readers, books of a lower reading level, alternative assignments, and so on.)
5. Do some people learn better from hearing material rather than having to read it? Do you think it is still important for these people to be able to read?

Extension Activities:

1. Have students make their own matching activity including typical reading assignments from classes they are currently taking. Students can exchange papers.
2. Have students calculate how much time (in minutes) is spent in direct reading activities for selected classes. For example, would you expect that a great percentage of time is spent reading (or on reading tasks) in Literature rather than P.E.? Take one designated day and keep a chart of the results. Any surprises?

Evaluation:

1. Give an example of a reading task for several of your school subjects. (Teacher may want to specify how many and which classes.)
2. Write a paragraph stating your opinion about the importance of reading in a particular class.

8.1   Reading for School

Directions:

Match the reading activity with the class for which it might be required.

_____ 1. Read the biography of a famous composer.   a. Physical Education

_____ 2. Read the rules for how to play tennis.   b. World History

_____ 3. Read the instructions for dissecting a frog.   c. Biology

_____ 4. Read about weapons used in World War I.   d. Music

_____ 5. Read the instructions for playing a game   e. Math
          using a certain disk.

                                                          f. Foreign Language
_____ 6. Read a short story.

                                                          g. Language Arts
_____ 7. Read examples of how to solve a word
          problem.
                                                          h. Computer Science
_____ 8. Read rules for which French words to
          capitalize.

8.2 Reading on the Job

Objective:

The student will identify reading tasks necessary or helpful for specific jobs or careers.

Comments:

There are tasks involved with almost any type of job that requires reading. True, some people can perform a job once they have learned how to do it without referring to a manual, but at some point reading is a part of acquiring knowledge about the job. Students are to think of ways that reading is a part of either performing a job or of more efficiently performing that job.

Introductory Activities:

a. Have students list ten occupations that require reading.   b. Have students list three to five occupations they feel do not require a lot of reading.

Activity:

The student will consider a list of common jobs and list possible reading tasks that would be important to complete the job.   *Answers (Examples):*   1. Being able to read the orders   2. Following instructions for feeding and exercise   3. Road signs   4. Alphabetizing names   5. Reading about the effects of medicine   6. Reading descriptions of the parts   7. Reading about the chemicals that are ingredients in some of the products   8. Following recipes

Discussion:

Students can discuss the different reading tasks they thought of for each of the jobs listed. Additional discussion questions include:

1. Can you think of any jobs that don't require any reading at all?   2. What type of reading materials would there be that a person could use to improve his or her skills? (Manuals, extra skills training, and so on.)   3. Which of the jobs on the worksheet also involved writing? (1, 2, 4, 5, 6, 7, 8; possibly 3.)   4. What are some jobs primarily based on reading? (Book editor, novelist, jobs for gathering information and research, and so on.)

Extension Activities:

1. "Job shadow" a parent or individual you know well. Find out what reading tasks are involved in his or her job. Is the reading task a vital part of the job?   2. Make a game along the lines of Twenty Questions, only using reading tasks as clues. Appropriate questions might include: "Do you read street signs on your job?" "Do you read from a dictionary on your job?" "Do you read papers written by students?" and so on.

Evaluation:

1. List five jobs performed by someone you know. List two reading tasks involved for each.
2. Write a paragraph describing a job you are interested in doing someday as a career. What reading tasks would be involved?

8.2   **Reading on the Job**

Directions:

Look through the following list of jobs. What are some reading tasks that would be required or important in order to do each job well? Write your ideas on the lines.

1. Working at a drive-up window at a fast-food restaurant

    _____

2. Taking care of cats and dogs at a kennel

    _____

3. Driving a truck across the country

    _____

4. Being a secretary

    _____

5. Being a doctor for children

    _____

6. Placing orders for computer parts ordered by customers

    _____

7. Running a beauty salon

    _____

8. Preparing food for a catering service

    _____

8.3 Improving Reading Skills

Objective:

The student will identify three to five ways to improve his or her reading skills.

Comments:

The best way to improve reading skills is to read, read, read. There are specific skills good readers have acquired, and students who would like to improve their skills can follow the model of good readers and read "smarter." In this lesson, specific reading skills and ways to acquire them are discussed.

Introductory Activities:

1. Have students rate themselves on their reading ability, from 0 (poor) to 5 (excellent).
2. Have students list specific things about reading they find difficult, or specific reading tasks they have trouble with (for example, outlining, answering questions, understanding words, and so on).
3. Have students estimate how much time (in hours or minutes) they think they spend in a day on reading activities.

Activity:

On the worksheet "Improving Reading Skills," students are to match a given reading skill with an example that shows how that skill might be taught. Be sure students understand the skills before completing the worksheet. *Skills:* sequencing—putting events in order; following directions—completing a task as specified; vocabulary (meanings)—identifying what a word means, synonyms, opposites, and so on; identifying new words—looking up the definition of a highlighted word; word attack—using phonics or decoding skills to pronounce or "take apart" a word; comprehension—understanding what was read, being able to summarize and remember.

Answers: 1. e   2. a   3. d   4. b   5. f   6. c

Discussion:

There are many specific reading skills. Likewise, there are many ways to acquire these skills. Have students do some thinking to devise ways to become a better reader. After reviewing the worksheet, go over the following questions:

1. What is the purpose of "word attack" skills? (To help identify unfamiliar words.)
2. Does being able to pronounce a word help you understand the word? (Yes, if you would have known the word when you heard it read aloud.)
3. What are some tasks you perform in school that require following directions? (Cooking, workshop, projects.)
4. What are some problems that could come up if you don't follow the directions carefully?
5. How would knowing synonyms and antonyms help you with reading? (Identify many more words, clarify meaning of what you read.)
6. What are some ways you can figure out the meanings of unfamiliar words without looking them up in the dictionary? (Context, word attack skills to pronounce them, and so on.)
7. What are some tasks that must be performed in a certain sequence? (Building, cooking, driving a car, dressing, and so on.)

8. What are some classes that require reading of material and then responding to comprehension questions? (Science, social studies, and so on.)

9. What are some ways to help remember the core or essence of what you have read, particularly if it was quite lengthy? (Take notes, outline, jot down important details.)

10. Why is it important to know synonyms and antonyms of common words? Why can't everything just be "big" or "good" if that's what you mean? (Makes more interesting reading to use different, more specific words; word choice also reflects more accurately what you mean.)

Extension Activities:

1. Keep a reading log for a week or two. How much time do you spend on reading? You might wish to have a separate "pleasure reading" journal in which you record the number of minutes spent on a daily basis.

2. Read different types of material. Make a list of at least ten different types—encyclopedia, newspaper, news magazine, directions for a task, and so on. Spend thirty minutes a day reading something you normally do not read.

3. Improve your vocabulary. There are self-help workbooks that concentrate on knowing word meanings and how words are used.

4. Tape-record yourself reading a passage orally. Practice reading fluently and clearly.

5. Browse through a volume of an encyclopedia. Find some topics that catch your interest and spend some time reading.

6. Get a book of crossword puzzles, word searches, and other word game activities. Work on them daily.

7. Practice skimming textbook material before you read. Look it over, read the headings, and form questions in your mind about what the content will be about. Then as you read, look for answers to your questions.

Evaluation:

1. Identify five reading skills and briefly explain what is involved in each.

2. For each of the skills you identified in (1), give one example of where or how you would use it in school and everyday life.

3. List two skills in which you feel you could improve and write a possible plan for improving those skills.

8.3   Improving Reading Skills

Directions: Here is a list of six important reading skills. Read each of the following examples and match it with the letter of the reading skill involved.

a. sequencing	d. identifying new words
b. following directions	e. word attack
c. vocabulary (meanings)	f. comprehension

Example 1. Circle the consonant blend in each word: trap   block   street   friend   thick

Reading skill _____

Example 2. Tom wanted to build a doghouse. First he made a list of the materials he would need. He figured out how much it would cost. Then he went to the lumber yard and placed his order. After getting his tools together, he and his father began to work on the project. A few hours later, Rover had a new home. What were the steps involved in making a doghouse?

Reading skill _____

Example 3. We went to the zoo to take a look at a marsupial. It was really cute. What is a marsupial?

Reading skill _____

Example 4. When you make your map, put a key in one corner that tells what your symbols mean. Use a ° to indicate a capital city. Use blue to show water. Be sure to include a compass to show the directions.

Reading skill _____

Example 5. Archery is a popular sport that involves shooting with a bow and arrow. In target archery, the archer tries to score points by hitting a target as close to the center as possible. If the archer hits the middle, he or she would score 10 points. That is called a bull's-eye. What is target archery?

Reading skill _____

Example 6.

What is the opposite of: direct   large   heavy

What is a synonym for: tired   cold   happy

Reading skill _____

8.4 Reading for Comprehension

Objective:

The student will identify specific comprehension skills when given examples.

Comments:

We often ask students, "Did you understand what you read?" and accept a nod of the head. When probed, however, the student may not be able to tell anything about what he or she just read. There are many different ways to view "understanding" of what you read; comprehension can encompass a lot of skills, from remembering specific details to being able to state the main idea in a few words. It is helpful to be precise with students as to what type of comprehension skill you are focusing on.

Introductory Activities:

1. Ask students to discuss a movie or book that most or all of them have read or viewed. Ask them to tell you what the subject was about using only one sentence. Connect this to the idea of "main idea."

2. Now ask students to tell what happened in the movie or book, in order. Connect this to the idea of "sequencing."

3. Continue by asking students to answer who, what, where, when, why, and how questions in the movie or book. Connect this to the idea of "important details."

4. Ask students to state whether or not they liked the movie or book. Talk about their reasons that helped them come to a decision. Connect this to the idea of forming a "conclusion."

5. Have students describe the movie in a short paragraph. Connect this to the idea of "summarizing."

Activity:

Write the terms *main idea, sequencing, details, conclusion,* and *summarizing* on the board. Explain that the activity "Reading for Comprehension" will involve understanding and identifying these terms.

Answers: 1. Important details   2. Summarizing   3. Sequencing   4. Conclusion   5. Main idea

Discussion:

Explain that there are many different ways to show that you comprehend or understand what you have read. When you give the students an assignment, also give them a clue as to how they will be expected to demonstrate their understanding.

1. In example 1, why were the details important? (Those are the clues that lead up to revealing the killer.)

2. If I had asked for the name of the murder victim, what type of comprehension skill would that show? (Conclusion.)

3. In example 2, what comprehension skill was demonstrated? (Summarizing.)

4. What are some other school assignments that would use summarizing as a comprehension skill? (Giving a book report, describing something in a written report.)

5. Example 3 uses the skill of sequencing. What other tasks would be important to do in a particular order? (Anything that is assembled, describing events that take place over several days.)

6. How does example 4 lead the person to come to a conclusion? (He has to read and understand facts, then put them together to come to a single answer or decision.)

7. What are some other tasks that involve considering several things before coming to one conclusion? (Deciding on a menu, playing chess, taking a test.)

8. The last example describes using the main idea to tell about a book. Why does a main idea need to be kept short? (You are trying to hit the highlight of the book, not tell every detail.)

Extension Activities:

1. As students are given various reading assignments, have them predict what type of comprehension skill might best fit the assignment. For example, when you have them read a short story, discuss they might use the skills of summarizing, sequencing, or main idea to give feedback on the story.

2. Discuss other comprehension skills such as paraphrasing, predicting, using vocabulary skills, reading between the lines (inferring, deducing), and using cloze (fill-in-the-blank) techniques.

Evaluation:

1. Give an example of an event or activity that has to be done in a specific sequence. List the steps in that event.

2. Write the main idea of a book that you have read recently or a movie that you have seen.

8.4   **Reading for Comprehension**

Directions:

These students are reading items for a specific purpose. Fill in the blanks with the reading skill that each student is using.

Main idea	Conclusion
Sequencing	Summarizing
Important details	

1. I have to read this murder mystery to find out who the killer is. I know I will have to pay attention to all of the little clues that are given. I really have to use the skill of paying attention to

   _____ when I read this.

2. I am reading five short paragraphs that each explain interesting habits of endangered animals around the world. I am going to tell the class five things about the animals. I am not going to tell

   every single detail because that would take too long. Instead, I will be _____ each paragraph.

3. I am reading a book on how to make an aquarium. I know that I have to assemble a lot of things, but it's really important that I do it in the right order. I know I won't get the fish first—I'll get them

   last! I am using the skill of _____.

4. I am reading a pamphlet that gives two sides of an issue in our community—how to use some land near the downtown area. One person believes that our community needs a new parking lot. The other person thinks that the land should be used to make a new park. I am going to read both sides and then I will decide what I think is the best way to use the land. I will come to my own

   _____.

5. I have been reading a long book with many chapters in it. My friends have been asking me what the book is about since I love it and I can't put it down. I don't want to give away anything that would ruin the story for them, but I want to tell them just very generally what the book is about.

   I will tell them the _____.

8.5 Following Written Directions

Objective:

The student will recognize whether or not a character has followed a written direction.

Comments:

Many directions come in the form of a written explanation, list, or assignment that, in turn, must be read and understood. In this lesson, students are given examples of people who have been given a written direction and must decide after reading the item whether or not the person read, understood, and followed the written direction.

Introductory Activities:

Inform students that for the next five minutes they are allowed to communicate only by writing on a piece of paper. Hand out blank paper, set a timer, and spend the next few minutes watching students experience communicating through the written word.

Write instructions for students on the board; for example: (1) go to your desk; (2) get out your reading book; (3) turn to page 50; (4) count how many times you see the word "the" on that page; (5) write that number on a piece of paper, circle it, and hold it up high.

Discuss how well students were able to follow written directions from these activities.

Activity:

On the worksheet "Following Written Direction," students are to decide whether or not the people on the worksheet followed the written directions and indicate their answer by writing Yes or No next to the items.   *Answers:*   1. No—she did not follow the directions right away.   2. Yes—he mailed the form in within the thirty-day period.   3. Yes—she responded right away.   4. Yes—he moved the car to a safe street.   5. No—they skipped the waiting part.   6. Yes—he got gas using the money left for him.

Discussion:

On the worksheet, it appears that the people were all able to read the instructions, but not all of them followed the instructions. Discuss why it is important (even urgent in some cases) to follow the instructions exactly as written.

1. In example 1, why didn't Tamara follow the instructions exactly? (She did other things first.) 2. Why do you think her mother wanted the hamburger taken out right away? (Might take awhile for it to thaw.)   3. In example 2, what was the written direction for Jeff to follow? (Mail the proof of purchase to the company.)   4. Why is it important to send in information like that on time? (The products are only under warranty for a specified length of time.)   5. How does using e-mail make it easy to respond to a written request as in example 3? (Very little effort is required to respond.) 6. In example 4, what might have happened if Jason didn't follow the instruction? (His car might have been towed.)   7. In example 5, what happened because the girls didn't follow the instruction? (The cake didn't turn out the way it should have.)   8. In example 6, what might have happened if Tony didn't read the instruction left for him? (He might have skipped mowing the lawn, asked his parents for money for gas.)

Extension Activities:

1. Assign students the task of finding five examples of written directions that they have seen or followed that day in school or around the house.   2. Have students write specific directions for someone else to read and follow. Choose a topic of interest to the students such as how to do/make/play something or how to get to their house from the school.

Evaluation:

1. Give an example of a written direction that you have been given.   2. Give a reason why it is important to follow the above direction carefully.

8.5　　　　Following Written Directions

Directions:

Write Y for Yes or N for No on the line if the person followed the written direction in each situation below.

_____ 1. Tamara picked up a note on the refrigerator from her mother that said: "Please take the hamburger out of the freezer as soon as you get home from school." She did her homework, called a friend, and then took the hamburger out.

_____ 2. Jeff got a new digital camera. It came with a warranty that said: "Mail this proof of purchase form with your sales receipt within 30 days of purchase." The following weekend he took a lot of pictures of the neighborhood on his way to the mailbox to send in the form.

_____ 3. Alyssa got an e-mail from a friend that said: "Don't forget we are having a book club discussion at my house tomorrow. Let me know today if you are coming." Alyssa clicked Reply, typed "yes," clicked Send, and then went to get a drink of water.

_____ 4. Jason usually parked in his car on South Street, but there was a sign nailed to a post that said: "No parking today—special event." He moved his car to North Street.

_____ 5. Jamie and Karissa wanted to surprise their friend with a homemade birthday cake, so they got an old family recipe that their great-grandma used to use for special parties. One part said: "Mix all of the ingredients together in a big bowl and set aside for 30 minutes." They were in a hurry, so they decided to just go ahead and put it into the oven. The cake came out flat and mushy.

_____ 6. Tony was taking care of the neighbor's yard while they were gone. They left instructions that said: "You will have to get some gas for the lawn mower. We'll leave you some money in an envelope by the door." Tony found the money, picked up a red gas can, and walked two blocks to the service station to get the gas.

Chapter 9

Writing Skills

9.1 Communicating Through Writing

Objective: The student will list and explain common forms of communication using writing.

Comments: Writing is communicating. A simple model of this process is: writer—message—receiver. In this lesson, the student is to identify some types of writing that are directed to a receiver.

Introductory Activities:

1. Have students list three things they have written lately.
2. Have students list three people to whom or for whom they have written something in the past week. What were the messages or assignments?

Activity: On the worksheet "Communicating Through Writing," students are given a task involving some form of writing. They are to identify what type of writing (for example, message, report, application) is required and who is the receiver of the message.

Answers: (examples) 1. Personal letter/Aunt Edna 2. Report/teacher 3. Job application/manager 4. Short message/mother 5. Business note/company 6. Book report/teacher

Discussion: There are many ways in which we communicate with each other through writing. Some may be quick and short-lived—a message jotted down, a comment; others are meant to endure—a special letter, a speech, and so on. Discuss with students how the type of writing and the message should fit the situation.

1. Which of the forms of communication are you most likely to use?
2. Which types of writing are the most formal? (Business application, report.)
3. What special considerations would you give to a more formal type of writing? (Check for neatness, spelling, and so on.)
4. Does knowing who will receive the message change the way you would write the message? (Probably—if it is someone you know well, you would not have to be so formal.)

Extension Activities:

1. Have students collect examples of formal writing such as job applications, business letters, and reports.
2. Have students research guidelines for writing different types of letters—business letters, friendly letters, thank-you notes, and so on. Then compile examples of each.

Evaluation:

1. List five examples of types of written communication.
2. Identify the examples in (1) as either formal or informal.
3. Specify a likely recipient of the message in each example.

9.1   **Communicating Through Writing**

Directions:

The following tasks involve writing. For each task, write an example of what type of writing might be used, such as a message, research paper, and so on. Then write who the information is directed to (received by), such as a teacher, parent, friend, and so on.

Task	Type of Writing	Received By
1. You want to let your Aunt Edna know how you are doing in school.		
2. You need to write a report about the political history of Haiti.		
3. You want to apply for a job at a restaurant.		
4. You should let your mother know you're going out for a few hours.		
5. You want to receive information from a company about its free offer.		
6. You want to give your opinion about a book.		

9.2 Everyday Writing Tasks

Objective:

The student will identify five to ten everyday writing tasks.

Comments:

Most students will face several types of writing tasks throughout the day. Writing is involved in simple tasks such as taking a phone message or writing yourself a note to remember something. This lesson provides the student with many examples of how writing is part of everyday life.

Introductory Activities:

1. Have students list three to five common writing activities they perform at school.   2. Have students list three to five common writing activities they might perform at home or for pleasure.

Activity:

The student will read a short story about a girl's activities at school and home. The student will list common examples of writing tasks that the girl encountered during the day.   *Answers:*   1. History outline   2. Write poem summary   3. Note to friend   4. Shopping list   5. Office form   6. Job application   7. Paragraph about self   8. Phone message   9. Address for information   10. Science questions   11. Thank-you note   12. Journal

Discussion:

This was probably not a completely "typical day," but there are many common examples of writing in this activity. Have students compare answers.

1. How many of your common writing activities are done with pen or pencil? Do you use a word processor for many of your tasks?   2. What additional "everyday writing tasks" could you add to this list? (Assignment sheet, other notes and assignments.)   3. Do you think writing is more difficult than reading for most people? Why/why not? (Writing may require more effort; it is self-generated, active, and so on.)   4. Which of the examples on the worksheet could be considered more formal? Which would be more informal?

Extension Activities:

1. Have students interview a parent or adult. What typical writing activities are part of their everyday life? How does this differ—or overlap—with a student's writing activities?   2. Have students spend time in the computer lab developing word-processing skills. Record improvement in rate and accuracy of typing!

Evaluation:

1. List at least five everyday writing tasks that would be performed at home, school, and/or work.
2. Write a paragraph explaining how you feel about one of the following topics:

   - Importance of Writing vs. Reading as a School Skill
   - Importance of Word Processing vs. Handwriting
   - Writing Skills of the Twenty-First Century

9.2   Everyday Writing Tasks

Directions:

Read the following short story. List as many examples of everyday writing tasks as you can find. Use the back of this sheet if you need more space to write.

Sara got up one morning and gathered her books for school. First hour, she had U.S. History. "Take out your outlines of Chapter 3," the teacher said. Sara handed hers in.

Second hour, she went to English. The assignment was to write a summary of a poem they had read. Sara spent about an hour working on that.

Later in the day, she had a study hall. "I want to make sure that Mike doesn't wait for me after school," she thought, dashing off a quick note for her friend Ellen to deliver to Mike. She decided she would use the rest of her study hall time making a list of ingredients she would need to pick up at the store to make chocolate chip cookies for her parents.

At lunch, she got her books and filled out a form at the office that stated she could leave early. She had an interview at the local veterinarian clinic for a part-time job.

She filled out a job application at the clinic. At the bottom was the question: "What special qualities do you have that you think would make you a good applicant for this job?" She thought for a minute, then wrote about her experiences taking care of animals for her parents' friends while they were on vacation.

After the interview, Sara went shopping, then home. The phone rang and the call was for her brother, Terry, as usual. She wrote the message and left it taped to Terry's bedroom door.

Then Sara began baking the cookies with the television on in the background. She watched a program about underprivileged kids and ways to help them. An address flashed across the screen at the end that showed where you could write for more information. She jotted down the address.

Sara's mother came in. "Hi, Sara," she called. "Here's a letter for you from Aunt Carol. There's some money in it, too, for your birthday."

After supper, Sara finished her homework—answering questions from the science book—and then wrote a thank-you note to Aunt Carol. Before going to bed, she pulled out her journal and wrote about her busy day.

_____

_____

_____

_____

_____

_____

9.3 Proofreading

Objective:

The student will identify several important features to proofread when reviewing written material.

Comments:

When writing, particularly on more formal pieces of writing, students should take care to avoid mistakes. Not only will mistakes result in a poor grade, but they can also change the meaning of a message. Proofreading can help the student be aware of common mistakes that should be avoided.

Introductory Activities:

1. Have students volunteer to tell about writing mistakes for which they have been corrected recently; for example, spelling, paragraphs, punctuation, and so on.
2. Have students come up with a working definition for proofreading. (Reading something written and making corrections.)

Activity:

On the worksheet "Proofreading," students are given several examples of ways to make their writing clear. Make sure students understand why writing should be: (1) neat—so it can be read; (2) well-organized—so the message makes sense; (3) appropriate—the style should be suitable for the receiver; (4) spelled correctly; (5) correct as far as punctuation and capitalization; and (6) written in clear sentences—again, so that the message is easy to understand. In this lesson, students are to circle the letter of the illustration that demonstrates the example.

Answers: 1. A   2. B   3. B   4. A   5. A   6. B

Discussion:

Students should explain why the illustration they chose demonstrates good proofreading and why the other illustration is incorrect.

1. On what writing tasks should you go to the time and trouble of proofreading? Would you bother with a shopping list? What about a letter to the President of the United States?
2. How important is correct spelling? What does this convey to the receiver? (On a formal piece of writing, it is extremely important; it conveys accuracy, professionalism, and knowledge!)
3. How does a "sloppy copy" (first draft) help when you are expected to write something formal? (Lets you get your ideas out without worrying about being perfect the first time.)
4. If you know you have trouble with spelling, what are ways you can help yourself avoid these mistakes? (Keep a personal list of difficult words, get familiar with a dictionary, have someone proofread your writing, and so on.)

Extension Activities:

1. Have students find and become familiar with proofreaders' marks. (These can be found in most dictionaries. They show symbols that are used to indicate changes in a piece of writing. Some that are appropriate would be indicating a new paragraph, inserting or deleting words, and using capital letters.) Prepare several pieces of writing with obvious mistakes and have students use proofreaders' marks to indicate corrections.

2. Make a classroom list of "spelling demons"—words that give students trouble! Post the list in a prominent place in the room. Students may also keep their own personal list of words that give them trouble.

3. Offer students the opportunity to work on spelling skills. Share "tricks" (such as mnemonic devices) for remembering hard words.

4. Have students exchange papers often and search for corrections in each other's writing. You may want to prepare a checklist of items to consider, such as the items on the worksheet. After checking, students should initial each item to show they examined it.

Evaluation:

1. Write a paragraph that explains the importance of proofreading something you have written.

2. List at least five items you should consider when proofreading a piece of writing.

9.3   Proofreading

Directions:

The following are examples of ways to make your writing as good as you can make it. For each one, circle the letter for the illustration that better demonstrates the example.

---

1. Your writing should be neat.

A the history of the old west is quite colorful and interesting.

B the ~~history~~ of the old ~~west~~ is west is quite colorful and ~~interest~~ interesting.

---

2. The message should be well-organized.

A The tennis club is starting. If you want to Join, you'll have to come to a meeting.

B The tennis club will meet this Wednesday after school in the gym

---

3. The message should be appropriate for the receiver.

A Hey Teacher—
Give me an A! This was a stupid assignment!

B Hey Mom,
Can you pick me up after track practice? thanks!
Love, Kathi

---

4. Check your spelling for mistakes.

A Go to the store on Friday when everything is on sale.

B The repare man will be hear on Thursday.

---

5. Check the punctuation and capital letters.

A It's important to have a good attitude at work. It makes the day go better.

B Many people go to work with a chip on their shoulder they wish every day were Friday

---

6. Make sure your sentences make sense.

A In home room our class talked. There are problems. We can think of ways. the parking lot is a big is messy.

B Today we discussed the problem of littering in the school parking lot. There is a lot we can do to make it cleaner.

9.4 E-mailing Dos and Don'ts

Objective:

The student will state five common courtesy tips to use when using e-mail.

Comments:

The use of online communication is increasing every day. Terms like *chat* (real-time conversations), *texting* (brief electronic messages sent by cell phones or other devices), and *IMing* (spontaneous instant messaging—another real-time communication feature between others who are a "buddy list") are part of most teens' conversations. Although most e-mails can be informal and fun, there is still a need to be familiar with a few basic rules of courtesy when using e-mail, especially when e-mailing an adult or regarding a job, or when the communication is a bit more formal.

Introductory Activities:

1. Raise your hand if you know what e-mail stands for. (Electronic mail.)
2. Raise your hand if you know what IM stands for. (Instant messaging.)
3. Raise your hand if you have ever texted someone. (Message via a keyboard from an electronic device.)
4. Raise your hand if you know what KPC means. (Keeping Parents Clueless.)
5. What is meant by "netiquette"? (Using etiquette or good manners when using the Internet.)
6. Can you think of any examples of bad manners using e-mail or other communication on the Internet?

Activity:

Pass out the worksheet "E-mailing Dos and Don'ts" to the students and review the seven rules on good manners for using e-mail. Have students match the numbered examples with the letters of the rules.

Answers: 1. f   2. d   3. b   4. a   5. f   6. c   7. e

Discussion:

Make sure that students understand the difference between informally e-mailing a friend and using e-mail to contact and communicate with someone with a more formal purpose.

1. In example 1, the person received an e-mail chain letter. What are some examples of chains or forwards that you have seen? Why are they annoying?
2. In example 2, the e-mail is all in caps. Why can this be rude? (It is harder to read, it gives the impression the writer is shouting.)
3. In example 3, the girl was in a bad mood when she wrote the e-mail, and even worse, she was wrong. How could this have been prevented? (Find out the facts first; stop and think before sending an emotional message.)
4. In example 4, how could the subject line be shortened? (Plans for tomorrow.)
5. In example 5, what was the beginning of this embarrassing moment? Could the person have prevented it? (The photograph was embarrassing to the person, but the one who sent out the e-mail is the one who broke the rule: he or she could have asked for permission before circulating the picture.)

6. What is the problem in example 6? (Document is too long for e-mail.) What could the sender use instead? (Type it up on a word-processing program and send it as an attachment.)

7. What is the problem in example 7? (The person did not use a spell check, and the position he wants involves proofreading.)

Extension Activities:

1. Have students research common hoaxes or myths that are circulated on the Internet. It can be fun to find out about some outrageous claims that might actually be true. Sources such as www.urbanlegends.com, www.mythbusters.com, or www.snopes.com are helpful and very interesting!

2. Acronyms are used as shortcuts for writing when using e-mail. Collect and list some common or interesting acronyms. Realize that even though they are fun to use, the recipients of some e-mails may not have a clue what you are talking about and think it is a foreign language. My favorite new acronym is BOCTAAE ("But of course there are always exceptions"). The website www.netlingo.com is very helpful.

Evaluation:

1. Why shouldn't you use all capital letters when sending an e-mail to someone?
2. Why should you be careful when you send a forward or attachment to others?

9.4   E-mailing Dos and Don'ts

Directions:

Review the netiquette list of good behavior when e-mailing. Which rule is violated in the following examples?

---

a. Keep the subject line short and to the point.

b. Don't write or send an e-mail when you are in a bad mood.

c. Keep your e-mails brief.

d. Don't use uppercase letters unless you want to indicate great emphasis, as if you're shouting.

e. Use spell check.

f. Think before forwarding attachments (hoaxes, jokes).

g. E-mails are not private.

_____ 1. *Oh great! Another stupid chain letter. If I don't forward this to five people within ten minutes, I will break my arm.*

_____ 2. E-mail: ARE YOU GOING TO COME OVER TO MY PARTY TONIGHT? DON"T FORGET TO BRING POTATO CHIPS AND A GOOD GAME.

_____ 3. E-mail: It was pretty mean of you to have a party and not invite Sharon. Sometimes you are so thoughtless! You think you are better than other people and I'm just sick of your attitude and the friends you think are so popular. Stuck up! What? Phone call for me? It's Sharon? She just got an invitation to the party? Oh dear . . .]

_____ 4. Subject: I am spending the night with my friend Tom and tomorrow we are going to a football game at his brother's high school.

_____ 5. E-mail: Wow! I just got a really embarrassing picture from our Halloween party sent to me online. I don't even remember having a red wig on my head and dancing on a table. I am wondering how many other people got that e-mail. Like, my sister?

_____ 6. E-mail: Here is my report. Would you look it over before I turn it in? It's about 50 pages long. Here we go. . . .

_____ 7. E-mail: I am intrested in aplying for the pozitin of assitent copy editor for your newspaper.

9.5 Using Computers to Improve Writing

Objective:

The student will state common computer/Internet features that will assist someone in creating a written document.

Comments:

Using the Internet and programs for writing (such as Microsoft Word), students can create, proofread, and polish their writing for school and other projects. Specific training on the computer program will of course be necessary, but this lesson presents some general ideas that may help students become familiar with some of the more common uses of word-processing programs. Although the Internet can provide facts and information, the important thing is what we do with that information—and that takes human intervention.

Introductory Activities:

1. Ask students to list some ways that a computer can help them with their writing projects. What features are they familiar with?
2. Discuss some advantages of computer-generated projects compared to handwritten projects. Discuss some disadvantages.
3. Demonstrate, using a computer, search engines such as www.search.yahoo.com, www.ask.com, and www.google.com.
4. Demonstrate how to find and use an online dictionary (www.wordcentral.com is a kid-friendly one), online encyclopedia (www.factmonster.com or www.encyclopedia.com are good), and Basic Word features such as choice of font, font size, bold/italic/underline features.
5. Demonstrate how to locate and import a picture.

Activity:

Some familiarity with using the Internet and a specific word-processing program is assumed as a basic skill for this lesson, as the emphasis is the *application* of some features rather than teaching how to use them.

The worksheet "Using Computers to Improve Writing" attempts to connect students' knowledge of features with examples of how they could be helpful when writing.

Answers (Examples):

1. Type in "Abraham Lincoln."
2. When was he born? When did he die? When was he president?
3. Go to www.wordcentral.com and type in the word in the search box.
4. Choose a font that is impressive, make it bold and large compared to the rest of the print.
5. Run the spell-check feature of the program.
6. Always save your work.
7. Use the Insert>Picture feature of your word-processing program.
8. The White House. "Biography of Abraham Lincoln." www.whitehouse.gov. 2009.

Discussion:

Depending on the students' abilities and opportunities to use computers, tailor your discussion to whatever is relevant to your class.

1. What is a search engine? (The feature that helps you find information; an index.)
2. What are some search engines that we commonly use? (Yahoo, Google, Ask.)
3. Can using an online dictionary be easier than looking up a word in a book? (Can be faster.)
4. How can you use different types of font, sizes, and even color to make your document look good? (Vary the style, call attention to certain parts of the report.)
5. Why is it a good idea to use a spell check? (Easy way to help proofread.) Why is it important to look over your writing even after you have used a spell check? (A spell check can be helpful, but won't catch everything.)
6. Why is it a good idea to always save your work, even if you don't think you will need it again? (Better to not have to redo all that work in the event that you need to use it again.)
7. Do you believe that everything you find and read on the Internet is true? Why or why not? (A lot of people can post whatever they want without verification.)

Extension Activities:

1. Give students plenty of opportunity to work with Word or other word-processing programs to become familiar with some of the more common features. The point is actually to become familiar with the process rather than the content. Let students type sentences with their spelling words in different colors, different fonts, different sized letters, and so on.
2. Invite students to submit questions about subjects that they are interested in, and assign small groups to try to find the answers on the Internet using different search engines.
3. To give practice with using an online dictionary or encyclopedia, have the class divided into teams and give each team a list of words or facts to define or explain and see which team can complete the list first.

Evaluation:

How can these computer/Internet features help someone with a writing project?

1. Online dictionary
2. Spell check
3. Search engine

9.5   Using Computers to Improve Writing

Directions:

Write a brief answer to the following situation that shows how a computer can be used to help with a writing project. (ornamental art: boy and girl working on a computer.)

David and Sarah are working on a paper for their reading class. The assignment is to research information about a famous person and write a report. The report should include historical information about the person, his or her contributions, and other interesting information. They should then type up a one-page report that can be copied and distributed to everyone else in the class.

David and Sarah chose to write a report about Abraham Lincoln.

1. What information could they type in to get started on a search engine such as www.search.yahoo.com or www.ask.com or www.google.com?

2. What specific questions might they ask?

3. If they wanted to find out what the word *fourscore* meant, how could they use an online dictionary?

4. When typing up the report, David wanted the title to stand out so it would be noticed. What might he do, using the document?

5. Before handing in the report, Sarah suggested they make sure everything is spelled correctly. How could they do that?

6. David wanted to save the document before printing it. Sarah said they probably didn't need to save it since they would have a copy that is ready to print and pass out. What do you think?

7. David wanted to put a picture of Abraham Lincoln on one of the pages of the report. What could he do?

8. The teacher asked them to include the references from whatever sites they used from the Internet. She wanted (a) the name of the person or group providing the information, (b) the title of the page used, (c) the Internet address, and (d) the date or year it was posted. How would they write this information from this site:

The information is updated daily, the page is called "Biography of Abraham Lincoln," the Internet address is www.whitehouse.gov, and the information is provided by the White House.

9.6 Writing and More Writing

Objective:

The student will complete several writing tasks, showing evidence of proofreading and producing a clearly written product.

Comments:

As with reading, the best way to improve writing skills is to practice writing. The student is given a long list of writing activities to work on. He or she should incorporate proofreading skills and demonstrate attempts to write clearly in order to produce a piece of writing that communicates well!

Introductory Activities:

1. Have students make a personal list of kinds of writing activities they enjoy. You may have to make suggestions to get them started—plays? riddles? letters? and so on.   2. Have students select one item from the list they would really like to spend time working on. Inform them that they will be given this as part of the activity.

Activity:

The worksheet "Writing and More Writing" lists twenty-five writing activities to get students started writing. You may wish to have students select five to ten activities and get a notebook specifically to be kept for these writing assignments. Add other items as students think of things they would be interested in writing.   *Materials:* writing notebook, pen or pencil—or computer and printer

Discussion:

Have students select writing activities and set aside time for students to work on them, on a daily basis if possible. Once students are well into the activities, discuss the following questions:

1. Once you get into the routine of writing, does it become easier?   2. What types of writing activities did you choose, and why?   3. Were you surprised to find you enjoyed trying to write something different? Perhaps a poem or play?   4. Are you using a proofreading checklist to help you produce a nice finished product?   5. What other items did you think of to add to the list?

Extension Activities:

1. Have students continue to add writing ideas to a class list. As times come up when students need ideas, refer to the list.   2. Establish a daily writing time for your students, perhaps just for five to eight minutes a day. There are many books available that supply topics, questions to answer, and thought-provoking ideas.

Evaluation:

As students complete the various writing activities, have them do a self-evaluation (Is this the best I can do?), work on proofreading, exchange papers (if the writing is not personal), and display (with permission) the students' efforts.

9.6   # Writing and More Writing

Directions:

Here is a list of twenty-five writing tasks. Choose some that sound interesting to you and sharpen your pencil or turn on the computer!

1. Make a list of everything you'd need to take for a week-long vacation in the Bahamas.

2. Write a letter to a local travel agency asking for a brochure on biking through France.

3. Choose a favorite sport. Write a paragraph explaining the rules of the game.

4. Pick a position on a hot topic in your community. Write a two-page paper explaining how you feel about it and why.

5. Write a paragraph that you could include on a job application that tells some interesting things about yourself. Include travel, interests, work goals, and educational plans.

6. Write a brief autobiography. What do you want others to know about you?

7. Keep a journal for a month. Keep track of your feelings, events, ups and downs, and any other information you would like to remember.

8. Follow the happenings of one important development in the life of your community. Keep a log of daily changes in that situation.

9. Write a news article for your school paper about something that is interesting around your school or community.

10. Interview your favorite teacher or coach.

11. Write a poem.

12. Write a short story.

13. From a book or an encyclopedia, write a one-page biography of a famous person.

14. Do a "Dear Abby" column within your class. Answer the questions and concerns of your classmates (submitted anonymously!).

15. Write an ad explaining why someone from another state would want to visit your town or school.

16. Write a thank-you note to a friend for doing something you appreciated.

17. Write a letter to someone famous asking him or her to visit your school.

18. Write directions for someone unfamiliar with your area for how to get to your house from the downtown area (or other landmark).

19. Copy down three or four of your favorite jokes or riddles. Exchange with friends.

20. Copy the Gettysburg Address.

21. Make an address book or phone book of everyone on your Christmas list.

22. Write your birthday "wish list."

23. Make up an assignment sheet for everything you need to do, get, remember, and complete for a month at school.

24. Send away for free information that you see advertised on television or in a magazine.

25. Make a list of the best things that have ever happened to you or things that make you smile.

9.7 Writing on the Job

Objective:

The student will identify ways that people in various careers would use writing skills.

Comments:

In most occupations, there are some writing tasks that are a part of carrying out the job. These may consist of writing out orders for someone else to follow, jotting down notes to remind oneself of something, or creating something for others to read. In this lesson, students are to think of how writing is involved in most jobs.

Introductory Activities:

1. Have students list ways that teachers use writing on the job. (Prepare tests, write out worksheets, and so on.)   2. Have students list ways that their parents use writing skills on their jobs.

Activity:

Students are given a list of ten careers on the worksheet "Writing on the Job." They are to list at least one way in which writing is used on the job.   *Answers (Examples):*   1. Write prescriptions. 2. Write trial notes.   3. Write comments about a photograph.   4. Write an ad to sell a product. 5. Describe a house for sale.   6. Write medical notes for a sick animal.   7. Write the conversations between cartoon characters.   8. Describe a vacation resort.   9. Write a biography of an artist. 10. Write directions for caring for a lawn.

Discussion:

Compare students' ideas about how writing is used on the job. Discuss the following questions:

1. Are there any jobs you can think of that do not involve much writing?   2. What are some jobs in which creative thinking or writing is important? (Advertising, writing stories, and so on.) 3. How do workers in jobs that require a lot of writing do these tasks more efficiently? (Form letters, use secretaries, use computers, and so on.)   4. If someone really liked to write, what type of jobs would he or she be interested in as a career? (Novelist, reporter, magazine writer, and so on.)

Extension Activities:

1. Invite an author or editor to visit the class and talk about how writing is part of the job. Have students prepare a list of questions to use to interview the author or editor.   2. Go through job files or books that describe occupations. Target five to ten unusual occupations. Get ideas for how writing is used on these jobs.

Evaluation:

1. List five occupations and one way in which writing is used on each job.   2. Write a paragraph describing an occupation you are particularly interested in and how writing is part of that occupation.

9.7   **Writing on the Job**

Directions:

How would people in these occupations use writing skills in their jobs?
List at least one idea for each.

1. Doctor

   _____

2. Lawyer

   _____

3. Photographer

   _____

4. Advertising person

   _____

5. Real estate agent

   _____

6. Person who cares for zoo animals

   _____

7. Cartoonist

   _____

8. Travel agent

   _____

9. Art gallery owner

   _____

10. Lawn care worker

   _____

Chapter 10

Math Skills

10.1 Everyday Math Skills

Objective:

The student will demonstrate knowledge of common math skills by stating at least one way that a given skill is used in everyday life.

Comments:

Math is an academic area with many practical applications to everyday life. It is important not only to know how to add and subtract, but also to estimate, solve problems, and apply operations to everyday situations.

Introductory Activities:

1. Have students make a list of common skills taught in math class (addition and other operations, perhaps some formulas, current topics discussed, and so on).   2. Have students list three to five activities they participated in today that involved numbers or math in some way.

Activity:

The student will read a list of math skills and write one example of how he or she would use that skill in daily life.   *Answers (Examples):*   1. Figuring out the total on a bill   2. Figuring out your score from 100 by subtracting the number wrong   3. Figuring out the number of cookies required if each student wants three   4. Splitting up money among friends   5. Grouping students into fourths for a project   6. Doing a lab in science   7. Calculating how much decoration you need to put around a bulletin board   8. Figuring out when school is out for the day

Discussion:

Compare students' ideas on the worksheet. Ideally, students will realize that math concepts are everywhere and apply to many situations.

1. Do you think math is hard or easy for you? Which parts?   2. Why is it important to know math facts quickly and to be accurate?   3. How important is it to know how to use a calculator to help solve problems?   4. Are there any parts of math you think are fun? What parts are they? 5. Do you know of any math "tricks" or ways to do math that help make it easier?

Extension Activities:

1. Arrange for tutoring of younger students in math. This could involve making math games, helping students with their work or math activities, going over flash cards, and so on.   2. Have students find and contribute math puzzles, brain teasers, or worksheets they have found fun, interesting, and useful. Laminate them and make a class learning center.

Evaluation:

1. List ten common math skills.   2. List two skill areas that are strengths for you.   3. List two skill areas that remain challenging for you.

10.1   Everyday Math Skills

Directions:

The following are some skills involving math. Next to each one, write one example of how you would use that skill.

1. Adding _____

2. Subtracting _____

3. Multiplying _____

4. Dividing _____

5. Using fractions _____

6. Measuring in ounces _____

7. Perimeter _____

8. Telling time _____

10.2 Improving Math Skills

Objective:

The student will identify specific techniques for improving math skills.

Comments:

Students are often their own best source for how best to learn something that is important to them. Some students learn by memorization, others by thinking things out, some by moving around, others by working with a partner, and so on. In this lesson, specific skills are considered and students are to match examples of ways to help learn those skills.

Introductory Activities:

1. Have students list two or three skills they feel they are good at. Ask for ideas for ways that they learned these skills.   2. Have students list their own personal preferences for learning math; for example, using notes? working with a partner? using a calculator? and so on.

Activity:

Students are to match specific skills involving math with a possible technique to help learn that skill on the worksheet "Improving Math Skills." Make sure students understand that these are just examples—there are lots of ways that people learn skills (refer them to the second Introductory Activity).   *Answers:* 1. d   2. b   3. f   4. e   5. h   6. g   7. a   8. c

Discussion:

Go over the specific answers with students. Ask students to give reasons for why they selected the answers on the worksheet.

1. How could you work with a partner to learn math facts? (Quiz each other.)   2. Why is it important to know common equivalences? (Some problems are given in one set of terms, some in another.) 3. What are some ways you can solve a "story" problem besides drawing a picture? (Underline key words, look for strategies.)   4. Why is it important to make sure you are given correct change when dealing with money? (Make sure you are not shorted.)   5. In what school classes would you use time and money?   6. Why is it important to be accurate when keeping a checking account? (So you aren't overdrawn, to avoid extra charges.)   7. Why would it be important to figure out your mileage when driving? (Make sure your car is running efficiently.)   8. What are some examples of when you would need to know the perimeter of something? (Carpeting, decorating, trimming, and so on.)

Extension Activities:

1. Teach students how to use a calculator to check their work. This will give them extra practice in working on concepts as well as teach them to become familiar with the calculator as a tool.
2. Have students make their own flash cards for math facts, formulas, key concepts, and so on.
3. Allow students time to use computer games to improve basic math facts as well as thinking skills.
4. Put up a "Brain Teaser of the Day." Encourage students to work together to solve puzzles.
5. Help students become aware of their own strengths and weaknesses in math. If students tend to

make the same mistake over and over, analyze the pattern; point out to the student exactly what he or she is doing wrong and give specific techniques for overcoming that particular problem.

Evaluation:

1. List two areas of math in which you could improve your skills.   2. Suggest at least two ways for each of the two areas in (1) that you could try to improve your math skills.

10.2   Improving Math Skills

Directions:

Match the skill on the left with a way you could improve your ability to use that skill.

1. Learn math facts quickly.

    a. Find out how many gallons your car will hold and how many miles you traveled on the tank of gas.

2. Remember equivalences (for example, 12 inches = 1 foot).

    b. Make a sheet with notes on it such as 3 feet = 1 yard.

3. Figure out a story problem.

    c. Make note cards with formulas for figuring out the perimeter of a square, rectangle, and so on.

4. Give change for a dollar.

    d. Make flash cards with math facts on them.

5. Figure out the time it will be in five hours.

    e. Watch carefully when a clerk gives you back money.

6. Maintain a checking account.

    f. Draw pictures to help yourself "see" the problem.

7. Figure out how far you can drive on a tank of gas.

    g. Enter deposits and amounts spent into your account; check for accuracy.

8. Find the perimeter of a figure.

    h. When making appointments for later in the day, figure out how much time will have passed.

10.3 Common Math Situations

Objective:

Given an everyday situation, the student will identify several ways that math skills are involved.

Comments:

Math is a part of many everyday activities—shopping, eating out, even counting the change in your pocket. In this lesson, students are to think of ways that math skills are involved in some common situations.

Introductory Activities:

1. Have students list five to eight activities they or their parents have done in the past few days that involved numbers.   2. Have students list two to four activities they or their parents have encountered in the past few days that involved reasoning or problem solving.

Activity:

Students are given six examples of common situations on the worksheet "Everyday Math Situations." For each, they are to think of several ways that math skills are involved.   *Answers:* Will vary.

Discussion:

Compare students' responses. There should be a wide variety of ideas for each. The following questions will be helpful for discussion:

1. Why is it important to understand the advertising that often accompanies products that companies want you to buy?   2. Is the "best buy" always the largest can or container?   3. What is "unit pricing"? (Figuring out how much something costs for one unit—one ounce, one pound, and so on.)   4. What is an easy way to figure out a 15 percent tip? (Find 10 percent and add half of that.)   5. What are some expenses that come with a car? (Repairs, insurance, and so on.) 6. What units of measure would probably be involved in cooking?

Extension Activities:

1. Collect menus from restaurants. Have students write math problems using the menus.   2. Borrow a pay stub from someone who is willing to share this. What are all of the deductions taken from the paycheck? What percentage is take-home pay?

Evaluation:

Choose one of the following everyday situations and list at least three ways that math skills are involved:

1. Going to a sports event   2. Going to the movies   3. Shopping for clothes   4. Playing a video game   5. Figuring out your report card grades   6. Planning a birthday party for a friend

10.3   Common Math Situations

Directions:

Fill in the chart with math skills you would use in the following activities.

10.4 Understanding Graphs

Objective:

The student will identify several types of graphs and the uses of each.

Comments:

A lot of mathematical information is shown clearly by using graphs and charts. In this lesson, four types of commonly used graphs are presented: bar graph, line graph, circle graph, and pictograph or picture graph. Students should be able to identify the type of graph presented and explain how the information is given on that graph.

Introductory Activities:

1. Dictate the following information for students to write: "On Monday, a music store sold thirty-seven CDs and eighty-seven cassettes. On Tuesday, it sold fifty CDs, twenty-eight cassettes, and nine posters. On Wednesday, it sold twelve CDs, thirteen cassettes, and four posters." Have students share how they recorded this information.

2. Have students make three columns on a sheet of paper. Label the columns "Monday, Tuesday, Wednesday" at the bottom of the paper. Have students total the number of items sold on each of the three days in (1). Construct a bar graph that shows the total number of items sold for the three days.

Activity:

Explain that you are going to show how to present information by using graphs. There are four graphs that you will be covering: (1) a bar graph—one bar represents one piece of information;   (2) a line graph—a continuous line connects pieces of information;   (3) a circle graph—shows how much (percentage) of a whole is designated for a given piece of information; and   (4) a picture graph—a simple picture as a code to represent how many of a given item are represented.

On the worksheet "Understanding Graphs," students are to match the type of graph with the example illustrated.

Answers: 1. picture graph   2. line graph   3. bar graph   4. circle graph

Discussion:

Go over the examples with students, paying attention to how each graph clearly depicts the information provided.

1. Why is it important to have a key when using a picture graph? (To show what the pictures stand for, how many items are depicted, and so on.)
2. What could be a good title for the graph in example 1? (The number of students in class.)
3. How does the graph show five students? (Half of a person.)
4. What could be a good title for the graph in example 2? (Amount of snowfall in January.)
5. Why is a line graph a good way to show this type of information? (It is continuous.)
6. What could be a good title for the graph in example 3? (The number of car sales in a week.)
7. What other type of graph would clearly show the information in example 3? (A line graph.)

8. What could be a good title for the graph in example 4? (Amount of money spent on county projects.)
9. Where does most of the money go in example 4? (Juvenile center.)
10. What other type of graph would clearly show the information in example 4? (Bar graph, possibly picture graph.)

Extension Activities:

1. Have students construct graphs to show information. Examples: (a) track the change in their height in inches over five years; (b) compare the population of three nearby states; (c) tally the number and kind of pet owned by students in the class; and (d) show the results of a survey asking for the favorite candy bar of students.
2. Look for examples of graphs in the newspaper and magazines. Label the kind of graph and give each a title (if not already provided).

Evaluation:

Construct one or more of the following graphs (remember to include labels and titles):

1. Make a bar graph showing the number of televisions serviced by a company in a year: January—13; February—11; March—3; April—14; May—10; June—19; July—13; August—20; September—15; October—16; November—11; December—11.
2. Make a circle graph showing the percentage of types of movies students enjoy: horror—12 percent; comedy—50 percent; romance—13 percent; science fiction—25 percent.
3. Make a line graph showing Mary's worksheet scores for one week: Monday—79 percent; Tuesday—90 percent; Wednesday—85 percent; Thursday—81 percent; Friday—70 percent.
4. Make a pictograph with one star representing five CDs. Show the number of CDs owned by each of these students: Jason—10; Mary—15; Marcos—25; Pete—7.

10.4   **Understanding Graphs**

Directions:

Write the type of graph (bar graph, line graph, circle graph, picture graph) shown in each example.

1.

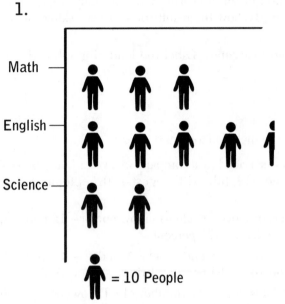

2.

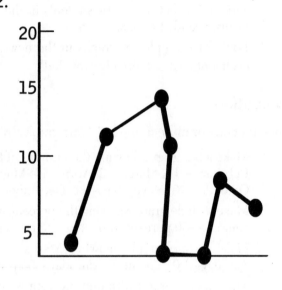

3.

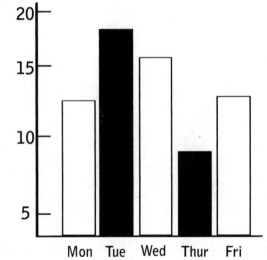

4.

10.5 Understanding Charts

Objective:

The student will construct and be able to interpret information on a chart.

Comments:

A chart is another way in which information can be presented. Students should not only be able to read information from a chart, but also, when given information, should be able to construct a chart to show this information.

Introductory Activities:

1. Do a quick survey of students to find out their favorite place to eat or get pizza. After tabulating the information, construct a simple chart with pizza places across one side and the number of students selecting that place underneath.
2. Conduct another survey of favorite toppings of pizza. Construct another chart, but this time divide the boys and girls into separate columns with the toppings across one side.
3. Obtain attendance information (if possible) for one week and construct a chart showing the number of students (divided into grade levels or boys and girls) absent Monday through Friday.

Activity:

The worksheet "Understanding Charts" depicts a chart showing the sale of items from a bookstore. Students are to use the numbers on the chart to answer questions.

Answers: 1. November (totals by month: 186, 153, 220, 241, 202) 2. October 3. pencils 4. $8.00 5. pencils (226 compared to 193 pens)

Discussion:

From this activity and the introductory activities, students should have experience on constructing and reading charts. The following questions should be discussed as a class:

1. How does a chart help make information easy to read? (Should be straightforward, uncluttered.)
2. When you construct a chart, why is it important to use labels? (To make it clear what information you are presenting.)
3. Could you put information on a chart other than numbers? (Yes; any type of description.)
4. What are some types of charts you could make?

Extension Activities:

1. Have students construct charts of any applicable information, such as grades or test scores in a certain class, sports results from teams, amount of money earned from fund-raising activities, favorite movies or books, and so on.
2. Collect charts that are in the newspaper and have students write questions using them. Exchange among students and grade for extra credit.

Evaluation:

1. Construct a chart using the following information of grades in four subjects for four students:

   - Mary, Kathleen, Todd, and Jamal are the students.

   - The subjects are math, reading, science, and history.

   - Mary's grades (in order) are 79 percent, 83 percent, 92 percent, and 82 percent. Kathleen's grades are 88 percent, 86 percent, 79 percent, and 94 percent. Todd's grades are 90 percent, 82 percent, 86 percent, and 77 percent. Jamal's grades are 79 percent, 78 percent, 90 percent, and 85 percent.

2. Answer the following questions using your chart:

   - Which student had the highest percentage in math? (Todd)

   - Which student had the lowest percentage in history? (Todd)

   - What was Kathleen's percentage in reading? (86 percent)

   - In what subject was Mary's highest percentage? (Science)

Name _____ Date _____

10.5 Understanding Charts

Directions:

Use the following Bookstore Report to answer the questions.

Bookstore Report

	Aug.	Sept.	Oct.	Nov.	Dec.
Number of pens sold	52	37	45	42	17
Number of pencils sold	36	29	58	70	33
Number of pads of paper sold	53	29	35	63	65
Number of notebooks sold	24	27	50	32	64
Number of rulers sold	8	12	8	18	15
Number of calculators sold	13	19	24	16	8

1. What month had the most sales of all items? _____

2. In which month were the most calculators sold? _____

3. What item sold the most in October? _____

4. If notebooks sold for $.25 each, how much money was made in November from that item?

_____

5. Were more pens or more pencils sold over the five months reported? _____

10.6 Sample Math Problems

Objective: The student will select and complete several types of math activities.

Comments: In this lesson, students are given a variety of activities using math skills. They are to select however many you feel are appropriate and try them out. You may wish to add plenty of activities of your own, depending on what you wish to emphasize in class.

Introductory Activities:

1. Have students list three to five types of math activities they enjoy doing.
2. Have students write one math problem they would give someone else to figure out.

Activity: Students are given lots of examples of math problems on the worksheet "Sample Math Problems." Depending on your specific objectives, you may assign them to work on several at their own pace.

Discussion: After students have been given time to work on several of the activities, discuss the process and their answers.

1. What did you find out about shopping for groceries? Did the amount of money it costs to buy food surprise you?
2. How far can your family's car go on one tank of gas? What factors would change this number? (Type of car, city or highway travel, condition of the car, and so on.)
3. How did your cookies turn out? Were the single and double batches different?
4. What is the current interest rate on savings accounts?
5. For problem 7, which types of soft drinks were the cheapest per ounce? Which were most expensive?
6. For problem 13, what amount did you get on January 31? ($10,737,418.24.) Were you surprised that it was this great?
7. For problem 17, how did you go about estimating the number of beans?

Extension Activities:

1. Add your own ideas to the math list. Include students' problems and ideas, brain teasers, and current events in math.
2. Post a "problem of the day" in your classroom. Have students work on it in their spare time.

Evaluation:

1. List one or two specific skill areas in math in which you would like to improve.
2. Specifically state what you will do or have done to improve your ability to solve math problems in (1).

10.6 Sample Math Problems

Directions:

Here are twenty math activities for you to try.

1. Shop for your family's groceries for a week. Estimate the total cost of the contents of your shopping cart before you find out the exact amount.

2. Figure out how far your family's car can go on one tank of gas.

3. Make a batch of chocolate chip cookies. Double the recipe for a larger batch.

4. Calculate how much money you would have if you deposited $100 into a savings account that paid back 4 percent interest each year and you kept the money in for one year.

5. Figure out your exact age in (a) months and then (b) days.

6. Estimate how far your house is from school. Then drive or bike the distance with an odometer to see how close your estimate was.

7. Make a chart that shows the unit prices of several different kinds of soft drinks.

8. Add up the number of calories you consume in one day.

9. Use a calculator to find the average height and weight of the people in your class.

10. Cut out five charts or graphs from newspaper articles. Write three to five questions that can be answered using them.

11. Collect menus from local restaurants. Plan an entire meal, including beverage, appetizer, and dessert. Calculate the cost. Don't forget the tip!

12. Check the classified ads for available jobs. What is the hourly wage of one that interests you? What would your weekly salary be? Monthly salary? Yearly salary?

13. If you are given a penny on January 1 and the amount doubles each day after that (for example, you would get 2¢ on January 2, 4¢ on January 3, 8¢ on January 4 and so on), how much money would you get on January 31?

14. Estimate (and then figure out) the total weight of everyone in the class if you all stepped on a scale at the same time.

15. If you weigh 1/6 of your normal weight on the moon, how much would you weigh?

16. How far is it around the perimeter of your classroom in feet? In yards?

17. Fill a small jar with jelly beans. Estimate how many beans are in the jar. Then count them.

18. Open a small bag of M&M's. Make a chart showing how many of each color of candy there are in the bag.

19. Record the temperature at the same time of the day every day for two weeks. What is the range in temperatures? Make a chart showing this information.

20. Read the sports section of the local paper. What is the percentage of completed passes from a football game? What is the hitting percentage (batting average) from a baseball game? What is the win/loss ratio of a favorite team?

Can you think of other math problems to share with your classmates? write one or two here.

_____

_____

_____

_____

_____

10.7 Using Computers for Math Information

Objective:

The student will identify and explain uses for several common online math tools.

Comments:

We all (teachers and students alike) have our favorite websites that we use to help us locate information. Sometimes websites have so many links and so much information that it may be hard for students to navigate them. This lesson contains information about a few tools (clock, timer, calendar, and so on) that students can readily find and use for math help.

Introductory Activities:

Ask students to tell you what tool would be helpful in the following math-related situations: Telling time (clock), figuring out how much you weigh (scale), knowing what the temperature is (thermometer), knowing what day of the week your birthday falls on this year (calendar), and figuring out how to multiply huge numbers (calculator).

1. Inform students that some of these tools are available online and that you will be visiting some sites to show them how to find them and how to use them.   2. Display or pass out individual sheets containing website addresses for the various math tools that will be discussed. Depending on your class, demonstrate how the tools work or have students explore on their own.

Activity:

While students are exploring the various online tools, ask them to think about how they might use these sites while they are doing math-related activities.   *Answers (Examples):*   1. Timing self on a math drill   2. Figuring out a story problem   3. Figuring out what time it will be in thirty minutes   4. Figuring out what day of the week spring break begins   5. Practicing making change for a job that requires handling money   6. Figuring out how to spend and save money   7. Practicing number drills

Discussion:

Have students share their experiences and ideas regarding these websites and the tools they have worked with on them.

1. Which tools were the easiest for you to find?   2. Which tools do you think you would use most often?   3. What are some math situations that would use these tools?   4. What would be the best way to remember where these tools are located?

Extension Activities:

1. Have students locate and evaluate these and other websites that contain helpful math tools. Often sites that look good at first want the user to subscribe to a service or buy a book. Try to come up with a helpful list for the class of easily accessible items.   2. Using the budgeting information, have students set up a sample budget given an arbitrary amount of money. Discuss how different students budgeted the same amount of money differently using the same basic budget plan on the computer. 3. For practice in using the calculator, have students work on solving basic operations problems with varying degrees of difficulty. The calculator will be of no benefit if the student is not accurate in using the keys.

10.7   Using Computers for Math Information

Directions:

Visit these online sites to find some tools that will help in solving math problems. Write how you might use these tools in school situations.

1. **Stopwatch:** www.stopwatch.onlineclock.net

   _____

   _____

2. **Calculator:** www.metacalc.com

   _____

   _____

3. **Clock (face and digital):** www.time-for-time.com/swf/myclox.swf

   _____

   _____

4. **Calendar:** www.timeanddate.com/calendar

   _____

   _____

5. **Making change:** www.mathplayground.com/making_change.html

   _____

   _____

6. **Budgeting:** www.capitateyourkids.com/budgeting_for_teens.htm Or www.moneyandstuff.info/pdfs/SampleBudgetforteens.pdf

   _____

   _____

7. **Flash cards (basic operations):** www.allmath.com/flashcards.php Or www.aplusmath.com

   _____

   _____

Chapter 11

Study Skills

11.1 School Tasks for Success

Objective:

The student will identify ten to fifteen skills that are important for success in school.

Comments:

Most teachers and students would agree that there are certain skills that separate the "good" students from those who have problems in school. In this lesson, students are to consider a list of student skills and rate themselves according to how well they think they are doing on each.

Introductory Activities:

1. Have students list three skills they think are important to doing well in school.   2. Have students list three skills they think their teachers would say are important to doing well in school. 3. Have students list three skills they think their parents would say are important to doing well in school.

Activity:

Students are given a list of typical school tasks on this activity. They are to rate themselves on a scale of 1 to 5 (with 5 representing the best) to show how well they see themselves performing each task.

Discussion:

Because this is a personal survey, students may or may not want to share their responses. You may inform the students that you won't even look at their responses, but hope that it will be helpful to them to improve their skills.

1. Which of the skills on the list would you pick as your biggest problem area?   2. Which would your teachers select?   3. Which would your parents select?   4. Which skills do you think are the most important for any student to do well at?   5. Do different teachers have different ideas or expectations of what they feel is important to do well in school or in their classes? 6. Are there any skills on the list that you feel are not important?

Extension Activities:

1. Conduct a class survey. Which skills are the hardest for most students to follow? Why? Which are considered the most important?   2. Add skills to the list. You may want to list different sets of skills for different classes.   3. Write a handbook for younger students explaining what skills are important for your grade level and how they can begin developing good student skills now. Illustrate the handbook with humorous drawings.

Evaluation:

1. List eight to ten important student skills.   2. Explain why five of the skills you selected are important to do well in school.   3. Write a paragraph selecting one student skill you would like to work on and outline a brief plan for how you could improve in that area.

11.1   **School Tasks for Success**

Directions:

The following is a list of skills or tasks that help someone do well in school. Rate yourself from 1 to 5 (1 = poor, 5 = excellent) according to how well you see yourself performing each skill.

_____ I am well organized; I can find my materials easily.

_____ I get my assignments done on time.

_____ I usually understand what I'm supposed to do on assignments.

_____ I get along pretty well with my teachers.

_____ I usually get along well with my principal.

_____ I get along well with other students at school.

_____ I can take good notes.

_____ I listen to what's going on in class.

_____ I ask questions if I don't understand something.

_____ I follow directions carefully.

_____ I do my assignments clearly and neatly.

_____ I usually put forth good effort into my work.

_____ I do my work right away; I don't procrastinate or put it off.

_____ I am on time to class.

_____ I do my homework.

_____ I turn in my work when it is due.

11.2 Tools for the Task

Objective:

The student will identify items (tools) that are necessary or helpful in completing a given task.

Comments:

Before we can complete or even begin a task, we have to know what materials are needed to do the job. In this lesson, students are given several tasks to complete and must identify what tools are needed.

Introductory Activities:

1. If you had to take a spelling test right now, what tools or materials would you need? (Paper, pencil, eraser.)   2. If you were going to clean out your desk or locker, what tools would you want to get ahead of time? (Wastepaper basket, paper towels, spray cleaner.)

Activity:

On the worksheet "Tools for the Task," students are to read and identify what common tools or items would be needed to complete the job.   *Answers (Examples):*   Task #1. Paper, resource books, possibly computer   Task #2. Poster board, colored markers, book with map of your state   Task #3. Recipe, food items, cooking utensils, oven, carrying case for food   Task #4. Poster board, tape measure or height/weight scale

Discussion:

Have students compare answers on the worksheet and possibly edit their own answers.

1. In Task #1, how many different tools did the class come up with?   2. Is it important to have everyone's project look exactly the same? Why or why not?   3. Why would it be helpful to have the needed items ahead of time?   4. In Task #3, why would it be important to know how you were going to prepare the food before starting the job? (Might need access to an oven or stove.) 5. What tools could be substituted if you didn't have markers, poster board, or a computer? (Could use colored pencils, crayons, butcher paper, library books, and so on.)

Extension Activities:

1. Assign groups of students a common task, such as #1 or #2 on the worksheet. Give each group the same tools to work with and compare how students used the same tools to come up with projects that looked very different.   2. Assign groups a task, but this time omit one tool. Have students brainstorm to complete the task by improvising or substituting tools to complete the job.

Evaluation:

List three tools that would be helpful to make a bulletin board that displays favorite books read by students in the class.

11.2   **Tools for the Task**

Directions:

For each of the following school assignments, list the tools that would be needed to get the job done.

Task #1: Write a two-page paper on an invention of your choice.

_____

_____

Task #2: Color and display a map of your state, showing the three largest cities and the capital.

_____

_____

Task #3: Prepare a traditional meal from a country of your choice for ten students to enjoy.

_____

_____

Task #4: Make a chart that compares the height of the boys and the girls in your grade at your school.

_____

_____

11.3 Taking Notes

Objective:

The student will demonstrate ability to read (or listen to) a short passage and take summary notes.

Comments:

The ability to listen to or read information and then understand it well enough to summarize it is a skill that is helpful throughout an entire school career. Much information is presented orally, especially in the upper grades. Some teachers use notes and chalkboards to list important information for students to know; others expect students to listen, analyze, and write information quickly and accurately. In this lesson, students are given an opportunity to write notes as if they were listening to a brief lecture.

Introductory Activities:

1. Have students list classes in which note-taking is a frequent activity.   2. Ask students how they know what information presented in a class is important to know. (Written on board; teacher says "You need to know this!" and so on.)

Activity:

The students are to "pretend" they are listening to a brief lecture given by a science teacher. You may want to read this to students from the worksheet "Taking Notes" or have them participate by reading it orally. The students are to jot down notes on the material on another sheet of paper.

Discussion:

Students will probably record the information in different ways. Some may use pictures with labels to help them remember; others may use words. Compare the ways in which students selected what they thought was important.

1. How did you know what was important to write down?   2. What clues did the teacher give that something was important? (Definition on the board, comment "Remember that.")   3. How did the pictures on the board help? (Something visual to go with the labels.)   4. What information about this material do you think might be on a test?   5. How do you organize your notes? 6. Is it easier for you to take notes from oral or written material? Why?   7. Is it important to be a good listener for oral information and a good reader for written information?

Extension Activities:

1. Have students pay attention in each class for clues or techniques that his or her teachers use to highlight important information. Make a list.   2. Prepare mini-lectures (or have students participate in this) with a quiz at the end. Practice emphasizing what notes should be taken and studied in preparation for the test.   3. Jot down an incomplete outline on the board before you give a lecture. As you talk, have students complete the outline on their own paper. Compare notes at the end.

Evaluation:

Have students use the notes they took on the worksheet to complete the following "quiz":

1. What is digestion?   2. How do the teeth and tongue help with digestion?   3. Where does food go after you swallow it?   4. What is the esophagus?   5. What is the stomach shaped like?

6. Where does food pass to after the stomach?   7. When does food go to the large intestine?
8. What is waste?   9. How does waste leave the body?

Answers to quiz:

1. Breaking down food   2. Moisten and crush it   3. Into the esophagus   4. A short tube that connects the throat and stomach   5. The letter j   6. The small intestine   7. After the small intestine   8. What the body does not use   9. Through the colon

11.3   **Taking Notes**

Directions:

Mr. Knowitall is giving a science lecture. What notes would you take if you were a student in his class?

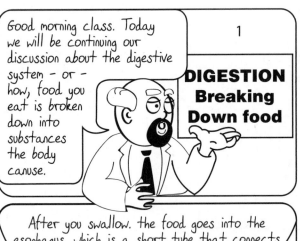

11.4 Studying Smarter

Objective:

The student will identify reasons why characters in examples are not studying effectively.

Comments:

On any given assignment, students in a class probably have about the same amount of time and length of work involved. However, some students use that time much more constructively—they study "smarter." This lesson highlights some problems that get in the way of being a good student.

Introductory Activities:

1. Ask students the following question: If you had fifteen minutes to learn the capital cities of ten European countries, how would you go about using that time to work on this task?
2. Ask students to list their ideas or techniques for "good studying." What are some ways they use their time wisely?

Activity:

On the worksheet "Studying Smarter," students are to examine the examples of students who are not studying in an effective manner. They are to pick out the problem in each.   *Answers:*
1. Disorganized   2. Procrastinating   3. Didn't keep quizzes or notes   4. Didn't plan ahead
5. Using time to socialize instead of studying   6. Not finding out instructions   7. Listening to music instead of concentrating   8. Joking around

Discussion:

Have students go over their ideas for each. Have them offer suggestions for a better use of the time.

1. How could each student on the worksheet study smarter?   2. Which are examples of problems of (a) time, (b) organization, (c) attitude?   3. How could you go about making changes if this were your situation?   4. Do you think some students study better with background music or TV? (Emphasize the word *background*!)

Extension Activities:

1. Have students role-play these and other situations. Have them come up with alternative endings that show good use of time.   2. Have students come up with a specific plan of attack for each student on the worksheet. What would they suggest for each?

Evaluation:

1. List two ways students can effectively use time to study efficiently.   2. List two ways students can effectively organize materials to study efficiently.   3. List two ways students can effectively use a good attitude to study efficiently.

11.4   **Studying Smarter**

Directions:

Each of these students could be a little smarter in the way he or she is studying. What is the problem for each of them?

1.

Where did my pen go?

2.

I'm tired. I'll just study for the test tomorrow. I'll have five minutes before class.

3.

The semester exam is tomorrow. I wish I had kept all of my notes and quizzes for the semester instead of tossing them away!

4.

Oh no! The 10-page report is due and the one book I need is checked out!

5.

I like studying with a partner. Hey – let's go see that new movie!

6.

I don't understand what I'm supposed to do on this worksheet. I'll watch tv instead.

7.

The capital of Wisconsin is what? Hey, hey, hey! Baby, baby!!

8.

Who was the first president?

ELVIS! Ha, ha, ha!

11.5 Following Directions

Objective:

The student will identify common school directions and possible consequences of not following them.

Comments:

The ability to follow directions is very basic to survival in school. Assuming the student understands the directions given, the next step is careful compliance with them. Students are given examples of common directions heard in school and are to think of what could happen if they were not followed correctly.

Introductory Activities:

1. Have students give examples of directions they have been given at home in the past few days (or hours).
2. Have students give examples of directions they have been given at school recently.
3. Have students give examples of directions that might be given by someone in position of authority such as principal, mayor, president, and so on.

Activity:

Students are given examples of directions on the worksheet "Following Directions" that might be given in school. They are to write a possible scenario of the circumstances in which they might be given the direction and to decide on a possible consequence of what might happen if the direction were not followed correctly.

Answers (Examples of consequences):

1. May do the wrong problems.
2. Answers might not be read correctly by the computer.
3. Reading more than you have to.
4. Getting some problems wrong.
5. May get filed with the wrong class.
6. Lose all of your computer work.
7. What should be a body of water may look like a country instead.
8. Unmelted butter won't mix easily into the popcorn.
9. Names will be out of order.
10. The teacher may be busy, and you would waste time when you could probably figure it out yourself.

Discussion:

Have students share their responses to the items on the worksheet. Be sure to praise creative answers!

1. Why would it be important to follow the directions given?
2. If you think you have a better idea, how could you suggest it in some of the situations?

3. What are some occupations for which it is extremely important to follow directions? (Life-or-death situations!)

4. If you did not understand the directions, what could you do to make sure you complete the task correctly? (Ask, watch someone else, and so on.)

Extension Activities:

1. Have students collect items for which there are extensive (and important) directions, such as assembling a model, playing a video game, driving a foreign car, mixing hair color, and so on. Have them present humorous scenarios that demonstrate what could happen if the directions were not followed.

2. Invite a guest speaker who works in a field with life-or-death consequences—perhaps a doctor, EMT/firefighter, military person, or airplane pilot—to talk about how important following directions is to his or her career.

3. Have students make puzzles in which sets of directions that must be followed sequentially are mixed up (cooking something, assembling something, and so on). Have students put them in the correct order.

Evaluation:

1. Give an example of types of directions given in classes such as math, science, P.E.

2. Write a paragraph describing what could go wrong if the following directions were not followed:

   - A surgeon performing open-heart surgery

   - A chef in a fancy restaurant trying out a new recipe

   - A mechanic working on a car

   - A lab technician testing evidence for fingerprints

11.5   **Following Directions**

Directions: When might you hear these directions being given? What is a possible consequence of not following the directions?

1. Do the odd-numbered problems only. Show your work.

   _____

2. Use a No. 2 pencil on the scantron sheet.

   _____

3. Read the passage first, then answer the questions.

   _____

4. Check your answers by randomly redoing some of the problems.

   _____

5. Put your name, date, and the subject in the upper right-hand corner of your paper.

   _____

6. Save your work on your disk.

   _____

7. Use the color blue to represent water on the map.

   _____

8. Melt three tablespoons of butter before pouring it over a bowl of popcorn.

   _____

9. Alphabetize the names by the last name.

   _____

10. If you're stuck, reread the chart in the book before asking the teacher for help.

   _____

11.6 Doing Homework

Objective:

The student will list several ideas that help with the task of completing homework.

Comments:

The downfall of many students is their failure to understand, complete, and return homework. Homework can be a time to reinforce concepts already taught at school, extra time allotted for completing tasks that weren't done at school, or a time to explore something new and related to activities introduced at school. In this lesson, students are asked to think about different ways to help make doing homework easier.

Introductory Activities:

1. Have students discuss how often they have homework.   2. Have students mention which classes most often assign homework.   3. Have students list several purposes of assigned homework.

Activity:

Students are given a list of several helpful homework tips. They are to match the tip with the picture that shows the idea being used.   *Answers:* 1. b   2. c   3. f   4. a   5. e   6. d

Discussion:

Go over answers with students. Discuss how the tip would be helpful in completing homework.

1. Is completing homework a problem for you? Why?   2. What specific problem areas do you have in doing homework?   3. What are some ways you could set things up before doing your homework to ensure that you know what to do and have all needed materials?   4. What are some safeguards you could have available to you in case you have trouble with understanding the homework? 5. How could you make sure you turn in homework correctly and on time?   6. What type of atmosphere is best for you to study in?   7. How can homework assignments help you get better grades or get a better understanding of the work?

Extension Activities:

1. Have students chart their homework for a month. They should record the class, assignment, completion percentage, and any other relevant information, including any problems encountered. 2. Have students record the number of minutes spent in homework (defined as any time spent working on or studying concepts for a class) for each class. Is there any connection between time spent studying and the grades achieved?

Evaluation:

1. Write three to five helpful ideas for doing homework.   2. Write a paragraph explaining how homework can be helpful to achieve learning in a particular class of your choice.

11.6   Doing Homework

Directions:

Here are some tips to doing homework successfully. Match the tip with the picture that shows a student following the idea.

_____ a. Know what to do.

_____ b. Have all necessary materials.

_____ c. Find a good place to work.

_____ d. If you have questions, ask.

_____ e. Do everything you are supposed to do.

_____ f. Put the work in a safe place where you'll have it to turn in.

1.

2.

3.

4.

5.

6.

11.7 Managing Daily Assignments

Objective:

The student will monitor his or her daily assignments for a specified length of time.

Comments:

Many students do not take the time to write down their assignments. They feel they can keep track of everything in their heads and do not need the extra work of writing things down. However, the use of a daily assignment sheet is often very helpful even for students who are capable of organizing themselves. This lesson consists of a project in which students keep track of their daily assignments.

Introductory Activities:

1. Have students describe any methods they use for recording daily assignments—notebooks, assignment sheets, specific pages, and so on.   2. Have students discuss which classes tend to give daily assignments, as compared to those that assign long-term projects or include participation as the major activity. How do daily assignments help students learn the material?

Activity:

Students are to keep track of their daily assignments for at least one week. You may wish to target only one or two classes at first, depending on the student and the likelihood of good record-keeping. The information on the worksheet "Managing Daily Assignments" includes the date, subject, specific assignment, room for a summary of the class's activity, notation for any homework, and a square to be marked off when the homework (if assigned) is done. You may wish to add other information that is pertinent to your situation.

Discussion:

After students have participated in this project for at least one week, discuss how helpful the assignment sheet is. Students may have ideas for adding other information or designing their own daily assignment sheet.

1. What classes tended to give daily assignments?   2. Why would briefly recording a summary of the class activity for that day be helpful?   3. What other information would be helpful to monitor on an assignment sheet?   4. Do you have a good idea what your grade or class performance is for each class?   5. How would an assignment sheet be helpful in case you were absent? 6. How would keeping an assignment sheet also help someone else keep up with homework?

Extension Activities:

1. Have students design a personal daily or weekly assignment sheet. Tell them to include their own personal touches such as a logo, motto, or any drawing that reflects their personality. Run off copies if possible and encourage students to use them.   2. Include good record-keeping as part of a class grade. Keep students posted often as to their performance in class.   3. At the end of the week, give a quiz on information that should have been kept on the assignment sheet, such as class summary information. Allow students to use their assignment sheets to answer the quiz questions!

Evaluation:

1. List two ways that keeping a daily assignment sheet can help a student get better grades.
2. List three to five pieces of information that should be included on a daily assignment sheet.

11.7   **Managing Daily Assignments**

Directions: Complete the following assignment sheet. Record all necessary information.

Date _____ **Subject** _____ Assignment _____

Summary of class:

Homework?   Done ☐

××××××

Date _____ **Subject** _____ Assignment _____

Summary of class:

Homework?   Done ☐

××××××

Date _____ **Subject** _____ Assignment _____

Summary of class:

Homework?   Done ☐

××××××

Date _____ **Subject** _____ Assignment _____

Summary of class:

Homework?   Done ☐

××××××

Date _____ **Subject** _____ Assignment _____

Summary of class:

Homework?   Done ☐

11.8 Managing Long-Term Assignments

Objective:

The student will plan a long-term (for example, several weeks' duration) assignment using a calendar and other resources.

Comments:

Planning and carrying out a longer assignment requires more effort than maintaining daily work. Especially if the student is given a lot of independence, he or she must organize the project, make deadlines, obtain materials, and keep on track. In this lesson, students are given an assignment to organize.

Introductory Activities:

1. Have students give examples of some long-term (at least several weeks, possibly a semester) assignments or projects. 2. Have students give examples of materials or resources that might be involved in a long-term assignment (library research, interviewing people, using a computer, and so on).

Activity:

Students are to examine a girl's long-term assignment for a class. They will use the sample calendar to help the girl plan how she will complete the steps of the project to get it completed on time.

Discussion:

Assume the project is assigned on October 1 and is due on November 30. Students may want to work in small groups so that they can discuss when they think certain deadlines should be made. Compare deadlines and activities that the students come up with. There is no "right" or "wrong" time schedule, but students should keep certain factors in mind; for example, when the library is open (weekends?), what materials need to be purchased, how much time might be needed for revisions, and so on.

1. After making a careful schedule, what problems could potentially come up that would throw things off? (Getting sick, someone not doing his or her part, and so on.) 2. Where would be a good place to keep the calendar? 3. What shopping or purchasing would you need to do? 4. What plans would you need to make to get access to a computer or typewriter? 5. What materials would you need for a map or other visual aids? 6. What might you put on the cover? 7. Can you think of other items or dates you should include on the calendar?

Extension Activities:

Have students organize a similar long-term plan for the following assignments. What tasks are involved? What materials are needed?

1. Prepare a fact sheet for each of the fifty states. Due in one month. 2. Design and give a "creative" book report. Due in three weeks. 3. Research and prepare a meal from another country. Due in two weeks. 4. Write and perform a play for another class. Due in one month. 5. Make a diorama of a scene from a favorite movie. Due in three weeks.

Evaluation:

1. Give examples of two or three long-term assignments or projects. 2. Select one of your examples and list the tasks and materials involved. 3. Using a calendar, make a sample outline of when each task in your example should be completed.

Name _____ Date _____

11.8   Managing Long-Term Assignments

Directions:

Here is Amy's long-term assignment for English and history. Help her plan how she will manage her time so that she will complete the project on time. Use the calendar that follows to help assign dates for the tasks.

October							
			1	2	3	4	
5	6	7	8	9	10	11	12
13	14	15	16	17	18	19	20
21	22	23	24	25	26	27	28
29	30						

November						
		1	2	3	4	5	6
7	8	9	10	11	12	13	14
15	16	17	18	19	20	21	22
23	24	25	26	27	28	29	30

Project: Write a research paper on a topic about the Civil War.

Due: In two months

Tasks:

- Pick a topic
- Find three sources
- Outline is due in one month—notes should be on 3 × 5 cards, must be turned in after outline
- Need to turn in one rough draft
- Need at least one map and two pictures or visual aids
- Final copy must be typed or on computer
- Must have a cover

Need to:

- Go to the library to do research
- Get cards
- Read books and other sources
- Get lab time on the computer
- Buy a cover for the report

Chapter 11: Study Skills   **231**

11.9 Completing Assignments

Objective:

The student will identify completed assignments and maintain a personal record of completed assignments for a designated period of time.

Comments:

Sometimes students may attempt an assignment but not complete it to specification. Turning in a partially completed assignment or doing an inadequate job on a task are problem areas for many students. Students are to identify correctly completed tasks in this activity.

Introductory Activities:

1. Have students give ideas for what a teacher looks for in a completed assignment (name on paper, neatness, all parts completed, directions followed, and so on).   2. Have students give examples of what types of assignments would need to be completed in their various classes (writing a paper, reading an entire book, painting a picture, and so on).

Activity:

On the worksheet "Completing Assignments," students are to read the assignments given and the description of what the character actually did. Then they are to determine whether or not the assignment was completed and circle Yes or No.   *Answers:* 1. no   2. no   3. yes   4. no   5. yes

Discussion:

After completing the worksheet, have students discuss why the characters did or did not complete their assignments.

1. Why didn't the boy complete the science assignment in example 1? (Didn't read the entire assignment.)   2. What was wrong with the assignment turned in by the girl in example 2? (Didn't follow directions.)   3. In example 4, what could the girl have done to complete the assignment? (Find sandpaper, finish staining.)   4. In example 5, how do you know the boy completed the assignment correctly? (The word "library" appears on the articles; there are five of them.)   5. What are some difficulties that you have from time to time with completing assignments in school?   6. What could you do to improve your completion of assignments?   7. Are there particular classes for which you have difficulty completing the work?

Extension Activities:

1. Collect various examples of daily, weekly, or monthly assignment sheets. How does each show assignment completion?   2. Have students keep track of their assignment completion on a regular basis—for at least a month. Teach them to calculate their percentage each week:

Number of assignments completed ÷ Number of assignments given

Evaluation:

1. Calculate the approximate percentage of assignments you have completed over the past two weeks. (Use your assignment sheets if necessary to calculate this percentage.)   2. List two specific ways you could improve your percentage of completed assignments.

11.9   Completing Assignments

Directions:

Did the following students complete the assignments they were given? Circle Yes or No for each.

1. Class: Science

   Assignment: Read Ch. 14, pp. 81–89.

   YES   NO

2. Class: Reading

   Assignment: Write a paragraph about a character in the story we read in class.

   YES   NO

3. Class: Math

   Assignment: Copy each problem! Solve page 54 (1–10).

   YES   NO

4. Class: Woodworking

   Assignment: Finish sanding and staining the wooden box.

   YES   NO

5. Class: Social Studies

   Assignment: Collect five news articles about the new library being built downtown.

   YES   NO

11.10 Good Student Behaviors

Objective:

The student will recognize and state behaviors that are characteristic of "good" students.

Comments:

Most students are probably able to come up with a list of behaviors they think are teacher-pleasing or characteristic of students who never get in trouble. But having "good behavior" is more than just being quiet or not getting caught misbehaving! In this lesson, several examples are given of what would constitute good student behavior.

Introductory Activities:

1. Have students list two examples of good student behavior they have observed recently. 2. Have students list two examples of poor student behavior they have observed recently.   3. Have students speculate on the consequences of the examples they listed.

Activity:

Students are given a list of student behaviors on the worksheet "Good Student Behaviors." They are to determine which they think are examples of good student behavior and mark them with a check mark. *Answers:* The checked good behaviors are 1, 2, 3, 5, 6, 10, 12, 13, 15.

Discussion:

After students have completed the worksheet, discuss why the behaviors were or were not examples of good student behavior. Discuss why the circumstances give clues as to whether or not the behavior would be appropriate at that time or not.

1. Why would being early to class be an example of good student behavior?   2. What would be the problem with situation 4?   3. Why would situation 9 be a problem in some classes? (Some teachers want extra time spent on their class material.)   4. Why would situation 10 be a good idea—in the right circumstances? (Good use of free time.)   5. How much depends on what each individual teacher will tolerate? (A lot!)   6. How can you tell what teachers expect of you and your behavior in their classes? (Usually they will give expectations at the beginning of the year; also observe who gets rewarded and punished in class.)

Extension Activities:

1. Have students add more items to the list. What other good student behaviors are important? 2. Have students perform skits demonstrating these behaviors (a) once the "right" way and (b) once the "wrong" way.   3. Select one good student behavior and design a management program for a week or two. For example, make it a point to stand outside your classroom and then award extra points for students who politely greet you each day and/or are in their seat when the bell rings, and so on.

Evaluation:

1. List five to eight examples of good student behaviors.   2. Select one good student behavior you feel is important and you could improve on. Design a plan you could carry out for at least one week to work on this behavior.

11.10   Good Student Behaviors

Directions:

Which of the following behaviors are examples of good student behaviors? Put a check mark in front of them.

☐ 1. Being on time to class

☐ 2. Being early for class

☐ 3. Saying hello to your teacher before class

☐ 4. Getting up to sharpen your pencil while the teacher is giving directions for the assignment

☐ 5. Asking questions in math if you don't understand what to do

☐ 6. Having extra paper

☐ 7. Coming to class with comic books to read in case you get bored

☐ 8. Getting up to talk to a friend in the hallway during class

☐ 9. Doing your social studies during math class while the teacher is talking

☐ 10. Bringing a reading book in case there is extra time at the end of class

☐ 11. Putting your head down to sleep

☐ 12. Copying notes from the board

☐ 13. Raising your hand to answer questions

☐ 14. Making jokes to get attention

☐ 15. Offering to help another student who is having trouble

11.11 Requesting Help or Information

Objective: The student will identify appropriate ways and times to ask for extra help.

Introductory Activities:

1. Have students think about a recent time when they needed help on a project or assignment. What type of help did they need? Who helped them? How did they ask for help?
2. Have students list different ways they can get extra help on their work (peer tutors, extra assignments, learning programs, and so on).

Activity: Students are to select the better way of requesting help or information.

Answers: 1. a   2. b   3. a   4. a   5. b

Discussion: Have students discuss why the examples are or are not appropriate times and ways to ask for help. In some cases, it may simply be a matter of good intentions but bad timing!

1. In situation 1, Sara is trying, but not getting the right answer. Why is (b) not appropriate? (The teacher has not intentionally given her a problem that's too hard for her to solve.)
2. In situation 2, why is (b) a good choice? (He can learn from his mistake.)
3. In situation 3, how is Alex saving himself some time by asking for information? (He doesn't have to study everything; he is narrowing down the assignment to what is important for the test.)
4. In situation 4, the guest is leaving. How does Renee show good behavior to try to get her questions answered? (She realizes this is not the best time for a lengthy conversation; she will wait for a convenient time for the guest.)
5. In situation 5, how is Donald showing flexibility in requesting help? (He is finding out when the teacher would have extra time in his or her schedule.)

Extension Activity: Have students observe quietly how many times other students request help of a teacher in a given classroom. Have them note (if possible) the different approaches taken—raising hand, demanding help, asking for help quietly, and so on. Encourage students to thank the teacher or other individual involved after they have given the help that the student asked for.

Evaluation: Your class has been studying the planets. You will be having a test on material you have learned in class about characteristics of the planets. Unfortunately, you have been sick for a few days with the flu and have missed some notes.

1. What are some specific ways you could get extra help?
2. When would be a good time to ask for extra help?
3. What specific questions would you ask?

11.11   Requesting Help or Information

Directions:

These students are working on projects, but they have run into problems. Which response shows the better way of requesting help or information in each case? Circle the letter.

1. Sara is working on a math problem, but she doesn't get the answer that is shown on the answer key in the back of the book.

   a. "Mrs. James? I have worked on this three times and I don't see how to get the answer."

   b. "Why did you give me such a hard problem? I can't do this."

2. Denny is working on a science program on the elements in the computer lab. The screen seems to be stuck on a certain frame and now it won't do anything.

   a. "May I just copy from Dena's computer so I won't do it again?"

   b. "Can you show me what I did wrong?"

3. Alex has a big social studies test coming up on Friday, but he isn't sure which chapters are on the test.

   a. "Hey, Frank, can I see your assignment sheet?"

   b. "Should I just take everything home and study all of it?"

4. Renee is interested in learning more about being a veterinarian. The guest speaker for the week is a vet, but she is just about ready to leave the classroom.

   a. "May I ask you some more questions about being a vet when you have time?"

   b. "Could you help me write my report?"

5. Donald's teacher said she would stay after school to give extra help on Mondays and Tuesdays from 3:00 to 5:00. Donald has piano lessons on Mondays and works after school for his uncle on Tuesdays. He is having trouble in class with math.

   a. "Why can't you help me on Wednesday?"

   b. "Is there another time that I could come to get some extra help?"

Part Four

Practical Living Skills

Chapter 12: Information Skills

12.1 What Do You Need to Know?

12.2 Where to Get Information

12.3 Information from Newspapers

12.4 Information from Magazines

12.5 Information from the Internet

12.6 Information from Books

12.7 Information from Television

12.8 Information from Other People

12.9 Taking Classes

Chapter 13: Money Skills

13.1 What Is a Budget?

13.2 Making a Budget

13.3 Paying Interest

13.4 "On Sale"

13.5 Unit Pricing

13.6 How Much Do Things Cost?

13.7 Writing a Check

13.8 Maintaining a Checking Account

13.9 What Is a Savings Account?

13.10 Credit Cards

13.11 Using Debit and Credit Cards and ATMs

13.12 How Much Money Will You Need?

13.13 Making Change

Chapter 14: Travel

14.1   Local Transportation

14.2   Overnight Travel

14.3   Traveling by Plane

14.4   Planning a Trip

14.5   Estimating Costs

14.6   Using a Timetable

14.7   Reading a Map

Chapter 15: Clothing

15.1   Caring for and Repairing Clothing

15.2   Buying Appropriate Clothes

15.3   Organizing Your Clothes

15.4   Washing and Drying Tips

Chapter 16: Living Arrangements

16.1   A Place to Live

16.2   Living with Parents

16.3   Home Upkeep

16.4   Home Repairs

16.5   Going Green

16.6   Decluttering

Chapter 17: Eating and Nutrition

17.1   Nutrition

17.2   Making Good Food Choices

17.3   Eating Out versus Eating In

17.4   Preparing a Meal

Chapter 18: Shopping

18.1   What Do I Need?

18.2   Smart Shopping

18.3   Comparison Shopping

18.4   Returning Items

Chapter 19: Exercise/Health and Hygiene

19.1   Exercise in Daily Life

19.2   Exercise Excuses

19.3   Personal Health Habits

19.4   Stress and Stressors

19.5   Stressful Events and Situations

19.6   Coping with Stress

19.7   Depression

Chapter 12

Information Skills

12.1 What Do You Need to Know?

Objective:

Given a situation, the student will identify what information is needed to complete the task.

Comments:

No matter how simple a task may appear at first, there is often a need to clarify what needs to be done to complete it. This is a matter of thinking through what is needed to accomplish the task—defining expectations, knowing what to get, doing things in sequence, and so on. This activity requires students to decide what information is needed to complete a given task.

Introductory Activities:

1. Tell students they are going to prepare a five-course dinner for some special guests. After they recover from the shock, ask them to list what they need to do.   2. Have students pretend they are going to take a cruise around the world next summer. What information is needed for this task?

Activity:

Students will read examples of situations in which a person needs to find out some information in order to complete the task. They are to write that information on the line next to each item.   *Answers (Examples):*   1. Shoe size   2. How many people will be there   3. Salary, hours, benefits   4. How long it should be, what type of book   5. Age of boy, interests   6. What type of computer   7. How many will be there, what you will be serving   8. Care instructions

Discussion:

Have students compare their ideas for what information is needed. There should be several different ideas for each one.   1. Why is it important to think about what information is needed before diving into a task? (Would save time, avoid mistakes.)   2. What information is important to know when buying a gift for someone? (What they are like, their interests, how much money you have to spend.)   3. Why do you think people are sometimes hesitant to ask for information, such as stopping to ask for directions? (Feel that it will embarrass them.)

Extension Activities:

1. Have students think of tasks but leave out at least one vital piece of information. Write the tasks on slips of paper, exchange them, and have students identify missing information.   2. Have students identify at least three tasks that are usually done at home or at school. What information is needed to complete these tasks?

Evaluation:

What information would be needed for the following tasks?

1. Decorating a room for a birthday party   2. Feeding your neighbor's pets while she's away for the weekend   3. Buying jeans for a friend

12.1   What Do You Need to Know?

Directions:

What information do you need to know for each situation?

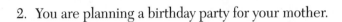

1. You are buying new shoes.

   _____

2. You are planning a birthday party for your mother.

   _____

3. You are applying for a job as a server at a pizza place.

   _____

4. You are supposed to write a book report.

   _____

5. You are buying a gift for your nephew.

   _____

6. You want to buy a new game for your computer.

   _____

7. You are cooking dinner for your family tonight.

   _____

8. You have some seeds to plant outside in your garden.

   _____

12.2 Where to Get Information

Objective:

Given a situation, the student will identify an appropriate source of obtaining information.

Comments:

Once it is established that more information is needed, the problem remains of finding out where to get the answers. In this lesson, students are given situations and must decide where the missing information can be found.

Introductory Activities:

1. Ask students where they would go to find out what was being served for lunch that day.
2. Ask students who they would talk to in order to find out what time basketball practice is this weekend.
3. Ask students what source they would use to find out who the nineteenth U.S. president was.

Activity:

Students are to read a list of questions inquiring about needed information. They are then to write one appropriate source where that information could be found.

Answers (Examples):

1. Television program guide or newspaper
2. Weather report on TV or in newspaper
3. Newspaper
4. Nutrition information on the wrapper
5. Encyclopedia or almanac
6. Sports magazine
7. Dictionary
8. Local bookstore

Discussion:

Compare responses. Students may have somewhat similar ideas for sources.

1. Did most of your responses involve people, places, or paper?
2. Who is someone whom you consider to be a good source of information about school? Sports? Life?
3. Why is the public library a good source of information? (Many types of materials are stored there.)
4. Do you think it is just as important to know where to find answers as it is to know the answers?
5. What is a good way to remember what things you need to look up or find out? (Jot down notes, make yourself a list.)
6. Are most of the sources you wrote down easy to obtain or accessible?

Extension Activities:

1. Set up a learning center or display table of almanacs, books of lists, and so on. Allow students time to browse through them. Make the assignment to write ten to fifteen questions based on interesting facts they have found. Devise a scavenger hunt in which students on teams must go through resource books to find specific information.

2. Make a *Jeopardy*-type game with five to eight different categories. Have students write questions ranging from easy to difficult for each of the spaces on the board. (See the example that follows.) Make sure students have a verified answer for each of their questions! Play the game with two teams.

Sports	Animals	People	Music	Movies	History
10	10	10	10	10	10
20	20	20	20	20	20
30	30	30	30	30	30
40	40	40	40	40	40
50	50	50	50	50	50

Example: Ten-point question for People—Name all four science teachers in our school.

Evaluation:

List an appropriate source for the following situations:

1. You want to know whether your painful arm is broken.
2. You are having trouble starting your motorcycle and aren't sure what the problem is.
3. You are interested in tie-dyeing a shirt, but have never done it before.

12. 2   Where to Get Information

Directions:

Here is a list of information you need to find out about. Write the name of an appropriate source where you could get the answer.

1. What's on TV on Thursday at 9 p.m. on channel 4?

   _____

2. What will the high temperature be for tomorrow?

   _____

3. What pet dogs are for sale at the pet store?

   _____

4. How many calories are in a Butterfinger candy bar?

   _____

5. What is the population of Zaire, West Africa?

   _____

6. Who is the first-string quarterback on the Green Bay Packers football team?

   _____

7. What are several meanings for the word *row*?

   _____

8. What are the current top three fiction bestsellers in the nation?

   _____

Chapter 12: Information Skills   **245**

12.3 Information from Newspapers

Objective: The student will identify three to five sources of information obtained from newspapers.

Comments: The newspaper is a source of an incredible amount of information—world news, national news, local news, weather, sports, editorials, and so on. In this lesson, students are to use a newspaper to locate information.

Introductory Activities:

1. Have students list as many newspapers as they can think of.
2. Have students list different features or sections of the newspaper.

Activity: Using a local newspaper (or whatever newspaper is convenient for class use), have students find the answers to the questions on the worksheet "Information from Newspapers."

Materials: pen or pencil, newspaper

Answers: Will vary for many of the questions

Discussion: Have students share their findings.

1. Were you surprised at how many different types of information were contained in the newspaper?
2. How is your newspaper organized? Are there different sections? What parts are always the same?
3. What is an editorial?
4. Who is the advice columnist?
5. How often do you read from the newspaper? What parts do you usually read?
6. Are there any special features in your newspaper?

Extension Activities:

1. Have students compare several newspapers, including some that are directed to special interests or organizations. What features are common to all? Which are particularly appealing and why?
2. Have students create their own class newspaper. Have fun designing and planning a unique publication!

Evaluation:

1. List five types of information that could be found in a typical newspaper.
2. List the names of three newspapers.

12.3   Information from Newspapers

Directions: Use a newspaper to answer the following questions.

1. What is the name of the newspaper? _____

2. What is the date? _____

3. What is the headline? _____

4. What is a sports story about? _____

5. What is the weather forecast for today? _____

6. What are the names of two comics? _____

7. What is one editorial about? _____

   _____

8. What does your horoscope say for today? _____

   _____

9. What is one car that is for sale? Find the price, condition, and other facts. _____

   _____

10. What is one house that is for sale? Find the price, location, and special features. _____

    _____

11. What is one sale that is going on this week at a large store? _____

12. What is one problem discussed in the advice column? _____

    _____

13. How many sections are in your paper? _____

14. On the back of this sheet, describe one photograph and write the caption under it. _____

15. How many births, deaths, weddings are reported? _____

12.4 Information from Magazines

Objective: The student will identify three to five sources of information obtained from magazines.

Comments: Most students are probably familiar with certain teen magazines. Strolling through the supermarket, one can see lots of magazines aimed at different populations. In this lesson, students are to examine different magazines and discover what types of information can be obtained from them.

Introductory Activities:

1. Have students list several different magazines with which they are familiar.
2. Have students list their favorite magazine and explain what they particularly like about it.

Activity: On the worksheet "Information from Magazines," students will match the magazine with the type of information typically contained within it. Even if students are unfamiliar with the magazine, they should be able to figure out the contents based on the title.

Answers: 1. d 2. c 3. g 4. b 5. e 6. h 7. a 8. f

Discussion: Go over the answers to the worksheet. Discuss how the examples given indicated which magazine they matched.

1. Which magazines do people in your family read or subscribe to?
2. What is the benefit of reading magazines for information rather than a newspaper? (More photographs, lengthier articles, different and more in-depth types of stories and features.)
3. What are some of the more unusual magazines you have heard of?
4. How does the cover of a magazine draw your interest? What types of photographs or pictures would be portrayed on a cover?

Extension Activities:

1. Have students bring in samples of lots of different types of magazines. Discuss what makes them appealing and to whom they would appeal.
2. Have students design a cover for a magazine they would like to see created. Who would be their target audience? Who (or what) will they feature on the cover?
3. Have students read a magazine they normally would not be interested in. Is the information clearly written and intriguing enough that—even though they may not be interested in the topic—they are still able to understand and appreciate the material?

Evaluation:

1. List five to ten different types of magazines (by title).
2. List a topic or type of information that would be obtained from each magazine listed in (1).

12.4   Information from Magazines

Directions:

Match each magazine listed on the left with an example on the right of information you might find in the magazine.

1. *People*

2. *Time*

3. *Horse Illustrated*

4. *TV Guide*

5. *New Woman*

6. *Sports Illustrated*

7. *Bon Appetit*

8. *National Geographic*

a. Recipe for a fancy chocolate dessert

b. Description of new fall television shows

c. What the U.S. President is doing

d. What the top-selling singer is doing

e. How to take care of your kids and keep your job

f. How people in New Guinea live and play

g. Benefits of different types of saddles

h. Predictions for the Super Bowl

12.5 Information from the Internet

Objective:

The student will recognize accurate statements about the uses and capabilities of the Internet.

Comments:

The Internet is vast! Huge! All-encompassing! There is so much information out there, it is mind-boggling when you realize how much knowledge is stored and is now accessible with a few clicks on a keyboard. Students need quick retrieval of important and desired information, especially when they are working on reports or looking for factual information. This lesson is a very basic introduction to the Internet and how it can be useful on a personal level.

Introductory Activities:

1. Ask students for examples of information that they have gotten from the Internet in the past few days. (Weather, news, sports information, games.)

2. Write an address such as http://www.kidsclick.org on the board. Discuss the parts of the address. Very briefly, "http" refers to a language that is used between computers on the Internet; "www" stands for the World Wide Web, which is not the same as the Internet but a collection of websites that can be accessed from the Internet; "kidsclick" is the domain name of the website which usually has something to do with the information; and the *extension*—the letters at the end of a web address, such as .org, .com, .mil, or .edu—refer to the type of organization (the military, government, business, school, and so on).

3. When searching for something with a search engine, a keyword is often used to locate information. Discuss what keyword(s) would be most helpful in finding information about: *Indian elephants* (not just *elephants*), the *weather in New York City* (not just *NYC*), or the names of the professional quarterbacks on your favorite football team (not just *quarterbacks*).

Activity:

The worksheet "Information from the Internet" can be used as a starting point to assess knowledge about the Internet or as a final quiz after having discussed and experienced some of the Internet activities.

Answers:

1. Yes
2. No (World Wide Web)
3. No; use "polar bears"
4. No
5. Yes
6. Yes; others are ask.com, search.yahoo.com
7. No (not ethically!)
8. No; links mean that there is more information
9. Yes
10. Yes (*bookmark* them or store them in Favorites)

Discussion:

Use the worksheet to start or continue discussing information regarding the Internet.

1. Why is it important to type in the site address correctly? (Every letter matters; could go to a completely different website than you intended.)

2. How is the World Wide Web different from the Internet? (It is a subset; the Internet refers to the millions of computers that communicate with each other, whereas the Web is mostly websites that share information.)

3. Why is it important to use a specific, rather than a general, keyword? (Gets you the information faster.)

4. Why isn't everything on the Internet true? (Anyone has access to it, can publish whatever they want to without validation.)

5. Why is it important to note what kind of website is providing the information; for example, .mil or .edu? (It would have information important to that source, military or education, rather than just general public information.)

6. How does a search engine work? (The engines use the keywords to search for documents or websites that contain the words you put in; it assembles a web page for the user listing sources that might be helpful to find what they are looking for.)

7. What is a link? (It is a word or phrase, usually underlined in blue or purple, that indicates there is more information available on another page or document; by clicking on the link you can find more information quickly.)

8. What information is on a homepage? (It might have a site map, tabs to indicate what information is on the rest of the website.)

9. What are some favorite sites that you like to use? For what purpose?

Extension Activities:

1. Have students write ten questions about topics that interest them and use the Internet to try to find the answers. How quickly can they find the information?

2. If you have a teacher webpage or a school website, show students its features, including the homepage, links, favorites, and other information.

3. Have students investigate these websites for more information about searching the Web or Internet: www.kidsclick.org (designed by librarians), www.kids.yahoo.com, www.askkids.com.

Evaluation:

1. What keywords might you type in to find out about black widow spiders?

2. What is some information that you might find on a website about spiders?

12.5   Information from the Internet

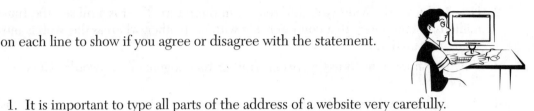

Directions:

Write Yes or No on each line to show if you agree or disagree with the statement.

_____ 1. It is important to type all parts of the address of a website very carefully.

_____ 2. WWW stands for the World Wide Wonderland.

_____ 3. If I want to learn about polar bears, I would use the keyword *animals*.

_____ 4. Everything I read on the Internet is probably true.

_____ 5. If a web page ends in .gov it means that the information is provided by the U.S. government.

_____ 6. A common search engine is called Google.

_____ 7. I can copy a complete report from the Internet and turn it in for an assignment.

_____ 8. Some websites contain links, which mean you have come to the end of the information.

_____ 9. A homepage usually tells you what information is on the rest of the website.

_____ 10. It is a good idea to keep track of sites that are helpful to you for future projects.

12.6 Information from Books

Objective:

The student will identify three to five types of information that can be obtained from books.

Comments:

Books are probably one of the most common sources of information. There are books available on almost any topic you can imagine. In this lesson, students are to go to a library and find examples of books on various topics.

Introductory Activities:

1. Have students list three topics they are interested in learning more about. Then, if they are familiar with some books, have them list a good book that would give information about each topic.
2. Have students give examples of a book they have read recently that they particularly enjoyed. What was the name of the book, what type of book was it (fiction or nonfiction, and so on), and what information did they learn from it?

Activity:

Students are to consider each subject listed on the worksheet "Information from Books" and browse through the local or school library to find the location of books on these topics. They are to give an example of a book that would provide information on the topic and then give an example of what type of information they could find in the book. You may need to help familiarize students with the layout of the library and where certain nonfiction books are found. Students may also do well on this activity if they work in small groups.

Materials: pen or pencil, access to a library

Answers (Examples):

1. How to care for iguanas
2. Where to vacation in Florida
3. What planes were used in World War II
4. How to take better outdoor pictures
5. Some healthy recipes for chicken
6. Where President Lincoln grew up
7. How the writer felt about his/her parents
8. The rules for playing golf

Discussion:

Have students go over the books and information they obtained from this activity. Allow students time to check out books they found—perhaps the books will spark some interest in new topics.

1. What did you find interesting or surprising about the books that were available on these topics?
2. How did you choose the book you selected as representative of each topic? What appealed to you about one book rather than another?

3. As you were looking through the shelves of books, what other topics or books distracted you? What else did you find intriguing?
4. When doing a research paper or project, why is it a good idea to use more than one source?
5. What is a problem with using older books as references? (Information can be outdated.)

Extension Activities:

1. Have students make a display of books that give information about a topic of their choice. Encourage them to use posters, lists of questions, models, and other aids to make an attractive display about a topic.
2. Have students write and display book reviews or book reports about topics interesting to them or relevant to something they are studying.

Evaluation:

What are three pieces of information you could learn from books with the following titles?

How to Build Your Own Backyard Birdhouse

All About Animals of Australia

Magic and Card Tricks

12.6 Information from Books

Directions:

Spend some time in your school or local library. Find an example of each category of book listed here. Then list at least one type of information you could learn from the book.

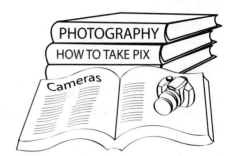

Subject	Example (Book Title)	What Information
1. Animals	_____	_____
2. Travel	_____	_____
3. Airplanes	_____	_____
4. Photography	_____	_____
5. Cooking	_____	_____
6. Biography	_____	_____
7. Autobiography	_____	_____
8. Sports	_____	_____

12.7 Information from Television

Objective:

The student will identify three to five types of information that can be obtained from television.

Comments:

Television is probably one of the more common sources of information, as it is readily available and appealing to viewers. In this lesson, students are to identify types of information that can be obtained from television.

Introductory Activities:

1. Have students list their top three favorite television shows. 2. Ask students to indicate what type of information can be gotten from the shows they picked. 3. Ask students to think of two or three shows that are primarily geared toward providing information. What information is given?

Activity:

Answers (Examples): 1. News bulletin 2. Sports program 3. Talk show 4. Game show 5. Educational or discovery program 6. News or trial coverage

Discussion:

Students may have some variety in their answers to the worksheet. Have them explain what clues were given in the cartoons to hint at the type of program.

1. Do you think most people watch television for pleasure or with the intent of learning something? 2. What programs have you watched that you think give a lot of information? 3. What type of information are you interested in learning about from television? 4. Do you have a television in the classroom? If so, how is it used? 5. How can television be used to provide information in a way that is different from radio, books, or people?

Extension Activities:

1. For a homework assignment, have students watch a specified show on some relevant topic— perhaps a documentary or educational program. In class, have students write a summary of what they remember. Compare students' writings. How accurate and how varied were their summaries? 2. Tape a provocative talk show episode. (Be sure of the content beforehand:) Have students watch the show, and periodically stop the program to have students write an opinion, evaluate a comment, or predict what they think will occur next. 3. If you have the equipment available, have students write, produce, and act in a television production about something of relevance to them, the school, or your community. Don't forget to include commercials!

Evaluation:

What type of information would the following television programs provide for the viewer?

1. An exercise show 2. A documentary about bullfighting in Spain 3. A debate between political candidates

12.7   Information from Television

Directions:

All of these television programs are giving information. What type of program is shown? Write your answer below each picture.

1.

2.

3.

4.

5.

6.

12.8 Information from Other People

Objective:

Given a situation, the student will identify an appropriate person who could provide information to answer the questions.

Comments:

People are a wonderful resource for information. People can teach skills, explain how to do things, give opinions about experiences they have had, and make recommendations. Students should not overlook this very important source of information.

Introductory Activities:

1. Ask students to give names of people (famous or not, living or deceased) whom they would like to have the opportunity to sit and talk with for an hour. Who would they choose? What would they ask?

2. Ask students to tell anecdotes in which a person helped them learn to do something or learn about something. How did this person assist them?

Activity:

Students are to list a person who would be an appropriate source of information to answer the questions on the worksheet "Information from Other People." In some cases, the name of a specific person (if known) is an acceptable answer. In other cases, a general type of person (someone of a certain age, someone who works a certain job, and so on) is sufficient.

Answers (Examples):

1. A veteran
2. A pilot
3. A music teacher
4. Someone who works at the Department of Motor Vehicles
5. Someone who has visited France
6. A friend who visited the Grand Canyon last summer
7. A pitcher for a professional baseball team
8. An English teacher
9. Someone who lived in Spain
10. Salesperson at a bike shop

Discussion:

Discuss and compare responses to the questions on the worksheet. Allow students time to share their experiences with types of situations presented.

1. How is talking to a person for information easier or better in some ways than using a book or other written source? (Can get feedback right away, can actually "see" how something is done, and so on.)

2. Just because someone is able to do something well, does that mean he or she is good at teaching or explaining to someone else? (No.)

3. Do you think you learn or understand better when someone explains something, or do you prefer to read instructions, think about them, try them out, and learn by doing?

4. Why is it important to keep in mind that someone's opinion of a task or event may differ from someone else's? (Both express what their perception was; neither may be true or both may be partially true; keep in mind that the person is explaining only what he or she perceived.)

5. What is also important to keep in mind when dealing with a person who has a job to do; for example, a salesperson for example 10? (That person may not be entirely unbiased!)

6. Before you consider a person's opinion or judgment on something, what should you know about the person? (Qualifications, reputation, experience, reliability, and so on.)

Extension Activities:

1. Invite people to visit your class and talk about what they do or specific skills they have. Prior to the visit, have students list questions they would like to learn about.

2. Have students write letters (fan mail?) to individuals whom they would like to learn more about. Sometimes celebrities will respond by sending at least a photo or form letter.

3. Encourage students to take lessons. School functions sometimes permit lessons in sports, music, and drama for very low cost. Let students know that teachers of many types of subjects are excellent resources for learning new skills.

Evaluation:

Who would be an appropriate person to help with the following tasks or questions?

1. What is necessary to adopt a stray kitten from the animal shelter?

2. How old do you have to be to join the Marines?

3. What customs or celebrations take place in Germany during December?

12.8   Information from Other People

Directions:

Who (specifically) or what kind of person (job, age, and so on) could give you information about the following topics? Write your answers on the lines.

1. What was the Vietnam war like?

_____

2. How do you fly an airplane?

_____

3. How do you play a guitar?

_____

4. What do you need to get or do to obtain a learner's permit for driving?

_____

5. What are some sights to see or visit in France?

_____

6. What is there to do at the Grand Canyon?

_____

7. How do you throw a curve ball?

_____

8. Is my story well written and interesting?

_____

9. Who would be a good tutor for Spanish class?

_____

10. What is the best kind of bike to get for riding cross country?

_____

12.9 Taking Classes

Objective:

The student will identify at least five types of continuing education classes that are available.

Comments:

Education can and should be a lifelong ambition. Even if someone is not a straight-A student in school, he or she can take advantage of weekend and evening classes available at community colleges, civic centers, local libraries, online, or through correspondence classes. We should always keep feeding our interests!

Introductory Activities:

1. Ask students to list some things that they are interested in learning about but that may not be taught in their school.   2. Help students list places in which alternative learning takes place in the community.

Activity:

The worksheet "Taking Classes" has a brief sample schedule of some noncredit classes that are typical of continuing education studies.   *Answers:*   1.   306, 319, and Watercolor I   2. Maybe 110, but might want to ask about prior experiences   3. 306 meets on Saturdays   4. 274, or Intro. to Yoga when offered   5. 107   6. Watercolor II, but only if you had Watercolor I first   7. Not yet   8. Any of the introductory classes

Discussion:

1. Why is it important to have some prerequisite experience for some of the classes?   2. Why would anyone want to take a class that didn't give you some kind of credit or certification? (Personal interest, no pressure of grades.)   3. What are some other reasons to take a class, other than for the learning? (Social.)

Extension Activities:

1. Locate a brochure of classes that are available in your community. Discuss the types of classes that are offered.   2. What type of class might students be interested in taking that is not on any of the existing lists? How might a person go about getting a class started?

Evaluation:

1. What type of class might someone who is very artistic be interested in?   2. What type of class might someone who likes sports be interested in?

12.9   Taking Classes

Directions:

Use the sample class schedule to answer the following questions about community classes.

Class No.	Name of Class	Meets	Prerequisites
107	Introduction to Gardening	Mon. 6–7 p.m.	None
110	French Cooking	Wed. 6:30–9:30 p.m.	None
274	Advanced Yoga Techniques	Tues. and Thurs. 7–8 p.m.	Introduction to Yoga
306	Ceramics for Fun	Sat. 9:30–11 a.m.	None
319	Watercolor II	Thurs. 7–8 p.m.	Watercolor I

1. If you were interested in art, what class or classes might appeal to you? _____

2. If you liked to cook, but didn't know anything about cooking, would any of these classes be helpful to you?

   _____

3. If you worked evenings, what class might be best for you? _____

4. If you were interested in yoga, what class might be appealing to you? _____

5. If you liked flowers, what class might be interesting to you? _____

6. If you were free only on Thursday nights, what class could you take? _____

7. If you were interested in learning to speak Italian, is there a class you could take? _____

8. What classes could you take if you had never taken a community class before? _____

Chapter 13

Money Skills

13.1 What Is a Budget?

Objective:

The student will be able to explain the following terms as they relate to a budget: *earned income, deductions, fixed expenses*, and *flexible expenses.*

Comments:

Understanding the purpose of a budget and how to devise one that will work for the individual is a harder task than it seems. Many of us have the tendency to spend everything that comes in—and more! In this lesson, students are introduced to some basic terms that relate to devising a budget.

Introductory Activities:

1. Ask students how many of them get an allowance or get money from working either at a job or for doing specific chores.   2. Have students volunteer to tell about how they allocate the money they receive.   3. Ask students to help come up with a definition for the term budget. (A plan for what you will do with income and expenses.)   4. Provide definitions for the following terms:

Income—money that comes in or is earned

Expenses—money that you must pay out

Fixed expenses—payments that are always the same amount of money; predictable

Flexible expenses—payouts of money that can change; they are not always the same amount

Deductions—money that is taken out of a paycheck to go to other designated sources (such as taxes or insurance)

Activity:

With teacher assistance, students are to familiarize themselves with terms on the worksheet "What Is a Budget?" as they relate to money and budgeting. Students are then to categorize the terms into one of four categories—earned income, deductions, fixed expenses, and flexible expenses. The number of answers under each category is shown by the number of lines.

Be sure that students understand the following definitions of the worksheet terms to help them make their selections:

a. Money that is usually taken out of a paycheck to pay for federal services
b. Money that is earned by working more than the usual number of hours
c. Expenses that go toward buying and maintaining clothing
d. Money that is usually deducted for state services
e. How much money a person earns each hour
f. The amount of money paid each month (usually) for a car
g. Taxes that are usually deducted from a paycheck to go toward the person's retirement or other work-related benefits
h. Payment for phone calls and services
i. Money paid toward a house (mortgage)
j. Money that is not from working, but still provides ability to buy things
k. Utilities (often a fixed expense)

l. Expenses incurred from traveling by car

m. Expenses that go toward running a house; for example, getting your carpets cleaned, mowing the grass, home repairs, and so on

n. Amount of money spent on either eating out or groceries

o. Expenses for leisure activities such as movies, roller skating, and so on

p. Money that is taken (usually from a paycheck) to go toward membership in a union, which is an organization that works to improve conditions of the members

Answers (Vary according to different conditions in your area): 1. Earned income: b, e, j   2. Deductions: a, d, g, p   3. Fixed expenses: f, i, k   4. Flexible expenses: c, h, m, n, l, o

Discussion:

Discuss why the items under each category would be an example of that category. In some cases, fixed and flexible items might differ.

1. What are other deductions sometimes taken directly from a paycheck? (Insurance, automatic payments, savings, and so on.)

2. If you were trying to tighten your budget, what area(s) would you concentrate on first? Why? (Probably flexible expenses, because you would have more control over those items.)

3. Why would the cost of flexible items go up or down? (Seasonal considerations, one-time purchases, and so on.)

4. How would a budget help you in planning for your expenses? (You would be able to decide ahead of time how much money you wanted to put toward something.)

5. How would a budget help you account for where your money goes? (You can see exactly how much is spent in each category.)

6. Do you think savings is an important part of a budget? Why? (Yes! Prepare for emergencies, plan for something you will need to pay for later.)

7. When would be a good time to make a budget? (When your income stabilizes or has changed.)

Extension Activities:

1. Have students find or think of other budgets other than personal and family budgets, such as school corporation, the U.S. government, local parks and recreation department, and so on. How is the money allocated?   2. Have students interview their parents about a budget. What guidelines do they use? What does most of the money go for? What percentage goes for housing and food? Do they have a savings plan?

Evaluation:

1. What is the purpose of a budget?   2. Give an example of income.   3. Give an example of a fixed expense.   4. Give an example of a flexible expense.   5. Give an example of a deduction.

13.1

What Is a Budget?

Directions:

The following is a list of terms that have something to do with earning and spending money. Assign each term to only one category below.

a. Federal taxes

b. Overtime pay

c. Clothing

d. State taxes

e. Hourly wages

f. Car payment

g. Social Security

h. Phone bill

i. House payment

j. Money from gifts

k. Electric and water bill

l. Gas for car

m. Household expenses

n. Food

o. Recreation expenses

p. Union dues

Earned Income

_____

_____

_____

Deductions

_____

_____

_____

_____

Fixed Expenses

_____

_____

_____

Flexible Expenses

_____   _____

_____   _____

_____   _____

13.2 Making a Budget

Objective:

The student will complete a suggested budget by calculating the percentage of money designated for each of several categories.

Comments:

Budgets can and should be tailored to fit the needs and goals of the individual. What is important (or necessary) for one person may have little or no value for another. In this lesson, students are given guidelines to complete a budget.

Introductory Activities:

1. Have students estimate how much money they have for income each month. (This may be based on allowance, working part-time, savings designated for spending, and so on.)   2. Have students prioritize at least three to five items they would include in a personal budget.

Activity:

Students are to complete a fictitious budget, based on a monthly income of $2,000. Using the questions and guidelines on the worksheet "Making a Budget," students should be able to calculate the percentage for each category. One point that students need to understand is converting a percentage to a decimal for ease in multiplication. Make sure that students follow the example.

Materials: pen or pencil, calculator

Answers: 1. $24,000   2. $1,320   3. $700   4. $175   5. $70   6. $105   7. $70   8. $70   9. $70   10. $49   11. $35   12. $35   13. $21

Discussion:

Have students share other "tricks" or ways to multiply to make finding the percentages easier.

1. Why is it important, when making a budget, to work with take-home pay rather than the gross (total) amount? (That is the "disposable" income; the rest is never seen.)   2. Why is it helpful to use percentages when making a budget? (Shows relative amounts of money designated to each account.)   3. What percentage do you think you spend most of your money on?   4. What do you think takes up most of people's money? (Probably housing.)

Extension Activities:

1. Invite a banker to speak to the class or obtain some typical personal finance information. What percentages are common or suggested for the main categories?   2. Have students make a personal budget. What categories should they include? How much money can they allocate to each? Then have them try it out for a month and make adjustments as necessary. Evaluate how well they estimated costs!

Evaluation:

Fred's paycheck is $3,500 for the month. His deductions total $1,200. His fixed and flexible expenses were exactly the same this month. How much would he spend on each? ($1,150.)

13.2   Making a Budget

Directions: Use this planning sheet to help Ed make a personal budget. He makes $2,000 a month (before deductions). Write your answers on the lines. Use the back of this sheet for your work.

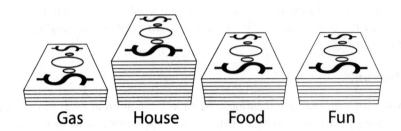

Gas   House   Food   Fun

1. What is Ed's yearly pay? _____

2. If his deductions total $680, how much does Ed bring home each month? _____

3. Ed has several fixed expenses. His apartment costs $550 a month and utilities (water and electricity) are $70 a month. How much is left now? _____

Ed would like to budget the remaining amount of his money. He wants to designate a certain percentage for each of the following categories. Remember that a percent can be changed to a decimal for ease in figuring out the dollar amount.

Example: 25% would be × .25; 15% would be × .15; and so on.

Expense Category	Percentage	Dollar Amount
4. Food	25%	_____
5. Clothing	10%	_____
6. Car/transportation	15%	_____
7. Household expenses	10%	_____
8. Savings	10%	_____
9. Church and charity	10%	_____
10. Phone	7%	_____
11. Medical and dental	5%	_____
12. Charge cards	5%	_____
13. Recreation	3%	_____

13.3 Paying Interest

Objective:

The student will calculate how much interest is added to a purchase in given situations.

Comments:

When people borrow money, especially from a bank or other commercial loan institution, usually a certain amount of interest is added to the transaction. In this lesson, students are introduced to the terms *principal* and *interest* and are given situations in which they must calculate how much money is added to the purchase price when interest is involved.

Introductory Activities:

1. Ask students to lend you $10.00 in cash. Tell them that you'll pay the money back sometime next week. Wait to see how many of them want to add a "service charge" or interest to the loan. 2. Ask students for their ideas about why people or banks charge interest when money is borrowed (for the privilege of using someone else's money for awhile).   3. Define *principal* (the main amount borrowed).   4. Define *interest* (a charge—usually a percentage—added to the amount borrowed).

Activity:

Be sure students understand how to convert percentage to a decimal for purposes of multiplying (principal times interest) to find the total amount to be repaid. In the examples on the worksheet "Paying Interest," they will need to convert 4 percent, 7 percent, 8 percent, and 10 percent to .04, .07, .08, and .10 (which will be multiplied by the principal amount).

Materials: pen or pencil, calculator

Answers: 1. p = $6,500, i = $260, t = $6,760   2. p = $35, i = $3.50, t = $38.50
3. p = $10,000, i = $800, t = 10,800   4. p = $18,500, i = $1295, t = 19,795

Discussion:

Go over the problems on the worksheet, making sure that students understand how to solve the problems and can make corrections if they get an incorrect answer.

1. Why is it important to find out the interest rate when purchasing something? (It adds significantly to the price.)   2. Would it ever be cheaper to buy an item with a higher purchase price but with a lower interest rate? (Maybe; you'd have to compare to figure out the bottom line each way.) 3. What are some items you would buy or transactions you would make that will probably have interest added? (Cars, credit cards, loans, mortgage, and so on.)   4. How is interest different from just having a service charge added to the cost of something? (The longer the money is borrowed, the more interest is paid; a service charge might not be so high or so profitable for the bank.)

Extension Activities:

1. Have students collect examples of sales ads in which interest is charged on the items; for example, cars, other vehicles, furniture or appliances with interest waived for a certain period, and so on. Figure out the total cost if the amount is financed for a year.   2. Make a poster comparing the actual cost of one item with different interest rates.   3. Find out the percentage charged on several major credit cards.

Evaluation:

Pretend you have borrowed $1,350 for a new snowmobile. You must pay back the loan plus 9 percent interest.

1. What is the amount of the principal? ($1,350)   2. What is the amount of interest to pay back? ($121.50)   3. What is the total amount of money you will have to repay? ($1,471.50)

13.3   **Paying Interest**

Directions:

Read the following situations. Figure out the principal, the amount of interest paid, and the total amount that must be repaid. Use the space below each problem for your work.

1. Tom borrowed $6,500 to buy a used car. He must pay 4 percent interest.

    Principal _____ Interest _____ Total _____

2. Elana borrowed $35 from her sister to buy some jeans. Her sister wants her to pay back the loan with 10 percent interest.

    Principal _____ Interest _____ Total _____

3. Mr. and Mrs. Martinez borrowed $10,000 to take a vacation in the Rocky Mountains. The bank charges them 8 percent interest.

    Principal _____ Interest _____ Total _____

4. Juan borrowed $18,500 to make a down payment on a house. He must pay back 7 percent interest.

    Principal _____ Interest _____ Total _____

13.4 "On Sale"

Objective:

The student will calculate the sale price of a given item.

Comments:

Buying "on sale" can result in substantial savings. Students can benefit from being able to figure out the sale price of items they are interested in purchasing. In this lesson, students are given the task of calculating the price of an item that has been marked down or is on sale.

Introductory Activities:

1. Have students discuss what items they are interested in at the moment that are on sale. What are they, and where is the sale?   2. Have students offer what would be considered a good sale price for some common items such as a popular compact disc, personal computer, designer jeans, a perm, and a video game. What would be the regular full-price cost of these items?

Activity:

Students are given two items on the worksheet "On Sale." The original price and the amount of the discount (percentage or fraction) are given. Students are to figure out the sale price. Make sure students remember how to use percentages (multiply by the equivalent decimal) and equivalent fractions (1/2 = 50% = .50; 1/3 = 33% = .33). Make sure students realize there are *two steps* involved in these examples—they must calculate the amount of the discount and subtract it from the original price!

Materials: pen or pencil, calculator

Answers: 1. $8.00, $72.00   2. $18.50, $55.50

Discussion:

Students may have some trouble with the mathematical calculations on these problems. If so, provide them with a helpful chart (perhaps on the board?) that shows the specific steps for solving these problems: (1) What is the original price? (2) What is the amount of the discount? Use decimals! (3) Subtract the discount from the original price. If necessary, provide a chart of common equivalences between fractions and decimals.

1. In problem 1, why is it relatively easy to figure out a 10 percent discount?   2. In problem 2, there is a half-price sale. Why do you need to know the price of both sweaters in order to figure out what each sweater would cost? (To find out what each one would cost, you must add the original prices of both, subtract half the price of one, then divide the result by 2.)   3. Why do stores have sales? (To get rid of old merchandise, get people to come to the store, promote other items, and so on.)   4. What are some items that go on sale seasonally? (Snowmobiles, swimsuits, coats, and so on.) 5. What are the pros and cons of waiting to buy something until it is on sale? (*Pro*: get a good price; *con*: not such a good selection, what you want might be gone.)   6. If something is sold "as is," how is that different from "on sale"? (Probably damaged.)

Extension Activities:

1. Have students walk through a mall and take an informal inventory of what is on sale. How do the stores promote their sale items?   2. Have students become detectives. Search for the same item that is sold in several different stores (for example, a two-liter bottle of soda, item of clothing). What is

the range of prices for the item? What is the average price? What is the best sale price?   3. Have students visit an outlet mall or store if there is one near you. Compare prices. What is the approximate discount for buying something that is "irregular" or not of the same quality?

Evaluation:

You are in a shoe store where there is a "buy one, get one at 1/2 price" sale. The shoes you like cost $35.00.

1. How much would the second pair cost? ($17.50)   2. What would your total cost be? ($52.50)

13.4 "On Sale"

Directions:

The following items are on sale! The regular prices are shown as well as the amount of the discount. For each problem, figure out the sale price. Use the bottom of this page for your work.

1.

REG. PRICE 80^{00}

10% OFF

Discount: _____
Sale Price: _____

2.

BUY ONE , GET ONE AT 1/2 PRICE

37^{00}

Discount: _____
Sale Price: _____

3.

THIS RACK 25% OFF

REG. PRICE 18^{00}

Discount: _____
Sale Price: _____

4.

14 K GOLD JEWELERY

EVERYTHING $\frac{1}{3}$ OFF

$27 $18 $36

Discount: _____
Sale Price: _____

13.5 Unit Pricing

Objective:

Given several examples, the student will be able to identify the unit used and the unit price.

Comments:

When is a "deal" a real deal? Although some buys may sound good, it is not until you really know what you are actually getting for your money that you can decide if it is truly a good purchase. In this lesson, students are introduced to the concept of figuring out the cost of an item based on the unit price—how much one ounce, one pound, one gallon, and so on, costs.

Introductory Activities:

1. Tell students that you have a deal for them—they can either have five cans of soda for $3.75 or a twelve-pack for $6.00. Which is the better deal? Why? (The unit price on the first is 75 cents, the second is 50 cents.)   2. Have students explain how they figured out which was the better buy. Ideally, they will understand that it boils down to how much you would have to pay for a single can.
3. Define *unit pricing* (the price for only one of a group of items).

Activity:

On the worksheet "Unit Pricing," students are to figure out what unit is being purchased (one can of soup, one candy bar, and so on) and the price for one item. Students may need a calculator to solve the problems. Be sure students have the unit correctly identified. Also, explain how you want the answer written if it does not come out evenly (for example, three cans for $1.00 would probably be 33 cents; .6666 would be rounded off to .67).   *Materials:* pen or pencil, calculator   *Answers:* 1. One can, 33 cents 2. One folder, 25 cents   3. One pizza, $4.00   4. One CD, $11.67   5. One candy bar, 24 cents   6. One gallon, $1.15   7. One pair of socks, $2.33   8. One drink, 25 cents

Discussion:

Be sure students understand how the correct answers were reached on the worksheet. Discuss any points of confusion.

1. Why is unit pricing helpful when you are comparing different brands of the same product? (Lets you see exactly how much the item costs when compared equally.)   2. What are some common units used when you buy food items? (Ounce, pound, and so on.)   3. What are some items usually packaged in quantities? (Soda, socks, small cereal packages, notebooks, pencils, gum, soap, and so on.)   4. Why isn't bigger always the best buy? (You might be paying more for each unit.)
5. Should you always get the item with the cheapest unit cost? What other factors should you consider? (Freshness, quality, taste, and so on.)

Extension Activities:

1. Have students bring in and set up a display table of grocery items. Figure out the unit cost of each.
2. Find and bring in items that come in different sizes; for example, cereal boxes, soda cans and bottles. Set up an activity for students to figure the unit cost of each and the better buy.

Evaluation:

Which is the better buy? Why?

    1. Three pads of lined paper, each pad containing 50 sheets, for $3.00   OR   2. 1 Super-Duper pad of lined paper with 250 sheets for $4.25

#2 is the better buy: each sheet is 1.7 cents compared to 2 cents each for #1.

13.5   Unit Pricing

Directions:

For each of the following examples, write the unit that is used and the unit price for each.

1. Chicken noodle soup: three cans for $1.00.

   _____

2. Pocket folders: twelve for $3.00.

   _____

3. Three pizzas for $12.00.

   _____

4. Buy two CDs, get one FREE! Your cost: $35.00.

   _____

5. Bag of candy: six bars for $1.44.

   _____

6. Twenty gallons of gas for $23.00.

   _____

7. Three pairs of socks for $7.00.

   _____

8. Boxed drinks: nine for $2.30.

   _____

13.6 How Much Do Things Cost?

Objective: The student will find out an approximate cost of common items around the house or in everyday situations.

Comments: Prices can vary greatly from store to store, by season, or generic versus name brand. Although there can be some variability, it is a good exercise to have at least a ballpark figure in mind of what some common items cost.

Introductory Activities:

1. Have students estimate what they think these items might cost: new tennis shoes, a hand-held calculator, an ice cream cone, and other items that you are interested in. Record their estimates. Use a local newspaper ad or other references to see how close students' guesses were.
2. Have students list reasons that might affect the cost of an item; for example, the season, special sales, buying in bulk, name brand, and so on.

Activity: The worksheet "How Much Do Things Cost?" will require some research to look up ads or to go to various stores to find out prices. You may want to have students estimate their answer before going out to do field work.

Answers: Will vary greatly.

Discussion: Record different answers on a class chart or graph to get a feel for the range of prices. If there is a lot of variability, you'll want to use an average price.

1. Which items were a lot more expensive than you thought they would be?
2. Were any items cheaper than you expected them to be?
3. Why do you think there is so much price variability on some of the items?
4. What kind of information affects how much something costs? (For example, on item 4 you would need to know the grade of gas; on item 13 you would need to factor in the ingredients for toppings, size, and so on.)

Extension Activities:

1. Play a type of *The Price Is Right* game by showing pictures of common items and having three prices displayed per item. Students must "come on down" and guess the correct price.
2. Have students experiment with a proposed budget of $100. How many pizzas are equivalent to one tire? How many eggs are equivalent to a can of root beer?

Evaluation: What is the approximate price of five common items that you use?

13.6   **How Much Do Things Cost?**

Directions:

Using appropriate sources, find out the cost of these common items listed below.

1. A twelve-pack of root beer _____
2. A tire for a car _____
3. A gallon of milk _____
4. A gallon of gas _____
5. A pair of jeans _____
6. A cell phone _____
7. A bottle of shampoo _____
8. A jar of peanut butter _____
9. A pound of chopmeat _____
10. A pair of socks _____
11. A paperback book _____
12. A bottle of aspirin _____
13. A large pizza from a restaurant _____
14. A haircut _____
15. A dozen eggs _____

13.7 Writing a Check

Objective:

Given the appropriate information, the student will correctly write a sample check.

Comments:

Some students may already have an active checking account; others may want to open one when they have incoming money or need to write checks for purchases. In this lesson, students are introduced to the information required on a check and are given practice in writing sample checks.

Introductory Activities:

1. Have students describe checks they have seen in use. (Personalized checks, humorous checks, checks with cartoons on them, and so on.)   2. Have students list occasions on which they or their parents have written checks. Why was a check used rather than cash or a charge? 3. Draw or make a large blank check for purposes of demonstration. Include blanks for: (1) the date, (2) the party to whom the check is written, (3) the dollar amount in numbers, (4) the amount in words, (5) signature, and (6) memo or purpose. Explain the purpose of each and demonstrate how each is used.

Activity:

Students will fill in blank checks on this worksheet with information given on each item. This includes who the check is written to, the date, the amount, and a signature.

Discussion:

Look over students' checks to make sure all information is filled out properly. Answer any questions about the checks.

1. How is using a check convenient for many people? (Don't have to carry cash, can keep track of spending, and so on.)   2. What types of places will usually take a check? (Grocery stores, department stores, gas stations, and so on.)   3. What identification is sometimes required to write or cash a check? (Driver's license, credit card.)   4. What happens if you write a check and don't have enough money in your account to cover it? (It will "bounce" or be returned with a substantial service charge added.)   5. What is a "blank check"? (A check that is signed but the amount is not filled in.)

Extension Activities:

1. Invite a banker to speak to the class or obtain literature from a local bank about opening a checking account. Find out what options are available for the customer. Is a minimum balance required? How much does it cost to maintain the account? List other questions.   2. Almost every interest group has a series of checks that appeal to them. Collect cancelled checks and display them.

Evaluation:

1. What are two benefits of using a checking account?   2. Use a blank check provided and write a check to your teacher for $100. Be sure to spell his or her name correctly! After your work is checked, void the check by writing "VOID" across it.

Name _____ **Date** _____

13.7   Writing a Check

Directions:

Use the blank checks on the next sheet to write checks for the following amounts and purposes. Look at the example for help. Use today's date.

1. Write a check to the Hobby Castle for $9.93 for a model airplane.

2. Write a check to Ms. Beamon for $17.54 for the class cookie sale.

3. Write a check to Friendly Fones for $39.00 for a new bedroom phone.

4. Write a check to Towne Outlet Store for $52.30 for school supplies.

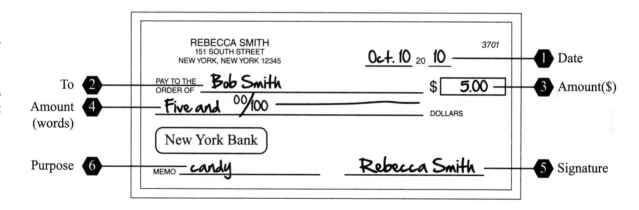

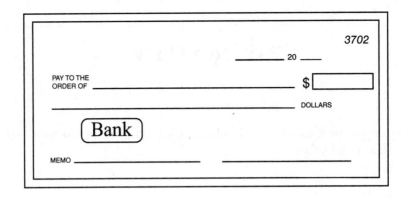

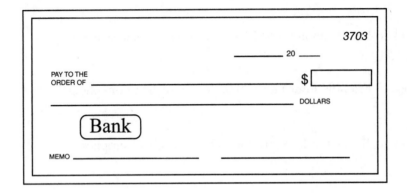

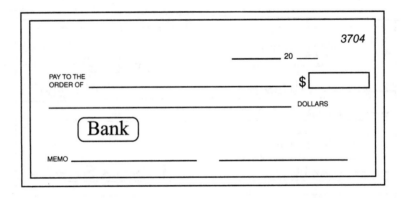

13.8 Maintaining a Checking Account

Objective:

The student will be able to correctly enter sample checks into a checking account ledger.

Comments:

Not only must students know how to fill out a check, but they must also learn to keep careful accounting records of how much money they have in the checking account. In this lesson, students are given a fabricated checking record to enter into a ledger.

Introductory Activities:

1. Have students raise their hands if they have a checking account.
2. Have students raise their hands if they would like to have a checking account.
3. Ask students to list some responsibilities they would have to live up to if they had a checking account. (Maintaining accuracy, making sure they have the money in the account.)

Activity:

Using the worksheet "Maintaining a Checking Account," students are to complete a checkbook register based on having an opening balance of $150.00 and subsequently subtracting checks and a service charge and adding a deposit. You may wish to go through the first check notation in the register together as an example.

Materials: pen or pencil, calculator

Answers:

The register should resemble the following:

Check no.	Date	Transaction	✓	150.00
101	10/1/10	Fred's Discount Shop		−8.89
		(balance)		141.11
102	10/1/10	Polly's Pizza		−15.42
		(balance)		125.69
103	10/2/10	Northfield High School		−17.00
		(balance)		108.69
104	void			
105	10/3/10	Harvell Oil Company		−40.30
		(balance)		68.39

Dep.	10/3/10	Paycheck	+150.00
		(balance)	218.39
106	10/4/10	Mrs. Violet Chandler	−10.50
		(balance)	207.89
Serv. Ch.	10/5/10		−8.00
		(balance)	199.89

Discussion:

Make sure students understand how to maintain the register and answer any questions they have about doing the math. Students may ask about the column with the check mark. Many people use this to reconcile their checks by placing a check mark in the column after the bank has cashed and returned the check.

1. How often do you think you should make sure your math is accurate? (After every few checks at least.)

2. How could you check your math? (Use a calculator.)

3. How could you use monthly bank statements to make sure your records are accurate? (Check your balance with the balance that the statement shows; after subtracting the checks that have not been cashed already.)

4. What do you think are some common sources of error? (Not lining up the decimal point, forgetting to subtract an amount, just making mathematical mistakes; for example, when the amount you are out of balance is divisible evenly by 9, chances are that you have transposed two numbers, such as writing "94" instead of "49.")

5. What should you do if you make a mistake on a check? (Write "void" across it, or if it is a minor error you can correct it and put your initial next to the correction.)

6. Sometimes there is a service charge as a penalty added if you do not have enough money in your account and the check "bounces." How could you avoid this? (Some banks have overdraft protection; better yet, make it a habit to update your balance each time you make a deposit or withdrawal, so you always know exactly how much money is in your account.)

Extension Activities:

1. Obtain examples of typical monthly bank statements. Have students figure out what information is contained on it and how this could help make sure their personal banking records are accurate.

2. Compare the features of checking accounts at two or three local banks. Find out which would be the best for students to start out with. Find out the policy for being overdrawn, overdraft protection, and any other relevant features.

Evaluation:

You open a checking account with a deposit of $100.00. Your first check is written for $37.92. What is your balance? ($62.08.)

13.8   Maintaining a Checking Account

Directions: Complete the following register from your checking account. Give yourself a starting balance of $150.00.

1. Write check #101 on 10/1/10 to Fred's Discount Shop for $8.89.
2. Write check #102 on 10/1/10 to Polly's Pizza for $15.42.
3. Write check #103 on 10/2/10 to Northfield High School for $17.00.
4. Void check #104—you made a mistake in the amount.
5. Write check #105 on 10/3/10 to Harvell Oil Company for $40.30.
6. Deposit $150.00 on 10/3/10. Note that this was a paycheck.
7. Write check #106 on 10/4/10 to Mrs. Violet Chandler for $10.50.
8. Subtract a service charge of $8.00 on 10/5/10.

Check no.	Date	Transaction	✓	150.00

13.9 What Is a Savings Account?

Comments:

Students may have had a savings account established for them when they were young and might continue to put money into this account. In this lesson, some features of a savings account are discussed and it is compared to a checking account.

Introductory Activities:

1. Have students raise their hands if they have a savings account. Ask when the account was first established. Some may have opened an account when they began working; others may have had an account opened for them by a parent when they were children. Share experiences.
2. Write "savings account" and "checking account" on the board and ask students to tell what they know about similarities and differences between these kinds of accounts.

Activity:

Students are to decide if each description on the worksheet "What Is a Savings Account" applies to a savings account, a checking account, or both.

Answer: 1. C, S   2. C, S   3. C   4. C   5. C   6. S   7. C   8. C, S   9. C   10. C

Discussion:

1. Why do you think many people have both types of accounts? (Want to pay bills from one, not draw from the savings.)
2. What are some goals or items that people might save for over a long period of time? (College education, home, vacation.)

Extension Activity:

What are some ways to get a better interest rate than a typical savings account offers?

Evaluation:

1. List one way a savings account is different from a checking account.
2. List one way they are the same.

13.9   # What Is a Savings Account?

Directions:

Read the following descriptions of the bank account. Write "C" if it could refer to a checking account. Write "S" if it could refer to a savings account. Both will be true for some of the items.

_____   1. You can deposit money into this account.

_____   2. You can take money out of this account.

_____   3. You usually get a better interest rate.

_____   4. You can write checks from this account.

_____   5. You probably would use this account quite often.

_____   6. If you had a large amount of money and weren't planning to spend it soon, you'd use this account.

_____   7. You have to maintain a minimum balance.

_____   8. You get a statement each month indicating how much money you have in the account.

_____   9. You may have to pay a service charge if you don't have a high enough balance.

_____ 10. You would use this account if you have a lot of bills to pay every month.

13.10 Credit Cards

Objective:

The student will use a sample credit card to answer information about its use.

Comments:

It is getting easier and easier for students to obtain credit cards. Unfortunately, the benefits seem to overshadow the risks that can be involved with easy credit. In this lesson, students are given a sample credit card and are asked to answer questions about its use.

Introductory Activities:

1. Have students list the names of familiar major credit cards. 2. Have students tell the percentage of interest charged on credit cards that they or their parents have or cards that have been advertised. 3. Have students figure out how much interest would have to be paid in a year on a balance of $4,890 if the interest rate was 22 percent ($1,075.80). Does this seem like a lot?

Activity:

Have students examine the information about the sample credit card on the worksheet "Credit Cards." Explain what the numbers refer to.

Credit limit—how much you can charge on the account

Annual percentage rate—the amount of interest charged annually on the balance of the credit card account

Annual fee—how much you pay each year for the privilege of having the card

Valid dates—when you first got the card and when it will expire

Account number—the sixteen-digit number that is the number of your account on this card

Answers: 1. 5231 0004 7586 3268 2. $10,000 3. $17.90 4. Once a year 5. August 2014 6. General Card 7. $209 8. $375 + 67.13 = $442.13 (rounded off)

Discussion:

Make sure students can calculate the interest rate (some numbers are rounded up). Answer any questions they have about the worksheet.

1. How is the use of a credit card helpful? (Convenient, gives you extra time for payment.) 2. How is use of a credit card more flexible than using a check? (You can spend money that you don't actually have yet; some places will take credit cards but not checks.) 3. What should you be aware of before running up a huge credit card bill? (How much the interest charges will add to your bill.)

Extension Activities:

1. Have students collect and compare features of having a major credit card. Compare items such as the annual fee, percentage rate of interest, other benefits, and so on. You may want to have students draw enlargements of the cards and list the features on posters. 2. Have students make a list of fifty local stores or nearby places that will accept a credit card.

Evaluation:

Write a paragraph listing several pros and cons of using a credit card for purchases.

13.10   Credit Cards

Directions:

Look at the sample credit card, then answer the questions.

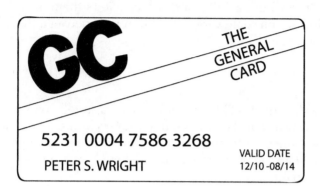

Credit limit: $10,000
Annual percentage rate: 17.9%
Annual fee: $50.00

1. What is the account number on this credit card?

2. How much can you charge on this card?

3. If you charged $100, how much interest would you have to pay in a year?

4. How often do you have to pay the $50 fee?

5. When does this card expire?

6. What type of credit card (name) is this?

7. If your balance is $219 and you have to make a minimum payment of $10, what would your new balance be (before interest is added)?

8. If your balance is $375, what would you owe after you figure out the interest you are being charged?

13.11 Using Debit and Credit Cards and ATMs

Objective:

The student will identify the most likely bank card to be used in a transaction.

Comments:

Older students may have access to cards that are linked to a bank, such as a debit card (which may also have the option of being used as a credit card) or an ATM card (which allows them to access cash that is linked to a bank account). This lesson focuses on some very basic differences between the bank cards and which are most appropriate for certain situations.

Introductory Activities:

1. Display a debit card, a credit card, and an ATM card. Ask students to tell you what they already know about the differences. On the board, make three columns for each card and list a few features; for example, **debit card**—takes money directly from your bank account, operates like a check; **credit card**—allows you to get something now and pay for it later, charges interest; **ATM**—allows you to get cash from your bank account.

2. For emphasis, tie or attach a ribbon or small rope to each card. Explain that the money that comes from each of these cards is not *free* money, but it is attached to a bank. It might be a local bank that services their checking or savings account, or in the case of a major charge card, it might be a bigger financial institution. Emphasize that no matter which card is used, the actual money comes from an account that they are maintaining.

Activity:

Keeping the visual display in front of the students, explain that they are going to use the worksheet "Using Debit/Credit Cards and ATMs" to try to figure out which card would be the best for each situation.

Answers (May vary, but go with general guidelines): 1. Credit   2. ATM   3. Debit   4. Debit   5. Credit   6. Trinity—debit; Zoe—ATM   7. Credit   8. ATM

Discussion:

1. Discuss each response and talk about how the selected card would help the student in his or her situation.

2. For the credit card answers (#1, #5, #7), discuss alternatives to help those students get what they want without using a credit card.

3. Are there situations in which using credit is the best or the only choice?

Extension Activities:

1. Anyone who has ever been in credit card debt can attest to the down side of being in that position (high interest rates, years of making minimum payments, and so on). Invite a financial counselor to speak to your class about alternatives to using a credit card, or using a prefunded card that operates like a credit card but has a preset limit.

2. Discuss some "emergency situations" in which using a credit card might be a good or necessary option, such as running out of gas in a car when you are in a new place, needing to sign up for a course right away, ordering something online, establishing identity, or finding something on sale that is just the right color!

Evaluation:

Give an example of a time when you would probably use each of the following:

1. A credit card
2. A debit card
3. An ATM card

13.11   Using Debit and Credit Cards and ATMs

Directions: These people are using cards to do their transactions. Circle **D** (for Debit), **C** (for Credit), or **ATM** to indicate which kind of card is being used.

1. Blake wants to buy a new bike, but he doesn't have enough money in his checking account. He will use a card to cover the full amount and pay it back as he can every month.

    D   C   ATM

2. Amy wants to go to a movie and have a pizza afterward with some friends. She only has $5 with her, so she wants to get some cash so she can pay for her evening activities. Which card will she use?

    D   C   ATM

3. Owen doesn't like to carry any money with him. He likes a small, thin wallet so he only has one card. He stopped at a bookstore to buy a book, but it is a small amount and he doesn't want to have to put the purchase on a charge card.

    D   C   ATM

4. Michelle always forgets to check her balance in her checking account, but she knows that every time she makes a purchase using this card she can check on the computer to see how much she spent and view her balance. She can also keep a receipt from each transaction that shows how much she spent.

    D   C   ATM

5. Aiden didn't know how much it would cost to go shopping for new clothes. He doesn't want to subtract money right away from his checking account, so he is using this card.

    D   C   ATM

6. Trinity and Zoe went roller skating and wanted to pay for their skates. Trinity handed her card to the cashier to pay by having money taken directly out of her checking account. Zoe used a card at a machine at the skating rink to get cash from her checking account. Which cards did they use?

    (Trinity) **D   C   ATM**   (Zoe) **D   C   ATM**

7. Devin wanted to buy a new stereo for his car. It was on sale, but it was still quite expensive, and he knows that he would need to work for a few months before he can pay for it. What card did he use?

    D   C   ATM

8. Jada's gas tank is almost on empty. She went to the gas station to get some money to fill up the car. What card did she use?

    D   C   ATM

13.12 How Much Money Will You Need?

Objective:

The student will estimate the amount of money needed for several items or situations, rounded to $5, $20, $100, or $500.

Comments:

Does a trip to Hawaii cost $100 or $1,000? Students may only have a vague idea of the price tags of some of their dreams. In reality, we need to know the cost—the real cost—of everyday activities, services, or items. Wild guesses won't work. In this lesson, students are given practice in categorizing items or services into one of four monetary categories.

Introductory Activities:

1. Ask students what they could buy with $1,000,000? (That's "a million.") They might answer "anything," but that is not true. Some people have garages that cost more than that! Keep a list of student guesses for research on the Extension Activities below.   2. Ask students (if appropriate) to talk about the most expensive purchase that they have made in the last week. What is the highest dollar transaction that students are familiar with?

Activity:

On the worksheet "How Much Money Will You Need?" the students are going to estimate the category that each item or service on the list would probably fall within. There may be some exceptions or qualifications—don't make that the issue here.   *Answers (May vary):* 1. B   2. A   3. D   4. B   5. B   6. D   7. C   8. D   9. C   10. B   11. C   12. C   13. C   14. D   15. C

Discussion:

Go over student responses and explain that these are just approximate categories—yes, you probably can get a video for 99 cents, but the lowest category is $5.

1. Why is it important to have some idea of how much something costs before you buy it? (Plan your budget, make adjustments.)   2. Were you surprised at how much any of these things cost? 3. Why do you think some people don't want to buy things on sale or during certain seasons? (They have the money, they need to get something immediately.)   4. When you know the cost of something ahead of time, how would that help you in your plan to get something that you want? (You have the goal.)

Extension Activities:

1. Use the Internet or other resources to find out an actual cost of owning dream toys such as a private jet, an island in the Pacific, a Rolls-Royce, and so on. Or, reverse the search and find out what you can buy with $1,000,000 and make a list.   2. Some items continue to need financial support or upkeep after the initial purchase (pets, appliances, cars, and so on). Go through the items on the worksheet to determine additional costs that one would have to consider. Can you go bowling without buying something to eat? Or buy jeans without a new sweatshirt?

Evaluation:

List one thing or service that you could purchase for:

$5_____ $20_____ $100_____ $500_____

13.12 **How Much Money Will You Need?**

Directions:

Circle the answer that is a good estimate of how much money would be needed for each of the following situations.

A = About $5   B = About $20   C = About $100   D = About $500

_____ 1. Buying a new hardcover book

_____ 2. Renting one video

_____ 3. Buying a brand-new bike

_____ 4. Taking a large pizza with three toppings

_____ 5. Playing a few games of bowling

_____ 6. Buying a new kitchen table with four chairs

_____ 7. Going to Walt Disney World for one day

_____ 8. Flying to a popular vacation spot

_____ 9. Buying a new iPod

_____ 10. Buying pair of jeans on sale

_____ 11. Buying small refrigerator for your room

_____ 12. Buying set of leather-bound classic books

_____ 13. Adopting puppy from the animal shelter

_____ 14. Buying original oil painting from a gallery

_____ 15. Tickets to a Broadway show

13.13 Making Change

Objective:

The student will be able to count out correct change for purchases under $20.

Comments:

Many businesses have cash registers that automatically provide the correct change for purchases. Counting out change is not a lost need, however; small businesses and informal situations (such as working the hotdog stand at a high school sporting event) still require the ability to make change. Learning to "count back" money efficiently requires practice and thinking.

Introductory Activities:

1. When was the last time you bought something and needed change back? (School cafeteria? Drug store?) Did the clerk dump the money into your hand or count it back to you?
2. Divide students into small groups. Have them each write down how they would give change in these situations:

Money owed	Money given	Type of coins
$1.45	$2.00	N, Q, Q
$3.70	$5.00	N, Q, $1
$.52	$5.00	P, P, P, N, D, D, D, D, $1,$1,$1,$1

In these situations, how did they come up with the most efficient way to give change? (Get to the nearest nickel/dollar, look for ways to group small coins, and so on.) Have students explain "tricks" or strategies that helped them. Counting back entirely in pennies will get the right answer, but is not a workable strategy. *Think:* efficiency!

Ideas: getting to the first (closest) dollar is the trickiest part; after that it's easier; start with pennies to get to the nearest 0 or 5, then you can use larger coins.

Don't worry about what "equivalences" you use—for example, using four dimes instead of one quarter, one dime, and one nickel is still 40 cents; use whatever you are comfortable with (within reason).

Activity:

There are two ways to provide change: counting back the balance, or using a calculator to find out the difference. In most cases, counting back is quicker, but if using a calculator works and is acceptable for a student/business, that is a great alternative. However, the student still has to count back the amount on the calculator correctly.

On the worksheet "Making Change," the students are to count back change using coins and dollars. There may be more than one answer, as some coin equivalences are interchangeable.

Answers (Will vary):

1. Q.
2. P, P, N, D, Q, Q, $1.
3. The penny eliminates the .01 right away; D, $1, $1.

4. P, P, Q, $1, $1, $1.
5. P, P, P, D.
6. P, D, Q, Q, $1, $1, $1, $5, $10.
7. The $5 bill takes care of the $5; that just leaves .50—Q, Q.
8. N, Q, $1, $5, $10.
9. P, P, N, D, Q, Q, $1, $1, $5.
10. P, P, P, N, D, D, D, D, $1, $1, $1.

Discussion:

Some students will struggle with making change by counting back and will have to resort to other techniques or aids if this is something they have to do.

1. In what situations do you need to know how to count back money? (Job, receiving change.)
2. Why is it a good idea to check your change when you make a purchase? (Make sure you got the right amount back.)
3. If you have trouble counting out change, what are some things you can do to help yourself? (Make a chart of common equivalences, carry a pocket calculator.)

Extension Activities:

1. Practice, practice, practice. The website www.mathplayground.com/making_change.html, already referenced for another topic (10.7, Using Computers for Math Information), is also a good practice resource for making change.
2. Provide frequent practice in giving change to the nearest dollar, as this is the first step in making change. Basically, you are setting up situations such as this: How do you get from 89 to 100 using coin equivalences? Answer: Penny, dime.
3. Use math money rulers to help students visualize the "steps" or coins that will help them:

   Q: 0, 25, 50, 75, 100
   D: 10, 20, 30, 40, 50, 60, 70, 80, 90, 100
   N: 5, 10, 15, 20, 25, 30, 35, 40, 45, 50, 55, 60, 65, 70, 75, 80, 85, 90, 95, 100

Evaluation:

What change would you provide for the following situations?

1. The customer gives you a $10 bill. The meal was $6.50 including taxes and tip.
2. You get a $20 bill from a friend; he wants $15.73 back to pay for a book you bought.

13.13   **Making Change**

Directions:

What coins and bills would be the most efficient to give the correct change in these situations?

Money owed	Money handed to you	Change given
1. $4.75	$5 bill	_____
2. $8.33	$10 bill	_____
3. $2.91	$5 bill and 1 penny	_____
4. $6.73	Two $5 bills	_____
5. 87 cents	Four quarters	_____
6. $1.39	$20	_____
7. $5.50	$5 bill and $1 bill	_____
8. $3.70	$20 bill	_____
9. $12.33	$20 bill	_____
10. $16.52	$20 bill	_____

Chapter 13: Money Skills

Chapter 14

Travel

14.1 Local Transportation

Objective:

The student will describe forms of transportation available in the community.

Comments:

Getting around independently is a worthy goal of any member of a community. Although some students may have bicycles or ride a school bus to get where they want to go, there are usually other modes of transportation that are available and should be investigated. These may include public buses, a subway system, taxis, and so on. In this lesson, students are to target places they frequently go to and note what form of transportation they use.

Introductory Activities:

1. Have students list ways people can get around in their community.   2. Have students put a check mark next to the ways they have used.   3. Have students put a dollar sign ($) next to the ways that cost money.   4. Have students put the letter **A** next to the ways that require an adult's help.

Activity:

Encourage students not to put down the same answer for all items. If necessary, if their first choice tends to be the same, have students put an alternative mode of travel for the items.   *Answer (Will vary)*

Discussion:

If your community is small, many students probably get around by foot or on a bike, or with the help of an adult driver. Encourage students to think about alternative modes of transportation. Is there a public bus system that could get them around? Do they ever carpool with a friend's parents? Look for alternatives!

1. Do you feel your town or community has adequate public transportation?
2. Are there any places you would like to be able to get to but can't? Is it because you need an adult, need money, or haven't learned to use that particular transportation system?
3. Do you feel you are able to use public transportation without major problems?
4. How much do you rely on adults or older siblings who drive to get you around?
5. Do you plan to have a car or access to a car when you are old enough? How?
6. Other than going to a friend's house or to school, where do you normally go on a regular basis that requires transportation?

Extension Activities:

1. Have students conduct a survey of their classmates regarding how they travel (a) to school and (b) for fun.   2. Have students compile a list of facts about public transportation in their community. Find out about rates, availability, schedules, and so on.

Evaluation:

1. List three forms of transportation available to you in your community.   2. Describe how each form listed in (1) is used by you and/or by others.

14.1   **Local Transportation**

Directions:

List ten places you go to periodically in your community or have recently visited. How do you get there? Write your answers on the lines.

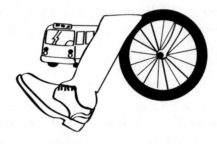

1. _____

2. _____

3. _____

4. _____

5. _____

6. _____

7. _____

8. _____

9. _____

10. _____

14.2 Overnight Travel

Objective:

The student will list several appropriate items that would be needed for specific overnight travel plans.

Comments:

When planning an overnight stay, students need to think about personal items (toothbrush, mouthwash), medication, amount and type of clothing, and any extra items that are specific to the destination (such as a book, fishing equipment, gift).

Introductory Activities:

1. Draw a large suitcase on the board. Give students three minutes to draw or write the name of items that they would take on an overnight trip.   2. Ask students to explain why these items might be important for overnight travel: alarm clock, deodorant, medication, extra socks, snack, iPod, book of crossword puzzles, contact lens solution.

Activity:

On the worksheet "Overnight Travel," students are to list specific items that they would take on an overnight trip with the specific destinations.   *Answers (Will vary):*   1. Pajamas, toothbrush, games, cell phone   2. Warm sweaters, books to read, iPod, lots of socks and underwear, jigsaw puzzle   3. Hiking boots, swimming suit, camera   4. Bug spray, flashlight, inflatable pillow, sleeping bag   5. Games, contact lens solution, pajamas, deodorant   6. Games, videos, appropriate pajamas, sleeping bag, bathrobe

Discussion:

The length of the overnight stay and the destination all affect what items someone should bring.
1. Other than clothes, what other things should you remember to bring when you will be away from home overnight?   2. What other factors do you have to think about when you are going to be gone? (Weather, activities.)

Extension Activities:

1. Find magazine pictures of travel destinations and have students cut them to fit the shape of a suitcase. Glue it onto a sheet of paper so that you can "open" the suitcase. Have students list items that would be specific to that destination.   2. Have students make a "personal overnight travel list" of items that are important for them to have even on a very short stay. The list might include medication, contact lens solution, personal shampoo and conditioner bottles, aspirin, an alarm clock, a retainer container.

Evaluation:

1. What personal items would you need to take with you on a one-night overnight trip?   2. What additional items would you take if you were on a one-week trip?

14.2   **Overnight Travel**

Directions:

List items that you would take for each of the following situations.

1. Spending a Friday night at a friend's house

2. Spending one week at your cousin's home during the winter, in a cottage on a ski slope

3. Flying with your family to a vacation home in the mountains

4. Going on a camping trip with a community group for 3 days

5. Staying with a friend for his/her birthday for an overnight party

6. Going to a group slumber party held in a church gymnasium

14.3 Traveling by Plane

Objective:

The student will use information to solve airline travel situations.

Comments:

Airline travel is a specific type of travel in which the traveler needs to become familiar with the rules and regulations of the airline industry. Some common things to know are: (1) bring proper identification, (2) arrive at least an hour ahead of time, (3) be prepared to remove some clothing items for security, (4) pack as lightly as possible, (5) know what items have to be in a zip-locking bag.

Introductory Activities:

1. Ask students to raise hands to indicate that they have flown on an airline. Give them a few minutes to talk about experiences and destinations.
2. Go over the airline travel tips and discuss why they are important.

Activity:

Some students may not have had the opportunity to fly anywhere. The worksheet "Traveling by Plane" includes questions that can be solved by applying given information to each situation.
Answers: 1. 29   2. $50   3. $75   4. 6:30PM   5. 9:30PM   6. Hand lotion, spray deodorant, bubble bath
7. Wear shoes that are easy to remove, light jacket, maybe leave off the belt

Discussion:

Airline travel must be safe for all passengers, and the rules and procedures must be followed. The more familiar students are with what is expected, the easier their experience will be.
1. Why do you think the airlines have so many rules? (Safety.)
2. What things do you have to be aware of when you are on a plane with so many other people so close together for probably several hours? (Not being annoying, watching personal space.)

Extension Activities:

1. Using the Departures chart, have students write questions for each other concerning times, flights, gates, and so on. Exchange questions with each other.
2. Have students research other airline regulations at www.tsa.gov to find out more information about traveling by plane. Have them share their findings with the class.

Evaluation:

What are three things you learned about traveling by plane from this lesson?

14.3   Traveling by Plane

Directions:

Use the information given to help you decide what Aaron should do to help him on his flight.

Flight Timings

Departures				
Flight #	**Destination**	**Scheduled**	**Gate**	**Status**
107	Orlando	11:30 A.M.	18	On Time
146	Chicago	1:40 P.M.	19	On Time
27	Milwaukee	6:20 P.M.	24	Delayed
29	Milwaukee	7:30 P.M.	24	On Time

1. Aaron is going to Milwaukee to visit a friend. He decided to get the latest flight possible to Milwaukee so he wouldn't have to rush. What flight will he get on?

2. Aaron has one carry-on bag and two checked bags. It will cost $25 for each checked bag. How much will he have to pay?

3. Aaron's carry-on bag is too big to fit in the overhead compartment, so he will have to check it. Now how much will he have to pay?

4. Aaron knows he needs to arrive at the airport at least one hour before departure. What time should he get to the airport for Flight 29?

5. If Aaron's flight is two hours, the plane departs on schedule, and there are no time zone changes, what time will he arrive in Milwaukee?

6. Aaron remembered that liquids, gels, and aerosol sprays have to be small (three ounces) and put into a clear plastic zip-locking bag to be checked at security. Which of these items should he put into his bag? Hand lotion, spray deodorant, hair brush, bubble bath, toothbrush, extra socks

7. Aaron has to take off his shoes, jacket, and belt and put them in a tray before he goes through security. How should he dress that day to make it easier to go through security?

14.4 Planning a Trip

Objective:

The student will list at least five considerations necessary for planning a trip.

Comments:

Whether planning to travel across the city, across the state, or across the country, one must consider the expense of travel. There are costs involved, not only in the actual travel, but in meals, hotels, and expenses for sight-seeing when the destination is reached. This lesson lists factors that must be considered when traveling.

Introductory Activities:

1. Ask students to list a place they would like to travel to someday. Allow time for them to share their ideas.   2. Have students list some ideas of what they would have to plan for before actually taking the trip. (Assume that money is not a problem.)

Activity:

You may wish to narrow the scope of this assignment by having students select a site within your state or possibly within another designated area. You may wish to have students work in small groups on this project.   *Materials:* pen or pencil, various guidebooks to cities or places

Discussion:

Students may come up with other items or considerations that are involved in taking a trip (tipping a taxi driver, car repairs, and so on).

1. Why did you select the particular destination for this project? Was this a pleasure trip? Sight-seeing? To visit someone?   2. How could you figure out the number of miles involved in the trip? (Atlas, map.)   3. If you drove and used 55 cents per mile as your estimated cost, how much would the trip cost to drive there and back?   4. Why is it usually cheaper to visit some places in the off season? (Not so popular, so tourist facilities offer better prices to attract customers.) 5. What are some other ways you can reduce the cost of a trip? (Stay with friends, take a bus, pack your own food, and so on.)

Extension Activities:

1. Have students contact a travel agency to collect brochures of interesting places to visit. Find out about ups and downs of costs and how you can save money by taking advantage of "package deals."   2. Find out about trips that are offered to school groups at a discount rate. How much money is saved by traveling this way rather than as an individual?   3. Have students collect photos and postcards of their designated trip. Make a display of the sights and adventures. 4. Research motel/hotel chains. Find out the relative costs of staying in several different motels/hotels in a given city.

Evaluation:

1. List five factors to consider in planning a trip.   2. List three cost considerations (involving money) you would have to keep in mind when taking a trip. (Meals, gas, tickets, tipping, shopping, and so on.)

Planning a Trip

Directions:

Select a destination for your trip. Then do some research to fill in the following information.

Destination (local/state/national/international): _____

Specific destination: _____

Length of time spent traveling: _____

Mode(s) of travel: _____

Number of miles traveled: _____ Cost of travel: _____

Number of meals involved: _____ Cost of meals: _____

Clothing required (list): _____

_____

Travel items (list): _____

_____

Number of suitcases needed: _____

Activities at destination: _____

People to visit: _____

Things to see: _____

Tourist attractions: _____

Who will accompany you on the trip: _____

Spending money: _____

Hotel/motel accommodations: _____

Cost per night: _____

Other considerations (parking at airport, tips, and so on): _____

Timetable (leaving, arriving, returning): _____

_____

14.5 Estimating Costs

Objective:

The student will estimate costs associated with travel (for example, meals, motel, attractions) to a designated destination.

Comments:

There are a lot of hidden costs involved in traveling, but adjustments can be made by staying in a less costly motel, eating at economical restaurants, traveling with others, and so on. In this lesson, students are to compare travel expenses to a specified destination by manipulating several variables.

Introductory Activities:

1. Have the class select four major cities that would be interesting to visit (for example, New York, Los Angeles, Denver, Chicago).   2. Have the class select a specified time for which they would like to pretend (or actually would like to go someday) to visit that city.

Activity:

Students should be divided into groups and assigned a major city to visit for a week (or whatever length of time you decide). Their object is to plan a visit to that city and estimate the costs involved on the worksheet "Estimating Costs." You may wish to have each group take a different city to compare how much it would cost a typical tourist to visit different places, or you may wish to have the different groups use the same city as the destination but each plan the excursion differently from the others. Students will probably need to get guidebooks for the city selected. It would also be helpful to have brochures on motel/hotel chains or other travel information.   *Materials:* pen or pencil, guidebooks for cities, maps, brochures on major motel hotel chains, other travel information

Discussion:

Students will probably have a lot of information to share on their "discoveries" about their cities. Ideally, they will also be somewhat enlightened as to how expensive meals and lodging can be.

1. Why are some cities more expensive to visit than others?   2. Did you find any good airfare rates?
3. What was the cheapest available way to get to your city?   4. What sights would you want to see in your selected city?   5. Who or what agencies can help you in planning a trip? (Travel agent, AAA.)
6. What was the range of prices for hotels or motels in the area?   7. What were some rates for rental cars? What determines the prices? (Kind of car, length of rental, adding insurance, and so on.)

Extension Activities:

1. Have students obtain and collect guidebooks for other interesting places. How much more would it cost to visit some places in Europe or other continents?   2. Have students find listings or books containing bed-and-breakfast establishments. Many of them are quite interesting, historic, and unique! Compare rates and places.   3. Some motel or hotel chains put out brochures advertising their amenities—a pool, spa/exercise room, elaborate room service, free breakfast, free newspaper, and so on. Have students investigate what special attractions some places of lodging offer.

Evaluation:

Pretend you are a travel agent working with a customer who would like to visit the city you have just studied. What advice would you offer him or her in planning a trip? What should he or she see there? What questions would you ask the customer to find out what the specific needs are?

14.5   Estimating Costs

Directions:

Divide into groups. Each group will select a destination or target city (for example, Chicago, New York, Denver, Los Angeles). Pretend you will spend one week at the selected city. Answer the following questions based on your city.

1. How much will it cost to get to your city?

2. How will you travel to get there?

3. How much would a hotel cost for your stay?

4. How much would meals cost?

5. What will you want to do or see in the city? What do you estimate these attractions will cost?

6. What will a rental car cost (per day/per week)?

7. What other expenses might you have to consider? Estimate them.

14.6 Using a Timetable

Objective:

The student will be able to read a given timetable of a public transportation system and solve situational problems.

Comments:

Reading a timetable is a useful skill for anyone who uses public transportation to get around. Decisions about arrival times, how long a layover may be, making transfers, and planning one's schedule around possible departures and arrivals are all considerations the user must be able to understand. This lesson provides a sample timetable and problems for the student to solve.

Introductory Activities:

1. Have students list vehicles or transportation systems that use a timetable. (Public buses, trains, delivery services, subways, and so on.)   2. Have students list information that would probably be contained on a typical timetable. (Vehicle number, arrival time, departure time, names of the stops, and so on.)

Activity:

For this activity, students will use a sample timetable to answer questions about situations involving train travel.   *Materials:* pen or pencil, perhaps a clock or clock manipulative   *Answers:*   1. 12:15 P.M. 2. A, B   3. C, D   4. 40 minutes   5. A—12 minutes, B—8 minutes, C—15 minutes, D—10 minutes   6. 38 minutes   7. A, B (C might be cutting it close!)   8. 1 hour, 33 minutes

Discussion:

Go over all of the problems with students, making sure they understand how to find the answers if they had any difficulty.

1. Why is it important to know how long a layover there will be at a stop? (In case you need to change trains, get off, and so on.)   2. How would knowing the schedule ahead of time help you plan your trip? (You'd know when to be there, what time you'll arrive, plan alternatives if necessary.) 3. Do trains (or buses or airplanes or anything else with a timetable) always adhere to the schedule? (Sometimes they may run late or early.)   4. Why should you allow extra time to make connections? (Because sometimes timed systems do not run on schedule.)

Extension Activities:

1. Have students bring in sample timetables from public transportation systems. Have them write and exchange problems and situations with each other.   2. Using a timetable, give students a desti- nation and time limit. Have them plan an efficient route.

Evaluation:

1. What are some systems of transportation that use a timetable?   2. What are three to five pieces of information contained on a typical timetable?

14.6   Using a Timetable

Directions:

The following is a sample timetable for trains in Fortville. Answer the questions based on the timetable.

Train	Leaves Fortville	Arrives Downtown	Leaves Downtown	Arrives River Ridge
A	8:02 A.M.	8:53 A.M.	9:05 A.M.	9:40 A.M.
B	11:30 A.M.	12:15 P.M.	12:23 P.M.	1:03 P.M.
C	1:29 P.M.	2:09 P.M.	2:24 P.M.	2:56 P.M.
D	6:15 P.M.	6:57 P.M.	7:07 P.M.	7:45 P.M.

1. What time does Train B arrive downtown? _____

2. Which trains arrive at River Ridge before 2:00? _____

3. Which trains could you take leaving from Fortville after noon? _____

4. How long is the ride from Fortville to downtown on Train C? _____

5. How many minutes does each train stay at the downtown station?

_____

6. How long does it take for Train D to get from downtown to River Ridge? _____

7. If you needed to be at River Ridge before 3:00 P.M., which trains would you take? _____

8. How long is your ride from Fortville to River Ridge on Train B? _____

14.7 Reading a Map

Objective:

The student will use a given map to answer questions about distance, directions, and locating information.

Comments:

Maps are another source of travel information. They can provide the user with location of specific sites, information about distance between points, and a good idea of how to get to one's destination. In this lesson, students are given a small map of a portion of Washington, D.C., to answer questions.

Introductory Activities:

1. Have students list various types of maps and their uses (weather map, road map, population map, and so on).   2. Have students tell about maps they have used recently or are familiar with (map of the school, city map, and so on).

Activity:

Students should examine the partial map of Washington, D.C., on the worksheet "Reading a Map." Make sure students can read the information on the map and are familiar with the scale of miles and compass.

Materials: pen or pencil, ruler

Answers: 1. Lincoln Memorial   2. Supreme Court, Library of Congress   3. Southeast
4. One inch = 1/2 mile   5. (Example) Go east on Constitution Avenue to 3rd Street, turn south/right until you get to Independence Avenue, turn east/left   6. Constitution Avenue, Independence Avenue
7. National Museum of American History   8. Northeast

Discussion:

Answer any questions students may have about the activity.

1. How could a map help someone get around in an unfamiliar place?   2. What information does a compass give? (Directions: north, south, east, west.)   3. Why is knowing the scale of miles important? (Gives distance.)   4. What other transportation information might be given on a city map? (Bus lines, subway stops, and so on.)   5. What other information might be contained on a map key? (Parks, roads, restrooms, phones.)   6. Where are some places that would distribute maps? (Zoo, museum, and so on.)

Extension Activities:

1. Have students collect various maps and make a display.   2. Have students play "Where Am I?" Give a map to students with a starting point and a set of directions. See if they end up at the intended destination.   3. Have students make a map of their neighborhood, community, state, or other relevant place.

Evaluation:

Have students refer to the Washington, D.C., map on the worksheet to answer the following questions:
1. About how far is it from 7th Street to 17th Street? (One mile.)   2. What direction is the Vietnam Veterans Memorial from the National Museum of American History? (West.)   3. What is the highway number of Constitution Avenue? (50.)   4. What direction do the numbered streets run? (North-South.)

14.7   Reading a Map

Directions:

The following is a map of highlights of Washington, D.C. Use the map to answer these questions.

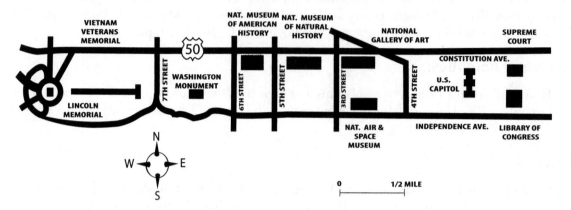

1. What national monument is on the west side of this map?

   _____

2. What two buildings are on the east side of this map?

   _____

3. What direction is the Lirary of Congress building in relation to the U.S. Capitol building?

   _____

4. What is the scale of miles? _____

5. Give directions from the National Museum of Natural History to the National Air and Space Museum.

   _____

   _____

6. What two major avenues run east and west?

   _____

7. What building is between 5th Street and 6th Street?

   _____

8. Where is the Vietnam Veterans Memorial in relation to the Lincoln Memorial?

   _____

Chapter 15

Clothing

15.1 Caring for and Repairing Clothing

Objective:

The student will demonstrate knowledge of how to care for or repair various clothing items.

Comments:

We all probably wish that our clothes would be self-cleaning (and could put themselves on hangers and go into the closet on their own); however, in order to look presentable we must periodically clean and repair whatever is necessary. In this lesson, students must think about how to take care of various items of clothing.

Introductory Activities:

1. Have students tell what they do with their clothes when they are done wearing them for the day. (Try not to be shocked!)   2. Have students tell who is primarily responsible for taking care of their clothes right now.

Activity:

Students are given a list of typical clothing maintenance or repairs on the worksheet "Caring for and Repairing Clothing." They are to suggest a way to take care of the problem.   *Answers (Examples):* 1. Take jacket to the dry cleaner.   2. Replace the zipper.   3. Sew on the button.   4. Hand wash the shirt.   5. Nest one of the socks into the other before throwing them into the wash. 6. Sew the rip.   7. Wash it off.   8. Spray prewash cleaner on the spot.   9. Replace the shoelaces. 10. Repair the hem.   11. Iron the shirt.   12. Darn the hole shut.

Discussion:

Some students may have more practical knowledge about doing minor repairs and cleaning than others do. Have students share their knowledge with the class.

1. Why aren't you wearing the same clothes now that you had five years ago? (Outgrow them, styles change, clothes wear out, and so on.)   2. Why is it a good idea to take good care of your clothes? (They will last longer, look better.)   3. Do you have a system now for taking care of your clothes? How does it work? How could it be improved?   4. When you shop for clothes, what things do you consider—cost, style, care?   5. What sources could you check if you weren't sure how to clean a specific stain? (Check clothing care books; call a cleaner; use Internet sources such as www.ehow.com, howtocleananything.com, or butlersguild.com.)

Extension Activities:

1. Have students write the specific steps for operating a washing machine and dryer.   2. Have students check advertisements or make phone calls to find out the cost of having clothing items dry-cleaned.   3. Have students run a load of clothing through a local coin-operated laundry machine.   4. Supply students with a needle, thread, a button, and a swatch of fabric and have them practice sewing on the button!   5. Have students write a short story entitled something like: "I Am Joe's Shirt"—describing a day in the life of a shirt from the shirt's point of view.   6. Have students compile a booklet of helpful cleaning hints. Copy and distribute the tips to students.

Evaluation:

1. List five typical clothing repairs that need to be done periodically.   2. List three typical clothing cleaning tasks that need to be done periodically.

15.1   Caring for and Repairing Clothing

Directions:

The following is a list of clothing maintenance or repairs that need to be done. What's your suggestion for what needs to be done?

1. Your suit jacket needs to be cleaned, but it says "Dry Clean Only" on the label.

2. Your skirt has a broken zipper on the side.

3. There is a button missing from your favorite shirt.

4. Your new red-and-white T-shirt is dirty but you are afraid if you wash it, it will come out pink.

5. Whenever you wash a pair of socks, you seem to lose one of them.

6. There is a little rip in one of your shirts.

7. You spilled some ketchup on a tie.

8. You were playing a little too roughly and got some blood on your jeans.

9. The end of your shoelace has completely unraveled and you can't get it through the hole anymore.

10. The hem of your slacks is coming out.

11. Your dress shirt is wrinkled.

12. There is a hole in the toe of your sock.

15.2 Buying Appropriate Clothes

Objective: The student will identify appropriate clothing for a given situation.

Comments: When buying clothing, it is important to keep some of these questions in mind: *How often will I wear this? What details about the event or place do I need to know? How much do I have to spend?*

Introductory Comments:

1. Divide students into two groups. Tell one group that they are going hiking. The other group is going to a rock concert. Each group has to list what they would buy on a shopping spree. Students might want to draw a composite picture of their "person."
2. Now inform students that the hiking group is going to a rock concert and the rockers are on a bus to go hiking. What problems or funny situations would they encounter?

Activity: Write the words *how often?*, *cost*, *type of event*, and *other details* on the board. As students select their answers on the worksheet "Buying Appropriate Clothes," have them refer to the key words to make their decision.

Answers: 1. Ski jacket 2. T-shirt 3. Comfortable dress 4. Nice white shirt 5. Tennis shoes with treads 6. Khaki pants

Discussion: For each answer, explain what factors the characters needed to consider in making their decision about the best choices of clothing.

1. What is the difference between casual events and formal events? What are some examples? (Wedding vs. hanging out with friends; meeting an employer vs. meeting one of your parent's friends.)
2. Why do you have to consider details such as climate or seasonal changes when buying clothes? (Each might require very different types of clothing.)
3. If you were on a very tight budget, what types of clothes would you buy? (Not too outlandish, clothes that would fit in most situations.)

Extension Activities:

1. Fashion shows display "what not to wear" pictures of celebrities. Have students come up with a parody making posters of "what not to wear" for students.
2. Jeans come in all prices, colors, and styles. Have students research and categorize jeans according to price, appropriateness, and appeal.

Evaluation: How are the types of clothing you should buy affected by climate? By cost? By the event at which you will wear the clothing?

15.2   **Buying Appropriate Clothes**

Directions: These students are shopping for some clothes. Read each situation and help them decide what to shop for. Circle the appropriate clothing for each situation.

1. Alexa is going skiing for the first time with some friends. She doesn't know if she will like the sport or not, but she wants to look good. Which jacket should she buy?

2. Adam is going to Florida and wants some new clothes to wear. What might he want to get?

3. Sierra is shopping for back-to-school clothes. She wants a cute dress to wear on the first day. What should she look for?

Chapter 15: Clothing

4. Diego is working at a restaurant. The dress code says he has to wear dark pants and a white shirt. What should Diego buy?

5. Vanessa is going hiking in the mountains. She needs something for her feet. What should she buy?

6. Cody is going on a job interview to work at a hotel. He needs to buy some pants. What should he buy?

15.3 Organizing Your Clothes

Objective: The student will state a suitable location for a given item of clothing.

Comments: Although shoving clothes under the bed, hanging them on a lamp, or rolling them up and tossing them on the bathroom floor might be a form of organization for students, it is helpful to at least identify a place where clothes can be kept in some kind of order. Grouping "like" clothes together or stashing off-season clothes in a storage box are examples of ways to categorize clothing.

Introductory Activities:

1. Give each student a blank sheet of paper. Ask them to draw their bedroom or bedroom closet to show how their clothes are organized.
2. Have students come up with different categories of clothing; for example, everyday clothes, socks and underwear, clothes for special occasions, and so on.

Activity: Explain that Blake is trying to organize his clothes on the worksheet "Organizing Your Clothes." Students will indicate where a clothing item could be stored by writing the letter of the appropriate storage place (dresser, closet, box, and so on). Go through each storage area and discuss what kinds of clothes you would expect to find in each area. For example, *occasional wear* means clothing that you do not wear all the time so it could go in the back where it is harder to get to. A shelf might be for shirts or pants that don't have to be creaseless; a rod might be better for shirts or sweaters that keep their shape better on hangers. Note that it is a summer day in the picture.

Answers (May vary): 1. F   2. G   3. A   4. C   5. G   6. E   7. D or B   8. H   9. A   10. F   11. B or D   12. E   13. E   14. E   15. E   16. H   17. B or D   18. B   19. possibly A or G   20. E

Discussion: There really isn't a "wrong" or "right" way to organize clothing, but it helps to be able to find what you are looking for with a minimum of searching.

1. What kind of clothes do you consider everyday wear?
2. What kinds of clothes are occasional wear for you?
3. If you don't have a storage box for off-season clothing, what else could you do with them? (Store them in the back of the closet or another room.)
4. What are some creative ways that your family organizes or stores clothing?

Extension Activities:

1. Have students make a map of their bedroom or closet to show how items are organized. Label each category and have students define or explain the attributes of each category.
2. Have students collect tips for organizing from other students, their parents, magazine articles, or other sources. Share ideas.

Evaluation: List three places that clothing could be stored for easy access.

15.3   **Organizing Your Clothes**

Directions: Help Blake organize his clothes by writing the letter (A–H) of the area where each item should go.

A. Dresser (socks, underwear)	E. Rod for hangers
B. Folded T-shirts	F. Occasional wear
C. Jeans drawer	G. Off-season box
D. Closet shelf for folded items	H. Shoe rack

_____ 1. Three-piece suit

_____ 2. Winter sweaters

_____ 3. Athletic socks

_____ 4. Jeans for school

_____ 5. Earmuffs

_____ 6. Nice shirt

_____ 7. Nice sweater

_____ 8. Running shoes

_____ 9. Black socks

_____ 10. Jacket for windy days

_____ 11. T-shirt from concert

_____ 12. Dress shirt

_____ 13 Dress pants

_____ 14. Uniform shirt for work

_____ 15. Uniform pants for work

_____ 16. Flip-flops

_____ 17. T-shirt for school

_____ 18. T-shirt with football logo

_____ 19. Swim suit

_____ 20. Tie

15.4 Washing and Drying Tips

Objective: The student will state two or three tips for washing and drying clothing.

Comments: A step toward independence is knowing how to do laundry. While hardly exciting, it is a task that, with experience, can be performed with some degree of efficiency and helps make clothes last longer. This lesson includes tips on washing and drying clothing.

Introductory Activities:

1. Ask students to raise their hands if they wash and/or dry their own clothes.
2. Ask students to tell stories about washing or drying mistakes that have ended up as humorous disasters. (Maybe you have a few of your own.)

Activity: The worksheet "Washing and Drying Tips" includes tips for washing and drying clothing or personal items (towels). The student should read each tip and decide whether the example shows someone following the tip or not.

Answers: Washing—1. No   2. Yes   3. No   4. Yes   5. No; *Drying*—1. No   2. No   3. Yes   4. No   5. Yes

Discussion: Depending on the student's level of experience, he or she may be quite familiar with washing and drying procedures. On the other hand, some may need specific instruction on how best to take care of laundry.

1. Why is it important to follow instructions on garments, such as how to wash or dry them? (The makers know the type of fabric and what conditions will preserve it best.)
2. Which washing or drying tips were new for you?
3. Do you have other washing or drying tips that you can share?

Extension Activities:

1. Have students write out the specific steps for operating washing and drying machines.
2. If possible, take students to a local laundromat and go through the procedures for a coin-operated washing and drying process.
3. Have students compile a humorous book of helpful dos and don'ts for cleaning, washing, and drying clothing. Copy and distribute to students.

Evaluation:

1. List two tips for washing clothing.
2. List two tips for drying clothing.

15.4   Washing and Drying Tips

Directions: Which of these examples show people who are following the tips for washing and drying clothing?

Washing

Tip #1   Sort your clothes by color: whites, darks, medium.
"Why is my white dress pink?"

YES   NO

Tip #2   Presoak heavily soiled items before you wash them.
"Oh good, that ketchup stain is gone. I loved the french fries, but what a mess!"

YES   NO

Tip #3   Check your pockets before you wash items.
"Oh, that's where my lipstick went to! And my gum!"

YES   NO

Tip #4   Make sure your clothing item is machine washable.
"DRY CLEAN ONLY. Hmmm. I'll put that in a separate pile."

YES   NO

Tip #5   Check the suggested temperature for washing.
"MACHINE WASH COLD. I'm just going to run everything on hot. . . .
Oh my, what happened here?"

YES   NO

Drying

Tip #1 Shake out items from the washer before putting them in the dryer.

"Strike one! Strike two! Get in there, you!"

YES   NO

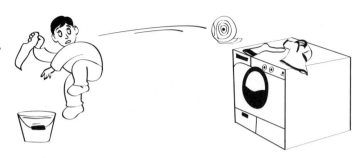

Tip #2 Don't overload the dryer.

"I am going to try to fill up the dryer with all four loads of wash!"

YES   NO

Tip #3 Put similar items together before drying.

"Towels over here, delicate stuff over there—I don't want clumps of thread on my socks!"

YES   NO

Tip #4 Dry clothes just long enough to remove wrinkles.

"Oh, I'll just get to that tomorrow. I don't feel like unloading or sorting right now."

YES   NO

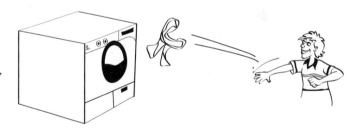

Tip #5 Keep the lint filter clean.

"Oh my, it has been awhile since I checked this. Now my clothes will dry much faster."

YES   NO

Chapter 16

Living Arrangements

16.1 A Place to Live

Objective:

The student will identify possible appropriate housing arrangements for given characters.

Comments:

Housing does not necessarily mean living in a house—there are all sorts of living arrangements that can suit people in various situations. In this lesson, students must match the character with an appropriate accommodation.

Introductory Activities:

1. Ask students to share their ideas about where they expect to live after they have completed their schooling or are working somewhere.   2. Have students list different types of housing or living arrangements for adults or people who are "on their own."

Activity:

On the worksheet "A Place to Live," students are to match the characters (who are given specific needs or situations as clues) with a housing possibility. Explain that not everyone can afford (or wants) to live in a house. Some people need to live close to their place of employment or on a bus line, or want to live with friends, or need to save money by staying with relatives.   *Answers:* 1. c   2. e   3. a   4. d   5. f   6. b

Discussion:

Go over the answers on the worksheet. Some answers may fit more than one character, but to make the answers come out even, the clues need to fit one particular response.

1. Why do many people start out by renting an apartment rather than buying a house? (Easier to get out of, cheaper payments, and so on.)   2. What are some disadvantages to living in an apartment? (Neighbors, parking, restrictions on pets, and so on.)   3. What are some advantages and disadvantages to living with relatives? (Save money, but may not have privacy.)   4. Why do you think some housing places have restrictions on kids or pets? (Tend to cause more damage, may annoy neighbors.)   5. How would you handle problem neighbors if you lived in an apartment? (Talk to manager, talk to the other tenants, talk to the problem people, and so on.)   6. How could you be a good neighbor to your neighbors? (Be considerate.)   7. How would you go about finding a place to live? (Check classifieds, friends' recommendations, and so on.)

Extension Activities:

1. Have students collect information on local apartment complexes. Compile and compare prices and amenities offered. How much is a one-bedroom apartment? A two-bedroom? Is there a pool? A game room? Do they allow pets?   2. Have students prepare and carry out an interview of someone who has recently taken a job, moved out of his or her parents' home, and/or is living independently. Find out if there were any surprises about finding a place to live or what is involved in living independently.

Evaluation:

Consider your needs and probable income. Make a list of what considerations will influence your choice of living arrangements when you are on your own.

16.1   **A Place to Live**

Directions:

Match the person on the left with a good place for him or her to live on the right. Write the letter of your answer on the line.

___ 1. Sally is going to college part-time at night. She works during the day. She shares a car with her sisters at home. She gets along pretty well with her parents

a. Westwood Apartments—close to town and right on a public bus line.

___ 2. David has a full-time job with good hours. He doesn't want to live alone, but he wants his own room. He has several good friends who are in the same situation.

b. Deluxe Mobile Homes—have your own small yard and share a community playground.

___ 3. Pete doesn't have a car, so he needs to live close to his job. He works during the day.

c. Live at home with parents and siblings.

___ 4. Alison wants to go to school in another city where she can get the classes she wants. She hopes she can save some money by staying with someone she knows.

d. Stay with Aunt Mary who lives in a big city, has lots of room, and won't charge any rent.

___ 5. Monroe moved to a new town. He would like to stay there for awhile, but he doesn't know the area well and doesn't really know where he would like to settle permanently.

e. Share an apartment with one or two friends.

___ 6. Shanelle wants her own place, and she really would like a yard, even if it is small. She has a small child and would like privacy.

f. Rent a room in a large house with several smaller apartments. You can stay only one month or as long as you like.

16.2 Living with Parents

Objective:

The student will identify common conflicts between parent and child living at home and provide a possible resolution.

Comments:

Older teens may be desiring increasing amounts of independence from their parents—yet they may not have the resources to move out or to even demonstrate competent living skills away from parental supervision. In this lesson, areas of conflicts with parents are explored and discussed.

Introductory Activities:

1. Ask students to name some things that their parents do or provide for them now that will stop when they move out. (Provide meals, car, pay bills.)   2. Ask students to suggest common areas of disagreement between a teen and his or her parents. List them and try to group them according to areas such as money, control of time, trust, chores, and so on.

Activity:

The worksheet "Living with Parents" provides examples of potential student-parent conflicts. The student should discuss the conflict from both viewpoints and suggest a way to resolve the issue.   *Answers (Will vary):*   1. Work at the store in the afternoons after school or on weekends during the day. 2. Seth might have to use alternative transportation and keep saving up his money.   3. Compromise on a plan to put some toward savings, some for spending.   4. Try a curfew, add additional thirty minutes as his parents trust Jake to be responsible.   5. Maybe Melissa could cook a few meals instead and offer to help supervise one of the other children to help with laundry.   6. Find out what Carson's problems are—is it academic? Does he need a tutor? Can a school counselor help?   7. Take care of a neighbor's pet for a week and see if it's as much fun as she thinks it will be.   8. Maybe Victor can fix up a room in the basement or attic to be his own place.

Discussion:

1. What does "compromise" mean? Which examples on the worksheet could be resolved by compromising? (Both parties giving up something.)   2. Do you think there are some things that a parent has the right to not compromise on? What? (Curfew for underage girls.)

Extension Activities:

1. Have students create their own survey about rights and privileges and ask adults to respond to their questions. They may want to interview their own parents. This could include questions such as: When should a teen be allowed to get a car? What time should a fifteen-year-old be allowed to stay out with friends? Do you think it is OK for teens to drink if they are not driving? Compile the results and come up with conclusions.   2. Collect articles from the local newspaper that are written about teen issues. What are some teen problems in your community? What are successes that teens are responsible for?

Evaluation:

1. What is a common source of conflict between a parent and teen living at home?   2. What would be a reasonable solution for that conflict?

16.2   **Living with Parents**

Directions:

How could these conflicts or daily situations when living with a parent be resolved?

1. Erin wants to work at a convenience store with night hours. Her father doesn't want her to work alone at night.

2. Seth does not have enough money to buy his own car, so he has to keep borrowing his dad's. His dad, however, works different shifts and the car is not always available.

3. Leslie wants to buy a lot of expensive clothes so she will look nice. Her mother thinks Leslie should be saving her money for college.

4. Jake and his parents do not agree on what time he should be at home during the week. Many of Jake's friends do not have a set time to be home, and Jake feels that he should be given the option of coming home when he wants to.

5. Melissa hates to do laundry, but her mother has asked her to help out with chores. There are four kids in the family and Melissa is the oldest.

6. Carson doesn't like school and would like to drop out. His father will not even talk about it with Carson.

7. Evelyn wants to get a pet puppy, but her parents are not thrilled with the idea, because they just got new carpeting. Evelyn insists that she will be able to care of it.

8. Victor has always had to share a room with at least one brother, and he would really like his privacy. He can't afford to move out on his own. His parents are willing to listen to his suggestions.

16.3 Home Upkeep

Objective:

The student will list ten to fifteen routine jobs that are necessary for properly keeping up a house or residence.

Comments:

It takes work to keep a place looking nice! Students may not realize how much work is involved in general cleaning, routine maintenance, and making improvements. In this lesson, students must make a list of inside and outside jobs that are necessary to keep a residence looking acceptable.

Introductory Activities:

1. Give students a blank sheet of paper and have them draw an abandoned house. Discuss what clues they gave that the house was abandoned.
2. Make a class list of maintenance work that would need to be done to improve their abandoned houses. Students may also have drawn a neglected yard to go with the house. Include yard work!

Activity:

On the worksheet "Home Upkeep," students are given a list of items or rooms that routinely need attention, such as the yard, carpet, plumbing, and so on. They are to list at least one specific routine job that needs to be done to keep the area functional, clean, and neat.

Answers (examples): Outside: mow the lawn, replace shingles, clean windows, paint fence, clean up after pets, weed, keep debris out of driveway; *Inside:* make sure spots or dirt are cleaned off walls, clean carpet, clean appliances, make sure the sink drains, dust and vacuum, clean windows, clean out refrigerator, launder sheets, sweep and mop the kitchen floor, clean toilets, take out garbage regularly.

Discussion:

Students may vary somewhat on the jobs they listed for the specific areas. Have students share their ideas.

1. Why is it important to keep your home looking nice? (Looks as though you are responsible, keeps property values up, safer environment, more pleasant to live in.)
2. How could letting your home deteriorate affect safety? (Things may fall apart, could lead to very expensive repairs, someone could get injured, a child may get into a place where he or she could get hurt, and so on.)
3. What goes through your mind when you see a house or apartment that used to be quite nice but is now run down? (The owners didn't care, perhaps couldn't afford to keep it up.)
4. Why do you think some people would rather live in an apartment or condominium than keep up with a house? (May be older, unable to physically do the work, don't want to spend the time.)
5. Some people enjoy doing yard work. Why? (Like to be outside, enjoy watching things that they have planted grow, and so on.)
6. What extra responsibility do pet owners have? (Keep their yards clean, exercise their pets, make sure the houses are clean if the pets are kept indoors, and so on.)

Extension Activities:

1. Have students make an extensive shopping list of items needed for a thorough cleaning (top to bottom!) of a house or apartment. Then do some research at a local store and figure out what it would cost.

2. From the list of jobs in (1), have students find out how long it actually takes to do the job (specify the particulars—clean the carpets in four rooms, wax one nine-by-twelve-foot kitchen tile floor, and so on). You may want to take a class average. It would also be interesting to have students take before and after pictures of their projects!

Evaluation:

1. List five to ten general routine jobs for keeping a residence livable and comfortable.

2. List two or three reasons why it is important to keep your living quarters looking nice.

16.3   **Home Upkeep**

Directions:

There is a lot to do to keep your place looking nice. List at least one job that needs to be done occasionally next to each clue word below.

Outside

Yard _____

Roof _____

Windows _____

Fence _____

Pets _____

Garden _____

Driveway _____

Inside

Walls _____

Carpet _____

Appliances _____

Pipes, plumbing _____

Dusting, vacuuming _____

Windows _____

Refrigerator _____

Bedroom _____

Kitchen _____

Bathroom _____

16.4 Home Repairs

Objective:

The student will make a list of home repairs that are routinely necessary and available resources for making the repairs.

Comments:

Unfortunately, things break, burn out, get lost, or fall apart with old age. Part of independent living is recognizing when there is a maintenance problem and taking steps to repair the damage. It isn't necessary to call in a professional in every case, but on the other hand, it is important to know when something is beyond your skills! In this lesson, students are to identify home repair problems and offer solutions.

Introductory Activities:

1. Have students make a class list of everything they can think of that can go wrong in a house or apartment.
2. Have students identify the last two or three things that needed to be repaired around their house.

Activity:

Students are to read the short story on the worksheet "Home Repairs" about a man who is faced with numerous housing repairs and to list them. Then they are to make a tentative list of professionals they may need to call or jot down what supplies they may need to get to do the job themselves.

Answers (Examples):

1. Broken coffee maker—take to appliance repair
2. Burned-out light—replace with new bulb
3. Spill on carpet—clean with towel
4. Broken garbage disposal—call appliance repair
5. No hot water—call plumber
6. Dirty windows—clean them
7. Gutters filled with leaves—clean them out
8. Loose hand rail—tighten loose parts
9. Broken cord—replace cord

Discussion:

We hope no one really has a day this bad! Students may differ on what jobs they think should be done by a hired professional. It is expensive to call a service person for every little job. Students should realize the importance of learning to do a few home repairs on their own.

1. Why is it a good idea to be able to do some home repairs by yourself? (Save money, save time waiting for repair person to show up.)
2. Why is it a good idea to call a professional service person to do some home repairs? (Get a guarantee, may do a better job, have the right tools and supplies, do the job faster, and so on.)
3. Why is it important to keep warranties on major appliances such as a refrigerator or oven? (It shows when and where you purchased the appliance, tells what is covered, may entitle you to free service within the warranty period, and so on.)
4. When shopping around for service, what qualifications do you think are important to find out about before having someone do the work? (If they are recommended to do a good job, provide a guarantee of their work, reasonable price, efficient workers, and so on.)

Extension Activities:

1. Have students watch a movie or television show parodying the hassles of being homeowners, such as the movie *The Money Pit* or the TV series *Home Improvement*.
2. Have students find out how much electricians, plumbers, carpenters, and/or appliance repair technicians charge for their services.
3. Have students obtain some books on do-it-yourself home maintenance and evaluate the books. Are they easy to understand? Are the directions accurate? Would they be helpful in making repairs?
4. Have students opt to learn one maintenance task from a friend, parents, older sibling, or other volunteer teacher. Expect a demonstration or report on this new learning!

Evaluation:

1. List five typical home repairs that will probably be necessary at some point.
2. List three to five professional service people whom you could call for repairs. Describe the type of maintenance or repair that the person would do.

16.4

Home Repairs

Directions: Pete is having a very bad day. Make a list of all the repairs he needs to do something about. Then next to each one, write who he should call or what he should do.

Pete's alarm went off, early in the morning. He rubbed his eyes and went into the kitchen to make coffee, but for some reason the coffee maker wasn't working. He decided to drink some orange juice. He opened the refrigerator, but found that the light had burned out and he couldn't see what was inside. He grabbed some juice, but as he turned around his dog knocked into him and he spilled the juice all over the kitchen carpet. He had some cereal for breakfast, and was going to dump the remains down his garbage disposal, but when he turned on the switch, nothing happened. He also realized that he was missing a spoon. He decided to wash his dishes, but when he turned on the faucet, only cold water came out—no hot water! There went his long morning shower! His dog was barking at something outside, and Pete went to look, but he couldn't see through the dirty windows. Leaves were falling all over the yard. He managed to wipe clear a little spot in the window on the second floor, where he could see that the gutters were completely filled with leaves. He turned to go back down the steps, and his hand slipped on the stair rail, which was loose. He tried to turn on the light at the bottom of the stairs, but his dog had chewed up the cord to the lamp. No light! He decided he would head on to work—where he hoped that everything would be in working order!

_____

_____

_____

_____

_____

_____

_____

_____

_____

16.5 Going Green

Objective: The student will recognize examples of ways to interact responsibly with the environment.

Comments: The environment is ours to take care of. It is important to teach students how to be efficient consumers and make wise use of resources as part of their everyday lifestyle. In this day and age, it is very convenient to recycle. There are many other small changes that we can make that contribute to ensuring a healthier environment.

Introductory Activities:

1. Divide students into two groups and have them compete to see how many items they can think of that can be recycled. Compare lists. Anything unusual?
2. Bring in examples of items that have been recycled; for example, cups that have become planters, everyday items turned into jewelry, and so on.

Activity: On the worksheet "Going Green," students are to choose the characters who are demonstrating concern for the environment.

Answers: Circled: 1, 2, 5, 6, 8, 9

Discussion: There is a wide spectrum of opinions about how best to live on the planet. The purpose of this lesson is to simply create awareness of simple, commonsense ways to not be wasteful or destructive.

1. What does the term *go green* mean to you? (Be friendly to the environment.)
2. What are some ways that you, your family, or your community is going green?
3. Were there any items on the worksheet that would be easy for you to do if you are not already doing them?

Extension Activities:

1. Research recycling—what types of items can be recycled, how and where are they recycled, and what can they be recycled into?
2. Have a Recycled Items Display. Find items that are a far cry from their original intention (a distributor cap is now a pen holder, typewriter keys are fashion jewelry, and so on) and set up an interesting display for others to visit.
3. Additional tips can be found on www.letsgogreen.biz (including all kinds of eco-friendly products) and www.earth911.com.
4. Find out how *going green* got started. Incidentally, *green* topped the 2008 list of banned words (twilightearth.com), with *carbon footprint* coming in second.

Evaluation: List three ways that you could go green in your home, school, or work lifestyle.

16.5   Going Green

Directions: Which of these students is showing respect for the environment? Circle the number of each one who is doing something "green."

1. **CARLA:** "I can just wash these plastic forks from the party and use them over again. I won't throw them away."

2. **BRAD:** "That was a great drink. Now where is that recycle bin?"

3. **ELLIE:** "Those new energy efficient light bulbs look really weird. I'll just use the old ones."

4. **JAMAL:** "I love these long showers! I could stay in here for at least an hour."

5. **MARIA:** "I'm using a reusable bag for shopping instead of getting a new plastic one every time I shop."

6. **TOMAS:** "I think I'll ride my bike to school today."

7. **AMANDA:** "This room is cold. I'll turn up the thermostat to 80."

8. **KEITH:** "I can use the back of these papers to jot down my rough draft for my report instead of using new paper."

9. **GRACIE:** "I'm going to dry these clothes by hanging them on a line outside. It's such a nice day."

10. **NICHOLAS:** "What am I supposed to do with an old ink cartridge? I guess I could take it to the recycle center, but it's three blocks away. I'll just toss it in the trash."

16.6   Decluttering

Objective:

The student will state ten to fifteen tips for keeping a living area organized.

Comments:

Is it just me or does everyone seem to have too much stuff? This lesson offers twenty tips for helping to stay organized and discard unneeded items. The less you have to organize, the faster you can get the job done!

Introductory Activities

1. Have students list, in one minute, as many items as they can think of that are in a bedroom or living room closet at home.   2. Have students take turns estimating how long it would take them to find the following items: their birth certificate, a pair of matching socks, a sharpened pencil, house keys, a flashlight, baby pictures of themselves (you may add other items, of course).

Activity:

Students should be given a copy of the worksheet "Decluttering" and asked to read and think about how each item might be helpful to them. They are then to draw a picture or write a brief description of how this could apply to them. (You may want to have them choose ten items instead of doing all of them.) *Answers:* Will vary.

Discussion:

Be sensitive to students who may not have a lot of possessions, or who may have had a tragedy (fire, tornado, and so on) that has destroyed their home.

1. Why do you think many people tend to collect and save a lot of items that they really don't need? (Too lazy to get rid of them, think they will use them later, like having a lot of things.) 2. What are some ways you could find new homes for unwanted or unneeded items? (Donate them, sell, give away.)   3. Which of the tips on the list do you think would be most helpful to you? 4. What types of organizing tasks are the hardest for you?

Extension Activities:

1. Have motivated students continue to find helpful organizing tips and arrange them into a booklet. They might have tabs (labeled, of course) and folders with pockets, and diagrams or pictures to help with the tips.   2. Have students challenge each other to clean up a disorganized room of their house (their own bedroom?). Take before and after pictures.   3. These websites are helpful in providing tips for getting and staying organized:

www.getorganizednow.com

www.pioneerthinking.com/household-organizers.html

Evaluation:

Write five ways that you could organize your schedule, your desk, your time, your cleaning habits, and your paperwork.

16.6   Decluttering

Directions:

Draw a picture or write an example of how someone could use these tips to help stay organized.

AUGUST

SUNDAY	MONDAY	TUESDAY	WEDNESDAY	THURSDAY	FRIDAY	SATURDAY
				1	② Meeting	3
4	5	⑥ Meeting	7	⑧ Party	9	10
11	⑫ Interview	13	14 Party	⑮ Account closing	16	17
18	19	20	㉑ Interview	22	㉓ Meeting	24
25	㉖ Meeting	27	28	㉙ Meeting	30	31

1. Use one calendar—put all of your appointments, due dates, and other scheduled events in the same place.

2. Label everything—your files, your keys, storage boxes, saved magazines.

3. Store similar items together—craft supplies, games, sports equipment, shoes.

4. Open your mail over a recycle bin—toss in junk mail, envelopes, and unneeded inserts; put bills or other needed items in one place.

5. Invite a friend over to help you clean—then return the favor and help him or her.

6. Have a special file for your receipts—you might need to return something; use the receipts for proof of payment, taxes, reimbursement.

7. Get a desk organizer, closet organizer, shower organizer—use these items to help you keep smaller items together.

8. Always keep important items in the same place when not in use—your glasses, your keys, your medicine, your homework, your bills.

9. Always have spare items of things you use often—laundry detergent, soap, cleaning supplies (then you won't have an excuse to not get started on cleaning!).

10. Get rid of your trash often—don't get used to seeing it around; know your trash day or where to dump your trash, and put that in your weekly schedule.

11. Put a laundry hamper in the bathroom—toss your dirty clothes there immediately, not on the floor.

12. Create reference lists—a list of birthdays, directions to places, websites that have been helpful, books you want to read, things you need to accomplish, people to call for help, gift ideas, and so on. Put the list in a folder, label it, and file it where you won't lose it.

13. Schedule cleaning tasks on a weekly basis—determine which tasks you will do each day of the week, then stick to your schedule.

14. Start organizing stuff that you may not need—put into piles of "give away or sell," "throw away," "keep," and "not sure." Box up the "not sure" items and see if you really miss having them after two or three months. If you haven't missed them, move them to one of the other piles.

15. Break down larger tasks into smaller steps—start organizing one drawer, one corner, one shelf, one file, one closet.

16. Make a photocopy of your credit cards (both sides)—if you lose one, you will have the numbers to refer to if you need to call to cancel them.

17. Put your TV remote in a basket on the coffee table or attach it with Velcro to the side of the TV so you won't lose it.

18. Set yourself a deadline for necessary tasks (especially those you don't want to do)—write it down on an index card and put it on your calendar.

19. Put things away; if you leave them out, they will still be there. Have hangers, boxes, files, drawers, and so on available.

20. Promise yourself to leave one area perfectly organized before you go to bed at night—your kitchen counter, your desk, your laundry room, your sink, the stand next to your bed.

Chapter 17

Eating and Nutrition

17.1 Nutrition

Objective:

Given guidelines, the student will plan a nutritious meal.

Comments:

In our hurried pace of life, planning and eating nutritious meals sometimes goes by the wayside. It may be easier to grab a little bag of potato chips and a candy bar than to take the time to eat something more healthy and full of nutrients. In this lesson, students are introduced to the food guide pyramid and will use that as a guideline to plan nutritious meals.

Introductory Activities:

1. Ask students to list the last ten things they can think of that they have eaten.
2. Have students put a check mark next to the items they think are considered nutritious.
3. Define *nutritious* (describing foods that contain nutrients—substances in food that provide material for maintaining the body and keeping it healthy; specific nutrients include fats, proteins, minerals, vitamins, and carbohydrates).
4. Have students reconsider the items they checked in (2) to see if they want to change their answers.

Activity:

On the worksheet "Nutrition," students will use a food guide pyramid to plan one day of nutritious meals.

Materials: pen or pencil, books on nutrition, calorie-counter booklets, and so on

Discussion:

Have students share their ideas on nutritious meals. They could exchange papers or evaluate volunteers' ideas as a class. Make sure students have included items from the food guide pyramid.

1. Why is it important especially for children to eat nutritious meals? (Their bodies are still growing.)
2. What are some benefits of eating well? (You'll feel better, maintain your weight, have a stronger body, fewer cavities, and so on.)
3. Not all foods that are good for you taste bad. What are some foods you like that you know are good for you?
4. Some menus in restaurants are marked "heart smart." What does that mean? (Low in fat, won't clog your arteries.)
5. What are some physical or health conditions that some people have that require special diets? (Heart diseases, obesity, diabetes, hyperactivity, and so on.)

Extension Activities:

1. Have students find out the number of calories contained in twenty food items (for example, candy bar, apple, serving of lettuce, and so on).
2. Have students find out the number of grams of fat in the same items.
3. Have students find out the recommended caloric intake for their age, weight, sex, and activity level.

4. Assign students the task of keeping track of everything they eat for one week. Look for trends. Are the foods nutritious?

5. Challenge students to take one week to give up fatty, sugary foods and eat only healthful foods. How do they feel at the end of the week?

6. Talk to school cafeteria personnel to find out what are the school's specific nutritious guidelines.

7. Have students research a topic involving nutrition. What foods are high in specific nutrients?

8. Prepare a book of nutritious meals using healthful guidelines.

9. Have students write to child-care organizations that promote nutrition in Third World countries. How do they help feed undernourished children?

10. Have students make a chart showing the nutritional value (including calories, vitamins, serving size, and so on) of several common foods.

Evaluation:

1. What are some guidelines to include when planning a nutritious meal?

2. Give an example of at least one item in each group of the food guide pyramid.

17.1   **Nutrition**

Directions:

Using the food guide pyramid, plan one day of nutritious meals—breakfast, lunch, dinner, and snacks.

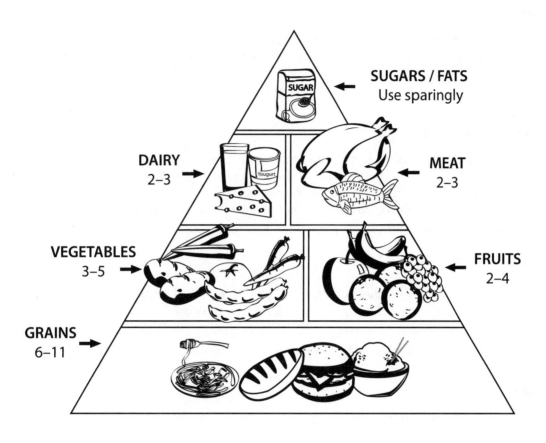

_____

_____

_____

_____

_____

17.2 Making Good Food Choices

Objective:

The student will be able to identify examples of healthy foods and provide good alternatives to unhealthy foods.

Comments:

Americans have an abundance of choice in their food decisions. Do I want fast food? A home-cooked meal? Do I feel like meat, or pasta, or soup? With all these decisions, sometimes it is easier to choose the fastest or easiest foods out of convenience, when these foods may in fact be the most unhealthy. Knowing which foods are healthy and good alternatives makes the decision-making process easier.

Introductory Activities:

1. Draw a picture of an apple, a carrot, and a fish on the board. Ask the students to list what nutritional values they know come from these foods. (Fiber, vitamins C and B, iron, potassium, fiber, protein.) More information can be found at www.nutritiondata.com.   2. Draw a picture of a candy bar, an ice-cream cone, and a hamburger on the board and have the students list the nutritional value of these. (There really is some, but stress the unhealthy fats and oils content in these foods.)

Activity:

Have students complete the worksheet entitled "Making Good Food Choices." Students will choose the better option between the two choices.   *Answers:*   1. Whole wheat bread   2. Lean turkey
3. Unsalted nuts   4. Steamed broccoli   5. Fat-free milk   6. Baked potato with salt and pepper
7. Salad   8. Bran flakes cereal   9. Water   10. Granola

Discussion:

1. Is it easy to tell if something is healthy or unhealthy?   2. What are signs that something may be unhealthy? (Oily, deep-fried, white flour, high in sugar, and so on.)   3. Can healthy foods still taste good? Give examples of some foods.

Extension Activities:

1. Take a group trip to the grocery store and walk around the perimeter of the store. Notice that most of the foods on the edge are "real" foods—that is, they are closest to their natural states. Then walk through the middle aisles and notice that most foods are boxed, canned, or processed. Have students point out healthy foods and unhealthy foods as you go.   2. Have students bring in boxed items or wrapped candy bars. List the ingredients in several of the items. Compare fat content, number of calories, and ingredients.

Evaluation:

1. Give an example of three healthy foods.   2. Give an example of three healthy snacks.

17.2   Making Good Food Choices

Directions:

Choose which of the two options is the healthier food. Circle your answer.

1. White bread   Whole wheat bread

2. Fried chicken   Lean turkey

3. Unsalted nuts   Honey-roasted peanuts

4. Butter-battered broccoli   Steamed broccoli

5. Fat-free milk   Chocolate milkshake

6. Baked potato with salt and pepper   Cheesy French fries

7. Pepperoni pizza   Salad

8. Blueberry waffles   Bran flakes cereal

9. Water   Diet Cola

10. Candy bar   Granola

17.3 Eating Out versus Eating In

Objective:

The student will state the advantages and disadvantages of eating in and eating out.

Comments:

Eating out is fun, easy, fairly quick, and requires little work; however, it can also mean large portions, greasy preparation, unnecessary expenses with taxes and tips, and fewer healthy options. Although eating out is something that most people do from time to time, it can be a bad habit to do regularly. Eating at home gives a person the opportunity to prepare foods in smaller portions and with healthier ingredients, and it costs significantly less.

Introductory Activities:

1. Ask students to estimate how many times or meals they ate out during the past week. Set a timer for one minute and have students (in groups) list as many fast-food restaurants as they can.
2. Making a "pros and cons" list on the board, have students list positive and negative aspects of eating out and eating in.

Activity:

Have students complete the worksheet "Eating Out versus Eating In." They should decide which character made the better food decision, and then write a reason why.   *Answers:*   1. GREG: He didn't choose the easy way out, but instead decided cooking could help him relax.   2. JANICE: She made the money go further and bought healthier items.   3. JOSE: He stopped eating after one serving. 4. HELEN: She chose something healthy.   5. FRANK: He was willing to try cooking and found that cooking can be easy.   6. PATRICIA: She made cooking at home a fun, social gathering.

Discussion:

1. What are some benefits to eating in and preparing your own meals?   2. What are some things that make this hard? (Takes time, requires planning, ignorance of recipes and how to prepare meals.)
3. Do you think many fast-food restaurants are now serving more healthy foods? Give some examples.

Extension Activity:

Collect menus from several local restaurants. Have students select items that would make a healthy meal. Total the calories, fat, and price.

Evaluation:

1. List an advantage and a disadvantage of eating out.   2. List an advantage and a disadvantage of eating at home.

17.3   **Eating Out versus Eating In**

Directions: Read each cartoon. Decide who made the better choice and then write why choice was better.

1.

Tony   Greg

2.

Marguerite   Jancie

3.

Jose   Brian

Chapter 17: Eating and Nutrition   **347**

4.

Catherine: "There's nothing in the refrigerator. I have some candy bars in my backpack."

Quick & Healthy

Helen: "I will pick up a salad from Quick & Healthy."

5.

Colin: "I am such a bad cook. I'm just going to eat somewhere where someone else will cook."

Frank: "Oh, I forgot I had this Easy Meal cookbook! I should try cooking something."

6.

Patricia: "I'm going to invite friends over for a make your own taco night. It'll be so much fun!"

Sienna: "What should we do, guys? Why don't we meet at that greasy place? I got food poisoning last time, but hey, at least I don't have to cook."

17.4 Preparing a Meal

Objective:

The student will list steps that demonstrate how to prepare a single meal that is healthy and well-balanced.

Comments:

It is important to know how to prepare meals that have food from every food group and portions that reflect the food guide pyramid. Having a good understanding of meal preparation makes it easier to plan in advance shopping for groceries, preparing healthy meals for individuals or families, and improving overall health. Eating well and in good proportions can help us feel better about ourselves and feel more in control of our eating habits and ability to make smart food decisions.

Introductory Activities:

1. Ask students to tell what their favorite food is. Ask, if they had the chance, would they eat only that one food for every meal.
2. Ask students to tell about a meal that they prepared or assisted in preparing.

Activity:

Have students split into small groups and read aloud the story of Donna's lunch on the "Preparing a Meal" worksheet. Then have them decide together the order of steps to prepare the different foods to make a whole meal.

Answers: The sandwich: 5, 2, 3 or 4, 3 or 4, 6, 1; *The apple:* 3, 1, 4, 2; *The milk:* 3, 2, 1; *The vegetables:* 1, 2

Discussion:

1. Discuss with students what their favorite part of Donna's meal was.
2. Was the meal easy or difficult to prepare? Could the students make a similar meal? With help?
3. Was it a healthy meal? What made it healthy? Was it balanced? If so, why?
4. Why was Donna's meal better than the pizza and chocolate cake she could have chosen?

Extension Activities:

Have students look up recipes on www.kidshealth.org/kid or in a food magazine and find their favorites. Prepare a few of the simple foods or even an entire meal in class and enjoy them together!

Evaluation:

1. What do you need in order to prepare a meal? (Time, food, knowledge of preparation.)
2. What food groups should be present to have a well-balanced meal?

17.4   **Preparing a Meal**

Directions: Read Donna's plan to make a healthy, well-balanced lunch. Then help Donna put the steps to preparing each food in the correct order.

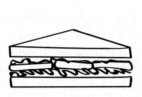 

Saturday afternoon, Donna stumbled into the kitchen, her stomach growling with hunger. She was famished after walking around the neighborhood with her dog Kip. "What should I eat?" Donna wondered. She opened the refrigerator and saw some leftover pizza and chocolate cake from her sister's birthday party the night before. But Donna wanted something healthy and didn't mind taking the time to make it. So she pulled out some lunchmeat and whole wheat bread to make a sandwich, grabbed an apple from the fruit bowl, and took out the milk carton to pour a glass.

"Yum, yum!" said Donna out loud. "I've got my fruit, my meat, my bread, and my dairy. What am I missing, Kip?"

Kip barked in response.

"That's right, boy. I need my vegetables." Donna pulled out a lettuce leaf for her sandwich and some carrots and celery. But how would she prepare it all?

The Sandwich

_____ Add a slice of meat.

_____ Spread a small amount of light mustard or mayonnaise on the bread.

_____ Add a single slice of cheese.

_____ Add a lettuce leaf.

_____ Place the remaining slice of bread on top.

_____ Place two pieces of bread on a plate.

The Milk

_____ Pour the milk into the glass.

_____ Open the milk carton.

_____ Find a tall, clean glass.

The Vegetables

_____ Open the bag of carrots and celery.

_____ Place several of each on your plate.

The Apple

_____ Cut the apple into slices.

_____ Find a ripe, unbruised apple.

_____ Place the slices on a plate.

_____ Wash the apple under lukewarm water.

Shopping

18.1 What Do I Need?

Objective: The student will identify several items that would be needed on a shopping trip in order to complete a task.

Comments: It is helpful to make and take along a list when you are going shopping for a specific purpose (to paint, to decorate, to build). First, it forces you to inventory what you need (and you might discover you already have some of the items), and second, it can help you stay focused on getting only what you have on the list.

Introductory Activities:

1. If I sent you shopping to get decorations for a Valentine's party, what would you get?
2. What if I told you that I had three boxes of decorations left over from last year's party? How would that affect your shopping for this year?

Activity: Students can focus on specific shopping needs with the worksheet "What Do I Need?"

Answers (Will vary):

1. Green paint, tarp, brush
2. Training book, collar, bowls
3. Warm sweater, mittens
4. Book, calendar, shirt, toy

5. Popcorn, beverages, small bowls
6. Posters, thumbtacks
7. Games, DVD
8. Book, bookmark, hot chocolate

Discussion: Emphasize that some items on a shopping list might have to be general until you see your choices. Listing the items will help steer you toward the right area.

1. Why is it important to take inventory of what you already have?
2. What is impulse buying?
3. Are there certain types of shopping that are repetitive? (Weekly meals, seasons.)

Extension Activities:

1. Have students compile a booklet of How to Do Things, including a list of materials. For example: How Do I Paint a Room? How Do I Throw a Good Party?
2. Have students design a cute shopping list form (generic or specific to tasks). Include sections for what I already have, what I need, where to shop.

Evaluation:

What items would you need to shop for if your aunt was visiting for a weekend and you know she likes pancakes and fresh flowers and enjoys playing games?

18.1   **What Do I Need?**

Directions:

What items would you need if you were in each of the following situations? Write some things on each shopping list.

1. Painting your bedroom green

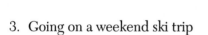

2. Preparing for a new puppy

3. Going on a weekend ski trip

4. Shopping for Christmas gifts for your family

5. Having a few friends over for a party

6. Decorating your room

7. Babysitting for some small children

8. Picking out a birthday gift for a friend who loves to read

18.2 Smart Shopping

Objective:

The student will name at least two ways that a shopper can get more for his or her money.

Comments:

Unless you enjoy paying full price for what you buy, it is important (and fun) to find ways to cut costs. Using coupons, looking for items off-season, visiting thrift shops, buying in bulk, and so on are good ways to save a little money.

Introductory Activities:

1. Do you or your parents ever use coupons when they shop? What do they buy? How much do you think they save?
2. If you didn't want to pay full price for clothes, what are some ways you could shop for clothing and save some money?

Activity:

Use the worksheet "Smart Shopping" to have students recognize ways to shop that can cut costs.

Answers: 1. e   2. g   3. a   4. b   5. c   6. f   7. b   8. d   9. h   10. f

Discussion:

Use the examples from the worksheet to discuss these questions about shopping.

1. What are some items that are "off season" for each season?
2. What are some pros and cons of using coupons?
3. What do you need to watch out for if you buy something that needs to be assembled or fixed up? (Be sure you know how or know someone who does.)
4. Sometimes people can find unique items at thrift stores or even at antique malls. What's the difference between junk and a bargain?

Extension Activities:

1. Go through the advertising section or promotions throughout your local newspaper. What items are on sale? What is "off season" right now? How big are the bargains?
2. Compare prices on an item; for example, a book that is (a) available in paperback, (b) sold at a thrift store, (c) sold "used" online, or (d) sold at bookstores, discount stores, and pharmacies, and so on. What is the range of prices for the same book?

Evaluation:

List two ways that a person can save money shopping and give an example of each.

Name _____ Date _____

18.2   Smart Shopping

Directions: How are these people being smart shoppers? Match the shoppers with their strategy.

a. Buy off-season.	e. Share with a friend.
b. Buy a larger quantity.	f. Use coupons or promotions.
c. Look for reduced price.	g. Buy after a holiday.
d. Look for something you can fix up.	h. Buy generic, not name brand.

___ 1. Hey, Yolanda—these paper towels are "buy one, get one free." Let's get two and we can each take one.

___ 2. I know this candy will go on sale right after the holiday is over. I'll just wait.

___ 3. I know that spring is coming, but all of the winter jackets are now on sale.

___ 4. The soup is four cans for a dollar. I could just buy one can at the sale price, but I have room to store them and I really like soup. I think I will buy four.

___ 5. This sweater is in the clearance pile. It looks fine to me!

___ 6. I have a coupon for that brand of cereal. I can save 75 cents on that box!

___ 7. One can of root beer is $1, but I can get twelve in a case for $4.99. I wonder what I should do?

___ 8. This table is a lot cheaper if I can put it together myself. I know that my dad will be able to help me. He has a lot of tools and likes to do stuff like that.

___ 9. These are really nice jeans. They don't have a designer label, but they look great.

___ 10. The store is having a promotion on this brand of soap. I don't usually buy that kind, but the price is great. I'll try it!

18.3 Comparison Shopping

Objective: The student will select an item from a pair of items that is a "better deal" and then give a reason why.

Comments: A bargain is a bargain only if it is something you need in the first place. It is great to buy something on sale, but is it something you want? In this lesson, students will try to decide what makes something a "good deal" by comparing similar items and deciding what factors to consider before making a choice.

Introductory Activities:

1. Ask students if they have ever bought something at a store and then changed their minds as soon as they walked out of the store. Why did they regret their purchase?
2. Ask students to describe what kind of sweatshirt they would like to have if they could have their choice. Include logos, hoods, size, color, price, name brand, and so on.

Activity: On the worksheet "Comparison Shopping," students will compare two items and discuss factors why each might be the better buy for someone.

Answers: Will vary.

Discussion: Have students discuss what factors were most influential in deciding which item was the better buy.

1. What factors were important to consider in the coffee cup example? (Price, color, condition.)
2. What factors were important in the sweatshirt example? (Logo, size, price.)
3. What factors were important in the TV stand example? (Assembly, availability, price.)
4. What factors are most important to *you* when purchasing an item?

Extension Activities:

1. Play "Find the Best Deal" by assigning students to find two similar items that vary greatly according to one of the factors discussed. Have them "promote" the items and let the student audience vote on the better deal. Then reveal the price and source of the items.
2. Send students out on a scavenger hunt to find the best local deal on a selected item—a book, sweatshirt, game, CD, or other popular item.

Evaluation: You are interested in getting a digital camera for yourself. Your aunt gave you $100 for your birthday to buy one. Camera A costs $100. It comes with a lot of accessories and you can do a lot with the pictures on your computer. It also has a printer. Camera B is $50 and is easy to use, but the pictures you take will not be as clear. Which camera is the better deal for *you*? Explain why.

18.3   **Comparison Shopping**

Directions:

Which is the better deal? Compare cost, value, need, and other factors. Explain your answers.

1. **Item A:** A set of four coffee mugs, the color you want, $25. You can also buy matching soup bowls later if you want.

   Item B: A set of four coffee mugs, a color you don't really like, but only $10. One of the cups has a loose handle.

2. **Item A:** A hooded sweatshirt with your favorite team's logo, a little bigger size than you normally wear, $40.

   Item B: A hooded sweatshirt from a thrift shop, fits perfectly, no logo, $15.

3. **Item A:** A TV stand, needs to be assembled, needs to be painted, available right now, $50.

   Item B: A TV stand, can special order it from the factory, completely assembled, but will have to wait about three weeks for it to come in, $35.

18.4 Returning Items

Objective:

The student will be able to give two or three helpful tips for successfully returning an unwanted item.

Comments:

Shoppers have the option to return unwanted items provided that they comply with the store's return policy. Some items cannot be returned without proof of purchase, such as a receipt. Other stores will take back items without any questions. Sale items usually cannot be returned. Buyers should be aware of the store's return policy and keep receipts, warranties, and other paperwork that might be necessary to return something.

Introductory Activities:

1. Ask students to give some "good" reasons for returning an item. (Wrong size, broken, doesn't meet your needs.)   2. Ask students to give some reasons why a store may not accept an item that you are trying to return. (Already been worn/read/used/opened; length of time between purchase and return is too long; lost receipt.)

Activity:

On the worksheet "Returning Items," students are to consider each situation and decide whether or not the person could probably return the item without a problem.   *Answers:* 1. No (worn)   2. Probably yes (if store can verify it is their product)   3. Yes   4. No (too long ago)   5. Yes   6. No (no returns of sale items)   7. No (was read)   8. Yes

Discussion:

Discuss return policies and how it helps both the customer and the store.

1. Why does it matter if you try to return something that you already wore or already read? (You used the item—now it is devalued.)   2. Why should you keep receipts for important purchases? (Shows when you bought something, where, price.)   3. What are some examples of things that you can't return? (Underwear that has been worn, opened food products, sale items.)

Extension Activities:

1. Survey several retail stores in your area. Have students find out the return policies and compare them.   2. Have students role-play situations in which one is a customer trying to return an item and the other is a shopkeeper. Practice being courteous (both parties!) and focused in the transaction.

Evaluation:

Which of these items could probably be successfully returned?

1. An unworn sweater   2. A magazine that you took home and read   3. An opened bag of potato chips   4. A set of markers from two years ago

18.4   **Returning Items**

Directions:

Each of these people wants to return an item. Circle YES if the item could be returned. Circle NO if it cannot be returned. If NO, why not?

1. "I would like to return this dress. It doesn't fit and I don't like the color. But I did wear it two times to a party. Here's the tag. There's a little stain on the back. Sorry." **YES**   **NO**

2. "This towel set is the wrong color for my bathroom. I threw away the receipt. I think I got it from this store, but I'm not sure." **YES**   **NO**

3. "I bought these jeans and when I got home I noticed that the zipper was broken. Here is the receipt." **YES**   **NO**

4. "I have a receipt for these curtains. I bought them three years ago." **YES**   **NO**

5. "I got this sweater from my aunt as a gift, but I really don't like the color and the size is too small. I would like to exchange it for something else." **YES**   **NO**

6. "I know the sign says NO RETURNS ON SALE ITEMS, but I decided I don't like this game and I would rather have my money back." **YES**   **NO**

7. "I bought this book last week for $15. I would like to return it and get my money back. The book really wasn't that interesting. Except it did have a good ending. But I've already read it, so I don't really want it anymore." **YES**   **NO**

8. "I was supposed to get vacuum cleaner number 2-848, and I picked up 2-484 by mistake. It's still in the box. I would like to return this and get the other one." **YES**   **NO**

Exercise/Health and Hygiene

19.1 Exercise in Daily Life

Objective: The student will identify ways to exercise and state at least two purposes for exercising.

Comments: Exercise is a key component to a healthy weight and healthy lifestyle. People exercise for a variety of reasons, including keeping weight down, enjoying the outdoors, being part of a team, feeling good about themselves, and being all-around healthy. This lesson encourages students to incorporate exercise into their lives.

Introductory Activities:

1. Have individual or small groups of students volunteer for a game of charades in which activities (both exercise and nonexercise) are acted out. Have students decide whether it was exercise (playing basketball) or not (sleeping, reading).

2. Have students list their favorite ways of exercising and state how often they do.

Activity: Students will look at the profiles of four different examples on the worksheet "Exercise in Daily Life." They will then answer questions about the exercise, equipment needed, and so on.

Answers:

1. Basketball; 1–2 hours; basketball, gym clothes; alone or on a team
2. Swimming; 30–90 minutes; pool, suit; alone or with friends
3. Walking; 30–60 minutes; walking shoes, comfortable clothes; alone or with friends
4. Weight lifting; 30–60 minutes; gym clothes, weights; with someone (need a partner for safety with weights)

Discussion: After students have completed the worksheet, discuss which of the four activities is most appealing. How could it become a reality?

1. What are some good reasons for getting exercise? (Health, social, weight.)
2. Why is it important to exercise daily? (Teaches good habits, good for body.)
3. What are some creative ways to exercise? (Take the stairs, jump rope.)
4. Are the dreams of these people possible? Does it matter?

Extension Activities:

1. Visit a local gym or recreation center to view the facilities. Demonstrate how the sport/equipment is used.
2. See how many forms of exercise the class can list, A through Z.

Evaluation:

1. List three types of exercise and give a purpose for each.
2. Write one personal exercise goal. What will you do *today* to get started?

19.1   Exercise in Daily Life

Directions:

Identify what kind of activity each student is doing, how long it may take them, what equipment is needed, and if it is done alone or with others. Parts of the charts are already filled in.

Paul	Jonda
Stats	*Stats*
Height: **6'1"**	Height: **5'2"**
Weight: **200 lb.**	Weight: **165 lb.**
Likes to exercise because: **Chicks dig it!**	Likes to exercise because: **Makes me feel good about myself.**
Dream: **To join the NBA**	Dream: **To learn the backstroke**
Activity:	Activity:
How long:	How long:
Equipment:	Equipment:
Alone/others:	Alone/others:

Lucy	Robbie
Stats	*Stats*
Height: **5'8"**	Height: **5'6"**
Weight: **125 lb.**	Weight: **160 lb.**
Likes to exercise because: **Helps keep my weight down**	Likes to exercise because: **Likes to set goals of lifting more weight**
Dream: **To walk a 5K race**	Dream: **To bench press 140 pounds**
Activity:	Activity:
How long:	How long:
Equipment:	Equipment:
Alone/others:	Alone/others:

19.2 Exercise Excuses

Objective: The student will identify several common excuses for not exercising and state a way to solve the problem.

Comments: We all make excuses for not exercising when there really are alternatives. It is important to know of other options for exercising and why excuses shouldn't keep us from living healthy. A person can exercise indoors, outdoors, alone, with a friend, with a TV program, with or without equipment, and in many creative ways.

Introductory Activities:

1. Ask students what types of exercise they have gotten in the past week.
2. Ask students to list excuses for not exercising. Write them on the board and code them: good excuse, bad excuse, or excuses that fall in the middle.

Activity: Students will complete the worksheet "Exercise Excuses" and choose a way to overcome each excuse by providing a solution.

Answers (Examples):

1. Wear a swimming cap.
2. Exercise at an off time when no one is around.
3. Ride her bike on some errands.
4. Participate in wheelchair sports.
5. Get a friend to try it with her.
6. Do Jazzercise indoors.
7. Start exercising slowly at first.
8. Go to the local park, which has exercise stations.

Discussion: Go over the student responses and compare creative solutions!

1. Why do people make excuses not to do something?
2. How can getting a partner or family member to join in help you get and stay motivated?
3. What goals could the individuals on the worksheet set to get started exercising?

Extension Activities:

1. Have students role-play the activities on the worksheet, with one being the resistant exerciser and the other being the voice of a coach, conscience, or health professional.
2. Make an "Excuse Board" and have students take turns shooting darts or rubber-tipped arrows at the excuses. Include comments such as "I'm too tired," "I don't like to get sore," and so on.

Evaluation:

1. List three excuses for not exercising.
2. List a solution for each of the excuses.

19.2   **Exercise Excuses**

Directions: How could you help these individuals with their excuses for not wanting to exercise?

1. Marsha doesn't want to go swimming because she'll get her hair wet.

   Solution: _____

2. John doesn't like lifting weights around football players because they have bigger muscles than his.

   Solution: _____

3. Sandy has too many errands to run today and can't work out.

   Solution: _____

4. Harvey is in a wheelchair and feels like he can't be athletic.

   Solution: _____

5. Karissa has always wanted to be a runner but is nervous about trying something new.

   Solution: _____

6. Janelle thinks the weather outside is cold; she would rather stay indoors and watch TV.

   Solution: _____

7. Fernando was sore for two days the last time he exercised.

   Solution: _____

8. Eleanor doesn't have the money to join a private gym to work out.

   Solution: _____

19.3 Personal Health Habits

Objective:

The student will complete a personal health survey and select two or three areas for improvement.

Comments:

Teens are going through many changes in their lives. Puberty affects their growth rate and triggers the onset of many other bodily changes. When you don't look like everyone else, it can lead to feelings of inferiority and confusion. In this lesson, students are to complete a self-inventory of some personal health habits to evaluate which areas are in need of attention.

Introductory Activities:

1. Ask students to tell what they ate for breakfast that morning. How many confess to eating candy bars, last night's pizza, or strange concoctions?   2. Ask students to share what time they went to bed last night. Calculate the number of hours slept. Compare answers.

Activity:

On the worksheet "Personal Health Habits," students are given a chance to complete (privately) a general inventory of habits for good hygiene, their self-assessments of weight, sleep habits, and regular medical maintenance. Be aware of some students who may be overweight or embarrassed about their looks. Some students may not have access to clean clothing, personal care items, or a stable home environment. (*Note:* Information for items 6 and 15 are discussed under Extension Activities.)   *Answers:* Will vary.

Discussion:

Go over the items on the worksheet in general terms. Do not ask students to share information that they are uncomfortable talking about in a group.

1. Why is it important to visit a dentist regularly? (Avoid pain, have nice appearance, keep your teeth all your life if possible.)   2. Why is it important to follow a doctor's instructions, especially for medication? (Monitor prescription drugs, know what is normal for you.)   3. Other than smelling and looking nice, why is it important to keep yourself clean?

Extension Activities:

1. Research BMI (body mass index) and help students calculate their weight. If 85 to 95 percentile is overweight, and over 95 percentile is obese, how many students are in an area of concern?
2. Sleep habits are different for teens! Research shows that a brain hormone is produced late at night that contributes to their tendency to keep odd hours. Have students make a list of good sleep health habits, including how to fall asleep.   3. Dieting is more than losing weight—it is eating healthy. Check into specific diet plans for teens and come up with ten tips for losing weight (small portions, watch out for sugary drinks, stop when you are full, and so on).
Helpful information for teens can be found on www.kidshealth.org/teen/food_fitness.com.

Evaluation:

List two or three personal areas of your health habits that could be improved. Explain how.

19.3   # Personal Health Habits

Directions:

Complete the following personal healthy inventory to see what areas might need attention.

- ☐ 1. I brush my teeth daily.
- ☐ 2. I visit my dentist at least twice a year.
- ☐ 3. I take all of my prescription medication regularly.
- ☐ 4. I get at least eight hours of sleep a night.
- ☐ 5. I fall asleep easily at night.
- ☐ 6. I am a good weight for my age and height.
- ☐ 7. I exercise regularly.
- ☐ 8. I eat breakfast every day.
- ☐ 9. I eat fruits and vegetables every day.
- ☐ 10. I take a bath or shower every day.
- ☐ 11. I use deodorant.
- ☐ 12. I wash my face every day.
- ☐ 13. I wash my hair several times a week.
- ☐ 14. I change my clothes every day.
- ☐ 15. I know how to lose weight safely.

19.4 Stress and Stressors

Objective:

The student will identify the stressor (something that causes us to feel stressed) in given situations.

Comments:

Stress is a part of life. Things that make us feel stressed are called *stressors*. This is not necessarily a negative thing; some people draw more energy, strength, and resourcefulness from being in what others might term a "stressful" situation. What is important is that each student can identify what is stressful and is able to cope with the situation. In this lesson, students are given stressful situations and are to select the stressor.

Introductory Activities:

1. Pretend you are in the following situation: Someone is chasing you. He is getting closer and closer. You are running as fast as you can, but your legs are getting tired and you can't go any faster. He is gaining on you! Now he is right behind you! You can hear him breathing! How do you feel? (Students may suggest fear, panic, excitement.)
2. Now let's continue the situation. The person grabs you and you fall down. Suddenly you hear cheering and thousands of people are yelling, *"Touchdown!"* Now how do you feel? (Happy.)
3. Did your perception of the situation change after you were given more information? Why? (In the context, it was not truly a life-threatening situation.)
4. Would you as the runner feel stress, even if you knew it was all a game? (Probably.)
5. Define *stress* (a feeling or response that results from some demand or pressure placed on you; could be pleasant or frightening).
6. Define *stressor* (something that causes you to feel stressed).

Activity:

In this lesson, students are to read on the worksheet "Stress and Stressors" examples of stressful situations. For each, they are to pick out the stressor and identify whether it is "good" or "bad" (pleasant/unpleasant; positive/negative).

Answers: 1. Test/negative   2. Accident/negative   3. Late bus/negative   4. School record/positive
5. Discipline by principal/negative   6. Too many tasks/negative

Discussion:

Have students reveal their thoughts about the stressors and their perceptions of each situation. Expand by having them tell about similar situations they have been in. Did they feel similarly stressed?

1. Is there a chance the stress that Otis feels in situation 1 would help him perform better? (Yes.)
2. If you knew that Terri took her father's car without permission and then got into an accident, would that increase her level of stress? (Probably.)
3. What if Terri had caused an accident by running into someone else? (Yes, increased stress.)
4. Why would Rolando in situation 3 feel anxiety? (There is nothing he can do to make that bus come faster.)
5. Do you think most athletes feel stress at times? (Probably.)
6. What are some causes of their stress? (Training rigors, desire to achieve, competing against others.)
7. What are some ways your body might show signs of stress, particularly in situation 5? (Red face, tightly clenched fists, increased heart rate, and so on.)
8. What could Wendy do in situation 6 to relieve her stress? (Take a deep breath, make a plan for getting the work done, cancel the babysitting, and so on.)

Extension Activities:

1. Have students compile a list of ten to fifteen activities that can be the cause of positive stress.
2. Have students compile a list of ten to fifteen activities that are usually the cause of negative stress. These activities could be at home, school, work, or leisure time.

Evaluation:

1. Define *stress*.
2. Define *stressor*.
3. Give an example of a situation in which the stressor is positive.
4. Give an example of a situation in which the stressor is negative.

Chapter 19: Exercise/Health and Hygiene

19.4   Stress and Stressors

Directions:

Read each of the following situations. Identify what is stressful (the stressor) about each situation and circle whether it is positive or negative.

1. Otis flunked his science test. He has a chance to retake it after school.
   If he does not get at least a C on the test, he will flunk the entire course and end up in summer school.

   Stressor: _____

           Positive   **Negative**

2. Terri borrowed her father's car to drive to the library. An elderly driver came out of nowhere and broadsided the car, leaving a smashed window and bent door. The other driver was hysterical, screaming and crying. Terri stepped out of the car, shaken but not hurt.

   Stressor: _____

           Positive   **Negative**

3. Rolando looked at his watch for the third time. If the bus didn't get here in the next minute, he would be late for his first day on the job. Where was that bus?

   Stressor: _____

           Positive   **Negative**

4. Christine took a deep breath. If she could do one more push-up, she would set a new school record. Her mouth was dry, her arms ached, but she was determined!

   Stressor: _____

           Positive   **Negative**

5. Dale and Karl sat side by side in the principal's office, giving each other occasional glares. "It was your fault," Dale hissed to the other boy. He received only silence. The shadow of the principal loomed over them. "You can come into my office now," boomed the angry voice.

   Stressor: _____

           Positive   **Negative**

6. Wendy looked at her assignment sheet. There was homework—lots of it!—assigned in every subject. She had to babysit for the McDermott triplets all evening. And she had promised her mother she would clean the entire house because she had had her friends over the night before. She felt overwhelmed!

   Stressor: _____

           Positive   **Negative**

19.5 Stressful Events and Situations

Objective: The student will identify common life events that are associated with stress.

Comments: Children, as well as adults, feel stress. For them, the stressor may be something as seemingly simple as moving to a new neighborhood or as devastating as experiencing the death of a parent. In this lesson, students are given a list of common stressors among children and are to take note of those that personally affect them.

Introductory Activities: Have students list what they consider to be one of the most stressful situations at home, at school, or among friends. (Be aware of your students' personal situations!)

Activity: Students are to read a list of stressful situations on the worksheet "Stressful Events and Situations" and indicate those that might be affecting them. Inform them that this is a personal inventory and will not be collected, but that they should be aware of the stresses they are under. Later lessons will discuss combating stress.

Discussion: Because the information is personal, students will not need to share their answers unless they want to discuss them in general terms. Be sensitive to their needs at this time.

1. Do you feel school puts a lot of stress on its students? How?
2. Would you rather have parents who put pressure on you to succeed, or parents who were more laid-back and let you work at your own pace?
3. Do you feel you work or perform well or even better under pressure?
4. Why is change—even if it is good or neutral—considered to be stressful? (Have to adapt to new things.)
5. How could success and achievement cause stress? (You might feel you have to live up to new expectations.)

Extension Activities:

1. Have students find a more complete list of adult life stressors. Some lists even provide a type of rating that indicates how intense that life event might be. (For example, the death of a spouse is usually at the top of the list, with a rating of 100. Divorce, marital separation, being in jail, being fired, retirement, and taking on a mortgage are also important stressors.) Although your students may view adulthood as far off, they or their parents will face these events before they know it.
2. Have students do a book report on the story of an individual who dealt with (and overcame) a stressful event.

Evaluation:

1. List at least ten important stressors that most people encounter in life.
2. Select a stressor that you can relate to personally and explain how it adds stress to your life. Is that stress positive in any way? If so, how?

Stressful Events and Situations

Directions:

Here is a list of stressful events and situations that occur throughout life. Put a check mark next to those that affect you.

☐ Moving or changing schools

☐ Having difficulty in school with academics

☐ Death of a close friend

☐ Death of a family member

☐ Change in the family (new baby, new siblings)

☐ Family crisis

☐ Family financial problems

☐ Alcohol abuse by family members

☐ Physical and emotional changes of puberty

☐ Domestic violence

☐ Living in a dangerous neighborhood

☐ Living in a single-parent household

☐ Parental separation or divorce

☐ Peer pressure

☐ Personal health problems

☐ Rejection by family members, friends, peers

☐ Ridicule by family members, friends, peers

☐ Change in sleeping habits (more, less, time of day)

☐ Change in eating habits

☐ Unrealistic expectations by parent or teacher

☐ Excessive discipline by parents

☐ Getting into trouble with the law

☐ Dealing with pregnancy

☐ Finding a job

☐ Getting married

19.6 Coping with Stress

Objective:

The student will be able to list and briefly explain at least three techniques for reducing stress.

Comments:

There are many techniques and programs available for stress reduction. These include everything from talking to yourself to hypnosis. Since our concern is students, the techniques presented in this lesson are fairly simple and straightforward. They can be learned and practiced within a school setting, with friends, or by individual study.

Introductory Activities:

1. Have students list some stressful occupations (surgeon, spy).
2. Have students suggest how those individuals might handle stress.

Activity:

Students are to read on the worksheet "Coping with Stress" a list of eight ways or techniques that may be helpful in dealing with stress. They are to answer the questions about each technique.

Answers (Examples):

1. Relaxation
   a. He could imagine himself winning.
   b. She could clear her mind of other thoughts.
2. Positive Practice
   c. She could rehearse all aspects of the speech.
   d. He could go through the arguments and anticipate all responses from the boss.
3. Talking to Yourself
   e. Encourage yourself not to get down about it; we all make mistakes.
   f. Dwell on the times when you succeeded; you will succeed again.
4. Assertiveness
   g. You wouldn't be confident enough to take a strong stand.
   h. You would gain respect for yourself.
5. Thought Stopping
   i. The person could train the mind to stop that line of thought.
   j. An explosive, laser beam.

6. Coping Skills

   k. Avoid whenever possible, continue to do your best, remind yourself it will be over someday.

   l. Find someone you can talk to; join Alateen.

   m. Practice time management to get everything in.

7. Learn New Skills

   n. Take a course; ask someone to teach you.

   o. Vocabulary, other self-help books.

8. Exercise

   p. The person could think through the problems of the day while moving around.

   q. Do something that involves the hands so he won't be tempted to eat.

Discussion:

Be sure to go over all the techniques and explain how each can work. Students may choose to target one to try. Some may already be employing some of the techniques in their experiences with stress.

1. Which of the techniques seem most appealing to you?
2. Which techniques have you already tried or currently use to reduce stress?
3. Can you think of other techniques that are helpful?

Extension Activities:

1. Steer students toward biographies of people who have gone through extremely stressful periods in their lives. How did these people cope? People like Anne Frank, Wilma Rudolph, Terry Fox, and survivors of the holocaust had experiences that are incredible.

2. Encourage students to try the techniques when they are in stressful situations. Have them report back to you (or the class) as to the success each has had. Practice them as a class if possible!

Evaluation:

List three techniques that can be helpful for reducing stress.

19.6   **Coping with Stress**

Directions:

Here is a list of some practices that can be helpful in managing stressful situations and/or the stressor itself. Read each carefully and then answer the questions.

1. **Relaxation:** Teach yourself to relax when you are in a stressful situation. Take a few deep breaths, close your eyes, imagine yourself floating.

   a. How could this be useful to a boy who is about to run a race?

   _____

   b. How could this be useful to a girl about to take a very important test?

   _____

2. **Positive Practice:** Before engaging in a stressful activity, go over it in your mind. Envision yourself performing each and every step, and always end with success! Do it so many times that it seems natural.

   c. How could this technique be used by a woman who has to give a speech?

   _____

   d. How could this be used by a man who has to present his side of a conflict to the boss or administrator?

   _____

3. ***Talking to Yourself:*** Get comfortable with the idea of giving yourself "pep talks" when you feel stressed. Keep repeating phrases such as "You are doing fine! This is something you can handle. You don't even need to worry about this." Say the things you wish someone else would say to you.

e. How could this work in a situation in which you made a mistake and are afraid to face your peers?

_____

f. How could this technique help someone who sometimes succeeds but sometimes doesn't?

_____

4. ***Assertiveness:*** Reduce your stress by standing up for what you believe is right. Handle the level of conflict by practicing saying what you believe and not backing down.

g. Why wouldn't this be a good technique if you weren't really sure how you felt or didn't know enough about the situation?

_____

h. How would it make you feel to know that others respected what you had to say?

_____

5. ***Thought Stopping:*** When you feel the symptoms of stress creeping in, imagine a lightning bolt flashing through the sky and bombarding that stressor to pieces. Imagine yourself screaming, "*Stop! That's enough!*" Forbid yourself to dwell on it anymore. "*Stop! Stop! Stop!*"

i. How could this technique be used by someone who daydreams a lot and ends up thinking about ways he or she is going to mess up or fail?

_____

j. What other mental images could be used to block or destroy a thought?

_____

6. ***Coping Skills:*** Pinpoint the stressor and logically decide how you can cope with it. If you have to sit next to that bully every day for the rest of the semester, make your plan as to how you can survive. Will you ignore him? Will you bring up a new, friendly topic of conversation? Will you combine other techniques, such as positive practice, to learn to handle this person in a way of your choosing? If you know there is going to be a problem, plan ahead of time to decide how you will handle it. Then stick to your plan.

k. How could you cope with a teacher who seems out to get you?

_____

l. How could you cope with a stepfather who is an alcoholic?

_____

m. How could you cope with a grueling work schedule for the next four weekends?

_____

7. ***Learn New Skills:*** Perhaps the stress comes from inability to perform. If a secretary is worried about making mistakes on the computer, perhaps taking a course in updating her skills would help handle the problem. People are capable of learning new things!

n. What skills could someone learn to overcome a fear of working with mechanical things? What about a fear of technology?

_____

o. If someone is embarrassed about appearing "dumb," what skills could he or she learn to improve this self-image?

_____

8. ***Exercise:*** Sometimes stress can be greatly alleviated by taking it out physically. Run! Play basketball! Work out! Do something to get your body on your side. Expend that energy in a positive, healthy way.

p. How could exercise help someone who works at a desk all day?

_____

q. What exercise would you recommend for someone who likes to eat when feeling stressed?

_____

19.7 Depression

Objective:

The student will define depression and identify several symptoms of depression.

Comments:

Everyone experiences moods of depression, particularly associated with sadness, grief, loneliness, or other traumatic events. But when the feeling of depression lasts for an extended period of time, it can cause other problems and may require treatment from a specialist. In this lesson, students are given a list of symptoms of depression.

Introductory Activities:

1. How would you feel if you came home from school and found out that a fish in your aquarium had died? (Probably sad for a little while.)
2. How would you feel if you came home and your favorite dog had died? (A little sadder than you'd feel about the fish?)
3. How would you feel if you found out your favorite uncle had died? (Very sad.)
4. How long do you think you would feel bad about the death of the fish? The dog? The person?
5. What would you think of a person who was still grieving over a dead fish three years later—grieving to the point that he or she couldn't eat, couldn't sleep, and didn't seem to care about anything? (You'd wonder about the significance of the fish, and you'd also advise the person to seek professional help.)
6. Define *depression*. (An emotional state in which the person feels sad, lonely, grief, or just "down." This is normal for short periods of time. When the symptoms persist, there is concern that it could be a more serious problem.)

Activity:

The term *depression* describes the behavior of anyone who is in a state of sadness, grief, or general gloominess. When used to refer to clinical depression, this is a much more serious type of depression that can be associated with other types of disorders and even suicide. In this lesson, students are to examine symptoms or signs of depression by matching them with a comment on the worksheet "Depression." It's hoped that this will create an awareness of the problem. Be sure to explain any terms with which students are unfamiliar.

Answers: 1. e   2. c   3. k   4. j   5. b   6. i   7. d   8. g   9. h   10. f   11. a   12. l

Discussion:

Everyone feels some of the symptoms of depression from time to time. Be sure students understand that this is normal.

1. Can you relate to most of the comments on the worksheet, at least at some time or another in your life?
2. When do you remember being the most depressed?
3. Do you know of anyone who was so depressed that he or she needed professional help?
4. What kinds of treatments are you aware of for depression? (Counseling, medication, perhaps shock therapy.)
5. Why wouldn't it work to tell someone to just "snap out of it!"? (It may be a chemical problem requiring medical treatment.)
6. Do children experience depression? (Yes.)
7. What are some causes of depression in children? (Children who suffer a significant loss, have low self-esteem, have family problems, or have an inherited tendency for depression.)
8. What would you think of someone who was on medication for depression?
9. Are people who are treated for depression "crazy"? (No, but they may need help.)
10. During the times when you were depressed, what got you out of it or helped a lot?

Extension Activities:

1. Have students research the treatments for depression. Have them find out in what ways other people (especially families) can help with a depressed individual.
2. Have students make a list of what they think are the most important factors of their lives that are associated with depression. Would a bad haircut make you feel depressed? Would losing a parent to cancer? Have them give this some thought. Answers will differ greatly among students.

Evaluation:

1. Define and explain *depression.*
2. List at least five symptoms or signs of depression.

19.7   **Depression**

Directions: The following is a list of comments that might indicate a depressed feeling and a list of symptoms of depression. Match the comment on the left with the symptom on the right.

1. "I don't care how I do on the test. It doesn't matter to me." _____

2. "I'm not hungry—I just don't feel like eating anything." _____

3. "I used to enjoy playing football, but I don't anymore. I don't enjoy basketball either anymore." _____

4. *Yawning:* "I'm sooooo sleepy." _____

5. "I don't feel like going out with my friends. I don't want to be around people." _____

6. "I'm trying to think of the right answer, but I just can't seem to stay on one thought for very long." _____

7. "My head hurts. My stomach hurts." _____

8. "Nobody likes me—and I don't blame them. What's there to like?" _____

9. "I've been crying for the past three days. I just feel like crying all the time." _____

10. "Nothing is going right. Even if I won the contest, I'd probably have to give the prize back." _____

11. "Why do you say I'm always in a bad mood? I'm not in a bad mood. Now get out of here and leave me alone!" _____

12. "I can't sleep at night. I just lie there and toss and turn. All night long." _____

a. Irritable, crabby

b. Socially withdrawn

c. Decreased appetite

d. Aches and pains

e. Apathetic, indifferent

f. Pessimistic, looks at the bad side of things

g. Low self-esteem

h. Long, severe crying spells

i. Inability to concentrate

j. Mentally and physically tired

k. Unable to enjoy activities once enjoyed

l. Insomnia, can't sleep

Chapter 19: Exercise/Health and Hygiene   **379**

Part Five

Vocational Skills

Chapter 20: Present Skills and Interests

20.1 My Strengths

20.2 My Interests

20.3 My Hobbies

20.4 Realistic Vocational Goals

20.5 Academic Strengths

20.6 Working with a Disability

20.7 Finishing High School

20.8 Extracurricular Activities

Chapter 21: Getting a Job

21.1 Searching for a Job

21.2 Vocational Vocabulary

21.3 Filling Out an Application

21.4 What Is a Resume?

21.5 Interviewing for a Job

21.6 First Impressions

21.7 Getting Work Experience

Chapter 22: Working

22.1 Having a Good Attitude

22.2 Being a Great Employee

22.3 Making a Mistake on the Job

22.4 Handling Criticism

22.5 Being Prepared for the Task

22.6 Changing Jobs: Why?

22.7 Changing Jobs: How?

Chapter 20

Present Skills and Interests

20.1 My Strengths

Objective:

The student will identify at least twenty things that he or she feels he or she can do well. This may include accomplishments, personality attributes, talents, and so on.

Comments:

When beginning the search for a job and hopefully a career, the student may start by looking at his or her own skills and interests. Although not everyone is lucky enough to find his or her job fascinating, it is a worthwhile endeavor to take inventory of what one is able to do well and is interested in doing. Perhaps later there will be some overlap between the job and the interest. In this lesson, students are to make a list of what they feel are their skills, talents, and/or things that they are knowledgeable about.

Introductory Activities:

1. Define *skill*. (Something someone is able to do well; this can be an acquired thing with learning.)
2. Define *talent*. (A natural ability to do something well; this is something that you have or you don't; it can be developed and enhanced, but it is more of something that is within the person.)
3. Define *job*. (A task that is performed usually for money; can be short-lived and may not involve a lot of training or skill.)
4. Define *career*. (A profession, usually involving training, that may last throughout a person's life.)

Activity:

Students will add items to a list of things that they are able to do well. This could include activities that they are good at, things they know something about, or even winning personality traits.

Discussion:

Provide time for students to share their ideas about their skills and interests. If some students say they cannot think of any, encourage classmates who know them to help them out.

1. Do you have skills or talents that seem to run in your family? If so, what?
2. Why do you think people in the same family might have similar interests? (Availability of resources.)
3. How did you become good at the things you are proficient in now? (Practice, good teaching, asking questions, and so on.)
4. Do you need other people to tell you that you are good at something or is it enough for you to recognize your skills yourself?
5. What are some skills that can be learned if you are willing to become a student or apprentice?
6. What are some examples of talents that some people just naturally possess? (Musical ability, athletic ability, and so on.)
7. What are some skills you have developed within the last year?
8. How did you learn a new skill?

Extension Activities:

1. Encourage students to take part in a workshop, mini-course, correspondence class, YMCA/YWCA evening class, cooking class at the community center, and so on. Many classes are free or are available for a small charge. Learn a new skill!

2. Help students offer their services for free to become an apprentice to someone who does something they are interested in or would like to learn more about. Try to help students hook up with an auto repair shop, riding stable, artist, and so on.

Evaluation:

1. List two skills in which you are competent that you have learned or developed in the past year.

2. List two talents you possess.

20.1

My Strengths

Directions:

Make a list for yourself of twenty to twenty-five (or more) things you are able to do well. Don't limit your-self to only things you can make or compete at; include things you know a lot about and your personality strengths.

Examples:

I am good with children.

I can fix things—a bike, VCR, and so on.

I know a lot about astronauts and the space program.

1. _____
2. _____
3. _____
4. _____
5. _____
6. _____
7. _____
8. _____
9. _____
10. _____
11. _____
12. _____
13. _____

14. _____
15. _____
16. _____
17. _____
18. _____
19. _____
20. _____
21. _____
22. _____
23. _____
24. _____
25. _____
26. _____

20.2 My Interests

Objective: The students will identify at least five to ten different interests that he or she currently has.

Comments: Some jobs come with a rather predictable work environment; a pilot, for example, may have a regular route, is responsible for the welfare of others, must be cool in a crisis, and should be familiar with the technology of the plane. A person who enjoys none of those qualifications would probably not seek a job in which he or she would be piloting an airplane. In this lesson, students are to identify some characteristics of a job that appeal to them.

Introductory Activities:

1. Have students write one career that is of interest to them.
2. Have students list at least three to five interests or skills that a person who performs that job would probably have.

Activity: On this worksheet, students will read a list of possible interests that people may have and then circle several that are appealing to them. The idea is to stimulate thought and discussion about their own interests.

Discussion: Clarify any items the students are unsure about. Remind them that this is just a preference list; there is no wrong or right.

1. What do you think are some major considerations for someone looking for a job? (Depends on the individual and his or her needs at the time; money, security, outlet for creativity, and so on.)
2. What are some ways you could take advantage of opportunities to try new things? (Read, volunteer, take a summer job, and so on.)

Extension Activities:

1. Have students look over the preferences they select. Have them identify at least one career that seems to fit their interests.
2. Assign a class project to select fifty careers. Provide a ten-sentence summary for each career that describes the probable characteristics of someone in that career.
3. Have students begin a personal career file: collect items on interesting careers such as news articles, school information, and brochures. Find out the salary, available training, and working conditions associated with each career.

Evaluation:

1. List three of your main career interests at this time.
2. Write a paragraph describing a time when you explored or tried something new and found out something about yourself.

20.2   My Interests

Directions:

Read the following list of interests you may have. Circle those that appeal to you.

1. Working with pets

2. Working with children

3. Being inside

4. Being outside

5. Being around people

6. Moving around

7. Sitting at a desk to work

8. Teaching someone how to do something

9. Traveling

10. Driving

11. Taking care of things

12. Working under high pressure, excitement

13. Having a calm, predictable environment

14. Being creative

15. Following a set schedule each day

16. Doing lots of different tasks

17. Doing the same task over and over

18. Being responsible for the welfare and safety of others

19. Making lots of money

20. Using a computer

21. Having a chance to learn new skills

22. Helping other people

23. Supervising other people

24. Working whatever hours I want

25. Getting raises and promotions

20.3 My Hobbies

Objective:

The student will describe how a specific hobby can be related or turned into a career.

Comments:

Sometimes things we do for fun and pure enjoyment can pay off in terms of being a vocational choice. Some hobbies are engaged in because they are a pleasant "break" from a demanding career (doctors playing golf?), and sometimes turning a hobby into a business can take away the enjoyment of the hobby. In some circumstances, however, it is nice to think of your work as something you truly enjoy doing. In this lesson, students are to specify how certain hobbies may be turned into careers.

Introductory Activities:

1. Define *hobby* (an activity that is engaged in primarily for entertainment).   2. Have students list five to ten hobbies with which they are familiar.

Activity:

Students are to match the hobby on the left side of the worksheet "My Hobbies" with a possible career listed on the right side that could grow from that hobby. Make sure students understand what is usually involved in the hobbies listed.   *Answers:* 1. f   2. h   3. c   4. d   5. i   6. e   7. g   8. k   9. a   10. 1   11. j   12. b

Discussion:

Make sure students did not have any trouble completing the worksheet.

1. What are some other examples of hobbies that can turn into careers?   2. Do you personally know of any people who have turned a hobby into a business or career?   3. Some people choose hobbies that are very different from their jobs. For example, a woman who works at a desk all day might go jogging for fun. What are some other examples of hobbies that would complement certain types of jobs?   4. What are some collections you can think of? (Stamps, dolls, antique cars.) 5. What would be the value of becoming an "expert" in a certain field of study if it was not part of your job?   6. What are some sports hobbies you can think of?   7. How could sports as a hobby be turned into a career other than by actually participating in the sport as a professional? (Advertising, sales of related merchandise, and so on.)   8. Why do people invest time and money in hobbies? (Serious fun!)   9. Think of some very exciting careers—race car driving, modeling, working on television, and so on. Do you think the people who are involved in these careers may have begun by dabbling in the career as a hobby? How?   10. Do you think people who are involved in exciting careers would have very different activities for their hobbies?

Extension Activities:

1. Organize a Hobby Fair for your class. Have students (or parents or adult friends or other interested community people) bring in collections, pictures, posters, brochures, and so on, about their hobbies. 2. Assign students the task of researching a new hobby. Let them find out about it and report back to the class.   3. Invite speakers to class to talk about their hobbies. How does the hobby fit into their life as a balance or supplement for their career? Does the speaker wish that the hobby could be his or her career?

Evaluation:

1. List three personal hobbies.   2. Describe how each of your hobbies could turn into a career for you.

20.3 My Hobbies

Directions:

Match the hobby on the left with a possible career listed on the right that could grow from that hobby.

_____ 1. Refinishing furniture

_____ 2. Collecting antiques

_____ 3. Training dogs

_____ 4. Painting with watercolors

_____ 5. Writing poetry

_____ 6. Cooking fancy meals

_____ 7. Playing football

_____ 8. Planting and growing flowers

_____ 9. Sewing

_____ 10. Doing aerobic dancing

_____ 11. Repairing cars

_____ 12. Horseback riding

a. selling patterns at a fabric shop; helping customers with their sewing needs

b. working at a store that sells saddles and bridles

c. working for the police department K-9 (canine) unit

d. selling paintings at an art gallery

e. running a catering business

f. selling furniture made of wood; doing repairs involving woodworking

g. coaching a high school sports team

h. working in a museum as a guide

i. being a freelance writer selling work to magazines

j. working in an auto body shop

k. managing a florist shop

l. teaching exercies classes at a health spa

20.4 Realistic Vocational Goals

Objective:

The student will identify problems with characters who have unrealistic career goals.

Comments:

Many children want to grow up to be actresses, sports heroes, rock stars, and millionaires! It seems glamorous and attainable to a child who doesn't realize that the odds are against him or her. In this lesson, examples are given of characters who have somewhat unrealistic aspirations.

Introductory Activities:

1. Have students volunteer to recall, when they were five or six years old, what they wanted to be when they were grown up.
2. Have students raise their hands if they have changed their minds about a career since they were little. If so, why?

Activity:

Students are given several situations to consider in which characters are not setting realistic vocational goals. They should identify possible problems and write their ideas on the lines.

Answers (Examples):

1. A small town may not support a huge factory; he doesn't mention having any resources to open a factory.
2. It appears as though the girl doesn't have much musical ability.
3. The product is not good.
4. He doesn't know much about his product.
5. He did not research the business; it may be a total scam.
6. He doesn't seem bright enough to be a scientist.

Discussion:

Have students explain how they selected the problems in each example. Some assumptions have to be made about the characters since not a lot of facts are given.

1. Is it wrong to have high aspirations? Why *not* plan to become a sports hero or rock star; obviously some people make it? (Try to be realistic—some make it, but many more do not.)
2. What types of skills or talents do you think are important when choosing a career? (Things that will fit into the career.)
3. Why is it important to know a lot about your product if you are selling it? (So you can be convincing to your customers.)
4. What lack of skills seems apparent in situations 2 and 6? (Musical ability, general intelligence.)

5. Do you think having someone tell you "You'll never make it" can work in a positive sense? How? (Might give the person incentive to try to beat the odds.)

6. What advice do you think someone who "beat the odds" would give to others who want to be where they are? (Keep trying, don't give up, and so on.)

7. What are some things you could be doing right now to help yourself toward whatever career or goal you are interested in?

Extension Activities:

1. Have students find and read interviews given by people who are successful in their fields. What advice do they offer to people who want to be successful?

2. Have students make a bulletin board emphasizing the importance of hard work toward achieving a goal. Use a "ladder" with words or phrases written on the rungs, such as *education, taking a risk, talking to people, learning, listening,* and so on.

Evaluation:

What is at least one realistic career goal for the following characters?

1. Joel loves music. He knows all of the artists and bands that are currently on the Top 40 list. He can't play an instrument, but he has a great memory for songs. (*Examples:* disc jockey, record store owner or manager.)

2. Rachel is good with numbers. She always has her checkbook balanced and handles investments for her family. She enjoys learning about how to make money by investing in the stock market. (*Examples:* stock market investor, accountant, financial advisor.)

3. Marta was abused as a child. She spent a lot of time in courts and eventually grew up in a foster home. Now she wants to help protect children from the type of abuse that she lived through. (*Examples:* lawyer, social worker.)

4. Tomas enjoys taking pictures. He has several cameras and has taken classes in photography. He would rather be behind a camera than anywhere else. (*Examples:* studio photographer; freelance photographer for books, calendars, and magazines.)

20.4   Realistic Vocational Goals

Directions:

The following characters are going to run into difficulty as they prepare for a career. What problems) do you see in each case? Write your ideas on the lines.

1. *It doesn't matter that I live in a town of 2,500 people —I'm going to become a business whiz and open a huge factory and make millions.*

_____

_____

_____

2. *I know Madonna won't be around forever. The world will be ready for the next great rock star! ME!*

_____

_____

_____

3. *How hard can it be to sell jewelry? I'll get this special "starter kit" and I'm on my way!*

_____

_____

_____

4. *Howdy. I'm selling...uhhhhh...well, let's see. Oh, heating products. Would you like to buy some?*

_____

_____

_____

5. *You tell me it costs only $10,000 to buy into this fast-growing business? What's the name of it again? Sure, I'll throw in my life savings to buy in.*

_____

_____

_____

6. *Yeah, I can be a rocket scientist. How do you spell "moon"?*

_____

_____

20.5 Academic Strengths

Objective: The student will review past and present report cards and state at least two academic strengths.

Comments: School records are important, especially because most high school transcripts will play a part in the student's further education. If students are in high school, you may be able to track their past records through your central office. Some students may have past report cards at home; if so, you may need to get parent permission to view them. Many schools send home standardized test information at the end of the school year as well. In this lesson, students are to look at their grades and determine which subject or subjects are a "strength." They may wish to view future career possibilities in light of what they are interested in and excel at in school.

Introductory Activities:

1. Have students tell about their best year in school. When was it? Why was it good?
2. Have students write what they think is their best subject in school.

Activity: Using past report cards and any other objective information about students' performance, students should summarize the information on the worksheet "Academic Strengths." Many report cards contain places to record attendance, which can affect school performance. Have students list semester or yearly grades for the main academic subjects and include other appropriate subjects in the last column. Make sure you do not embarrass students who may not have good grades.

Materials: reports cards, standardized test results (if available), attendance reports, pen or pencil

Discussion: Since grades may be a rather personal issue with some students, have students volunteer to reveal their thoughts and answer questions. Have students go over the discussion questions at the bottom of the worksheet.

Extension Activities:

1. Have students find out if there is a connection between attendance and grades. If possible, provide students with information about attendance and grades from anonymous students in their class. Do good students have good attendance? Do poor students have poor attendance? Have them define their terms and decide what limits support their conclusions.
2. Have students interview teachers in the school or collect examples of grading procedures for their classes. How much control does a student have over the grade he or she gets in a class? (Some teachers may grade on a contract basis, others use percentage of points, and so on.)

Evaluation:

1. List two of your academic strengths as indicated by report card grades.
2. Select one of your memorable classes and grades. Explain in a paragraph what you remember about that class. Why was it memorable? Was the grade you received a fair one? Why?

20.5   Academic Strengths

Directions:

Using old report cards and standardized testing if available, complete the following academic profile of your grades over the past few years. Be objective!

```
REPORT C          RT CARD
  2000-20          02-2003
            REPORT CARD
ENGLISH     2001-2002        - C
MATH      ENGLISH  -  A      - B
SCIENCE   MATH     -  A      - A
HISTORY   SCIENCE  -  B      - C
READING   HISTORY  -  A      - A
          READING  -  B
```

School Year	Attendance (excellent/good/poor)	Grades				
		Math	Reading/English	Science	Social Studies	Other

1. How was my attendance overall?

2. In what areas do I have the best grades?

3. Is this an area that I am interested in learning more about?

4. In what areas do I have the worst grades?

5. What is my explanation for those grades?

6. Do I feel these grades are a fair representation of my abilities and knowledge in these areas?

7. At this point, am I interested in further education, such as college?

8. Am I interested in further education, such as technical or vocational training?

9. Are there ways to improve my grades? How?

10. Am I interested in putting more effort into academic classes if it would improve my chances for further education?

20.6 Working with a Disability

Objective:

The student will explain how a person with a disability could make adaptations to do well in school or on the job.

Comments:

Just because a person has a disability (physical, emotional, learning, and so on) does not mean he or she cannot still achieve success at school or on the job. There are many adaptations that can and must be made for people with disabilities. In this lesson, students are given examples of characters who have a disability. They are to explain how the character is coping with school and work in spite of the disability.

Introductory Activities:

1. Have students make a list of disabilities with which they are familiar.
2. Have students look over their list and note how many of these are physical disabilities.
3. Have students give examples of any individuals they know who have a disability and how that person functions with adaptations, if necessary.

Activity:

Students are to read five examples on the worksheet "Working with a Disability" about people with disabilities in a school or work situation. They are to identify the disability and explain how the character is coping with it in each setting.

Answers (Examples): 1. physical disability—uses elevator 2. learning disability—taped material 3. epilepsy—medication 4. emotional disability—small class 5. deaf—hearing aid, translator

Discussion:

Go through each example and clarify each disability if students are unfamiliar with the basic handicapping condition.

1. Do you know of anyone with a disabling condition? What is it?
2. Does this person's disability stop this person from doing what he or she wants or needs to do in any way?
3. What special adaptations (if any) are made for this person?
4. Do you think having a disability should stop someone from succeeding in school?
5. What are some ways schools can help a person with a disability?
6. What types of jobs might be out of the realm of possibility for the people on the worksheet? Why?

Extension Activities:

1. Have students work in groups and research a handicapping condition. Have them find the definition of the handicap, ways that people with this disability can overcome or work around it, famous people who have had this condition, and other topics. Ideas may include: deafness, blindness, cerebral palsy, epilepsy, mental retardation, emotional disturbance, physically challenged, and so on.

2. Have students volunteer to spend time working in a classroom with children with special needs. The experience may be quite enlightening!

3. Have students read selected books written by or about people with disabilities. What limits (if any) did the people put on themselves?

4. Find out what community resources are available to help people with disabilities. Is there a group home? Sheltered workshop? Vocational training?

5. If you know of someone who would be willing to come in to talk to the class about his or her disability and how it affects everyday life, invite this person to school. Prepare your class for appropriate questions. Perhaps someone in your class has a disability—be sensitive to his or her feelings.

Evaluation:

1. List examples of at least three common disabilities.

2. For each, give an example of how a person with that disability might still perform school and work tasks.

20.6

Working with a Disability

Directions:

Read the accounts of the following students. Identify each disability. Then explain how each is coping with his or her situation at school and on the job.

1. Mark is in a wheelchair. He was injured in an accident many years ago, but has complete use of his upper body. At school he has classes on the first floor and uses the school elevator to get where he needs to go. He attends regular classes at school.

2. Amanda has a learning disability. She finds it extremely difficult to read and understand any kind of written material, although she excels in math. Her teachers allow her to take tests orally, and she often listens to books read on a tape recorder. Her grades are average. Only her closest friends even realize that she has a disability.

3. Charlie has epilepsy. He cannot get a driver's license, but he has no other restrictions. His seizures are completely controlled with medication. He does average or above-average work at school and has two part-time jobs: delivering the local newspaper and helping his uncle at a gas station.

4. Kanisha is in a class with other students who have not done well in a traditional class setting. She has an emotional handicap that prevents her from learning as easily as some other students. The class is small, and she takes most of her academics from one teacher. They also do some "job shadowing" several times a week, in which Kanisha can assist people at the local hospital.

5. Eric is partially deaf. He has a small hearing aid in both ears and communicates primarily through signing. He attends several regular classes with the help of a translator. After school Eric helps out at the YMCA with teaching swimming to young children with and without handicaps.

20.7 Finishing High School

Objective:

The student will give at least two reasons why it is important or beneficial to complete high school.

Comments:

There are a lot of reasons why teenagers drop out of high school. Among these are the facts of pregnancy, poor grades, truancy, getting into trouble at school, boredom, seeing no relevance, and a simple lack of motivation. In this lesson, students are asked to respond to comments about completing high school.

Introductory Activities:

1. Have students raise their hands if they intend to graduate from high school.
2. Have students raise their hands if they have a close friend who has dropped out of high school.
3. Have students raise their hands if they have a brother or sister who has already dropped out of high school.

Activity:

Students are to read the twelve statements on the worksheet "Finishing High School." They are to circle Agree or Disagree to show how they feel about the statement. These are all opinion statements, so inform students that they will not be scored "right" or "wrong."

Discussion:

It may be quite surprising to hear your students' views on completing high school. While some may be overly optimistic that they of course will complete high school (even with poor attendance, poor grades, low motivation), others—particularly those without support from home—may already be planning to quit. Without being judgmental or "preachy," listen to the students' comments and opinions. Extension activities may prove to be quite enlightening to some of these students!

1. What do you think is the main purpose of high school?
2. If someone close to you has dropped out of school, why would that make it more likely that you would also drop out of school? (That's your model; you may think of this as "freedom"; you may already have a job.)
3. Do you think there is a connection between the amount of education a person has and his or her earning potential?
4. What other kinds of training are available after high school besides a regular four-year college program? (Two-year degrees, vocational schools, apprentice programs, and so on.)
5. Do you feel your parents value a high school education?
6. Why is a high school degree sometimes important to parents or grandparents who never got one? (They might feel as though they have missed an opportunity.)
7. What are some ways that classes and schools try to make learning more relevant? (Offer on-the-job programs, work/study, and so on.)

8. Do you know of anyone who has completed the GED program? What comments did this person have about the program?

9. If someone has quit high school, how easy do you think it would be to return—especially after having a baby or working for awhile? (Probably difficult—new responsibilities, less time, more stresses.)

10. What advice would you give to someone who is struggling in high school, but still wants to stay in and try to finish? (Get help—talk to a counselor, teachers; get tutoring, and so on.)

Extension Activities:

1. If possible, have a counselor come in to explain the GED (equivalency) program. Some students may think this is an easy way to get through high school. Find out about the history of the program (military program during World War II), the restrictions, time involved, level of material, and commitment of time that is necessary to complete the program.

2. Have students research the earning potential of students with and without high school degrees.

3. Have students find out reasons why teenagers drop out of high school. How many plan to return? How many actually return?

4. Invite speakers to your class who have made the decision (or felt it was necessary) to drop out of high school. Do they regret the decision? What factors were involved in their life at the time? What are they doing today?

Evaluation:

1. List at least two reasons why it is beneficial to complete high school.

2. List at least two reasons why teenagers may choose to drop out of high school.

3. Write a paragraph explaining your intentions about finishing high school.

20.7 **Finishing High School**

Directions:

Complete the following survey by expressing your opinions and reactions to the following statements about high school. Circle **Agree** or **Disagree** after each statement.

1. It is important to have a high school diploma. **Agree Disagree**

2. You can still get a good job without a high school degree. **Agree Disagree**

3. High school is a waste of time if you don't plan to go to college. **Agree Disagree**

4. Most high school classes don't have any practical value. **Agree Disagree**

5. It is easy to get a GED (equivalency degree) if you drop out of school and then want to get a degree. **Agree Disagree**

6. There are ways to get help if you want to finish high school. **Agree Disagree**

7. A lot of my friends either have quit or intend to quit high school. **Agree Disagree**

8. One or both of my parents did not finish high school. **Agree Disagree**

9. I have a brother or sister who quit school. **Agree Disagree**

10. I would consider leaving high school, but only if I had a job already lined up. **Agree Disagree**

11. The only reason I am in high school is because of the activities and my friends. **Agree Disagree**

12. If you really want to get a high school diploma, you will find a way. **Agree Disagree**

20.8 Extracurricular Activities

Objective: The student will list at least five to ten extracurricular activities available at his or her school and how involvement in those activities is beneficial to vocational planning.

Comments: Schools, no matter how small, generally offer a range of extracurricular activities for students to participate in. Many colleges look for evidence of participation as part of the application process. It is important for students to be well-rounded, to try different things, and to be part of groups. Getting involved and being part of a team are important qualities to future employers. Plus, it can be fun! In this lesson, students are to complete a word search that includes many examples of extracurricular activities.

Introductory Activities: Have students guess which activity you are referring to by giving the following clues:

1. "Go! Team! Go!" (Cheerleading.)
2. "Would you please grant an interview, Ms. Principal?" (School paper.)
3. "There are other ways to have fun without drinking!" (Students Against Drunk Driving—S.A.D.D.)

Activity: Students are to try to find the words in the word search puzzle "Extracurricular Activities." All the words are examples of typical extracurricular activities at schools. Inform students that not all of the activities may be available at your school. Clarify any terms with which students are unfamiliar.

Answers:

```
a c x h f o o t b a l l x l m
l h c m l h o l h c s r t f h
a e r h o b a n d c o m l l t
h s e m x h o i a m c h j h w
c s t o r n b a n a c m a n n
a d a b s t k m c r e l b b s
v d e b a t e m e s r l u m b
s t h o d h l o r v s i l a u
k s t u d e n t c o u n c i l
j w e n n i t t h l o m l x c
e i l e p h r a e l r q r u p
c m h e e r a s e e c h a l e
n t a b c d m u r y h r y a p
s e l m o h u x l b e h l o l
s a w d o g r d e a s f r a n
x m r s t h a m a l t o l y h
s l e e p h l m d l r x h o o
t r s h c a s o i o a p w w o
o u t a n y p t n d o e k m h
j e l o l k r e g s d b h b l
l i i c c h o i r g w e l t r
p l n h i h o k l e w h i c h
d a g l s y d r l h c s l h x
```

Discussion: After completing the activity, have students talk about which activities they are interested in or involved in. Perhaps some students are unaware of the activities available at your school.

1. What are some of the benefits of being involved in an extracurricular activity? (Fun, be on a team, learn a new skill, and so on.)

2. What might it cost you in terms of time and money to become involved in an extracurricular activity? (Time for practices, travel time, money for uniforms, and so on.)

3. What is fun about being part of a team? (Other people accept you, support you, might enjoy being on a winning team, and so on.)

4. What skills might you learn from being a part of a group that an employer would be interested in? (How well you get along with others, whether you are a leader, whether you can learn new things.)

5. Why do you think potential employers want to know which activities you were involved in when you were in high school? (Want to know your interests, what type of skills you have, and so on.)

6. Are there certain groups at your school that are considered to be desirable? Which groups?

7. Are there certain groups at your school that are laughed at or not respected?

8. If you were going to start a new extracurricular organization at your school, what would it be?

Extension Activities:

1. Have students research and then prepare a display showing the different activities available at your school. They may want to interview people who are involved in the club or group (or they may be members themselves); to find out the restrictions, membership responsibilities, services provided, and skills taught; and so on.

2. Encourage students to join an activity—perhaps something they never really gave any serious thought to before. Give it a try!

Evaluation:

1. List five to ten extracurricular activities available at your school.

2. For each, specify at least one skill that would be used when pursuing that activity.

3. Select one of your activities and explain how (or why) an employer might be interested to know you were involved in that activity at school.

20.8   Extracurricular Activities

Directions: There are a lot of extracurricular activities in the following word search. Can you find them all? Look for the words horizontally, vertically, diagonally—and backwards!!

```
a   c   x   h   f   o   o   t   b   a   l   l   x   i   m
l   h   c   m   i   h   o   l   h   c   s   r   t   f   h
a   e   r   h   o   b   a   n   d   c   o   m   l   l   t
h   s   e   m   x   h   o   l   a   m   c   h   i   h   w
c   s   t   o   r   n   b   a   n   a   c   m   a   n   n
a   d   a   b   s   t   k   m   c   r   e   i   b   b   s
v   d   e   b   a   t   e   m   e   s   r   l   u   m   b
s   t   h   o   d   h   i   o   r   v   s   i   l   a   u
k   s   t   u   d   e   n   t   c   o   u   n   c   i   l
j   w   e   n   n   i   t   t   h   l   o   m   t   x   c
e   i   l   e   p   h   r   a   e   l   r   q   r   u   p
c   m   h   e   e   r   a   s   e   e   c   h   a   l   e
n   t   a   b   c   d   m   u   r   y   h   r   y   a   p
s   e   l   m   o   h   u   x   l   b   e   h   i   o   j
s   a   w   d   o   g   r   d   e   a   s   f   r   a   n
x   m   r   s   t   h   a   m   a   l   t   o   i   y   h
s   l   e   e   p   h   l   m   d   l   r   x   h   o   o
t   r   s   h   c   a   s   o   i   o   a   p   w   w   o
o   u   t   a   n   y   p   t   n   d   o   e   k   m   h
j   e   l   o   i   k   r   e   g   s   d   b   h   b   i
l   i   i   c   c   h   o   i   r   g   w   e   i   t   r
p   i   n   h   i   h   o   k   l   e   w   h   i   c   h
d   a   g   i   s   y   d   r   i   h   c   e   i   h   x
```

band
orchestra
football
volleyball
theater
dance
wrestling
SADD
intramurals
choir
debate
chess
pep club
student council
swim team
cheerleading
newspaper
art club
soccer

Chapter 21

Getting a Job

21.1 Searching for a Job

Objective:

The student will identify at least five ways to begin searching for a job.

Comments:

For many students, it may seem overwhelming at first to enter the world of work after the structure and safety of high school life. Some may already have jobs lined up, but many probably must go in "cold"—beginning that search for the first real job. In this lesson, students are given examples of ways to begin looking for a job.

Introductory Activities:

1. Have students raise their hands if they are planning to inherit the family fortune after they finish high school and never work another day in their life.
2. Have students raise their hands if they are already working somewhere and plan to continue to work there after high school.
3. Have students raise their hands if they have a good idea of what they will be doing right after high school.
4. Have students raise their hands if they think they could benefit from some help getting a job after high school.

Activity:

Students will consider a list of ways to find a job. They should provide an example of how each way could be helpful and write their answers on the lines.

Answers (Examples):

1. Find out if there is an opening at a business in your area for which you are qualified.
2. Put your own ad in the newspaper or online.
3. Your friend or relative may know the person who does the hiring and put in a good word for you; this lets the employers know you are available.
4. A counselor can help match you with a job.
5. There may be a job placement service after training is completed.
6. A social worker may be able to find you a position.
7. Sometimes businesses will hire temporary helpers; this can help someone get a foot in the door.

Discussion:

Have students share their ideas and/or experiences with getting a job. They may have additional suggestions as well.

1. How much time do you think is involved in job-hunting? (Could be a lot!)
2. What are some ways you can be systematic about looking for a job? (Keep a list of places you have tried or want to try.)
3. Whom are you probably competing with to find a job? (Other recent graduates, unemployed adults in the community, other skilled workers, people who have been laid-off in your area, and so on.)

4. Do you think the job will come to you or will you have to do some work to find a job? (Unless they are in a family business, they will probably have to do some work.)

5. How could job-hunting be a discouraging experience? (Getting turned down, being told you don't have enough experience.)

6. If the place you are interested in working at requires experience, how could you go about getting experience if they won't hire you? (Find something somewhat related.)

Extension Activities:

1. Have students interview five adults to find out how they got their first jobs.

2. Go through your local paper's classified ads for employment. Have students systematically go through them to find what types of jobs are available, the range of salaries, which are entry-level positions, how many require specific experience, and whether any will provide training. For how many of the jobs are students qualified right now?

3. Contact an employment agency to find out the terms for finding a job through this means. Is a fee involved? How much? What types of jobs are listed?

4. Check out www.myfirstpaycheck.com and www.coolworks.com for more tips on getting a job and for some "dream jobs" that might get students thinking!

Evaluation:

1. List two possible jobs in which you are interested.

2. List three ways you could begin a search for finding one of those jobs listed in (1).

21.1   Searching for a Job

Directions:

The following is a list of ways to find a job. Write an example of how the method could help you (or someone you know) find a job.

1. Reading the classifieds in the newspaper

2. Putting your own ad in the newspaper or online

3. Asking friends and relatives if they know of any openings where they work

4. Going to businesses, factories, and other places of work and asking for applications

5. Talking to a counselor at an employment agency

6. Signing up for job training in your community

7. Finding out whether you are eligible for any government-sponsored work programs

8. Working for a temporary-help agency

21.2 Vocational Vocabulary

Objective:

The student will match common vocabulary terms associated with getting a job with their definitions.

Comments:

Terms such as *résumé*, *cover letter*, *background check*, and *character reference* are all commonly used when someone is seriously trying to get a job. This lesson focuses on explaining what the words mean and how they relate to getting a job.

Introductory Activities:

1. Ask for three students to volunteer for a skit. With one student (the job-seeker) in the middle, position a female on one side to represent his mother, and a male on the other side to represent a former boss. Discuss with the student audience how both of these individuals know the job seeker, but may have different things to say about him. Continue to play out the different roles that each has and different responses that each have to the same question. (*What is he like? Is he a good worker? What are his strengths? Is he trustworthy?*) Explain that what these individuals say about the student represent a character reference (mother) and a job recommendation (boss).

2. Pass out the "Vocabulary Help Sheet" to students to refer to while you discuss the terms.

Activity:

When student seem familiar with the "Vocabulary Help Sheet," pass out the worksheet "Vocational Vocabulary" and have students match the term with the definition.

Answers: 1. c   2. e   3. b   4. g   5. f   6. h   7. a   8. d

Extension Activities:

1. Write each vocational term on an index card and have students randomly pick them and explain, demonstrate, act out, or otherwise perform to show their understanding of the term.
2. Check out www.jobsearch.about.com/cs/justforstudents for lots of helpful information about all aspects of vocational searching for students. There are sample forms, letters, online search information, and sample applications.

Evaluation:

1. What is the difference between a letter of recommendation and a character reference?
2. What are some ways that an employer finds out what a possible employee is like?

Vocabulary Help Sheet

Follow Bob through his attempt to find a job!

BOB: I saw an advertisement on the mall bulletin board that the Farm Store is hiring help for the summer. I am interested! I will go over to the Farm Store and see what I need to do.

BOSS: Hi. I'm glad you're interested. First, you will need to fill out a job application so we know a little bit more about you.

BOB: No problem. Here you go.

BOSS: Thanks. We'll be in touch or else give us a follow-up call or letter in a few days.

A few days later . . .
BOB: Well, I haven't heard anything. I will send them a copy of my résumé so they will know about my work experience. I'll send a cover letter to remind them that I stopped in and that I am still interested in the job.

A few days later . . .
BOSS: Hello, Bob? Come on in for an interview. We will need a letter of recommendation and a character reference when you come.

BOB: Let's see . . . I can get a letter of recommendation from Mr. Jones who was my boss when I worked at the pizza place. He always liked me. And then I'll ask my teacher to write a character reference for me.

Chapter 21: Getting a Job

The next day . . .

BOSS: Bob, we like what we have found out about you. Now we would like you to take a career assessment test to see if you have the math skills and the personality skills that would help you on this job. It won't take long.

BOB: This is not too hard. I just have to put down what I would do in each situation.

Later . . .

BOSS: OK, Bob, it looks like everything checks out. We just need to do a background check and a drug screening to make sure you qualify for our company.

BOB: I don't take drugs. Why do you have to do that?

BOSS: You will be dealing with the public. Also, we want to make sure you have good attendance and don't have any problems that would affect your performance on the job. It is routine; everybody has to pass that.

The next week . . .

BOSS: Bob, I am happy to say that everything checked out great! Welcome to the team!

BOB: You won't be sorry you hired me! Thanks!

21.2   **Vocational Vocabulary**

Directions:

Match the description on the left with the term on the right.

___ 1. A short (one-page) paper summarizing your personal information and work experience.

___ 2. A letter written by you to an employer explaining your interest in a job.

___ 3. A form that you fill out for a certain job to give the employer information about you.

___ 4. A letter written to your employer by someone who knows you, telling about your personal skills and character.

___ 5. A letter written by someone who has worked with you telling about your job skills.

___ 6. A check on your background activities to see if you have ever been arrested.

___ 7. A lab exam to see if you have drugs in your system.

___ 8. A test that helps to find out your strengths and weaknesses for a particular job.

a. Drug screening
b. Job application
c. Résumé
d. Career assessment
e. Cover letter
f. Letter of recommendation
g. Character reference
h. Background check

21.3 Filling Out an Application

Objective:

The student will complete a sample job application accurately and neatly.

Comments:

Most job searches begin with an application. This requests information regarding the applicant's education, work experience, and personal information. When entering the world of work, a student should be prepared to provide the necessary information. Also, an application should be filled out completely, honestly, and neatly. All of these are factors in making a good first impression—which is often what the application serves as. In this lesson, students are to work on completing a job application.

Introductory Activities:

1. Ask students how many of them have ever walked into a place of business, thrown out their arms, and yelled, "I'm ready to work! When do I start?" and have gotten a job.
2. Ask students to explain why filling out a job application is usually the way many companies begin their search for employees.
3. Ask students to list what information they think is generally included on a job application.

Activity:

Students are to complete the sample application for employment on the worksheet "Filling Out an Application." They will need to know or obtain their social security number, names and phone numbers of references, and dates of previous employment.

Discussion:

Have students ask for clarification about any parts of which they are unsure. They may need a day to get missing information such as their social security number. Encourage students to write as legibly as possible. Also inform them to be honest and accurate on the application.

1. Why is it very important to write legibly on the application? (The reader needs to know how to contact you or the references, has to be able to read the information.)
2. What else can help make a good first impression on the application? (Using one color of ink or even typing it, staying within the lines, overall neat appearance.)
3. Why would an employer want to know of any physical defects? (They need to know if you can perform the job you are applying for.)
4. What are some jobs that require someone to be over twenty-one? (Serving alcohol in the United States.)
5. Why would they want to know your hobbies or interests? (To see what kinds of activities you are involved in.)
6. Why would they want to know if you have a criminal record? (The job may involve handling money or checks, involve some sort of security, and so on.)

7. Why are you not to include activities that indicate your race or religion? (Should not be a factor in getting the job.)

8. Why is it important to have good references from your previous employers? (They probably will be contacted.)

9. Why would they want to know how many days were lost from work? (They want to know whether attendance will be a problem.)

10. What factors are prohibited from being discriminated against, as written on the top of the application? (Race, creed, color, national origin, ancestry, age, sex, physical or mental handicaps, and so on.)

Extension Activities:

1. Collect and bring in examples of applications for employment from several businesses or organizations. Have students check them out and figure out what things are similar among them.

2. Have students prepare a personal information sheet they can use to complete applications. Have them record references, names and addresses of previous employers, and so on.

Evaluation:

How would you revise the following responses to an application for employment:

1. What interests you in working for our company?
   "I am hoping to get free food and be able to talk to my friends while I am working."

2. What are your hobbies or special interests?
   "I have no hobbies. I am interested in boys."

3. What is your reason for leaving your last job?
   "My boss was a jerk."

Directions: Here is a sample job application for an entry-level position at a fast-food restaurant. Complete the application to the best of your ability.

BURGER HAVEN

RESTAURANT OPERATIONS
HOURLY EMPLOYEE
APPLICATION FOR EMPLOYMENT

Discrimination in employment because of race, creed, color, national origin, ancestry, age, sex, physical or mental handicaps, or liability for service in the armed forces of the U.S. is prohibited by federal legislation and/or by laws against discrimination in some states.

AN EQUAL OPPURTUNITY EMPLOYER - M/F/H

PERSONAL

LAST NAME	FIRST		MIDDLE INITIAL	PHONE
STREET ADDRESS	CITY		STATE	ZIP CODE

SOCIAL SECURITY NUMBER

NAME AND PHONE OF PERSON TO BE NOTIFIED FOR EMERGENCY

KNOWN PHYSICAL DEFECTS WHICH COULD AFFECT YOUR ABILITY TO PERFORM POSITION BEING APPLIED FOR

IS YOUR CITIZENSHIP OR IMMIGRATION STATUS SUCH THAT YOU CAN LAWFULLY WORK IN THE U.S.?   ☐ YES   ☐ NO
IF HIRED CONTINUED EMPLOYMENT MAY BE DEPENDENT UPON PROOF OF CITIZENSHIP OR PRESENTATION OF AN ALIEN REGISTRATION NUMBER.

ARE YOU   ☐ 14–15   ☐ 18–17   ☐ 18 OR OLDER   IF UNDER 18, PROOF OF AGE MUST BE PROVIDED PRIOR TO HIRING

EDUCATION

NAME OF SCHOOL AND ADDRESS	# OF YEARS COMPLETED	GRADUATED YES	GRADUATED NO	NUMBER OF COLLEGE CREDITED HOURS	MAJOR	AVERAGE
JUNIOR HIGH						
HIGH SCHOOL						
COLLEGE						
OTHER						

EXTRA CURRICULAR ACTIVITIES	CURRENTLY ENROLLED IN HIGH SCHOOL/WORK/STUDY PROGRAM ☐ YES ☐ NO

GENERAL/ACTIVITIES

DATE AVAILABLE TO START

DAYS AND HOURS AVAILABLE TO WORK	DAY FROM TO	SUNDAY	MONDAY	TUESDAY	WEDNESDAY	THURSDAY	FRIDAY	SATURDAY
	FROM							
	TO							

WHAT INTERESRED YOU IN BURGER HAVEN?

WHAT ARE YOUR HOBBIES, SPECIAL INERESTS, AND ACTIVITIES?
(Do not Include those indicating race, creed, nationality or religion)

HAVE YOU BEEN COVICTED OF A FELONY OR MISDEMEANOR OTHER THAN A TRAFFIC VIOLATION?   ☐ NO   ☐ YES
IF YES STATE CHARGE,COURT,DATE AND DISAPPOINTED OF CASE.

EMPLOYEMENT/WORK EXPERIENCE

COMPANY NO. 1 (Present or most recent employer)		ADDRESS/PHONE NUMBER	
EMPLOYED (Month & Year) FROM TO	RATE OF PAY START ENDING		AVERAGE NUMBER OF HOURS WORKED PER WEEK
POSITIONS HELD		SUPERVISIOR'S NAME / POSITION	
DESCRIBE YOUR DUTIES			
MAY WE CONTACT THIS EMPLOYER? ☐ YES ☐ NO	DAYS LOTSFROM WORK		
REASON FOR LEAVING			
COMPANY NO. 2 (Present or most recent employer)		ADDRESSS /PHONE NUMBER	
EMPLOYED(Month & Year) FROM TO	RATE OF PAY START ENDING		AVERAGE NUMBER OF HOURS WORKED PER WEEK
POSITIONS HELD		SUPERVISEORS NAME/ POSITION	
DESCRIBE YOUR DUTIES			
MAY WE CONTACT THIS EMPLOYER? ☐ YES ☐ NO	DAYS LOTS FROM WORK		
REASON FOR LEAVING			

THE INFORMATION I AM PRESENTING IN THIS APPLICATION IS TRUE AND CORRECT TO THE BEST OF MY KNOWLEDGE, AND I UNDERSTAND THAT ANY FALSIFICATION OR MISREPRESENTATION HEREIN COULD RESULT IN MY DISCHARGE IN THE EVENT I AM EMPLOYED BY BURGER HAVEN. I AUTHORISE BURGER HAVEN OR ITS REPRESENTATIVES TO CONTACT ALL FORMER EMPLOYERS AND TO FURTHER INQUIRE AS TO ANY INFORMATION GIVEN BY ME ON THIS APPLICATION.

APPLICANT'S SIGNATURE ———————————————————————————————   DATE: ————————————

DO NOT WRITE BELOW THIS LINE - FOR BURGER HAVEN USE ONLY

			GOOD	AVERAGE	POOR
COMPANY NO. 1 REFERENCE CHECK					
APPLICANT ELIGIBLE FOR REHIRE:	☐ YES ☐ NO	ATTENDANCE:	☐	☐	☐
DATES OF EMPLOYMENT VERIFIED	☐ YES ☐ NO	PERFORMANCE:	☐	☐	☐
CHECKED BY		CONTACTED	DATE :		

			GOOD	AVERAGE	POOR
COMPANY NO. 2 REFERENCE CHECK					
APPLICANT ELIGIBLE FOR REHIRE:	☐ YES ☐ NO	ATTENDANCE:	☐	☐	☐
DATES OF EMPLOYMENT VERIFIED	☐ YES ☐ NO	PERFORMANCE:	☐	☐	☐
CHECKED BY		CONTACTED	DATE :		

MANAGER'S/INTERVIEWER'S NOTES:

21.4 What Is a Résumé?

Objective:

The student will construct a brief résumé including education, work experience, interests, and other relevant information.

Comments:

A résumé is a simple one-page document that introduces the hopeful employee to the prospective employer. Although the format may vary, the following information is usually included: position sought, personal information, work experience, education, and references. In this lesson, students examine a sample résumé.

Introductory Activities:

1. Define *résumé* (a brief account of one's work experience and qualifications).   2. Ask students to give their ideas of what an employer would want to know about them before hiring them for a job.

Activity:

Students are to look at a sample résumé and answer specific questions about it. Emphasize that a résumé is a quick look at a person's skills, interests, and experience and will not contain a lot of information. *Answers:*   1. High school graduate.   2. He has a wide variety of interests and abilities—is athletic, musical, probably smart!   3. Probably a favorite teacher; owner of the construction company he worked for.   4. He was given some responsibility, is able to make repairs.   5. 18 (in 2004).

Discussion:

Answer any questions about the information Michael included on his résumé. Then go over the following questions.

1. Why is it usually important to keep the information on a résumé to only one page? (Gives a lot of information in a little space, employers don't have to spend a lot of time reading it.)
2. Why should a résumé be neat and easy to read? (It's the first impression you give of yourself.)
3. Why it is helpful to list the duties you performed on your jobs? (So the employer will know exactly what you were responsible for.)   4. Why is it good to include some personal interests and achievements? (This may set you apart from other applicants, shows your strengths.)
5. What personal information might you include on a résumé? (Birthday, family information, phone, address, and so on.)

Extension Activities:

1. Collect and display different examples of résumés. Discuss with students what is distinctive about each. What information is common to them all?   2. Have students compose a personal résumé. Have them experiment with different styles. Display them to the class, with permission.

Evaluation:

1. What are you most proud of that you would include on your résumé?   2. What references would be most helpful on your résumé?   3. What are some unique things about you that would set you apart from others on your résumé?

What Is a Résumé?

Directions: The following is a sample résumé. Look it over carefully and then answer the questions.

Michael A. Kenner

1124 North Orchard Street

Milwaukee, WI 53213

(414) 476-9988

Education

Graduate of Milwaukee North High School, 2004

Extracurricular Activities

Football team, 2002–2004; Swing Choir, 2001–2004; Debate Team, 2003–2004; Chess Club, 2002–2003

References

Camille T. Sabato, teacher (414) 883-2959

Alexander Smith, Smith Construction owner (414) 783-2990

Work Experience

Smith Construction Company, summer 2003: carpenter's assistant

Dairy Barn, after school 2002–2004: assistant manager

Pete's Bike Repairs, summers 2001-2002: helped take orders, made minor repairs

Interests

Bike riding, sports, hunting

Personal Information

Born May 20, 1986

Oldest of three children

21.4 What Is a Résumé? (*Continued*)

1. What do you know about Michael's education?

2. What can you tell about Michael from his interests and extracurricular activities?

3. Why do you think he selected the references he did?

4. What do you know about him from his work experiences?

5. How old is Michael?

21.5 Interviewing for a Job

Objective:

The student will give at least five important considerations to keep in mind during the interviewing process.

Comments:

The interview is the first step in the door toward getting a job. It is at this point that the prospective employee has a chance to make a face-to-face impression with someone who may have the authority to hire him or her for the job. In this lesson, the student is to evaluate ten different steps in the interviewing process and state appropriate ways to handle each step.

Introductory Activities:

1. Ask students to give their opinions as to what a job interview is.
2. Ask students to give reasons why making a good impression at an interview is important.

Activity:

Students are to complete the worksheet "Interviewing for a Job" by providing the character with appropriate comments (or actions) related to performing well at an interview.

Answers (*Examples*)::

1. Be polite, be specific.
2. Be on time or early.
3. Dress for the type of job—don't overdo it, don't look too casual.
4. Say "Good morning," not "Yo!"
5. Express interest; don't ask about salary right away.
6. Tell why you came for the job.
7. Tell what you have done that might be relevant.
8. Express some personality.
9. Say "Thank you for your time."
10. Thank them for the interview and reaffirm your interest in the position.

Discussion:

Go through each of the steps and talk about what would be considered appropriate or inappropriate at each point.

1. Why is it important to be on time or early for an interview? (Their time is valuable, you want to appear conscientious.)

2. What would be appropriate dress if you were applying for a job at an office? (A suit jacket, with either pants or skirt, or a businesslike dress; a shirt and tie.)

3. What would be appropriate dress if you were applying for a counselor's position at a sports camp for kids? (Something more casual.)

4. Why would it be important to ask questions about the position? (Shows that you are interested, have given it some thought.)

5. Why shouldn't you ask about the salary right away? (It would appear as though that was your only reason for wanting the job.)

6. If the interviewer tells you right away that you won't get the job, why should you still be polite when you leave? (There might be another job opening later.)

7. Why is it a good idea to send a follow-up letter or make a phone call? (To find out what they have decided, make another good impression.)

Extension Activities:

1. Practice mock interviews, with students taking turns interviewing each other. Have them fabricate the type of job they are offering and make a list of questions. Have students participate by interviewing and evaluating the interviews of others.

2. Have students work in groups to illustrate various positive and negative points about being a good interviewee. Videotape the skits and have students evaluate them. This can be a fun activity!

3. Invite a business friend to talk to the class about what he or she looks for in a person who is interviewing for a job. What specific things turn them off? What is impressive?

4. Here are two web pages that offer video tips on interviewing: www.videojug.com/film/job-interviews-why-should-we-hire-you and www.videojug.com/film/job-how-can-I-make-a-good-first-impression-2.

Evaluation:

1. What are some important things to prepare for before the interview?

2. What are some ways to make a good impression during the interview?

3. Why is an appropriate appearance very important during an interview?

21.5   **Interviewing for a Job**

Directions:

Alison is interviewing for a job as a typist in a business office. What advice would you give her at each step of her interviewing process?

1. Calling to set up a time

   _____

2. Being on time

   _____

3. Appropriate appearance

   _____

4. Polite greeting

   _____

5. Asking good questions about the position

   _____

6. Explaining her interest in the job

   _____

7. Stating her qualifications

   _____

8. Telling personal things about herself that are interesting and unique

   _____

9. Politely leaving

   _____

10. Sending a follow-up letter

   _____

21.6 First Impressions

Objective:

The student will recognize that appearance, attitude, and honesty are important factors when making a first impression.

Comments:

When being considered for a job, a student should do everything possible to create an appropriate appearance (dress for the type of job you want), attitude (portray your strengths, but be respectful), and honesty (don't try to pass yourself off as something you are not). This lesson gives examples of characters who need to improve in these areas.

Introductory Activities:

1. Write *appearance*, *attitude*, and *honesty* on the board. Have students give examples of how each could affect making a good first impression.   2. Display pictures of random people. (Try to get a cross section of different "looks.") What is your first impression of each?

Activity:

Use the "First Impressions" worksheet to have students decide which area (appearance, attitude, honesty) needs to be improved.   *Answers:*   1. Appearance—should wash hands and use a lint brush. 2. Attitude—doesn't seem motivated.   3. Attitude—the picture doesn't really reflect his job skills. 4. Honesty—is afraid of animals.   5. Attitude—is telling the boss what to do.   6. Attitude— should wait for instructions.   7. Appearance—it might be better to dress down.   8. Attitude—is more concerned about breaks than the job.

Discussion:

1. What are some ways that you could adjust your appearance to make it appropriate for the job you are trying to get? (Check your hair and clothing, find out how casual or formal the job is.) 2. What are some ways that you could show a willing, respectful attitude?   3. How can you answer questions honestly without seeming to be (a) bragging or (b) not qualified for something?

Extension Activities:

1. Role-play the examples on the worksheet to show both an inappropriate impression and a better impression.   2. Check out www.videojug.com/film/how-can-I-make-a-good-first-impression-2 for video tips (with a British accent) on body language. Another interesting video is www.videojug.com/film/job-interviews-why-should-we-hire-you. These are primarily for adults, but have tips that teens can use, too.

Evaluation:

Explain how appearance, attitude, and honesty can affect making a good first impression and give an example of each.

21.6   **First Impressions**

Directions: How could these characters improve their first impression on these job interviews? Keep in mind: appearance, attitude, honesty.

1. Victor is applying for a job at a bookstore. He forgot to wash his hands after brushing his dog, and he has dog hair all over his sweater.

2. Melissa is applying for a job at a video store. She told the interviewer that she is interested in the job because she likes to watch movies and thinks it will be easy.

3. Carson wants to work at the community pool; he brought pictures of himself swimming on a beach.

4. Evelyn is hoping to work at a pet store. She told the interviewer that she loves animals, although she is really afraid of cats and gerbils.

5. Dan wants to work with a crew that is raking yards. He told the interviewer that he knows how to rake, so don't bother telling him what to do.

6. Melanie wants to be a babysitter for a family with three small children. She told the mother that she will spank the kids if they get mouthy with her.

7. Colin wants to work at a car wash. He showed up wearing a nice suit and tie.

8. Melinda is applying for a job as a cashier at a drug store. When the interviewer asked if she had any questions, Melinda wanted to know how many breaks she would get.

21.7 Getting Work Experience

Objective:

The student will list several ways to get work experience.

Comments:

There are opportunities available all around for young people to get work experience—which is sometimes a prerequisite for someone to hire them for another job! Some of the jobs may not pay much (and some may involve volunteering just for the experience), but the experience gained can be beneficial and look great on a résumé. In this lesson, students are to think of lots of ways they can gain work or leadership experience.

Introductory Activities:

1. Have students think of ways or times when they have been in a leadership position. List them.
2. Have students raise their hands if they have ever babysat, cleaned out a garage, walked a dog, or washed a car. Inform them that they have work experience!

Activity:

Students are to read the worksheet's partial list of suggestions and think of other possible ways to get work experience.

Discussion:

Ask students to share their ideas. See if students can come up with at least twenty different ways they can gain work experience.

1. How many of the ways you thought of involved earning money for your services?   2. How important is it for you to have money for what you do? Would you consider working for free if you got good experience?   3. What are some unusual experiences you have had that would apply to a job you might eventually do?   4. What are some organized volunteer programs in your community? (Meals-on-Wheels, hospital gift shop, and so on.)   5. What does the fact that you have done part-time work and volunteer work say about you to a potential employee? (You are creative, resourceful, interested in others, and so on.)

Extension Activities:

1. Have students find out about volunteer programs in the community. Encourage them to sign up to give it a try for the experience.   2. Set up peer tutoring or cross-age tutoring within your school. Provide training for helping the students learn to be tutors and start them off with a volunteer experience.
3. Have students contact some local businesses to find out whether there are part-time work/study positions available. Some businesses will work with a school as "partners in education."

Evaluation:

1. List at least five possible work/leadership experiences you have already participated in or would consider doing.   2. What are at least two reasons why volunteering is a helpful experience for both you and the agency for which you are working?

21.7   **Getting Work Experience**

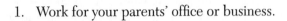

Directions: The following is a partial list of ways you can get some work experience that might help you with future jobs. Add to the list with your own ideas.

1. Work for your parents' office or business.

2. Ask your relatives for part-time work.

3. Be a camp counselor in the summer for children.

4. Volunteer to work with handicapped children after school.

5. Teach a Sunday school class for children.

6. Help out on a farm.

7. Tutor children at your school.

8. Offer to care for neighbors' pets or houses while they are on vacation.

9. Be a library assistant at your local library.

10. Become involved in summer sports programs as a manager, batboy, and so on.

11. _____

12. _____

13. _____

14. _____

15. _____

16. _____

17. _____

18. _____

19. _____

20. _____

Working

22.1 Having a Good Attitude

Objective:

The student will rewrite comments reflecting a bad attitude toward work to make them positive or acceptable.

Comments:

Not every job is a worker's dream. Some jobs, especially entry-level positions, might involve doing tasks that are less than glamorous, are low in pay, and may be tedious. Employees who have the attitude that they are "too good for the job" (and express this feeling) are probably not going to last long. Students need to realize that having a good attitude is important on any job. In this lesson, students are to rewrite negative comments to make them reflect a better attitude.

Introductory Activities:

1. Present students with the following scenario: "You just started a new job. Your boss comes to you and says that she noticed you were late. She warns you not to let it happen again. What will you do?" Write students' responses on the board.

2. Next to each response, decide whether it reflects a *positive attitude* (taking the criticism politely, without defiance, and so on) or a *negative attitude* (responding in a sullen or defiant manner).

3. Have students speculate what might happen to the employee if each of the possible responses listed was followed.

Activity:

The characters on the worksheet "Having a Good Attitude" reflect a negative attitude in terms of being defiant, lazy, self-seeking, or appearing as if they think they are too good for the position. Students are to decide what is wrong with the attitude expressed and then rewrite the characters' comments to reflect a better attitude. Students may argue that the employee is in the right and should not have to put up with unfair treatment, and so on. For the sake of completing the worksheet, inform students that there will be a lesson later on handling problems with the boss.

Answers (Examples):

1. At least this job is a start and I'm getting a paycheck.
2. I can learn to go to bed earlier at night.
3. I'll try to keep my mouth shut when I'm upset around that man.
4. I'll do the best I can, even though the work is dull.
5. If I do good work on this job, I'll probably get to do something better later.
6. Fred will understand that I need this job.

Discussion:

Students may feel the employee has a right to pick and choose whatever job he or she wants. Indeed, if someone is in a position to have a lot of choice, there is no reason to stay at a job that makes life miserable. On the other hand, if one is beginning the world of work, it is crucial to make a good impression, practice good work skills, and learn the social skills needed to be a good employee—if only to work one's way out of that job into a better one.

1. If someone feels he or she is too good to do a certain job, what other options does he or she have? (Look for something else, put up with it for the time being, and so on.)
2. If you have no other work options at the moment and are stuck in a low-paying, boring job, what could you do? (Learn to adapt, try to make it as interesting for yourself as you can.)
3. Why do some people feel work rules have to bend to fit their personal rules—such as what time they will start, what they will wear, and so on? (They probably have been used to calling the shots and haven't been used to following school rules either.)
4. Is getting a paycheck the only reason to stick it out on a job you don't like? (It might be enough in some cases, but it's also a good idea to stay around long enough to get a good recommendation and experience.)
5. How can you reflect a good attitude toward your coworkers? (Be friendly, do your share, be positive about the work.)
6. If you bring a bad attitude to work with you, how does that affect the people you work with? (It might rub off.)
7. How does the bad attitude affect your job performance? (Probably makes you not want to care or do a good job.)
8. Can you think of any ways to change a bad attitude? (Realize that you need the job more than it needs you, calm yourself down and rethink your goals, and so on.)

Extension Activities:

1. Have students talk to their parents about their work. If their parent is an employer, have them give examples of employees who have good attitudes on the job. If their parent is primarily an employee, look for examples of how they reflect a good attitude. Share these ideas with the class.
2. Collect, write, and display positive attitude comments around the room. These can be useful for school situations as well as work. Colorful signs that display sayings such as "I can do that!" or "Here's my best work!" can reflect a positive attitude about your classroom.

Evaluation:

Rewrite the following comments to reflect a more positive attitude:

1. "This work is stupid. Whoever thought of doing this was really an idiot."
2. "No one will notice if I leave ten minutes early again. I work hard enough that I am owed that time anyway."
3. "I don't care that the boss said to do it his way—I think my own way is better."

22.1   Having a Good Attitude

Directions: What is wrong with the attitude expressed by these employees? Rewrite their comments to reflect a better attitude!

1. *There's no way I would work at that place – they hardly pay anything and the work is too hard. I'm better than that!*

    _____

    _____

2. *I'm not taking any job where I have to get UP before noon.*

    _____

    _____

3. *I don't like that boss. He reminds me of a teacher I used to hate.*

    _____

    _____

4. *This work is boring. Forget it!*

    _____

    _____

5. *I like animals, but cleaning out all these cages is not what I had in mind. I wanted to play with them and pet them.*

    _____

    _____

6. *I can't work overtime! I have a date with Fred!*

22.2 Being a Great Employee

Objective:

When given examples of pairs of workers, the student will select the better of the two employees and state why.

Comments:

Having a good attitude is only one factor in being a good employee. There are a lot of other factors, such as being punctual, performing well, getting along with the boss, getting along with coworkers, and so on. In this lesson, students are given pairs of employees to compare and must select the better one.

Introductory Activities:

1. Have students list characteristics of a good employee (you may start the list with "good attitude"). Students can give examples.   2. Have students list characteristics of a poor employee. They can add specific examples if they choose.

Activity:

In this activity, students will read the comments of two employees in a similar situation. They are to circle the one in each pair who demonstrates the behavior of a good employee.   *Answers:*   1. Second employee—comes to work ready to work   2. First employee—is recognized for performance 3. First employee—team player   4. Second employee—polite and respectful to boss   5. First employee—gets along with coworkers   6. Second employee—comes to work on time

Discussion:

Go over the examples on the worksheet and have students explain what characteristic the good employee is demonstrating.

1. How would you feel if the first worker in example 1 was a brain surgeon who was going to operate on you today? (Frightened!)   2. Why is it important to be mentally and physically ready to work? (You owe that to your employer; it's important in order to do a good job.)   3. In example 2, why do you think the second employee never gets noticed? (Maybe he never does anything well.) 4. In example 3, the second worker says the company does not care. Who else does not care? (The worker.)   5. Both employees greeted the boss in example 4, but what is the difference? (One was sarcastic, the other was sincere.)   6. Do you think the second employee example 4 is being phony or just trying to get in good with the boss? (Could be; it all depends on the attitude of the employee.) 7. What characteristic is demonstrated in example 6? (Being on time.)

Extension Activities:

1. Have students write and present (or videotape) a humorous skit in which two employees are vying for the same position. Both could go overboard trying to impress the boss.   2. Have students come up with a checklist for at least ten skills they think are indicative of a good employee. Which of these skills also apply to being a good student?

Evaluation:

1. List at least five characteristics of a good employee.   2. Choose one characteristic and explain how this contributes to being an effective employee and producing a better product or service.

22.2   **Being a Good Employee**

Directions: Read the comments of each pair of employees below. Circle the one who is the better employee of the two. Explain why with your classmates.

22.3 Making a Mistake on the Job

Objective:

The student will give examples of how to cope with making mistakes on the job and provide an appropriate way of handling the situation.

Comment:

Everybody makes mistakes! We're all human, and sometimes things just don't go right—even on the job. However, there is a right and a wrong way to handle our mistakes, to notify those in charge, and to deal with the frustrations we may feel. Making mistakes can actually be a very helpful way of learning how to do your job better and a chance to make you a more careful worker. It's all in how you respond to the mistake.

Introductory Activity:

Play a game of Simon Says with the students, in which Simon tells them to perform activities that would be normal in the work environment ("Simon says to type on a computer," "Simon says to mop the floor," "Simon says to wipe off a table," and so on). When a student "messes up" and performs the task without Simon saying to do so, have the student sit out until all players are done. Then discuss with the group how it felt to make a mistake.

Activity:

Have students complete the "Making a Mistake on the Job" worksheet. They should identify what mistake was made, give a suggestion of a positive way to handle or correct the mistake, and suggest what can be learned from the mistake.   *Answers:*   1. *Mistake:* Broke glass. *How to handle:* Notify boss, ask for assistance if needed, sweep up all pieces of glass. *What to learn:* Be careful when working with glass. 2. *Mistake:* Spilt drink on customer. *How to handle:* Apologize, get towels for customer, clean up spill, notify manager, offer to give customer a free drink. *What to learn:* Be careful not to spill when working with beverages.   3. *Mistake:* Filled the bag too full of heavy items. *How to handle:* Apologize, pick up items, replace any damaged foods, repack in careful manner. *What to learn:* Be careful not to pack too full or too heavy.   4. *Mistake:* Put items in wrong section. *How to handle:* Put items in right place. *What to learn:* Be aware of particular places for particular items.

Discussion:

1. Is it okay to make mistakes? What can you learn from making them?   2. Should you notify your boss if you make a mistake?   3. Why should you not be afraid to tell your boss if you've made a mistake?

Extension Activity:

Create scenarios for the students to act out, where they can make a mistake. Have them respond in a bad way and then in a good way.

Evaluation:

1. Give an example of making a mistake on the job.   2. Give an example of how to correct that mistake.

22.3   **Making a Mistake on the Job**

Directions:

For each of the following scenarios, tell what the worker's mistake was, how the worker should handle it, and what the worker might learn from the mistake.

1. Mistake:

    _____

    _____

    _____

How to handle:

_____

What to learn:

_____

2. Mistake:

    _____

    _____

    _____

How to handle:

_____

What to learn:

_____

22.3 Making a Mistake on the Job (*Continued*)

3. Mistake:

____

____

____

How to handle:

____

What to learn:

____

4. Mistake:

____

____

____

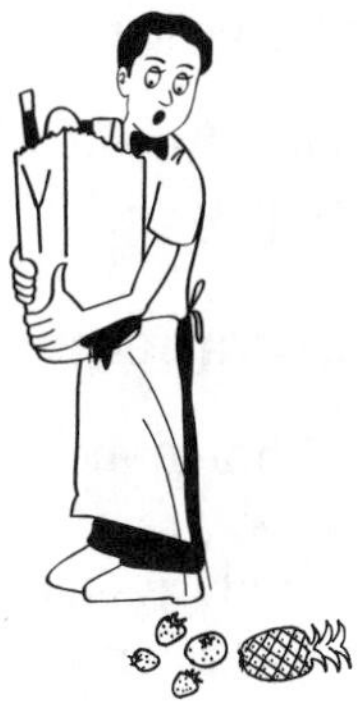

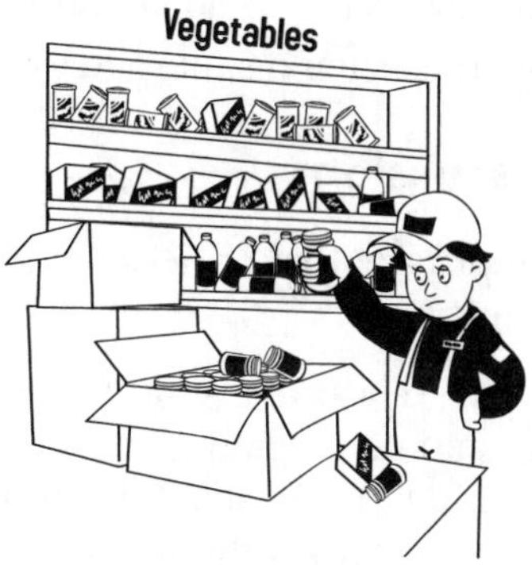

How to handle:

____

What to learn:

____

22.4 Handling Criticism on the Job

Objective:

The student will identify positive ways of handling criticism on the job in an effort to become a better employee.

Comment:

Although none of us likes to receive criticism for our work, sometimes that is the very thing that helps us to be proactive about changing our bad habits or recognizing when we've made a mistake. Criticism does not always have to be harsh and mean; it can be constructive and helpful for us at work. Regardless of the way the criticism comes, it is up to us to use it for our good, to make us better employees.

Introductory Activities:

1. Have students give examples of when they have had poor customer service and what criticism they may have felt or wanted to express.   2. Have students give an example of positive (constructive) criticism and criticism that is meant to be hurtful.

Activity:

Students should complete the "Handling Criticism on the Job" worksheet and note which way of handling criticism is best in that situation.   *Answers:*   1. c. Cheri knows that being late is jeopardizing her job and should make an extra effort to be early.   2. b. Ted should realize that he is behind and should focus on catching up on his work.   3. a. Frank should make an effort to be clean and well-groomed every day.   4. b. Molly should not rush through her tasks just to get done, but should go at a pace that allows her to do her best work.   5. c. Donny should be proud of his role as the first person guests meet; he should smile and welcome everyone.

Discussion:

Emphasize that criticism does not necessarily mean "critical," but that it can also mean giving a helpful opinion.

1. Why can hearing criticism be hard? (We take it personally, it seems unfair, we only like hearing positive and not negative, and so on.)   2. Why can some criticism be good? (It can point out a mistake we didn't know about, it can help us to a better job in the future, make us better employees, and so on.)   3. Discuss with the class a time when you've received criticism on the job and how you either handled it well or poorly.

Extension Activity:

Have students watch an episode of *Mr. Bean* or another TV show in which the character makes a lot of mistakes. Pause the show right after each mistake and have the students criticize him. Then have the students say what he should do instead.

Evaluation:

1. Give an example of a bad criticism on the job.   2. Give an example of a constructive criticism on the job.   3. Give an example of a bad way of handling criticism on the job.   4. Give an example of a good way of handling criticism on the job.

Chapter 22: Working

22.4   **Handling Criticism on the Job**

Directions:

Choose the best way of handling each example of criticism on the job. Circle the letter of your answer. Then discuss with classmates what can be learned from that criticism.

1. "You're ten minutes late again, Cheri. You know I like my employees to be on time."
   a. Cheri runs to the bathroom crying.
   b. Cheri makes an excuse, saying that it was the traffic's fault.
   c. Cheri apologizes and then makes sure to be early the rest of the week.

2. "Ted, your performance is down. We need twenty boxes packaged, and you've only done fifteen."
   a. Ted says, "Well, if Billy could keep up, then maybe I could get my work done, too."
   b. Ted focuses on his task at hand and tries hard to catch up.
   c. Ted throws the boxes on the ground and leaves.

3. "You really need to keep up on your grooming and hygiene, Frank. I have been receiving complaints that you smell bad."
   a. Frank apologizes and then comes to work showered and well-groomed the next day.
   b. Frank takes his shoes off, so that the room smells even worse.
   c. Frank goes on working, ignoring his boss.

4. "It looks like you've been rushing through your cleaning duties, Molly. I'd like you to go slower and do a better job."
   a. Molly throws down her towel and sits on the ground in defeat.
   b. Molly slows down in her work and tries to do a better job.
   c. Molly speeds up even faster.

5. "Donny, I'd like to see you smile more as you greet our guests. After all, yours is the first face they see."
   a. Donny complains, "But I don't feel like smiling today."
   b. Donny refuses to greet any more guests.
   c. Donny takes pride in his role and welcomes the guests happily.

22.5 Being Prepared for the Task

Objective:

The student will identify steps that show how to be prepared for tasks on a job.

Comment:

Once you have a job, you will want to do that job well. This can lead to impressing your employer, a possible promotion or pay raise, pride in your work, mastering a skill, and many other rewards. One of the best ways you can do your job well is to be prepared for each task that you have. Though these tasks may vary, you can learn how to be prepared and excel at your job.

Introductory Activity:

Write several activities of a typical morning routine on the board (brushing teeth, getting dressed, eating breakfast, and so on). Have the students tell how they would prepare for each one of these tasks.

Activity:

Have students complete the worksheet "Being Prepared for the Task" by listing ways to prepare for each task in a given profession.   *Answers (May vary):*   1. Leroy should put on his gym clothes, do some stretches, and dribble the ball around.   2. Miss Violet should clean the board off, get some good markers, decide which problems to write, and then write them on the board.   3. Oscar should get the ingredients for the muffins, bake them in the kitchen, decorate them, and then display them.   4. Mr. Dell should wake up early, measure out the right amount of food, put the food in the cows' troughs, and give them water.   5. Sally should get soap and water and clean off all the table tops, locate napkins and silverware, roll them napkins, arrange on the tables.   6. Dan should locate some free weights and a couple of stretching bands, find a space big enough to work in, wear comfortable athletic clothes, bring charts and necessary paperwork.

Discussion:

1. What might happen to the people in the worksheet if they don't come prepared for their tasks? (They might lose business, animals go hungry, customers get angry, lose their job, and so on.) 2. Why is it good to be prepared at work?   3. What kind of preparation can be done in your head before you actually work on the task? (Give thought beforehand, time, organization.)

Extension Activities:

1. Think of a family vacation you would like to take. List all the ways you would prepare for your trip—what you would pack, what you would need to buy, whom you would need to tell, how much money you would need to bring, who would take care of your pets, and so on.   2. Have students pick some way-out occupations and divide into small groups to list some of the more unusual tasks that might come with the job. (TV shows such as *Dirty Jobs* might inspire some creative thought!)

Evaluation:

1. What are the benefits of being prepared for a task?   2. Pick an occupation that interests you and list three tasks that would come with the job.

22.5   **Being Prepared for the Task**

Directions: Each of these people has a different profession. Notice the task they are going to do, and list how they can prepare themselves for each task.

Name: Leroy Davis

Profession: Professional basketball player

Task at hand: Leroy needs to shoot some free throws before his game.

How to prepare:

_____

_____

Name: Miss Violet

Profession: Third-grade teacher

Task at hand: Miss Violet needs to write some math problems on a dirty board.

How to prepare:

_____

_____

Name: Oscar Cupcake

Profession: Baker

Task at hand: Oscar needs to bake a dozen muffins for the display case.

How to prepare:

_____

_____

Name: Mr. Dell

Profession: Dairy farmer

Task at hand: Mr. Dell needs to feed his forty cows.

How to prepare:

_____

_____

Name: Leroy Davis

Profession: Professional basketball player

Task at hand: Leroy needs to shoot some free throws before his game.

How to prepare:

_____

_____

Name: Miss Violet

Profession: Third-grade teacher

Task at hand: Miss Violet needs to write some math problems on a dirty board.

How to prepare:

_____

_____

22.6 Changing Jobs: Why?

Objective:

The student will identify several reasons why people change jobs.

Comments:

There are lots of reasons why people change jobs—it may be due to work environment, boredom with the job, additional training that qualifies one for a new job, or change in location. Most people do not keep the same job (or even career) for their entire working life. It is important to keep options open and, if the opportunity presents itself to move to another job that is, in some respects, better, it is perfectly acceptable to do so. In this lesson, students are given examples of people who are ready to change jobs or want to do so.

Introductory Activities:

1. Ask students to give examples from personal experience of their parents or relatives of times when they changed jobs.   2. Ask students to give reasons why people might change jobs. 3. After listing reasons, have students try to categorize them; for example, personal reasons, professional concerns, and so on.

Activity:

Students will match the person who wants to change jobs with the reason for the job change. *Answers:* 1. c   2. b   3. d   4. a   5. f   6. e

Discussion:

After students have completed the worksheet, see how the reasons compare with the reasons students listed in the introductory activities. What other reasons did they give that were not on the worksheet?

1. Some people keep the same job for their whole lives. Why? (No other options, enjoy the work, work for family, and so on.)   2. What are some good or positive reasons for job changes? 3. What are some negative reasons for changing a job?   4. What else might change with a new job that demands more responsibility? (More money, power, respect, time demands, and so on.) 5. What stresses might be involved in a job change? (Moving, getting to know different people, learning a new job, and so on.)

Extension Activities:

1. Have students interview at least five adults who have had job changes. Find out the sequence of jobs—have most been improvements? Were they the same types of jobs? What contributed to making a job change?   2. Have students prepare a bulletin board entitled "Climbing the Ladder of Success" (or similar theme) showing how an entry-level position can lead (with additional training, skills, and some luck) to different positions. For example, a principal may have started out by being an assistant to a teacher, then became a student teacher, teacher or coach for a high school, and eventually a principal. Have students find out other paths that careers can follow.

Evaluation:

1. List three to five reasons why a person may want to change jobs.   2. Write a paragraph explaining at least one negative aspect and one positive aspect of changing jobs.

22.6   **Changing Jobs: Why?**

Directions:

Match the person on the left with the reason for the job change on the right.

1. I'm bored with my present position of planting seedlings. I would like to do something different, like plan how a garden will look when it is finished.

    a. Higher pay

2. I just can't work with that woman anymore. She criticizes everything I do. I go home feeling like I'm worthless.

    b. Get away from an unpleasant situation

3. It's too far to work at that supermarket. Now that one is open one block from my home, I'm going to apply for a job there.

    c. More interesting job

4. Hey! I can make $2 more an hour for the same job at that factory. It's time for a change!

    d. Better location

5. Now that I've completed this training, I should be eligible for a supervisor's position.

    e. Benefits

6. If I guarantee that I will stay on the new job for a year, they will pay for my training and get me started in this new office. Sounds good to me!

    f. More responsibility

22.7 Changing Jobs: How?

Objective:

The student will list at least three ways or steps that a person can take to make a job change.

Comments:

Once the decision to change jobs has been reached, it is then time to begin the job search all over again; however, there is one difference—now the person has had at least one job and has experience! Even if the experience was negative and the person realizes that this is not the job for him or her, at least that is a starting point. In this lesson, students will complete paragraphs to indicate how to go about changing jobs by improving skills, getting additional training, or using other available resources to make that change.

Introductory Activities:

1. Have students write a probable job they are capable of holding right now or perhaps work at part-time.
2. Have students indicate by raising hands if they would like to keep that same job for the rest of their lives. Why or why not?

Activity:

Students are to complete the worksheet "Changing Jobs: How?" by filling in the blanks in paragraphs with words from the selection at the bottom of the page. When completed, the paragraphs will give ideas for ways to make a job change.

Answers: 1. experience 2. training 3. help 4. recommendation 5. job 6. classifieds 7. move 8. consider 9. night 10. quit

Discussion:

Changing jobs does not indicate that you are disloyal or hard to get along with—it may only indicate that you are willing to move up or move on to something else that comes along that is better for you. Have students discuss the following questions.

1. If you are happy with your present job, why even bother looking for something else? (It may not meet your needs for the future, you may want to earn more money, have more prestige, and so on.)
2. What are some jobs that have built-in advancement? (Some entry-level jobs provide training, management positions, and so on.)

3. Do you think some companies would like to keep their good employees so they make arrangements for them to stay to have a better job? Why? (Yes—good employees are hard to find!)

4. If you knew that your boss could recommend you for a better position within the same company, how could you go about using this resource? (Ask for an evaluation, talk to boss about your desire to change jobs, and so on.)

5. What are some ways to get additional skills that would qualify you for a better job within a company? (Ask around, check with the personnel office, look for in-service opportunities, and so on.)

6. Sometimes factories or businesses close and the job goes with it. If your position is terminated because of those factors, how would this affect your looking for another job? (Still use the references, explain that it was not your fault that you're out of a job, and so on.)

Extension Activities:

1. Have students check with their parents or other adults who and bring in examples of on-the-job or in-service traning that is available to employees. How does this help both the employee and the company?

2. Find out what evening school courses are available at local community colleges. How could a person maintain a day job and still get traning to help him or her advance to another position?

Evaluation:

1. List two or three ways a person could change jobs once already employed.

2. Write a paragraph explaining how satisfactory (or superior) job performance on a present job can benefit someone when he or she is changing jobs.

22.7   **Changing Jobs: How?**

Directions:

Fill in the blanks in the following paragraphs to find some ways to change jobs. Use the words in the word box at the bottom of the page.

You are bored with your present job. If you could get some more **(1)** _____, you would be qualified to do something else. You might want to find out about some

(2) _____ that is offered on your present job that would help you move on to something new.

You like your boss and do very well at what you do. Perhaps your boss can

(3) _____ you find another job at the same place. You can always ask for a good **(4)** _____ from him or her. This will help you find another

(5) _____.

There is nothing in your town besides the same old jobs. You look through the

(6) _____ and find out that you can do a similar, but more interesting job if

you are willing to **(7)** _____ to another city. You are alone and don't have a

family, so you might **(8)** _____ it!

If you are willing to go to school at **(9)** _____, you can take some evening

classes in a new area that interests you. This way you won't have to **(10)** _____ your present job, but you can try out something new.

recommendation	night
training	help
experience	move
classifieds	job
quit	consider

Part Six

Problem-Solving Skills

Chapter 23: Handling Problem Situations

23.1 Understanding the Problem

23.2 Coping with Surprises

23.3 Adjusting to Change

23.4 When the Problem Is You!

Chapter 24: Making Decisions

24.1 Decision-Making Factors

24.2 Needs versus Wants

24.3 Immediate Needs versus Waiting

24.4 Following Through

24.5 Changing Bad Decisions

Chapter 25: Resource Management

25.1 What Are My Resources?

25.2 Reliable Resources

25.3 Fact versus Opinion

25.4 Time Management

25.5 Staying on Task

Chapter 26: Goal-Setting

26.1 What Is a Goal?

26.2 Setting Priorities

26.3 Doing Things in Sequence

26.4 Realistic Goals

26.5 Adjusting Goals

Chapter 27: Risk-Taking

27.1 What Is a Risk?

27.2 Why Take Risks?

27.3 Acceptable Risks

27.4 Handling Fear

Handling Problem Situations

23.1 Understanding the Problem

Objective:

The student will demonstrate understanding of a given problem situation by identifying the problem(s) involved.

Comments:

All of us find ourselves in problem situations at one time or another. A first step toward resolving the problem is identifying what the problem consists of. Few problems are simple enough to reduce to one little event; most involve larger situations in which several factors interplay to create problems. In this lesson, students are given problem situations to consider and must pick up the specific factors involved in contributing to that problem situation.

Introductory Activities:

1. Have students think of one problem situation that is important as it relates to their school.
2. Have students write the names or positions of the main people involved in the problem situation.
3. Have students share their ideas and opinions as to what problems face the school at this time.

Activity:

Students are given four problem situations to read on the worksheet "Understanding the Problem." They then are to list the specific factors contributing to the problem situation. In each case there is no simple single factor that is the problem; there are many contributing forces that affect the situation.

Answers (Examples):

1. Some employees don't like the new boss, some do (personality conflicts); there is resentment between employees; the boss seems to have favorites; the atmosphere is tense in the office; there is a loss of personal privileges.
2. Terry spent a lot of money on Angela, which she accepted; they apparently were not communicating about their expectations of the relationship;
3. The first teacher is a friend of the family; Phyllis's skills have improved to the point that the first teacher is not adequate; the first teacher thinks everything is fine; Phyllis has a chance to take lessons with a better instructor; Phyllis is fearful about talking to the first teacher.
4. Everyone has been cheating without penalty, Jason was not involved in this incident (but he has cheated before); parents are involved in being upset about the discipline policy; a big deal is being made about something that Jason thinks is not even a problem; people have different opinions on what cheating is.

Discussion:

Have students share their thoughts about the problems involved in each situation. Point out to students that there are several factors contributing to each problem situation.

1. How could you condense each of the four problems into a simple statement? (For example, a new boss contributed to work problems, Angela didn't want to have sex with Terry, Phyllis wanted to dump her tennis coach, the teacher was upset with a class for cheating.)
2. How does oversimplifying the situations change the whole way you look at the problem? (It makes you miss a lot of the subtleties that still contribute to the problem.)

3. Do you think most problems involve lots of little factors, rather than one main problem? (Probably—life is complex!)

4. Is there a simple solution to the problem situation in example 1? Why or why not? (Many people are involved.)

5. Does every person involved in that work situation have some choices? What? (Choice to comply, complain, talk to the boss, and so on.)

6. Does only Angela have a problem in situation 2? (Both are involved.)

7. Did Angela owe Terry an explanation of her feelings early on in the relationship?

8. Does Angela owe Terry sex in return for the expensive dinners and presents?

9. Does Phyllis owe loyalty to the first instructor in situation 3?

10. How could Phyllis make the problem worse? (Keep going behind the instructor's back.)

11. In situation 4, is the problem with cheating or *being caught* cheating?

12. What values are esteemed by the students and the teacher?

13. Is there a way to handle this situation so that each and every student is treated fairly? (Not unless everyone confesses.)

14. Should Richard be punished even though he didn't copy from anyone himself?

15. Should Jason be punished even though he didn't cheat on this assignment? Is the punishment directed toward cheating in general or cheating on this specific activity?

Extension Activities:

1. Have students role-play the situations on the worksheet, taking care to explain how each of the participants might feel under the circumstances. You may want to have several groups of students redo the role-plays, showing different endings.

2. Look through headlines of articles in the newspaper. Have students demonstrate how problems are brought to attention through a simple statement, and then elaborated on in the article to reveal more complex factors.

Evaluation:

Demonstrate how each of these "simple" problems could be expanded to reveal complex factors affecting the situation.

1. You've been cut from the varsity football team.
2. You didn't get a scholarship you were counting on.
3. The rent in your apartment just went up $50 a month.

23.1   **Understanding the Problem**

Directions:

Read the following situations. List several specific factors or problems that contribute to making the entire situation a problem.

1. Everything seemed to be going along fine at the office until a new supervisor was hired. He wanted the employees to work faster, take no personal phone calls while on the job, and not talk about things that were not work-related. The entire atmosphere at the office changed. While some workers felt they were pressured unfairly to work harder, others felt rewarded and noticed for their dedication to the company and their performance. Those who liked the new boss were unfriendly to those who did not like the new boss. Every day there were people either talking of quitting, refusing to talk to other employees, or competing to get attention from the boss.

What problems do you see in this situation?

_____

_____

_____

2. For the first few weeks that Angela dated Terry, everything was fun. He spent a lot of money on her every weekend, taking her out to expensive restaurants and buying her gifts. Angela liked Terry a lot as a friend, but wasn't sure she wanted to get more involved. Terry began pressuring her to have sex, and when she resisted, he became angry and hurt. Angela felt confused and hurt, also. Now they are not even talking at all to each other.

What problems do you see in this situation?

_____

_____

_____

3. Phyllis was taking tennis lessons from a friend of the family who used to play a lot when she was in high school. Phyllis was getting to be quite good—in fact, she was at the point that she was probably better than her instructor. She wanted to move up to a new level of training, but she didn't want to hurt her current instructor (who was planning to set her up in a city tournament). Phyllis found out about an instructor in town who was a professional player for awhile and is excited about taking Phyllis on as a new student. Phyllis is afraid to talk to the friend of the family about this.

What problems do you see in this situation?

_____

_____

_____

4. Almost everyone in Jason's English class has been cheating on the last research assignment. They copied from Richard, who was making some money by selling copies to people in the class. Jason, however, did not copy from this person this time, although he has in the past. The teacher found out what was going on, and is furious. The school board is threatening to start expulsion procedures, and parents are in an uproar about that, too. Jason thinks it is unfair for everyone to be punished, especially because *he* did not cheat on this assignment. Everyone does it—why should the teacher be upset about this one time?

What problems do you see in this situation?

_____

_____

_____

Chapter 23: Handling Problem Situations   **449**

23.2 Coping with Surprises

Objective:

The student will identify an appropriate coping strategy, given problem situations.

Comments:

Even though we may make elaborate plans, there are always things that can and do go wrong. Part of being a good problem solver is the ability to cope with mistakes or surprises that happen. This is a time to think, regroup, assess the situation, and attempt to get back on track. In this lesson, students are given problem situations and are asked to identify a coping strategy.

Introductory Activities:

Have students consider the following situations. What possible things could go wrong?

1. Planning an outdoor wedding
2. Inviting your friends out to dinner without checking the prices on the menu
3. Having two dates on the same night

Activity:

Students are to read on the worksheet "Coping with Surprises" the examples of unpleasant surprises that can happen and to write a way to cope with the situation. Ideally, the students should try to focus on getting "back on track" toward the original plan.

Answers (Examples):

1. Continue to entertain your friends by watching a movie on TV.
2. Ask the coach for more time if possible.
3. Use humor to announce that you are going to speak from the heart!.
4. Call for a ride, either with a cell phone or by finding a pay phone, or wait for a friend's to come to the parking lot and get a ride to a safe place.
5. Make the best of it, and have a good time with the ones who are there.
6. Try to find another truck (and another friend!).
7. Explain your situation to the supervisor; get a doctor's excuse.
8. Get up early and get to the school copier or another copier.
9. Get off at the first stop and get going in the right direction; make phone calls if necessary to let people know where you are.
10. Call a friend who is in your class and borrow his or her book.

Discussion:

Things can go wrong unexpectedly. In each case, have students share their ideas for ways to cope with the problems and get back on track. In some cases, they may just have to accept the situation and make the best of things. In others, they can actually try to do something to find another way to achieve the goal.

1. Why does it seem as though things go wrong at the worst possible time? Is this really true, or does it just seem that way? (Things may be more crucial at an important time.)

2. How can you prepare for mistakes to happen? (Think ahead, go through all of the things that might go wrong.)

3. When things are beyond your control, how can you use your personality to cope? (Show a sense of humor, ask for help, show strength and determination, and so on.)

4. Do you think people are sympathetic to your situation when you are in an embarrassing position? (Probably.)

5. In situations where you learn to cope with the unexpected, how do you think this could turn into a positive experience? (Prepare you for the same type of situation happening again, cause you to be more resourceful, and so on.)

Extension Activities:

1. Have students locate copies of "Murphy's Law," a humorous interpretation of how things go wrong. Have students write a few laws of their own as they apply to their situations.

2. Have students locate cartoons, such as *The Far Side*, which also depict situations in which things go horribly awry. Perhaps you have some artistic students who can draw their own renditions of humorous situations.

Evaluation:

How could you cope with the following situations?

1. You are in the middle of a math test. Suddenly the batteries in your calculator are dead.

2. You are watching volleyball intramurals after school. A friend comes up to you and says, "Aren't you supposed to be babysitting for Mrs. Peters?" You realize you are an hour late and you totally forgot.

3. You are out on a date at an amusement park with someone you think is really special. Your date sees an old friend and disappears for a very long time. You are not sure whether your date is coming back.

23.2   Coping with Surprises

Directions:

Here are situations in which unplanned surprises come up. What could you do in each situation to cope with the problem and get yourself back on track?

1. You are showing a video at a party to your friends when suddenly the VCR shuts off and the tape is jammed inside.

2. You're on the track team, ready to run the biggest race of your season when you notice your shoe lace is about to break and one of the cleats is broken off.

3. You are giving a speech to ask students to elect you for Student Council president when you realize you have forgotten your notes and don't even know what your next sentence will be.

4. Your car won't start after play practice in the evening. It's dark, late, and you're alone. The parking lot is nearly empty.

5. You planned a huge surprise party for your best friend. Everyone said they would come, but only three people show up.

6. Fred promised you could use his pickup truck for your club's float for the parade. At the last minute, he informs you that he lent it to somebody else.

7. Your throat hurts a lot. You want to call in sick to work, but you've missed a lot of work lately and you're afraid you'll lose your job.

8. You're supposed to make copies of your report for the class, but the library copier is broken. It's 8 o'clock at night and nothing is open.

9. You're running late to get downtown. Suddenly you realize that you are on the wrong bus. You're headed uptown!

10. You have a huge algebra test tomorrow. You brought every book home from your locker—except the algebra book!

23.3 Adjusting to Change

Objective:

The student will identify positive coping strategies that are necessary to handle changes in situations.

Comments:

Life is not predictable. There are often changes in schedules, personnel, resources, timing, and numerous other changes, many of which are unpredictable. Before allowing these unforeseen changes to throw us into a wild frenzy, it is helpful to stop, think, and decide how these changes will affect us. Some things will need to be done immediately; others may take longer. Coping with changes is a sign of maturation as well as a necessary life skill.

Introductory Activities:

How difficult would it be to adjust to these changes?

1. Changing a dentist appointment from 4:00 to 5:00
2. Going from blonde hair to black hair
3. Transferring to a high school in another state
4. Finding out your single parent is getting married again
5. Finding out that you have juvenile diabetes

Activity:

The worksheet "Adjusting to Change" gives situations that involve changes. Students are to read the two possible responses for each situation and circle the one that better depicts the person coping well with the change.
Answers: 1. First   2. Second   3. First   4. Second   5. First   6. First

Discussion:

Students should discuss why the chosen response reflects the better choice of behavior or attitude in the matter and why the other response is not appropriate.

1. How many of the examples involve a change in attitude on the part of the main person? (Really, all of them involve having an attitude of wanting to work out the problem.)
2. Some of the changes were a result of someone else's mistake. Which ones? (#3, #4.)
3. Even if something is not your responsibility, do you still have a responsibility to deal with the change? (Yes, if you're involved at all.)
4. How could a display of temper cause even bigger problems? (Might anger other employees, make a small problem seem larger, does nothing to solve the problem.)
5. Why do you think many people dislike change? (They get used to doing something one way, get good at it and don't like to have things done differently.)
6. If you knew that change in the way you did something would be hard at first, but would eventually make your life easier, would you do it? (Hopefully.)
7. What are some technological changes that older people today are resisting or having difficulty with? (DVDs, computers, ATMs, and so on.)

Extension Activities:

1. Have students look at a set of blueprints from the design of a house or other building project. Have them figure out why this is a good time to make changes, if changes are going to be made. What parallels can they determine between blueprints for a building project and planning other types of projects?

2. Have students think of examples of other changes that occur all the time. For example, substitutions of players in a basketball game, food substitutions at lunch, substitute teachers, and so on. How do these changes affect others involved?

Evaluation:

Write a paragraph describing a change in your life that affected you deeply in some way. Did this change affect others also? Would you view this as a positive change now?

23.3   Adjusting to Change

Directions:

Here are six situations that are causing problems because there has been a change. Read the two possible responses for each and circle the one that shows the better coping response to the change.

23.4 When the Problem Is You!

Objective: The student will recognize characters who are causing a problem and state a solution.

Comments: It is easy to blame others when things go wrong. It is much harder to see ourselves in a situation—how we appear to others and how our behaviors (attitudes, comments, habits) affect others and the situation. In this lesson, students will focus on (1) problem-causers and (2) how to recognize themselves in a problem situation.

Introductory Activity: Set up scenarios in which four students participate in a role-play. One of the students is secretly designated the problem-causer. Have the rest of the class be the audience to pick out the problem-causer and discuss how he or she could better participate. Possible situations: a person who disagrees with everything; a person who is inappropriately loud; a person who forgets to bring needed materials.

Activity: On the worksheet "When the Problem Is You!" the student will read each scenario and identify the reason why the problem-causer is causing a problem.

Answers: 1. d   2. b   3. a   4. e   5. c

Discussion: Emphasize how the problem-causer could become aware that he or she is causing or contributing to a problem.

1. What kind of change would you like to see in these problem-causers?
2. Do you think those characters realize that they are causing problems? Why, or why not?
3. How have you handled situations in which one person is a problem?
4. Have you ever been the one to cause a problem when everyone else is OK?
5. How would you want to be informed if you were causing a problem?
6. What would make you want to change?

Extension Activity: Have students keep a journal for a few days or weeks, recording their thoughts about their own participation in causing problems for others or in situations affecting others. Questions to ponder might include: Am I sometimes the cause of a problem? For whom? Do I care? What do others probably say about me? What do I think about myself? What could I do to change my behavior (attitude, comments, habits)? What is a new approach I could try?

Evaluation:

1. What is one way that you could know that you were causing a problem?
2. What is one step you could take to change?

Name _____ Date _____

23.4   **When the Problem Is You!**

Directions:

One person in each of these examples is causing a problem. Match the type of problem with each example.

a. being rude	d. arguing
b. not doing your share	e. making mistakes
c. being late	

1. I think we should paint the poster black.   No, let's make it red.
   Why don't we make it a little bigger?   No, it's already too big. Make it smaller.
   We could put it up in the hallway.   No, it would look better in the gym.

_____

2. Who brought pretzels for the party?   I did!
   Who brought drinks?   I did.
   Who brought napkins?   Oops, I forgot again. Sorry. I forgot last week, too, didn't I?

_____

3. This is my friend Alicia.
   I'd like you to meet Jessie. She's new.

Hey. (Bored)
Yeah, whatever.

_____

4. No one can figure out your directions.
   We need to have that for our group project
   to be right. There are mistakes all over it.

Well, you can figure it out. I'm not doing it over.

_____

5. (Teacher) Late again? Every day this week.

Sorry, Laurel always has to comb her hair and
makes us wait for her.

_____

Chapter 24

Making Decisions

24.1 Decision-Making Factors

Objective:

The student will identify examples in which individuals have considered several factors that would affect the outcome of the situation.

Comments:

For many decisions, especially minor ones, there is probably little thought or planning that goes into the process of making that decision. But for more important decisions, one must consider a lot of factors. Sometimes how you "feel" at the time is not the way to make a productive decision. One should consider whatever factors are involved in that situation (price, efficiency, other people, deadlines, and so on). In this lesson, students are to identify individuals who have used a systematic plan to make a decision.

Introductory Activities:

1. Present students with the following situation: If you had the choice between taking $500 cash or a one-hour shopping spree in your favorite store, which would you choose?
2. Have students list what factors were involved in making their decision.
3. Present students with this situation: There is a $100 bill hidden in the room. How would you go about trying to find it? List some of their strategies.

Activity:

Students are to read the situations on the worksheet "Decision-Making Factors" that involve an individual making a decision. The students are to decide which examples show the person considering the factors involved in the decision as opposed to those who are haphazard, or without a plan.
Answers: 1. No   2. Yes   3. Yes   4. No

Discussion:

Have students give and explain their responses to the worksheet.

1. Did all of the examples show a plan, even if the plan was haphazard or unworkable? (Yes, you could argue that even a bad plan is still a plan.)
2. In situation 1, if the word "some" was changed to "all," would that be a more systematic plan? (Yes.)
3. What are the important factors to consider in situation 1? (Academic goals, how much money you have to spend, geographic location, and so on.)
4. Do you think this individual will make a good decision or will the decision be made for him? (Sounds like this is a passive person who probably won't get accepted to anything!)
5. In situation 2, did you think this was a systematic plan? (Yes.)
6. What factors did the person consider to be important? (Work qualifications.)
7. In situation 3, what important factors were considered? (Flight times, rates.)
8. Did the person in situation 4 have a plan? (Sort of—just working on what he felt like.)
9. What could go wrong with that system? (If you felt like quitting, your work would not get done.)
10. Do you think most people put a lot of thought into daily decisions? (Probably not—choose by habit.)
11. Does any decision have important factors that affect it? (Yes.)
12. Does the process of identifying the important factors that affect a decision help make the best decision more clear? (Ideally, it should.)

Extension Activities:

1. Have students look through the national news section of the newspaper. What important decisions do government officials have to make? What are some of the important factors that must be considered before making a decision?

2. Have students watch some of the congressional debates on television. What is involved in the decision-making process as far as considering important factors?

3. Have students list five to ten decisions they have directly or indirectly been involved in during the past week. Have them rate the importance of the decision (for example, setting up the time of a dental appointment versus selecting a new car) and list the factors involved in making that decision.

Evaluation:

What factors are involved in making the following decisions:

1. Whether to buy a St. Bernard puppy from a pet store or adopt a homeless adult small dog

2. Whether to go to a movie you don't really want to see with a person you are interested in or go out to an expensive dinner and special event with someone you really don't like

24.1   **Decision-Making Factors**

Directions:

Each of these individuals is trying to make a decision. Decide which of them are considering the factors involved and which are not. Circle YES or NO next to each situation.

I'm not sure which college to go to. I guess I'll just apply to some of them and see where I get accepted.

YES   NO

I can only hire one assistant. I'll go through their résumés, set up interviews with the ones who sound good, and then I'll pick one.

YES   NO

There are four flights to New York. I'm going to check the times of arrival and departure to see which fit my schedule. Then I'll check rates for the flights and try to find a good deal.

YES   NO

All this homework! I'll work on whatever I feel like for awhile. It will all get done.

YES   NO

24.2 Needs versus Wants

Objective:

Given examples, the student will differentiate a *need* from a *want*.

Comments:

Sometimes it is hard to distinguish between a need and a want. Do we *need* those new jeans, or can we live without them? Is it necessary for our survival to have expensive shoes, or is it important because everyone else has them? Again, making a good decision must involve considering the factors. You have to have clothes, but you must consider the appropriateness of the occasion, cost, quality, and so on. In this lesson, students are to consider situations that can roughly be divided into wants and needs and to categorize them.

Introductory Activities:

1. Inform students that a special holiday is coming early and they can have five things they want. Have them make their lists.
2. Inform students they are being sent to the moon for a week. Have them make a list of five items they would take with them.
3. Have students compare the items on the lists. What would qualify an item as a *want* or a *need*?
4. Have students come up with working definitions for the terms "want" and "need." A want could be considered something that would be helpful to have, but not necessary to accomplish a certain goal. A need could be something that is crucial to the completion of a goal. In that respect, new shoes may be a want if a person already has shoes for walking around, but specific shoes may be a need if the person must have a certain type of footwear to play a sport.

Activity:

Students are to read the statements on the worksheet "Needs versus Wants" in which a desire for something is expressed. From the context, they are to determine whether the item involved is a "want" or a "need." The purpose of the lesson is not so much to sort through the responses but to look for additional factors that would indicate what the goal is in each situation.

Answers:

These are suggestions; allow for discussion to clarify the student's responses and thinking.

1. Need (socially expected).
2. Want.
3. Want.
4. Need (proper clothing).
5. Need (medicine).
6. Want.
7. Need (tools for completing assignments).
8. Depends on the situation—because it is the "ultimate," we can assume that the buyer has some choices and *wants* this specific item.
9. Need (hygiene).

10. Want, but depends on the situation—if a car is the only way that the individual can get to school, it would be a need.

11. Could be either—does the coursework depend a lot on using a personal computer for assignments?

12. Need.

Discussion:

In each of the examples on the worksheet, there are other questions that can and should be asked to clarify the situation. Depending on that situation, either answer could be justified. Encourage students to think!

1. What are some examples of items that would be considered needs in terms of social behavior? (Gifts, cards, bridesmaid dresses, taking someone out to dinner, and so on.)

2. Besides oxygen, water, food, clothing, and shelter, what are some other needs that humans have? (Need to be loved, need for friendship, need to play, and so on.)

3. Is it wrong to want something expensive if it is available in a cheaper model? (Not necessarily—if you have the money to buy something nice, it's not a problem.)

4. If your goal is to be the best football player in your school, what might be some of your equipment needs? (Padding, shoes, helmet, and so on.)

5. What would be some of your other needs? (Time for training, good coaching, adequate sleep, proper nutrition, and so on.)

6. Is it wrong to want things? (Not necessarily.)

7. When you make decisions, should you consider "wants" as well as "needs"? (Absolutely! Focus on your goals!)

Extension Activities:

1. For each of the examples on the worksheet, have students construct a situation in which the item is a want and then a need. By manipulating the situations, each item could conceivably fit into either category.

2. Have students investigate Abraham Maslow's hierarchy of human needs. Make a chart indicating this theory of what humans need and what is included at each level.

Evaluation:

1. Give an example of something that is a need for you. Explain your example.

2. Give an example of something that is a want for you. Explain your example.

Name _____ Date _____

24.2   Needs versus Wants

Directions:

Read the following statements. Does each indicate something that the person **needs** or something that the person **wants**? Write your answer in the space below each statement.

1. I got invited to Sarah's birthday party. I must decide what to get her for a gift.

2. That was a great dinner. What shall I order for dessert?

3. Oh, that little kitten is so cute. I'll take her home with me.

4. This sock has a huge hole in it. I'll get new ones.

5. Where is my cough medicine? Cough, cough, cough!

6. I love how this perfume smells. And it's only $40 an ounce!

7. Shoot! This pen ran out of ink! I'll have to replace it.

8. This is the ultimate stereo system. I don't care that I have to make many payments—it's worth it!

9. I like this brand of toothpaste.

10. How am I going to get to school if I don't have a car?

11. Everyone in the class has a personal computer but me.

12. My calculator stopped working. It needs new batteries.

Chapter 24: Making Decisions   **465**

24.3 Immediate Needs versus Waiting

Objective:

Given a decision-making situation, the student will identify possible short-and long-term effects of a choice.

Comments:

Sometimes students are tempted to make decisions that seem to be great for immediate satisfaction, but are not best in the long run. It might be hard to take the time to think through the consequences of making a decision, especially when a choice might yield something desirable right away. In this lesson, students are to consider situations that may yield better results if a choice is put off until a better time.

Introductory Activities:

1. Ask students if they would rather have $1,000 right now or $1,000,000 in ten years. Tally their responses.
2. What would be the benefits of having money right away?
3. What would be the benefits of waiting and having a much larger sum?
4. What might be a drawback of waiting for the larger amount of money?

Activity:

Explain to students that they are going to consider some situations on the worksheet "Immediate Needs versus Waiting" in which individuals must make a decision about some aspect of their life. They are to answer questions that direct them to consider short-term effects and long-term consequences.

Answers (Examples):

Situation 1

a. Whether he can join the truck driving program later or it has to be right now, whether he has any other sources of money, whether he can work and go through training at the same time.
b. He would have to do the training program later, he would have money to pay his rent, he could start saving money.
c. He might have to borrow the money until he is finished with the training and can get another job.
d. Students may suggest that Jeff work part-time and try to get into the program later. Because he doesn't have any money saved up, he may need to learn to budget his money and activities.

Situation 2

a. Whether Kari is going to work, how much money they have saved up, how much free time they want to spend with each other.
b. Yes.
c. Kari thinks she would have someone to take care of, maybe would not have to work; Sam would have to have a secure income to support the family; they might be spending a lot of time at home instead of going out.
d. They could save money, have time together, get to know each other, plan for children when they are more settled.

Situation 3

  a. How much she needs the job, whether there is potential for advancement in the company, how much of her day is spent directly involved with the boss, how much she enjoys her work.

  b. She would start all over looking for work but she might be directed toward a better job and better situation.

  c. Learn patience, get respect from other employers who understand her situation, save money until she's in a better position to leave.

  d. Talk to another supervisor, possibly talk to the boss, ask for a transfer within the company.

  e. Students may say that the stress is not worth the job. If Elinor is a good worker, she will probably be able to find another job.

Discussion:

Students may have varied responses to the worksheet. Have them discuss how they arrived at their conclusions.

Extension Activities:

1. Waiting seems hard to do, especially for a teenager. Have students make personal lists of things they consider worth waiting for. Depending on the student, this may include a college degree, marriage, sex, buying a house, and so on.

2. Have students write endings for the situations on the worksheet. There are ways for all of the decisions to end positively.

Evaluation:

Explain your feelings about the following well-known adages:

He who hesitates is lost.

Fools rush in where angels fear to tread.

Look before you leap.

24.3   Immediate Needs versus Waiting

Directions:

Each of these individuals needs to make a decision about something in his or her life. The decision must be made right away; each individual needs your help to figure out the consequences of doing something immediately or waiting.

Situation 1

Jeff can work at a hardware store for minimum wage right away, or he can enroll in a technical program that will train him for truck driving, which is what he really wants to do. However, he does not have any money saved up and needs to pay rent.

    a. What factors does Jeff need to consider?

    b. If Jeff decides to work at the store, what effect would that have on the factors in (a)?

    c. If Jeff goes to truck driving school, how could he handle the factors in (a)?

    d. What do you think Jeff should do?

Situation 2

Sam and Kari have been married for a few months. Kari wants to have a baby right away and wants to stay home to take care of it. Sam has a pretty good job, but he's not sure he wants to be a father so soon.

    a. What factors do Sam and Kari have to consider?

    b. Is it important that Sam and Kari agree on their decision?

    c. What are some immediate results of having a baby right away?

    d. What are some reasons for them to wait?

Situation 3

Elinor works for a man whom she detests. He is often unfair with how much work he gives her to do, never compliments her on a good job, and has temper tantrums. Elinor likes her work, but she comes home stressed and edgy. Every day seems to get worse.

    a. What factors does Elinor have to consider?

    b. What results would probably happen if Elinor quit?

    c. What benefits might occur if she stayed on the job?

    d. Is there anything Elinor can do to change her situation?

    e. What do you think Elinor should do?

24.4 Following Through

Objective:

The student will state the importance of following through on a decision, particularly when it involves a commitment to others.

Comments:

Sometimes decisions can, and should, be reversed. If new information comes in, or something happens that changes original plans and goals, decisions may have to be adjusted. When one is in a position of making decisions that affect other people and require planning, however, it is a good idea to recognize when to stick with the decision. In this lesson, students are given situations to evaluate.

Introductory Activities:

Ask students to rate the following situations according to how important the decision is:

1. Deciding to order pepperoni pizza and then changing your mind to sausage pizza
2. Deciding to marry Tom and then changing your mind to marry Wayne
3. Deciding to negotiate trade agreements with a European nation and then changing your mind to declare nuclear war instead

Activity:

This lesson involves following through on a decision. In the examples on the worksheet "Following Through," the decisions are from the point of view of a person in a decision-making role; that is, others are subject to the effects of that decision. The decision is stated and the person is identified. The student must then decide which of the two responses indicates that the person is following through on the decision.

Answers: 1. B   2. A   3. A   4. B   5. A

Discussion:

Each situation involves identifying a group of people who are affected by the decision. The decision itself may also be questioned. Use the following questions to discuss students' ideas about the importance of following through on a decision.

1. Would you say that the more people who are involved in a decision, the more important that decision is? (Possibly, but each individual decision that a person makes is very important to him or her.)
2. In example 1, do you think the decision is unfair? (Depends on whether or not employees were abusing the privilege.)
3. If some of the employees were spending half of their time talking on the phone, how would that affect the business?
4. Do you think the boss would allow exceptions?
5. In example 2, how many people are affected by the coach's decision? (The players.)
6. If the situation changes, as it seemed to in the example, why shouldn't the coach change his mind? (The other players are expecting a certain play or pattern.)
7. How would a last-minute change in plan affect the other players? (They might be confused, caught off guard.)

8. In example 3, do you think the teacher's changing a due date is unfair to students? (Probably, unless the students had a few months' notice or were able to negotiate the due date with the teacher.)

9. Do you know of examples of teachers changing assignment dates to make them later? How do you feel about that if you are one of the people who had planned to be finished on time?

10. How many people are affected by the bride's decision in example 4? (The dressmaker.)

11. When alterations have already been made, is it a fair policy to make someone purchase the dress if the person changes her mind? (Yes, because the alterations took time and involved work; there's usually a policy stated up front about this.)

12. In example 5, what types of decisions needed to be made resulting from the decision to go to Florida? (When to go, reservations, time off from work, and so on.)

13. Why would changing the geographical location of a vacation be an important decision? (Clothing, tickets, other plans.)

14. In this case, if everyone involved agreed they would rather go skiing, is anyone inconvenienced by the change in decision? (Not particularly.)

Extension Activities:

1. Have students tell of examples of decisions that are important to follow through on. They may have some anecdotes from personal experience about decisions that were not followed up on, leading to some interesting consequences.

2. People are constantly making decisions. Many daily decisions are seemingly of little consequence; for example, what to wear, what to eat, what route to take walking home, and so on. Yet in particular situations, these decisions could be crucial (dietary restrictions, social events, who might be waiting along a certain route home, and so on). Others may involve a lot of people, time, or consequences. Have students make a list of twenty to thirty decisions that they have made in the past twenty-four hours. Have them rate the personal importance of each and describe the factors on their "rating scale."

3. Have students write and perform humorous role-plays in which a character cannot make up his or her mind about a decision. ("I'll have a strawberry shake. No, wait, make that chocolate. Well, maybe peach sounds good. No, wait—I'll have what she's having.")

Evaluation:

Write a possible consequence of the person in each of these examples not following through on his or her decision:

1. "I know my doctor tells me I need to have gallbladder surgery, but I've changed my mind. I don't want an operation."

2. "I've decided not to sell the house after all."

3. "No one in the company is going to get a raise this year."

24.4   **Following Through**

Directions:

In each situation below, which response shows the person following through on a decision? Circle A or B.

1. ***Boss.*** *Decision:* There will be no more personal phone calls made on office time.

A

"Maybe that was a bad decision—emergencies do happen from time to time."

B

"People will plan their time better if they make phone calls during breaks."

2. ***Coach.*** *Decision:* Stretch Roberts will try for the last basket during this basketball game. He is the best shot on the team.

A

"Give Stretch the ball!"

B

"Wait! Ace is in a better position—throw it to him."

3. ***Teacher.*** *Decision:* The research paper will be due at the end of the semester.

A

"Everyone knows the due date and should be finished. That will give you four months to prepare."

B

"I'm planning to go on vacation—I'll make the paper due in three weeks."

4. ***Bride-to-Be.*** *Decision:* I'll take that wedding dress. It will need alterations, however, or it won't fit me just right.

A

"I want my deposit back—I found another dress I decided I like better. I'm sure you can sell it again to someone who is my size."

B

"There are so many things to plan; I will stick with this dress."

5. ***Father.*** *Decision:* We're going to Florida over spring break.

A

"Here are our plane tickets, hotel reservations, and new suitcases. I'm working on plans for what we'll do."

B

"Let's go skiing instead. We'll all need new clothes."

24.5 Changing Bad Decisions

Objective:

The student will offer at least one option available to a given individual who had made a bad decision.

Comments:

Unfortunately, not all of our decisions turn out to be the "right" ones. In retrospect, we can sometimes see that we should have asked more questions, thought a little longer, or maybe done a little more homework before making a decision. In this lesson, students are given situations in which an individual made a decision that turned out to be a mistake. They are to come up with a new decision to better the situation.

Introductory Activities:

1. Tell students: "I want everyone in the class to jump out of their seats and squawk like a chicken." Observe the chaos for a minute or two and then try to get their attention back!

2. Have students decide whether or not that was a good decision. (Probably not.) Why? (Loss of classroom control.)

3. Ask students to predict what would probably happen if you (the teacher) asked students to toss pencils around the room and scream at the top of their lungs. (They would probably do it.) Why is it likely that you would not make the decision to ask them to do this, especially when your class was being observed? (From the first episode, you were able to see that the class was willing to follow crazy orders; also, it would make your discipline very questionable if the class were to be observed.)

Activity:

Students are to read the situations on the worksheet "Changing Bad Decisions" and decide what each person in the example could do to make the best of a bad decision. In each case, have students think about making a new decision, hopefully with new knowledge of the situation.

Answers (Examples):

1. Decide to take back the keys until further notice.
2. Decide to tell his parents that he doesn't know Amanda very well.
3. Decide to keep the puppy at home until she has housetrained it.
4. Decide to call home and get a ride with someone else.
5. Decide to take back the game and get a gift certificate instead.
6. Decide to politely inform them that they weren't expecting this number of people.
7. Decide to pick up her daughter and look for a new babysitter.
8. Decide to talk to the girl ahead of time about the problem and mention that there might be hard feelings.

Discussion:

Students may have various creative ideas for the situations. Listen to them and try, together, to come up with some good solutions.

1. In situation 1, Mr. Wu felt he had made a bad decision. Why? (His daughter was not a careful driver.)
2. If he had thought about the situation more carefully ahead of time, would he have been able to figure this out before buying her a car? (Probably.)

3. What made this a bad decision? (His daughter was not a good recipient of a car; it would only get her into trouble.)

4. Is a bad outcome the same thing as a bad decision? (It could be thought of that way; the outcome would determine the value of the decision.)

5. In situation 2, at what point did Fred realize he had made a bad decision? (When he saw the way she was dressed.)

6. Is there any way he could have foreseen that situation? (Possibly not; he didn't know her very well.)

7. Could the problems in situation 3 been thought of ahead of time? (Yes, puppies are somewhat predictable in that department.)

8. What was Debbie's bad decision? (To get into the car.)

9. In situation 5, what could Peter have done ahead of time to pick a more appropriate present for his cousin? (Asked around to see what kind of games he liked.)

10. In situation 6, the Robertsons made an attempt to do something nice for their neighbors, and apparently were taken advantage of. How would this affect what they will do the next time they invite someone to dinner? (Probably specify how many are invited.)

11. What decision will Mrs. Greenberg make the next time she looks for a babysitter? (Decide to ask for references, observe the babysitter before deciding to use her or him.)

12. In situation 8, do you think Paula will redo her next birthday list more carefully? (Probably.)

13. How could Paula still end up with a successful birthday party? (Make sure everyone will behave themselves, uninvite the key problem girl.)

Extension Activities:

1. Have students look for examples of bad decisions. They may find examples from politics; in particular, in political cartoons. Have them explain why the outcome was particularly bad for the individual who made the decision.

2. Have students share anecdotes of their own dealings with decisions they have regretted.

3. Have students talk to older adults who probably have some regrets about decisions they have made. If willing to share their ideas, have the adults talk about some of them in class.

Evaluation:

Write a paragraph describing a decision in which you were involved that you would consider to be a bad decision. What was the outcome? Were there any clues that this decision would give this result? What would you do differently the next time, with this new knowledge?

Name _____ Date _____

24.5   **Changing Bad Decisions**

Directions:

What could each of these people do to make a change in plans after realizing that he or she had made a bad decision? What new decision could be made?

1. Mr. Wu had decided to buy his daughter a new car. He soon realized that she was going to end up crashing it because she was not a careful driver.

2. Fred realized he had made a mistake when he asked Amanda out for a date and she showed up at his parents' house wearing outrageous clothes, with purple-and-green striped hair.

3. Jill bought a new puppy and didn't think twice about taking it over to her girlfriend's apartment—until it had several "accidents" on the floor.

4. Debbie got into the car with Eddie and realized he had been drinking. She hoped he would get her home safely.

5. Peter bought a video game for his cousin for a birthday present and then noticed that the cousin already had the game. The cousin made the comment that it was really a stupid game that only babies would play.

6. Mr. and Mrs. Robertson invited their new neighbors over for dinner and were surprised when they showed up with their seven children, eight in-laws, and three of their friends.

7. Mrs. Greenberg dropped her young daughter off at the new babysitter's and turned around to wave good-bye. The babysitter was already yelling at her daughter and threatening to spank her.

8. Paula had sent out invitations to a birthday party at her house for Saturday night, when she realized that several of her friends were angry at one of the other girls she had invited because she was dating their boyfriends.

Resource Management

25.1 What Are My Resources?

Objective:

The student will identify at least ten different resources available to him or her.

Comments:

Many types of resources are available to most people if they will stop and think about them. Not only are people available to help, but there are other resources, such as publications, institutions, possessions, and intangibles such as time, one's own skills, and creativity. In this lesson, students are to think about types of resources available to them.

Introductory Activities:

Ask students what they could do in these situations:

1. You need $10 to buy something. (Write a check, go to the bank.)
2. A button comes off of your shirt. (Sew it back on, take it to your mother.)
3. A friend asks if you will teach him or her how to play tennis. (Get the friend a book, go out on the court and spend time teaching.)

Define *resource* (something that is available to help relieve a situation or achieve a goal; examples are people, skills, tools, institutions, equipment, publications, and so on).

1. What resources did you come up with for #1? (Money, a bank.)
2. What resources did you come up with for #2? (A skill, a parent.)
3. What resources did you come up with for #3? (A skill, a book.)

Activity:

Make sure students have a fairly good idea of what is meant by a resource. Explain that they will now have some situations to consider that require the use of resources to solve. They are given one example of a possible resource on the worksheet What Are My Resources and are to think of two additional resources. They can discuss how the resources can be used to solve the problem.

Answers (Examples):

1. Realtor, neighbor
2. Friend, brochure
3. Tuxedo shop, other clothes
4. Friend who just turned eighteen, post office
5. Department of motor vehicles, police department
6. Friend, phone book
7. Teacher, computer tutorial
8. Bus station attendant, phone call
9. Community bulletin board, friends
10. Doctor, information that came with the medicine

Discussion:

Have students share their ideas of resources that would help solve the problems on the worksheet. You may want to keep a running list of what type of resource was selected; for example, person, skill, institution, and so on.

1. What personal resources—your talents, abilities, personality—do you have?
2. What kinds of problems or needs would someone who was new in town encounter? (Where to live, work, how to find places, and so on.)
3. What are some community resources that would help someone in this situation? (Maps, phone book, neighbors.)
4. What people are available as resources to you in situations in which you need advice or someone to listen? (Friends, family, counselor.)
5. What people are resources for you if you needed help with physical tasks, such as moving, painting, or getting a ride? (Friends, neighbors.)
6. In what ways could these resources be helpful to someone: the local YMCA, library, a workshop, computer lab, newspaper, correspondence school classes, computer, ability to touch-type, huge bank account?

Extension Activities:

1. Have students take personal inventory of the resources available to them. Do they have a sister who can cut hair? A driver's license? A savings account? A car? Have them come up with at least fifty different items.
2. To help students remember the categories or types of resources, have them collectively or in small groups work on a wall poster, with drawings, magazine pictures, photographs, and so on depicting resources. You may want to title categories, such as People, Skills, Places, Tools, and so on.

Evaluation:

1. What is a definition for a resource?
2. Give an example of a person who is a resource for you, a tool that you have used, a building or institution, and a skill or talent that is a personal resource. Explain how each has helped you achieve a goal or resolve a problem situation.

25.1   What Are My Resources?

Directions:

Read the following problems. Next to each one is listed a possible resource that could help solve the problem. Add two other resources for each problem.

Problem

1. You are unfamiliar with a city that you have just moved to. You want to find a place to live.

2. You are responsible for planning a group trip to an amusement park. You think you heard something about a discount for more than ten people.

3. You need to rent a tuxedo for a wedding that you will be in, but you are not sure of your size.

4. You just turned eighteen and want to register to vote.

5. You have to renew your driver's license.

6. Your car is making funny noises, and you want a recommendation for a good mechanic in town.

7. You are having trouble with your math and are afraid you aren't going to pass.

8. You need to know what time the last bus leaves for the next town.

9. You want someone to help you paint your house.

10. You have a high fever, stomach ache, and dizziness. The medicine you took is making you feel worse.

Resources

City map

Phone book

Friend who does alterations

City hall

Parents

Gas station manager

Tutor

Bus schedule

Newspaper

Pharmacist

25.2 Reliable Resources

Objective:

Given examples, the student will identify reliable resources and explain why they are reliable.

Comments:

"You can't believe everything you hear." Likewise, anyone can hang out a shingle but it is no guarantee that the person is a competent, trustworthy individual. Students need to learn to evaluate whether or not a resource is truly reliable. This might mean checking credentials, asking a friend for a recommendation, obtaining a written warranty, and considering the personal relationship of the person giving the comments. In this lesson, students are to evaluate resources and decide whether or not they are reliable.

Introductory Activities:

Give students the following choice to consider:

> They are taking a trip and are going to fly. They can choose between a flight on Airline A, which has a perfect flight record for the past thirty years, but is more expensive; or a flight on Airline B, which uses old planes with old parts and has the worst flight record of all major airlines, but offers economy rates.

Which airline would students probably choose? (Airline A) Why? (They value their life, it has a better record, it is more *reliable*.)

Activity:

Have students complete the worksheet "Reliable Resources," which has examples of statements describing some resources. They must decide whether or not the resource sounds reliable or not.

Answers:

These are suggestions—students may be able to justify different responses!

1. No   2. Yes   3. Yes   4. No   5. No   6. No   7. Yes   8. Yes   9. Yes   10. No   11. Yes   12. No   13. No   14. Yes   15. Yes   16. No

Discussion:

Have students explain the reasoning for their answers on the worksheet. In some cases, more information about the situation would be helpful, but is not given.

1. What makes a resource seem reliable?
2. Why would you tend to doubt the reliability of a person who was trying to sell you a watch in a parking lot? (Don't know his reputation.)
3. How important is reputation in evaluating a resource? (Very important.)
4. How does a warranty or guarantee of a product or service protect your safety? (Can take it back if it's defective; it's like a promise that it will be satisfactory.)
5. How important are credentials when checking out the services of a doctor, dentist, contractor, or other provider? (Very important.)

6. How could you go about checking on the credentials of such a person? (Ask friends, ask questions, check with the Better Business Bureau, and so on.)

7. Why might you trust the opinion of someone who was a family friend rather than someone with whom you did not get along personally? (The family friend would probably have your best interests in mind; the other person may not care.)

Extension Activities:

1. Have students collect and display magazine ads of products that try to declare their reliability; for example, watches that "keep on ticking."

2. Have students take note of television commercials that promise services, such as personal injury lawyers. Have them evaluate whether or not, based on the ads, those services seem reliable.

3. Have students examine warranties on items such as a car, pet, appliance, and so on. What does the small print indicate?

Evaluation:

Give an example of:

1. A reliable person
2. A reliable product
3. A reliable form of transportation
4. A reliable piece of equipment

Explain your choices.

25.2   **Reliable Resources**

Directions: Do these items sound like examples of reliable resources to you?
Circle Yes or No.

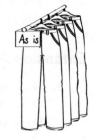

1.   A doctor who got his license from a mail order magazine. **YES   NO**

2.   A builder who has built several houses in your neighborhood that appear to be very nice.
     YES   NO

3.   A phone number in the local phone book. **YES   NO**

4.   A salesperson for a used car dealership that is being investigated by the Internal Revenue Service
     for tax fraud. **YES   NO**

5.   A story about aliens coming to Earth to steal people. **YES   NO**

6.   An old car that is covered with rust, has a flat tire, and has a gas gauge on "empty." **YES   NO**

7.   The local weather report for tomorrow. **YES   NO**

8.   The number of calories in a candy bar as reported by the wrapper. **YES   NO**

9.   The warning label on a bottle of prescription medicine. **YES   NO**

10. The personal habits of your neighbor as reported by the town gossip. **YES   NO**

11. A thirty-day warranty on game parts for a computer game you purchased at a department store.
     YES   NO

12. A pair of jeans that is purchased from a rack marked "As Is." **YES   NO**

13. A watch from a man in a trench coat in a parking lot behind a bar. **YES   NO**

14. A kitten purchased from a pet store with a two-month guarantee of good health. **YES   NO**

15. The opinion of the wiring in your house from an engineer who is a good friend of your father.
     YES   NO

16. The opinion of your piano-playing ability from someone who can't stand you. **YES   NO**

25.3 Fact versus Opinion

Objective:

The student will correctly identify statements as being either fact or opinion.

Comments:

Part of making a judgment as to the reliability of a resource is considering whether the information is a person's opinion or if it is a fact. Some people can be very convincing and give seemingly logical arguments for statements that are not true. In this lesson, students are to examine statements and decide whether they are fact or opinion.

Introductory Activities:

1. Define *fact* (something that is always true, based on evidence that no one can argue with).   2. Define *opinion* (an expression of how someone feels about something; may or may not be true).   3. Have students give an example of a fact about something in the classroom (such as the time shown on the clock, the color of the walls, and so on).   4. Have students give an example of an opinion on how they feel about the school cafeteria food.

Activity:

Students are to examine the statements on the worksheet "Fact versus Opinion" and decide whether it is an example of a fact or an opinion. Have them look for "clue words" or other subtleties that may indicate the comment is an opinion.   *Answers:* 1. Fact   2. Fact   3. Fact   4. Opinion   5. Opinion   6. Opinion   7. Fact   8. Opinion   9. Opinion   10. Fact

Discussion:

Make sure students understand the reasoning behind the examples. Clarify any questions.

1. Where is a good place to hear opinions expressed? (Cafeteria, pool hall, church socials, and so on.)
2. When is a good time or during what events would you hear opinions expressed? (Political elections, debates, and so on.)   3. Who or what would be a good, reliable resource to give you factual information about investing your money? (Banker, investor.) About buying a good car? (Consumer reports, friend in the business.) About traveling to a foreign country? (Travel agent.)   4. If someone appeared to be truly sincere, would that make him or her more believable? (Probably.)   5. Why do we take into account the way a person acts and looks as much as the words they use? (We tend to look at the whole person.)   6. What were some clues on the worksheet that tipped you off that it was an opinion being expressed? ("I think"; words like "always," "never," "everyone," and so on.)

Extension Activities:

1. Have students come up with a list of twenty facts and twenty opinions. Have them cite their sources for the facts.   2. Have students circulate quietly in populated areas, listen for opinions being expressed, and write down the examples they hear (for example, "I think the Bulls will win this year," "I like pizza," and so on). Compare findings.   3. Tape and discuss television commercials. How much of what is presented is factual? How much is opinion? Does it depend on the product?

Evaluation:

1. What is a fact?   2. What is an opinion?   3. Give three examples of facts.   4. Give three examples of opinions.   5. Take one of your opinions and turn it into a fact.

25.3   **Fact versus Opinion**

Directions:

Are the following statements examples of facts or opinions? Circle FACT or OPINION.

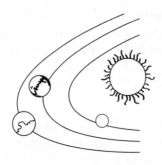

1. The owner's manual states that you should rotate the tires on a car and change the oil regularly to maintain it properly. **FACT**   **OPINION**

2. Earth is the third planet from the sun. **FACT**   **OPINION**

3. There are about 140 calories in a can of non-diet soda. **FACT**   **OPINION**

4. When buying an appliance, you should purchase the most expensive warranty possible. **FACT**   **OPINION**

5. Fish make better pets than cats or dogs for people who live in apartments. **FACT**   **OPINION**

6. It is easy to drive through Chicago in the middle of the day. **FACT**   **OPINION**

7. Thomas Jefferson was our third president. **FACT**   **OPINION**

8. I think First Bank and Trust will give you a good deal on a car loan. **FACT**   **OPINION**

9. No one in New York City is friendly to strangers. **FACT**   **OPINION**

10. Blood travels in the body through the circulatory system. **FACT**   **OPINION**

25.4 Time Management

Objective:

The student will be familiar with several strategies for using time efficiently when given several tasks to complete.

Comments:

It seems as though there is never enough time to get everything done. Students may have their days filled with school, sports, working, friends, chores at home, and numerous other activities, all of which are important. Much can be accomplished if time is valued and used efficiently. In this lesson, students are introduced to several time-saving strategies.

Introductory Activities:

1. Ask students what they would do if they were given an extra hour in their day.
2. To have students experience at least one dimension of "time," select two or three volunteers and have them put their heads down on cue and, when they think one minute is up, raise their hands quietly. The rest of the class can observe. Did time seem to pass slowly for these students?

Activity:

On the worksheet "Time Management," students are to read the story of a girl who has mismanaged her time to an extreme. They are to note (this can be done by underlining specific passages in the story) instances in which the girl in the story got "off-track" or did not use her time efficiently.

Answers: overslept, had not done homework from night before, had not done laundry, slept through study hall, looked through magazine instead of studying, watched more TV than necessary, forgot soap at the store, shopped for nail polish

Discussion:

Have students compare instances they selected as representative of mismanaged time.

1. At what point did this day begin to go off-track for Sandy? (When she overslept, but she had set herself up for problems when she didn't do her homework or laundry the night before.)
2. What could she have done the night before to be better prepared for this day? (Laundry, homework; perhaps gone to bed earlier so she wouldn't oversleep.)
3. What activities could have been shortened? (Length of time she slept in, watched TV, or shopped.)
4. What activities could have been rearranged? (Prepare food for dinner before doing homework or talking with a friend.)
5. What activities could have been eliminated? (Shopping, talking with friend, watching TV.)
6. How could making a list have helped Sandy with shopping and other chores? (Could have helped her shorten her shopping time, kept reminding her of what she was supposed to be doing.)
7. Are there other shortcuts she could have taken to get everything done? (Ask friend to help with chores, shop on a different day.)
8. What is an example of activities that Sandy can and did do at the same time? (Walking dog and thinking about science project.)

9. What are some other activities that could be done simultaneously? (Doing laundry and thawing out frozen food, watching television and preparing food, walking the dog and practicing a speech, and so on.)

10. What do you think is Sandy's basic problem? Is she lazy, disorganized, or just too busy?

11. What would you suggest Sandy do to get ready for tomorrow? (Make sure she has clothes ready and homework done, sets the alarm, talks to mother about dinner plans, and so on.)

Extension Activities:

1. Have students figure out approximately how many hours they spent on a typical school day involved in certain activities, such as sleeping, studying, recreation, and leisure. Help them construct a circle graph depicting the different categories.

2. Have students design and maintain a daily time planner or schedule. Try it out for a week. Have them look for patterns of time that could be used in different ways.

3. List the various strategies for efficiently using time, and have students make a conscious effort to try using them. You may want to make a colorful poster and put it in a conspicuous place. Strategies: shorten tasks, rearrange tasks, eliminate tasks, do tasks simultaneously, list tasks, prepare for tasks.

Evaluation:

1. List and describe at least three time-management techniques.

2. List at least two activities you would like to spend more time doing. How could you plan to give yourself more time?

3. List at least two activities you could manage much more efficiently. Describe how you could do this.

25.4   **Time Management**

Directions:

Here is a day in Sandy's life. Look for examples of how she did not use her time wisely to accomplish everything she wanted or needed to do that day. Underline those examples.

The day started out when the alarm clock went off and Sandy rolled over and went back to sleep. When she woke up again, she realized she had overslept, missed the bus to school, and did not have time to do the homework she had left over from the night before. She got up, found the laundry basket, and took out some clothes to wear. She wished she had remembered to get the laundry done the night before. Her mother was busy working overtime and wasn't able to do as many chores around the house as she used to.

After getting a late pass from the office, Sandy went to the first class of the day—study hall. Since there were only ten minutes left of class, she didn't feel she had time to start anything, so she put her head down and tried to catch up on some missed sleep.

Later in the day, she realized she had a test (which she had put off studying for) and a paper that was due. She told herself she would get it done that night and turn it in the next day for at least partial credit.

After school, Sandy had basketball practice. She got a ride home with a friend who wanted to know if she could stay for a while and work on math together. Sandy thought that would be fine, but instead of working on math, they decided to look through a magazine and pick out new hair styles.

Soon, Sandy heard her mother's car pulling into the driveway and she panicked when she realized her mother had asked her to take out frozen meat and let it thaw after school. She quickly ran into the kitchen and put it in the microwave, hoping it would begin to thaw.

Sandy, her friend, and her mother called for a pizza to be delivered and watched television for an hour to relax. Sandy's friend left and Sandy was about to get out her homework, but the TV movie sounded really interesting and she decided to watch it with her mother instead.

The dog scratching at the door reminded her that she needed to feed Bozo and take him for a walk. While walking, she thought about what she would choose to do for her science project. She thought that an experiment comparing two detergents would be good—and besides, she needed to catch up on the laundry so she would have something to wear to school tomorrow.

After the walk, Sandy's mom asked her if she would run to the store to get some soap. Sandy did, and stopped to look at the new nail polish and perfume that had just come in. She decided that these would be good birthday gifts to get for her friend. When she got home, she realized she had forgotten to get soap.

It was getting late, so she told her mother she would shop right after school tomorrow—if she had time!

Chapter 25: Resource Management   **487**

25.5 Staying on Task

Objective:

The student will identify several reasons why it is understandable to get off task and will identify several strategies for staying on task.

Comments:

Many problems would be solved if the task causing the problem was simply completed. Task completion is sometimes complicated by factors such as a student's being distracted, tired, hyperactive, hungry, unfamiliar with the work, or just plain bored. Teachers can try to make material interesting, but at times there is work that simply must be done. The student needs to accept the importance of the task and stick with it until it is completed. In this lesson, students are to identify possible reasons why characters are off task.

Introductory Activities:

Inform students that you want them to take out a piece of paper and pencil and begin writing numbers counting by 3's (3, 6, 9, 12, 15, and so on). As they are writing, begin to tap a pencil on your desk, quietly and inconsistently at first, then making it louder and more distracting. Look for signs of students coming off task. If necessary, run over to the window and cry, "Look at that!" Do you have any students who are still on task?

Activity:

Inform students that on the worksheet "Staying on Task" they are going to look over examples of people who are having trouble staying on task. They are to identify a reason why the person is off task.

Answers: 1. Boring work   2. Meaningless work   Distracted by person   4. Distracted by hunger   5. Distracted by noise   Basically hyperactive   7. Not understanding what to do   Work appears too hard   9. Tools broke   10. Work seems too long

Discussion:

Have students share their ideas for being on task.

1. Why is it possible for someone to be unable to complete tasks at school but be able to watch television without blinking an eye for several hours? (Interest, motivation, time of day, less need for effort, and so on.)

2. What are some tasks people have to do that are not especially interesting, but are necessary? (Laundry, other chores, maybe schoolwork, and so on.)

3. How can you make dull tasks more interesting for yourself? (Think about something else that you will do when you are finished, time yourself, do it with a friend, and so on.)

4. What are some ways to stay on task for a long period of time, especially when you are doing homework or studying? (Find a quiet place, eat a snack, move around once in awhile.)

5. In each example on the worksheet, what could be done to help the person complete his or her task?

Extension Activities:

1. Have students come up with specific ideas for helping themselves stay on task. Ideas include the following:

   - Reward yourself for completing a task, perhaps at the end, or perhaps when you reach a half-way point (allow yourself to get a snack, take a break).

- Work with a partner (agree to stay on task and help each other stay focused).

- Break the task down into smaller steps (make a check mark on your list after each smaller task has been completed).

- Be sure to ask questions if you don't understand what to do.

- Allow yourself a certain amount of time to complete a task; set a timer and stick with it.

- If you're going to take a break, decide how many minutes long it will be.

2. Have students select a task they find hard to stick with. Gradually increase the time spent on that task. Using a chart and a timer, set goals for how many minutes, laps, math problems, pages (or whatever unit is appropriate for the task) will be the ultimate goal.

Evaluation:

1. List three tasks that are hard for you to complete.
2. For each, give a reason why you find this task difficult to complete.
3. What suggestion could you give yourself for staying on task for each of the three tasks selected?

25.5   **Staying on Task**

Directions: Each of these people is experiencing difficulty in staying on task. What do you think is the problem in each case?

1.

2.

3.

4.

5.

6.

7.

8.

9.

10.

Goal-Setting

26.1 What Is a Goal?

Objective:

The student will give at least one example of an appropriate goal for specific situations or events.

Comments:

A goal can be thought of as simply the endpoint of a quest. It could be an educational degree, the acquisition of a desired possession, or a feeling of personal satisfaction in having achieved something. It can be different things to different people. In this lesson, students are to think about goals and how they relate to different situations.

Introductory Activities:

1. Ask students to help define what a goal is. List their ideas on the board.   2. Define a goal as the endpoint of a quest or target.   3. Have students give examples of some personal goals they have set for themselves.   4. Have students give examples of some goals that others have set for them.

Activity:

Students are to write at least two examples of goals that would be appropriate for the situations given on the worksheet "What Is a Goal?" At this point, the goals do not have to be extremely specific, but they should represent someone working toward the achievement of something. It may help them to think: "I would like to…" *Answers (Examples):*   *Family:* get along better with my father, to write more often to my aunt   *Hobby:* complete my art project, to get to the next level in karate   *School:* have perfect attendance, to pass all of my classes   *Sports:* get to all practices on time, to score fifteen points in the next game

Discussion:

Ask students to share their goals for the different areas represented on the worksheet.

1. Do you think most people have goals whether or not they are actually aware of them?   2. What are some goals that students contend with every day? (Classes, homework, passing tests, and so on.) 3. Do you think goals mean more if you set them yourself rather than having someone else decide them for you?   4. How does actually setting a goal (for example, putting it in writing) help you achieve it? (It would be more specific, help you realize what it is that you need to do, and so on.) 5. What are some ways you can keep your goals in mind or stay aware of them? (Write them down, put the list on the refrigerator.)   6. How often do you think your goals change? (Probably pretty often.)   7. Do you think it is important to set goals for yourself?

Extension Activities:

1. Have students find interesting photos in popular magazines that indicate something or someone working toward a goal. It may be a monkey reaching for a banana, a secretary working on a computer, or any other type of picture. Have students share their ideas. (This may make a good bulletin board activity.)
2. Have students select a personal or educational goal that can be shared with the class. Write the goal in huge letters and put it up somewhere in the room. You may want to have students come up with class goals for themselves and/or a personal goal they want to work on for the next grading period.

Evaluation:

1. Define *goal*.   2. Give two examples of goals. For each, indicate whether it is a personal goal, educational goal, and so on.

Name _____ Date _____

26.1   **What Is a Goal?**

Directions:

For each of these aspects of life, identify at least two goals that would be appropriate.

Example:

School—to read five books about Russia, to get a high school diploma

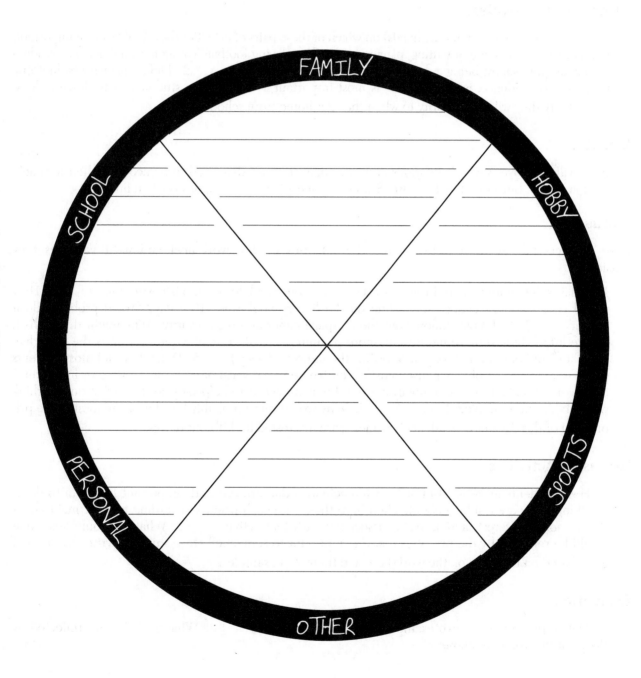

26.2 Setting Priorities

Objective:

Given a situation and list of activities, the student will arrange them in a logical order of priority.

Comments:

It is important to have defined goals so that we know when we have reached them. Part of goal-setting is figuring out what is truly important to us or what is worthy of being a goal.

Introductory Activities:

1. Have students vote (by raising hands) on which of these pairs of activities they think is more important: math or science, reading or writing, playing baseball or playing football, voting for a politician or reading a book on philosophy, being a doctor or being a lawyer, and so on.   2. Define *priority* (something that takes precedence, is done first or is most important).   3. Have students write down at least one activity they will give priority to when they get home from school/work.

Activity:

Students will read over several situations and prioritize the tasks that need to be accomplished for each. Answers may vary, but should make sense. Students can explain their responses when finished.

Discussion:

Have students talk about how they rated the activities on the worksheet and what variables they considered.

1. What is the limiting factor in situation 1? (Time—one week to accomplish everything.)   2. How would your priorities change if the fine on the library book was $10 a day? (You'd probably do it sooner.)   3. Did most students put the ten-page paper as a high priority? Why might this be high on the list? (Might require more time, more planning.)   4. For situation 2, what is the main factor that would determine how you prioritize the items? (Money.)   5. What item did most students put first and why? (Probably house, most expensive item—or vacation, most interesting or important.) 6. For situation 3, if time and money are not the main factors to help set priorities, what do you think would be in this example? (Interest.)   7. Why would there probably be a lot of variation in the prioritizing of this list among students? (Students are interested in different things.)

Extension Activities:

1. Have students make a list of at least ten activities that are presently important for them to do or are things they are thinking about. Then have them rate each priority according to what main factor (time, money, interest, and so on) is associated with that activity.   2. What are some goals that would be reflected by the priorities that are important to someone? Have students write examples of goals based on the ideas on the worksheet and their own examples.

Evaluation:

1. Define *priority*. Give two examples of personal priorities.   2. What goal(s) is/are reflected by the priorities you have chosen?

Name _____ Date _____

26.2   **Setting Priorities**

Directions:

Read the following situations and prioritize the items by using numbers (1, 2, 3, and so on) to indicate what you would do first, second, third, and so on. Your answers may be different from those of other people.

Situation 1

You have one week to get the following things done:

_____ Return a library book that is overdue at 10 cents a day.

_____ Jog a mile.

_____ Write a ten-page paper.

_____ Get ice cream for a party tonight.

_____ Get your hair cut.

Situation 2

You have $100,000 to spend.

_____ Buy a toothbrush.

_____ Buy a dog.

_____ Buy a car.

_____ Buy a house.

_____ Plan for your vacation.

Situation 3

You have some free time to do some things you normally may not have time to do. Money is not a problem. Don't feel rushed, either—you have all the time in the world to get everything done.

_____ Cook a meal.

_____ Go to a movie with your best friend.

_____ Clean the toilet.

_____ Ski the slopes of Vail, Colorado.

_____ Learn to do ballroom dancing.

Chapter 26: Goal-Setting   **495**

26.3 Doing Things in Sequence

Objective:

Given a specific goal as an example, the student will identify several steps that should be done in sequence to accomplish that goal.

Comments:

Once a goal is determined, the steps needed to reach that goal must be thoughtfully sequenced. Some goals, of course, may not require many steps—a short-term goal may be accomplished simply and quickly. Other goals, however—such as completing a longer project, more intensive activity, or acquiring a skill—may require more steps. In this lesson, students are to list steps that would be involved in working toward a goal.

Introductory Activities:

Have students list the steps that would most likely be involved in a major project, such as building a house, planning a surprise anniversary party, making a yearbook for the school, painting a huge mural of the major events of the year, and so on.

Activity:

Students are to consider the goals on the worksheet "Doing Things in Sequence" and list several steps that would lead to the attainment of the goal. The point of the lesson is to put the steps in order, not just randomly list activities. Students may need some clarification of this.

Answers (Examples):

1. Study daily notes every day after class, review with a friend two days before the test, skim the notes the night before the test
2. Start an exercise program cautiously, increase the intensity gradually, join a vigorous exercise program
3. Clear off all food items, throw old papers into the trash, organize papers into files, put away all remaining loose items
4. Take tennis lessons, practice often, play with a partner who is a good tennis player, try out for the team
5. Set up a time to visit your grandmother, get the recipe, get the items on the recipe, have your grandmother show you any special tricks she uses

Discussion:

Have students compare their responses to the examples on the worksheet.

1. Some tasks are easier to organize sequentially. What are some examples of such tasks? (Making something that results in an end product, such as sewing, cooking, building, repairing, and so on.)
2. What are some examples of tasks or goals that don't necessarily have to be done in a particular order? (Cleaning a room, preparing a surprise party, collecting specimens for a nature collage, doing homework for several subjects.)
3. Why is it important to follow steps in order? (Some later steps may depend on getting the first ones done right.)

Extension Activities:

1. Have students write short plays (and then role-play them!) indicating what could happen if tasks were done with the steps in the wrong sequence. Skits might involve cooking, dressing, driving a car, and so on.

2. Have students make a list of at least ten other important goals. What steps should be taken to complete the tasks necessary to reach the goal? Do they need to be done sequentially?

3. Students may enjoy making a short (four-panel) cartoon depicting someone doing the tasks involved in reaching a goal. Depending on the interest and ability of the students, they may enjoy making a sort of "puzzle" out of the sheet by cutting the panels apart and having other students put them in the correct sequential order.

Evaluation:

What are three important sequential steps that are necessary to complete the following goals:

1. To learn to write a report using the word processor
2. To teach my dog to come when he hears me ring a bell
3. To take orders and deliver chocolate bars to neighbors for a fund-raising project for the school

26.3   **Doing Things in Sequence**

Directions:

Consider each of these goals. List at least three steps that should be taken in order to help accomplish that goal.

 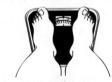  

Goal 1: To get an A on the next science chapter test

_____

_____

_____

Goal 2: To become more physically fit

_____

_____

_____

Goal 3: To organize the mess all over my desk

_____

_____

_____

Goal 4: To make the varsity tennis team

_____

_____

_____

Goal 5: To learn how to cook lasagna the way my grandmother does

_____

_____

_____

26.4 Realistic Goals

Objective:

Given situations, the student will identify and give examples of realistic goals.

Comments:

Part of good goal-setting is making sure that the goals are reasonable and attainable. Not everyone can become a president, rock star, millionaire, or bank president. Factors such as education, luck, training, personality, physical ability, and lots of others can affect how realistic a goal is for someone. In this lesson, students are to identify whether or not suggested goals are realistic for the individuals in the examples.

Introductory Activities:

1. Hold up a huge book for students and inform them that your goal for them is to read the entire book by the next day and turn in a fifty-page paper explaining your opinion of the book. After a pause, ask them how they feel about your goal for them.

2. Have students comment about why a goal may be attainable for one person but not another.

Activity:

Students are to read examples of individuals and their goals on the worksheet "Realistic Goals." They are to decide whether or not the goals seem realistic for the people involved.

Answers: 1. Yes   2. Yes   3. No   4. No   5. Yes   6. No   7. No   8. Yes

Discussion:

Have students explain their responses. In some cases, students may have a difference of opinion as to whether or not the individual could attain the goal. Some may insist that with hard work or good luck, a goal could be attained. Try to keep students directed toward using only the information given on the worksheet.

1. Do you think any goal is attainable if someone tries hard enough or works long enough toward that goal? (No—sometimes other factors work against you, such as a physical disability.)

2. What if you don't have any ability in a certain area? Would you still experience some success if you worked toward a goal even if you didn't make the original goal? (Probably—and that is a good reason for adjusting the goal.)

3. Why is it important to consider your abilities and interests and other resources before making your goals? (You want to set yourself up for success.)

4. What about people who "beat the odds" and do well even though others never thought they would reach their goals? How can you explain that? (This happens, but not very often!)

5. There are other factors you must consider when thinking about goals. What factor is important for Alvin in situation 1 if he is to reach his goal of working the night shift? (He must perform well at night, he still has to get to work on time, and so on.)

6. In situation 2, what is required besides simply having artistic ability for Andi to be successful as a fashion designer? (She may need some experience, further training, good luck.)

7. Why is situation 3 probably unrealistic for Pete? (He just does not have the required physical type and ability.)

8. How likely is it that Pete will "beat the odds"? (Not likely.)

9. What could happen? (He could grow, practice a lot, and so on.)

10. What might be a more attainable goal for Pete? (Become a good sports statistician or sports commentator.)

11. What is one reason it would be difficult for Alana in situation 4 to become a doctor in a foreign (for her) country? (Language barrier.)

12. What is the main reason this goal is probably unrealistic for Alana? (She doesn't enjoy science, and there is a lot of science involved in training to become a doctor.)

13. How could the language problem be resolved for Alana, even if she decided not to pursue medicine? (She could take English classes, get a tutor, spend some time in an English-speaking country.)

14. What is the problem with Amanda's goal in situation 6? (She hates to do the activity that would be the primary responsibility for the job.)

15. Could Amanda still be successful at being a chef even though she did not enjoy it? (Sure.)

16. Could someone be good at doing a job, even if he or she didn't enjoy the job? (Yes.)

17. How much is enjoyment a factor in being successful in reaching a goal? (It is sometimes not even related at all.)

18. What do you see as David's problem in situation 7? (He is not dedicated to following a plan that will help him reach his goal.)

Extension Activities:

1. Have students complete a "Goal Grid" containing examples of the following information:

Goal	Realistic for	Realistic but unlikely for	Unrealistic for
1. To become president	Political families	A poor child from the ghetto	Someone who is not a U.S. citizen
2. To play professional football	An exceptionally good athlete	Someone with some ability and a good attitude	A legless person in a wheelchair

Teacher: Add other goals as desired.

2. Have students complete a personal "Goal Grid." Have them select at least three areas such as educational, social, personal, and so on.

Evaluation:

1. Give an example of a goal that is realistic for you in the area of school.

2. Give an example of a goal that is desirable, but unrealistic for you in the area of sports.

26.4   Realistic Goals

Directions:

Read the following situations. Do you think the individuals have set realistic goals for themselves? Write Yes or No after each situation.

1. Alvin doesn't like to get up early in the morning. He would like to find a job working the night shift at a factory. Is this a realistic goal for Alvin?

2. Andi is very artistic. She would like to go to art school to learn how to draw better and then become a fashion designer. Is this a realistic goal for Andi?

3. Pete is short and not very athletic. When he is older, he wants to play on a professional basketball team. Is this a realistic goal for Pete?

4. Alana is from a country where Spanish is spoken. She does not know very much English, although she is quick to learn. She is planning to stay in the new country and wants to become a doctor. She does not enjoy science classes. Is this a realistic goal for Alana?

5. Rich likes to work on cars. In fact, he is very good at fixing all kinds of machines. Some day he would like to open a repair shop for small engines. Is this a realistic goal for Rich?

6. Amanda hates to cook. When she tries, though, she can follow a recipe pretty well. She wants to open a restaurant and be the main chef. Is this a realistic goal for Amanda?

7. David wants to lose ten pounds quickly. He has started jogging, eating salads for lunch, and limiting his other meals to having only three desserts. He followed this plan for two days. Is this a realistic goal for David?

8. Danielle is very pretty and outgoing. She likes to be the center of attention and is doing well in her modeling classes. She has decided to try out for a small part in a local movie. Is this a realistic goal for Danielle?

Chapter 26: Goal-Setting   **501**

26.5 Adjusting Goals

Objective:

The student will identify reasons why individuals may need to adjust their original goals.

Comments:

When it is evident to an individual that a particular goal is not realistic, attainable, or appropriate, it is important to recognize that a new goal is needed and to make those adjustments.

Introductory Activities:

1. Announce to students that you have decided to play professional hockey for a living. After comments have died down, ask students to explain why they think that goal may not be appropriate for you. (Probably unrealistic.)   2. Have students assist you in developing a new, but related goal. Perhaps you will play another sport, perhaps you will become a passionate hockey fan, and so on. 3. Have students list reasons why your original goal may be unrealistic for you. (Ability, interests, geographical location, and so on.)

Activity:

Students are to match situations with reason & for adjusting their goals.   *Answers:* 1. c   2. b   3. a   4. e   5. d

Discussion:

Go through the situations with students and have them select specific clues that indicated why the individual needed to adjust his or her goal.

1. How often do you think people change their goals? (All the time.)   2. Are the reasons that people need to change goals periodically all bad or negative? (Not at all—one may outgrow a goal that is too easy to achieve.)   3. When you adjust a goal "downward," isn't that lowering your standards or just giving up? (Not necessarily; it could be more appropriate for the ability and interests of the individual.)   4. Can you think of some examples of when you changed goals because you became interested in something else?   5. What are some examples of changing a goal because you learned something new or obtained information that changed what you thought about something? 6. Have you had any unpleasant experiences that encouraged you to change your goals?   7. Why is it important to know when it is a good time to change your goals? (So you don't waste a lot of time pursuing something that is not really what you want.)

Extension Activities:

1. Have students write a short story in which a character (perhaps based on a true experience) has a major change in goals. Have the other students identify the reason(s) why the change was necessary or beneficial.   2. Have students find cartoons (as in the Sunday paper) for examples of characters changing goals. Comics such as *Garfield* and *Peanuts* are good sources!

Evaluation:

1. List three reasons why someone might have to adjust an original goal.   2. Give an example of each of the three reasons you listed above.

26.5   **Adjusting Goals**

Directions:

These people have to adjust their goals for various reasons. Match the reasons on the right with the situations on the left.

1. "Ace" couldn't make the varsity basketball team, so he decided to try out for the junior varsity team.

   _____

2. Jennifer realized that working a paper route was not going to get her enough money for her class trip in the spring, so she got several jobs cleaning houses, which earns her more money.

   _____

3. After going to a concert, Belinda decided that she no longer wants to be an actress—she wants to sing!

   _____

4. Fred wanted to become a surgeon until he took his first medical class and got poor grades, hated the thought of blood, and was told by his professors that he would never make it.

   _____

5. Carter didn't realize he could get a scholarship that would completely pay his way through college until he talked to his counselor. Then he decided he wanted to transfer to the state school that offered the scholarship.

   _____

a. Changing a goal because of a new interest

b. Changing a goal because the original goal is off-track or won't bring you toward a larger goal.

c. Changing a goal to match your ability

d. Changing a goal because of new information

e. Changing a goal because of an unpleasant experience

Chapter 27

Risk-Taking

27.1 What Is a Risk?

Objective:

The student will define a risk and give at least two examples.

Comments:

Life is filled with risks. Every time you cross a street, sign your name, or smoke a cigarette you are dabbling with some form of risk. In this lesson students are given a simple definition of a risk—something associated with danger or loss—and consider several examples of risks.

Introductory Activities:

1. Ask students to raise their hands if they want to volunteer. Do not mention what they are volunteering for. Inform them that those with their hands up are risk-takers! 2. Ask students to consider the following situation: They have to pick Door 1 or Door 2—behind one of them is a million dollars, and behind the other is something that will cause them great pain. Ask students to raise their hands if they would participate in this "experiment." Are these students risk-takers? 3. Define *risk* (something that potentially could involve danger or loss).

Activity:

Students are to consider the goals and situations on the worksheet "What Is a Risk?" and decide which of the two risks that would help attain the goal is more costly or is the greater risk. They are to put a check mark in front of that answer. *Answers:* 1. Second—you don't know the reputation of the person. 2. First—assuming that you do not have a recommendation of the work of this facility. 3. First—a signal is much safer. 4. First—there are many dangers associated with hitchhiking. 5. Second—this doesn't really prove anything. 6. Second—young horses can have attitudes and accidents! 7. Second—this is a definite commitment, perhaps one that could/should be tried later. 8. Second—it is putting off something that needs to be done soon.

Discussion:

Have students discuss why the various responses are or are not risky toward achieving the goal.

1. What are some examples of risks that you take every day? 2. How dangerous are these risks? (Probably not very.) 3. Are there any activities that people do that do not have some element of risk? 4. Does every risk involve a goal? (Of some sort!) 5. When you get in the habit of doing something often—for example, crossing a busy street in the middle—why does it seem to be less risky? (Becomes a habit, you get good at it.) 6. Are there things that are risky for one person but may not be for another? Explain. (Yes—skill is associated with how much risk is involved, for example, sports, driving, and so on.)

Extension Activities:

1. Have students cut out magazine or newspaper articles that show someone taking a risk. Try to decide what the goal is behind the risk being taken. 2. Have students list 15 risks they will probably face during that day.

Evaluation:

1. Define or explain what a risk is. 2. Give two examples of risks you have taken recently. 3. Explain what goal was behind each of the two risks.

27.1   **What Is a Risk?**

Directions:

Read through these goals and some risks that could be associated with achieving them. Decide which of the two is the greater risk. Put a check mark in front of your choice.

  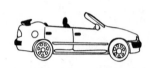  

1. *Goal:* to make some money

☐ Invest in a certificate of deposit.

☐ Withdraw some of your savings to give to a well-dressed stranger who says he knows of a good investment.

2. *Goal:* to get your car fixed

☐ Take your car to "Speedy-Fix."

☐ Take your car to a reliable mechanic whom you have used before for repair.

3. *Goal:* to cross a busy street

☐ Look both ways, then run for it.

☐ Cross at the corner with a signal.

4. *Goal:* to travel to another state

☐ Hitchhike.

☐ Buy a ticket for a train.

5. *Goal:* to make the football team

☐ Give up other sports and practice as much as you can.

☐ Don't warm-up or wear any padding to prove how tough you are.

6. *Goal:* to purchase a winning racehorse

☐ Check the horse's track record.

☐ Buy a young horse so it will have time to be trained well.

7. *Goal:* to free hostages

☐ Negotiate with the hostage-takers.

☐ Storm the building with weapons.

8. *Goal:* to maintain a healthy heart after you have had a diagnosis of clogged arteries

☐ Arrange for recommended surgery.

☐ Hope that time will heal your heart.

27.2 Why Take Risks?

Objective:

The student will state three to five reasons why people take risks.

Comments:

People take risks for a variety of reasons. Some may include: excitement or the thrill of danger; desire to improve their situation in some way (for example, gaining money); peer pressure; lack of knowledge; desire to push themselves to learn or become something different; or perhaps because there seems to be no other alternatives. In this lesson, these motives are examined.

Introductory Activities:

1. Pass out a $1 bill (can be counterfeit or play money!) to each student. Inform them that they can give you the dollar to get a ticket that reveals whether they are the winner. The winner will get $100. Do they want to play? (Most will say yes.) Why? (The odds are good, the consequences are good, the risk is small.)
2. Repeat the activity, but this time tell students that everyone will get a consequence, including one of the following: $100, a slow painful death, an hour's detention, a candy bar, a free concert ticket of their choice, or thirty hours of community service. Do they want to play? (Some will probably have mixed emotions now—the risks are greater and not predictable.)

Activity:

Several reasons why people take risks are listed on the right-hand side of the worksheet "Why Take Risks?" Students are to match the risks on the left with a possible reason why someone would take that risk from the choices on the right. There are several possibilities for each risk; students should explain their thinking.

Answers (will vary; examples): 1. a, d   2. a, b   3. b   4. b, c, e   5. a, d, e, f   6. a, d   7. b, d   8. c, e
9. a, f   10. a, d, e   11. b, e   12. d, f   13. a, b, d   14. a, f   15. e   16. a, d, f   17. c, f   18. b, e

Discussion:

The students' responses should generate quite a bit of discussion, as their answers may vary widely.

1. What risks do you consider exciting?
2. Do you consider yourself a risk-taker or someone who is more conservative and likes to play it safe?
3. What situations on the worksheet involve danger?
4. What risks could you take in your life that would improve your situation—for example, change your job, gain you more possessions, and so on?
5. What is stopping you from taking those risks?
6. Have you ever been in a situation in which you felt there was only one alternative—and that was risky? (Perhaps involving disease or an accident.)
7. What risks are a result of peer pressure in your group?
8. What would happen if you resisted peer pressure from your group?
9. Why would it be a risk to break away from peer pressure?

10. What risks would you take to improve yourself? Do you desire to make self-improvement changes?

11. What are ways to combat ignorance? (Experience, education, asking people for advice, and so on.)

12. Why do you think some people are so hesitant to ask others for information that could prevent them from getting into a risky situation? (Embarrassed.)

Extension Activities:

1. Have students write a paragraph or short story about the most exciting risk they have taken. What was it like? Was the outcome good or bad? Would they do it again?

2. Have students do a book report on a famous risk-taker (for example, a race car driver, stunt person, aerialist, escape artist such as Harry Houdini or Criss Angle, and so on). What motivation drives these people to take risks?

3. Have students make a personal list of at least five things they would like to do but are afraid to try or are unwilling to risk.

Evaluation:

Give one example of a risk that could be taken for each of the following reasons:

1. Thrill
2. Improve your life
3. Last resort
4. Peer pressure
5. Self-improvement
6. Being unaware of the risk

27.2   **Why Take Risks?**

Directions:

Match the risks on the left with the reasons or motives on the right. There may be more than one possible correct answer. Be able to justify or explain your responses.

Risk

___ 1. Riding a roller coaster without holding onto the bar

___ 2. Buying a lottery ticket

___ 3. Investing money in the stock market

___ 4. Having surgery

___ 5. Taking recreational drugs

___ 6. Drinking more alcohol than you really want or intend to

___ 7. Joining a union

___ 8. Giving a speech in front of people you don't know

___ 9. Having sex without using protection

___10. Getting a very different haircut

___11. Going back to school after you had quit

___12. Not wearing a seatbelt

___13. Gambling with a small amount of money

___14. Gambling with your life savings

___15. Refusing to join in a group that is teasing someone else

___16. Driving 100 miles an hour along a country road

___17. Introducing your boyfriend/girlfriend to your very pretty/handsome cousin

___18. Taking a class on how to sell real estate

Reasons

a. Desire for thrill, excitement, attention

b. Wanting to improve your life or situation

c. No other alternatives

d. Peer pressure

e. Wanting to change yourself, improve self

f. Being unaware of the risks

Chapter 27: Risk-Taking   **509**

27.3 Acceptable Risks

Objective:

The student will give a reason why a situation is or is not an acceptable risk.

Comments:

There are times when taking a risk might result in a good or acceptable outcome. On the other hand, taking a foolish risk might end up costing you money, pride, time, or other loss. Wisdom is being able to look at the whole situation and take a risk that you are willing to live with.

Introductory Activities:

1. Write "acceptable risk" and "unacceptable risk" on the board. Ask students to assign each of these situations to the appropriate category:

   A. Crossing a busy street blindfolded

   B. Sampling five different types of candy bars to pick the best

   C. Letting your mother choose your clothes for your next date

   D. Swimming across a lake

2. Every risk involves the possibility of some loss. Have students tell what is at stake in the examples above. (Life, stomach pain, status, safety.)

Activity:

On the worksheet "Acceptable Risks," students are to read the examples and decide whether or not the risky situation is an acceptable risk. Discuss why or why not.   *Answers:*   1. Acceptable, if the teacher has been willing to accept changes in the past.   2. Not acceptable—it will be hard not to bring up the situation after spending so much time together.   3. Not acceptable—puppies chew. 4. Not acceptable—friend doesn't have a good record for repaying.

Discussion:

What is "acceptable" for one person might not be tolerable for another. Be sure to have students explain their opinions.

1. What are some risky things that would involve personal safety? (Jumping out of an airplane, physical activities, getting into a fight.)   2. Why would it be important to understand the risk before getting involved? (Make sure you are up to the challenge.)   3. What are some activities that you might find an acceptable risk but someone else might have a problem with?

Extension Activity:

Have students conduct an informal survey called "Would you ever…?" and include items such as: Would you ever get in a car with a drunk driver? Would you ever eat something if you didn't know what it was? Would you ever jump out of an airplane? Get students talking about risk-taking and how others view a risk.

Evaluation:

Give an example of an acceptable risk and an unacceptable risk. Explain your answers.

27.3   **Acceptable Risks**

Directions:

These characters need to make a decision about taking a risk. Which decisions do you think would be acceptable risks for each one?

1. Landon has a report due and his teacher wanted it done on a computer. Landon didn't get to the computer lab before it closed, so he handwrote the report. His teacher usually is pretty understanding about schedules, so he thinks it will be OK if he turns it in as it is.
    Acceptable risk   Not acceptable

    Why: _____

2. Melanie doesn't want to hurt her friend's feelings, so she isn't going to tell her about the party that everyone else is going to. She is supposed to spend the night with her friend, and they are going shopping after school together.
    Acceptable risk   Not acceptable

    Why: _____

3. Dennis didn't want to pick up his clothes, even though his new puppy chews on everything. He left a brand-new shirt on the floor along with a good pair of jeans. And here comes the puppy.
    Acceptable risk   Not acceptable

    Why: _____

4. Aaliyah's friend wants to borrow some money from her. The last time she lent her friend money, it took about two months for her friend to pay her back. She had to keep bothering her friend to get the money because her friend always had excuses for why she couldn't pay.
    Acceptable risk   Not acceptable

    Why: _____

27.4 Handling Fear

Objective:

The student will state several ways to handle a frightening situation.

Comments:

People are fearful of many things—snakes, roller coasters, scary movies, new people, new places, unpleasant surprises, and so on. Special learners may need extra coaching and strategies to help cope with frightening situations.

Introductory Activities:

1. Ask students if they have ever watched the TV show *Fear Factor*. What are some common things that people are afraid of? (Some good ones to get them started are spiders, heights, darkness, storms.)
2. Talk about examples of fearfulness in these situations: speaking in front of people, taking responsibility, having a confrontation, getting into trouble. What are some other things that cause people to be afraid?

Activity:

There are some tips for handling scary situations on the worksheet "Handling Fear." Students should consider each example and try to use at least one or two tips for each to show how the person could handle his or her fear.   *Answers:*   1. a—Find out the schedule. c—Ride with someone at first. 2. c—Swim with someone else. d—Know when he is too tired to go on.   3. a—Find out how old the child is, what he's like, and so on. e—Babysit for a short time with the parent close by.   4. a—Find out what the girl is interested in. c—Go up to her with a friend.   5. a—Find out how long the speech has to be. d—Talk about something you know well.   6. a—Find out whether the principal is angry or just wants information. d—Don't go in with an attitude.   7. a—Ask someone to help. b—Watch someone else work the machine.   8 a—Be prepared, find out where they will be. c—Walk with a friend if you can.

Discussion:

1. Sometimes things you are afraid of will not be so scary if you are prepared ahead of time. Which examples on the worksheet fall into that category? (1, 5, 7)   2. If people or situations are frightening to someone, it can be helpful to have another person around. Who would be some people that you can count on for moral support?

Extension Activities:

1. Have students predict and then research common fears. The site www.faceyourfearstoday.com lists common fears and phobias, A through Z. How many of them did you already know?   2. Have students write a short paper, "Facing My Fear." Why is their particular fear bothersome to them? What have they done about it? How have they shown bravery?

Evaluation:

1. What is one situation that makes you fearful?   2. What is one tip that would help you in this situation?

27.4   **Handling Fear**

Directions:

How can these tips help someone who is frightened in the following situations?

a. Ask questions.   b. Watch someone else.   c. Have a partner.   d. Know your limits.   e. Take a small step first.

1. Vanessa is afraid to use public transportation.

   _____

2. Connor is a good swimmer, but he isn't sure he can swim the length of the pool.

   _____

3. Amanda was asked to babysit for a small child.

   _____

4. Eric wants to talk to a new girl in class, but he feels nervous.

   _____

5. Angelina is worried about giving a speech in front of the class.

   _____

6. Ian is called into the principal's office for being involved in a food fight in the cafeteria.

   _____

7. Michelle is not sure she knows how to work the cash register for her job.

   _____

8. Whenever Devin walks home from school he is bullied by some boys who live near him.

   _____